Paulo Freire
& the Cold War Politics of Literacy

Paulo Freire

& the Cold War Politics of Literacy

Andrew J. Kirkendall

The University of North Carolina Press Chapel Hill

Library of Congress Cataloging-in-Publication Data
Kirkendall, Andrew J.
  Paulo Freire and the cold war politics of literacy / Andrew J. Kirkendall.
    p. cm.
Includes bibliographical references and index.
ISBN 978-0-8078-3419-0 (cloth : alk. paper)
1. Freire, Paulo, 1921–1997. 2. Literacy—Political aspects.
3. Literacy—Political aspects—Latin America 4. Cold War.   I. Title.
LB880.F732K57 2010
302.2'244—dc22
2010006640

Portions of this work appeared previously in somewhat different form in
Andrew J. Kirkendall, "Entering History: Paulo Freire and the Politics of the
Brazilian Northeast, 1958–1964," Luso-Brazilian Review 41:1 (Summer 2004):
168–89; Andrew J. Kirkendall, "Paulo Freire, Eduardo Frei, Literacy Training
and the Politics of Consciousness Raising in Chile, 1964–1970," Journal of Latin
American Studies 36:4 (November 2004): 687–717; and Andrew J. Kirkendall,
"Paulo Freire, l'Unesco et la Lutte Contre l'Analphabétisme des Adultes dans
le Monde de la Guerre Froide," 60 Ans d'Histoire de l'Unesco: Actes du Colloque
International, Paris, 16–18 Novembre 2005 (Paris: UNESCO, 2007). They are
printed here with permission from the publishers.

14 13 12 11 10   5 4 3 2 1

To Meg Reynard, light of my life,
and in memory of Joan Carol Nelson Kirkendall

Contents

Illustrations

Acknowledgments

My visits to the Instituto Paulo Freire in São Paulo were critical to the development of my ideas. I am not sure that the institute had ever had a foreign historian in their midst, and they seemed to have been intrigued by my insistence on squeezing the last drop out of their resources over several visits. My time spent reading in Freire's first personal library, which is located there, was particularly valuable. I am grateful to Moacir Gadotti and Angela Antunes for their encouragement and generosity. No one did more for me there than Lutgardes Costa Freire, Freire's youngest child. I am proud to consider him a friend. His letters also helped me gain access to materials at the Superior Tribunal Militar in Brasília, where, unfortunately, much that should be in Brazil's Arquivo Nacional is located. I have deposited copies of my copies at the institute. I thank him also for the use of photos. While I doubt that many at the institute will agree with a good deal of what I have written, I am extremely grateful for the warm welcome I have always received on my visits.

Waldemar Cortés Carabantes and Jacques Chonchol were both kind enough to meet with me when I was doing research in Chile, although it should be clear that what I have written about them was based on documents and not on oral history interviews. The archives of the World Council of Churches in Geneva, Switzerland, have a wealth of material on Freire. Stephanie Knecht and Laurence Diehr allowed me to roam among the shelves and find things on my own. I am grateful for their trust.

In too many places where I did research, I was struck by the difficult conditions under which many archivists and librarians operate, particularly in northeastern Brazil. All treated me professionally, and I regret that I do not have the names of many who helped me in a matter-of-fact way and without ever suggesting that it was something that required special thanks. I fear that Paulo Santos at the state archives in Rio Grande do Norte in Natal will have to stand for those who go unnamed here. I must emphasize my debt to Gonçalo Marcelino de Lira Neto of the military tribunal archives; Ana Paula of the Centro de Ensino Supletivo Virginia Correia de Oliveira in Recife; and Maria Joselita da Silva of the Instituto Nacional de Estudos e Pesquisas

Educacionais Anísio Teixeira in Brasília. Marcília Gama helped me with the political police records for the state of Pernambuco; unfortunately, the file on Freire himself has gone missing. Thanks as well to Margarita Vannini and the exceptional staff of the Universidad Centroamericana's Instituto de Historia de Nicaragua y Centroamérica in Managua. My involvement with the UNESCO historical conference in 2005 grew out of my research in Paris in the UNESCO archives in 2004; many thanks to archivists Jens Boel and Mahmood Ghander for their support.

In the United States I want to thank David Kuzma of the Special Collections and University Archives at Rutgers University, Stephen Plotkin of the John F. Kennedy Library, and Regina Greenwell of the Lyndon Baines Johnson Library. I am also grateful to the interlibrary loan department of Evans Library at Texas A&M University.

Other people who helped in a variety of small but important ways include Justin Wolfe, Emily Story, Caitlin Fitz, Jim Green, Jeff Lesser, Barbara Weinstein, Éric Morier-Genoud, Maria Escobar-Lemmon, Celso Castilho, Steven Kyle, Renato Aguilar, and Lesley Bartlett. Special thanks to Mary Ann Mahony, who got me started writing on this project early.

Thanks also to Celia Barlow, the *Journal of Latin American Studies*, and Cambridge University Press; the *Luso-Brazilian Review* and the University of Wisconsin Press; and UNESCO for permission to reproduce material that originally appeared in their publications. Thanks in particular to the anonymous reviewers for *JLAS* for their suggestions.

I thank the Texas A&M College of Liberal Arts for a faculty research enhancement award that financed the first research trip on this project back in 2001, and for helping to defray some of the production costs. I also thank the history department and the Glasscock Center for Humanities Research for supporting me with small research grants over the years. I thank department head Walter Buenger for supporting my leave of absence. Thanks, as always, to Jude Swank for help with the computer, Barbara Dawson for help with reimbursements, and to Judy Mattson, who has provided invaluable help for years. Thanks to Jude, Judy, Robyn Konrad, and Rita Walker as well for lending sympathetic ears in difficult times.

My career would have been very different had it not been for the efforts of my colleagues Terry Anderson, Al Broussard, and Chester Dunning. Their rare example of solidarity and bravery when an injustice was being done is much appreciated and it is a reason why I find so much of the resistance literature ultimately unsatisfying. I hope they know how much I value them.

Other colleagues have helped in other ways: Jim Bradford for his truly encyclopedic knowledge; Hank Schmidt for his inspiring example of pioneering cultural historical scholarship; and R. J. Q. Adams, Chuck Brooks, Jeff and Kate Carté Engel, Rebecca Schloss, Roger Reese, Glenn Chambers, Jason Parker, Robert Resch, Molly Warsh, John Lenihan, Chip Dawson, David Hudson, and others in the department already named for general camaraderie. Those colleagues who were not yet tenured back in 2002–3 also provided thoughtful commentary on the project early on, and I appreciate it.

I thank my editor, Elaine Maisner, the manuscript's anonymous reviewers, Tema Larter, Mary Caviness, and all of the other good folks at the University of North Carolina Press for helping make this a book. I hope that the anonymous readers for the press know how much I appreciated their professional and close readings. I alone am to blame should errors remain.

I should also note the help provided by Mr. Peavey of the Austin Driving School for his own role in improving life during the years I was writing this.

I thank my father, Richard Stewart Kirkendall, for providing funds for much of the research I undertook during the 2004–5 academic year. I could not have done it without him.

The years in which I researched and wrote this book were difficult ones for my wife and me. She made too many sacrifices for my career. I hope that the coming years will see more times like the week we spent in Paris during the UNESCO sixtieth anniversary conference in November 2005. Meg and I lost three special people during these years, her parents and my mother. Paul Reynard was the most giving man I have ever met. Kathy Reynard became a second mom to me. They have left such a hole in our world. We miss them so much. Mom died as I was making some of the final corrections on this book; I owe her so much, including my love of books. It amazed me how those light-green and very heavy bookends in her apartment triggered so many memories after she died. I still keep expecting to be able to call and talk to her about the latest St. Louis Cardinals game. She cannot be replaced. (Many thanks to brothers Tom and Ted for invaluable help in part of the incomplete healing process.) The children were growing up as I wrote this. I hope that they realize that I have loved them immensely if not always wisely. They have taught me so much. The hours I spent reading to them when they were younger were among the most precious moments of my life. May we always share common interests.

Abbreviations

AP	Ação Popular (Popular Action)
CCPD	Commission on Churches' Participation in Development
CEPLAR	Campanha de Educação Popular da Paraíba (Popular Education Campaign of Paraíba)
CIA	Central Intelligence Agency
CORA	Corporación de Reforma Agraria (Agrarian Reform Corporation)
COSEP	Consejo Superior de la Empresa Privada (High Council of Private Enterprise)
CREFAL	Centro de Cooperación Regional para la Educación de Adultos en América Latina y el Caribe (Center for Regional Cooperation for Adult Education in Latin America and the Caribbean)
EPA	Ejército Popular de Alfabetizadores (Popular Army of Literacy Instructors)
FAO	Food and Agriculture Organization
FARP	Forças Armadas Revolucionários do Povo (Armed Forces of the People)
FRAP	Frente de Acción Popular (Popular Action Front)
FSLN	Frente Sandinista de Liberación Nacional (Sandinista National Liberation Front)
IBAD	Instituto Brasileiro de Ação Democrático (Brazilian Institute of Democratic Action)
ICIRA	Instituto de Capacitación e Investigación (Institute of Training and Investigation)
IDAC	Institut d'Action Culturelle (Institute for Cultural Action)
INDAP	Instituto del Desarrollo Agropecuario (Institute of Farming and Livestock Development)
INEP	Instituto Nacional de Estudos e Pesquisas Educacionais (National Institute of Pedagogical Studies)
ISEB	Instituto Superior de Estudos Brasileiros (Higher Institute of Brazilian Studies)
JDC	Juventud Democrata Cristiana (Christian Democratic Youth)
JUC	Juventude Universitária Católica (Catholic University Youth)

MAPU	Movimiento de Acción Popular Unitario (Movement for Popular Unity)
MCP	Movimento de Cultura Popular (popular culture movement)
MIR	Movimiento de Izquierda Revolucionario (Movement of the Revolutionary Left)
MLSTP	Movimento de Libertação de São Tomé e Príncipe (Movement for the Liberation of São Tomé and Príncipe)
MOBRAL	Movimento Brasileiro de Alfabetização (Brazilian Literacy Training Movement)
MOVA	Movimento de Alfabetização de Jovens e Adultos (Literacy Movement for Youth and Adults)
PAIGC	Partido Africano da Independência da Guiné e Cabo Verde (African Party for the Independence of Guinea-Bissau and Cape Verde)
PCB	Partido Comunista Brasileira (Brazilian Communist Party)
PDC	Partido Democrata Cristiana (Christian Democratic Party)
PSD	Partido Social Democrático (Social Democratic Party)
PT	Partido dos Trabalhadores (Workers' Party)
PTB	Partido Trabalhista Brasileira (Brazilian Labor Party)
SESI	Serviço Social de Indústria (Industrial Social Service)
SIDA	Swedish International Development Authority
SUDENE	Superintendência do Desenvolvimento do Nordeste (Northeastern Development Agency)
UCA	Universidad Centroamericana (Central American University)
UDN	União Democrática Nacional (National Democratic Union)
UN	United Nations
UNE	União Nacional de Estudantes (National Students Union)
UNESCO	United Nations Educational, Scientific, and Cultural Organization
USAID	United States Agency for International Development
WCC	World Council of Churches

Paulo Freire
& the Cold War Politics of Literacy

In a makeshift school built out of coconut trees in 1963 in the poor northeastern Brazilian city of Natal, a group of adult students sat and worked on their ABCs. This was no ordinary night class. As these men and women, many of whom were new to urban life, learned to recognize the words they spoke in letters and syllables, they began to perceive a chance of changing their worlds. Slides depicting scenes from their daily life projected onto a screen prompted them to discuss their realities and to understand them as having been made through human action and therefore capable of being *changed* through their own actions. Their "consciousness," in the language of the time, was being "raised." If expectations were being raised as well, within a year they would be dashed by a military coup that put an end to these lessons. Many of these students' teachers would be imprisoned. Politicians who had supported these literacy programs usually lost their political rights and went into exile.

The man who designed the literacy program, Paulo Reglus Neves Freire, also ended up in prison. In the decade and a half spent in exile following his time in prison, Freire became one of the foremost intellectuals from what was for many decades called the Third World. He became a key player in world events because of his creation of new techniques for literacy training and consciousness raising. He sought to transform educational practices that reinforced the status quo and demonstrated a belief that knowledge was something that was deposited in inert students and that tended to "domesticate" them. In theory at least and generally in practice as well, Freire wanted to create questioning, critical, active adults. Literacy training, moreover, was serious business during the Cold War. In a later literacy campaign with which he was associated in Nicaragua under the Sandinistas in 1980, teachers were targeted for execution.

Freire himself has been variously described as everything from a subversive to a saint, a reformist, a populist, or a Leninist, his techniques depicted as little more than brainwashing and nothing less than the answer to the problem of how to create truly democratic societies in poorer countries. Even before his death he was in danger of becoming a myth.[1] In the following pages, I provide an examination of him as a historical actor of global importance. While his ideas have become widely known, his national and transnational political activities and the ways his ideas were used in particular political contexts is understudied (and, too frequently, misunderstood). His techniques have been employed by people of widely varying ideological commitments for different ends, even, as we shall see, at the same time in roughly the same context. Freire became an international figure because of the conjuncture of local and national circumstances in his native Brazil and an international climate in which adult illiteracy became of transcendent importance. The Cold War era was marked by a competition between countries to prove that their models of economic, political, social, and cultural organization were superior.[2] The proliferation of mass media made people throughout the world more aware of their relative states of economic and technological development. Having large illiterate populations, as illiteracy came to be considered a disease or disability, became not only a symbol but presumably a cause of a nation's backwardness. The speed of modern life and communications lent a new urgency to dealing with social issues, and nations focused on illiteracy as never before.[3] Literacy training programs became a major part of what one historian has called "the vast international undertaking known as development."[4]

During Freire's lifetime, the meanings of illiteracy and the methods employed to eliminate it became hotly contested political issues, important enough to figure in the overthrow of governments (as in Brazil in 1964), in the polarization of forces in a pluralistic democracy (Chile in the latter half of the 1960s), in the building of nations (in newly independent African countries in the 1970s), in the construction of a revolutionary order (Nicaragua in 1980), and in the reconstruction of civil society after decades of dictatorship (Brazil once again in the 1980s and 1990s). This book provides both a political biography of Paulo Freire and an examination of the politics of literacy during the Cold War. It is also a story of the transformation of a Latin

American new left, one that was deeply humanist and often tied to a changing Catholic Church; that was committed to profound change in the short term; and that generally did not admire the Soviet Union as a previous generation had but was prone to embracing uncritically Third World governments created by liberation movements. Freire personified this Left, which, at its best, could work to further democratize pluralistic societies and, at its worst, could be rather obtuse about the dangers posed by one-party states. Literacy training, as we shall see, was understood not solely as a factor in economic growth but also as a means of political mobilization. But, depending on the circumstances, mobilization could be either empowering or controlling.

Freire's career must be understood within the larger twentieth-century drive for development and the role that education has played in it. While nations can become literate through long-term processes of social and cultural evolution, there have certainly been shorter time periods in history, during the Protestant Reformation, for example, in which nations have made dramatic leaps forward in the numbers of people who could read and write.[5] The twentieth century was defined by impatience. Moreover, it was a time in which a new faith in state planning replaced or at least modified liberal capitalist beliefs in the ability of the market to resolve social and economic problems.[6]

Along with five-year plans came the establishment of mass literacy campaigns intended to bring less industrialized nations into the "modern" world. Literacy campaigns have been launched to modernize, as well as to mobilize, populations. They have sought to preserve social order as much as to empower individuals or groups. Literacy campaigns can be used (and misused) for partisan purposes. They can employ professionals or volunteers. They may be embraced by a wide variety of community, political, and religious groups that may or may not have similar or complementary goals. Mass literacy campaigns, as we shall see, often involved large-scale interaction between people of different social classes. University and high school students frequently played a disproportionate role in these campaigns in providing the energy and the expertise to make them work. While self-consciously trying to achieve certain goals, as stated in their official discourses, states and their agents have had to take into account people's motivations for learning to read and write (and for continuing to do so). Indeed, this book could have been written as a story of public and personal ambitions and how they do or do not mesh. These ambitions often, although not always, reflect the degree to which a society is urban or rural, whether the nation has achieved a level of cultural identity, and the extent to which its people already see themselves as citizens.[7] Early on, Freire, as we shall see, saw the transformation of people and their understandings of themselves to be an even more important part of what he was trying to achieve than the mere acquisition of reading and writing skills. If, from a historian's perspective, it is often maddeningly difficult to determine to what extent any of the campaigns Freire advised really succeeded in teaching people to read and write, it is often even more difficult to determine how much they led to a changed political consciousness.

Freire, like any historical actor, must be understood in terms of his actions within particular social and political contexts and the allies he made within the partisan or ideological struggles in which he engaged and about which he rarely reflected upon in as concrete a way as a historian would like. In my effort to understand Freire, my approach has been to look at the man in his times using his writings from particular historical moments rather than (as has often been done) his retrospective writings (while not neglecting his frequent attempts at writing what were, to a large extent, memoirs). Because Freire spent so much time in exile, much of his correspondence is not available. (The best single collection of his letters is located at the World Council of Churches' archives in Geneva, Switzerland, where he spent the 1970s, and I am the first scholar to have consulted it.) This book also draws on official government documents and speeches, as well as the textbooks used in the various literacy campaigns, to understand what political actors were trying to achieve and how these goals came into conflict with others' visions.

To understand Freire's rise to prominence, we must also examine the larger twentieth-century context of comparative state projects. The first half of the twentieth century saw a variety of attempts to achieve mass literacy. In its first two decades of existence, the Soviet Union made eliminating illiteracy a central component of its attempt to transform Russian society. H. S. Bhola, in his comparative study of literacy campaigns, considers the Soviet Union's efforts "the ancestor of all modern mass literacy campaigns." If literacy rates were not as low under the Romanov dynasty as Communist Party propagandists later made them out to be, they were nevertheless, by any measure, inadequate. In its approach to literacy, the Soviet government often relied on military models and metaphors, considering literacy the "Third Front" (a pattern that, as we shall see, was replicated in later campaigns, including the Freire-inspired campaign launched by the Sandinistas in Nicaragua in 1980). Under Vladimir Lenin in the early years, there was a concern about "over-politicizing the literacy campaign." The campaign went through a series of phases and reorganizations, some more coercive than others, in the Lenin and post-Lenin eras. During the era of the New Economic Policy in the 1920s, there was an attempt to focus on young adults, who, it was believed, could more easily make the transition to a changing economic order. The Red Army itself became a major focus of literacy efforts. For Joseph Stalin, literacy was closely tied to the need to modernize the economy at any cost to the society. Although the numbers of people literate by the late 1930s looked good, the quality of education was poor. As Ben Ekloff has suggested, "Under Stalin, people learned how to read and write, but seldom to learn from reading." Historians disagree about the extent to which there was a "genuine transformation of values, tastes, and cognitive orientations" in the Soviet Union during this time period and whether, indeed, a so-called New Man with a transformed "consciousness" ever existed.[8]

Decades later, the Chinese Communists, for their part, also placed a major emphasis on literacy. The party began with insurgent army and party cadres in the 1920s and 1930s. For Mao Zedong, political education and organization took precedence over literacy training per se among the general population. Following the triumph of the Communists in 1949, there was an attempt to move forward with reforms that simplified the written language. In the 1950s, literacy campaigns became a valuable tool in the organization of the population and the legitimation of the regime. Teaching the populace to read and write was combined with an effort to eliminate "false consciousness." Illiteracy rates seem to have been cut in half in the first decade of Communist rule.[9]

Whatever the quality of the education in the two major Communist countries, the long-term trends in literacy in both the Soviet Union and Communist China were positive. This gave these nations a good deal of prestige. Many nations during the Cold War era were convinced that the Soviet model, which had transformed a rural society and turned it into one of the world's superpowers, provided a quicker route to modernity than that offered by the United States. The worldwide experience of the Great Depression had left its mark on people's thinking about the social and economic roles of government. Many leaders around the world looked to the Soviet Union and China as they sought to transform their countries, even if they did not define themselves as Marxist-Leninists. The language of "consciousness raising" and "false consciousness" would be adopted by many who were not themselves Marxists.[10]

In many parts of the world, literacy campaigns often were designed by the state, but some were associated with nongovernmental organizations, and particularly with the activities of missionary organizations. Undoubtedly, the major figure in this regard was the Pennsylvania-born Frank Laubach, who had worked as a teacher and a missionary in Muslim areas in the Philippines in the 1930s. There he developed a phonetic method of teaching people to read words commonly used in daily life. It was adopted for many languages in the developing world. His "lightning literacy" method, along with the philosophy of "each one, teach one" (employing volunteers and often the newly literate as instructors), quickly began to spread throughout the world through the work of the Committee on World Literacy and Christian Literature. The loss of the Philippines to Japan during the Second World War forced Laubach to concentrate his energies on Latin America, where some of his partisans credit him with the explosion of literacy programs that took place in the mid-1940s in the region. Laubach, to a certain degree, paved the way for Freire to follow. He raised expectations and suggested that long-standing problems like illiteracy could be resolved in fairly short order and with relatively limited resources.[11]

In Latin America, I have argued elsewhere, control over language, the more ornate the better, had marked a man as a legitimate wielder of power since the nineteenth century.[12] Many historians have focused on the ways in which public education served as a mechanism for social control during this time period, but one might also argue that the inadequate diffusion of even arguably authoritarian schools during much of the region's history also served as an instrument for the depoliticization of the masses and a curb on the formation of a sense of active citizenship.[13] In the early twentieth century, Latin American college students played an important role in establishing what were often called popular universities, which sought to integrate the urban poor into the larger society. In Mexico, Latin America's major revolutionary experience in the first half of the twentieth century provided an opportunity for experimentation with educational possibilities on many levels. As the postrevolutionary, "class-conciliating" state sought to legitimize itself, it focused on some measure of "political domestication and socialization," as well as on "consciousness-raising and peasant and worker mobilization." According to historian Mary Kay Vaughan, the focus was on "individual advancement and increased productivity," as well as "class harmony." Despite attempts to improve popular literacy in the cities and organize people in the countryside, the contradictions of the Mexican state project limited the transformative impact of education by the beginning of the Second World

War. (It should be noted here that one of the early influential proponents of literacy programs in the United Nations Educational, Scientific and Cultural Organization [UNESCO] was Director-General Jaime Torres Bodet, a Mexican educator, intellectual, bureaucrat, and diplomat who was greatly influenced by his country's experience.)[14]

After the Second World War, nongovernmental and intergovernmental organizations, as well as various kinds of foreign aid programs, proliferated, many of which focused on education and illiteracy in particular. The most important of these was UNESCO. UNESCO was founded, along with the United Nations (UN), in 1945, building on the examples of previous organizations like the International Institute of Intellectual Co-operation and the International Bureau of Education, both created in 1925 (the latter eventually merged with UNESCO in 1969). After the twentieth country ratified UNESCO's constitution, the organization officially was born 4 November 1946. It would come to have "both a standard-setting responsibility and a technical-cooperation function concerning adult education generally and adult literacy more specifically."[15] Concerted state action to address issues such as adult illiteracy became a mainstay of governments from all points on the political spectrum. After the immediate postwar needs of reconstruction were addressed, "development" became an almost universal aspiration during the 1950s, in part because of the need felt by nations during the Cold War years to prove that their economic and political systems should be the model for others to adopt if they wanted to achieve "First World" status. A mainstream and internationalized liberalism placed a greater emphasis on education as a solution to global problems.[16]

In much of the Western world, a theory of stages of development took hold. Development economics was, indeed, largely a postwar creation, but what became known as modernization theory became particularly important in the late 1950s and early 1960s. Prominent theorist W. W. Rostow argued for a five-stage linear progression through which all countries could pass in becoming "modern" (in other words, more like the United States and the major countries of western Europe). Rostow emphasized the growth of an economy's productive capacity, which was easier to measure than other development indicators. Rostow optimistically argued that poorer countries, after a certain amount of economic aid from developed countries, would, at some point, "take off" and not need further aid. (It should be noted here that Rostow later became an important adviser to U.S. presidents John F. Kennedy and Lyndon B. Johnson.) From the perspective of many in the Third World, the experience of the disruption of the global economy brought on by two world wars and a depression had taught the lessons that development could not any longer simply come from emphasizing the export of primary products; industrialization was essential. Many Latin American countries had begun to produce goods for the domestic market that they had previously imported. (Freire was born in what became one of the most industrialized nations in Latin America, Brazil, and he would do some of his most important work in one of the others, Chile.) Agriculture was to some degree neglected; where it was not, however, the assumption was that peasants needed to be weaned from subsistence agriculture. Although there were certainly already thinkers in Latin America who feared that the region's economic problems were relatively intractable, the period from the late 1950s through the late 1960s, which are discussed in the first three chapters of this book, was a relatively optimistic one. Problems during this period on even a fairly large scale were believed capable of resolution with appropriate state action, whether through foreign aid or through domestic state intervention in the economy.[17]

UNESCO eventually turned its attention to development, as well. One of its primary concerns in its first decade of existence was to promote what it called "fundamental education." The United Nations included education as one of the rights enumerated in its 1948 Universal Declaration of Human Rights. Although the concept of fundamental education was later abandoned as being too vaguely defined, an increasing connection was being made between education and development. The focus on development would expand UNESCO's horizons and tax its resources. An important component of this focus was on literacy itself. In the mid-1950s, a statistical survey of world illiteracy rates noted that roughly 75 percent of the world's population of illiterates lived in Asia, 15 percent lived in Africa, and roughly 6 percent lived in the Americas. While many Latin American countries had declining illiteracy rates, the total number of illiterates was still increasing.[18]

Latin America was now becoming linked with a large group of new nations just emerging from decades of colonial rule to become part of what became known as the Third World. Some of these former colonies would align themselves with the "First World" or the industrial West; Latin America as a region would remain part of the U.S. sphere of influence as it had been for decades before the Cold War began. Other newly independent countries would align themselves with the "Second World," or the Soviet Union and its allies. Many sought an elusive nonalignment.[19] The countries of the Third

World came to have an increasingly prominent role in the United Nations and UNESCO. Paulo Freire eventually would identify with a Third World Left that sought independence from both camps.

In Latin America, regional development concerns led UNESCO to initiate a "Major Project for the Extension and Improvement of Primary Education in Latin America" in 1957. The goals of the project, which lasted until 1965, were to help governments and the general public understand the impact of education on social and economic change; governments could then include educational spending as part of broader development programs. Teacher training courses were provided. Normal schools would also receive financial aid. UNESCO officials made grander claims for the project at times; the Assistant Director-General Malcolm S. Adiseshiah in 1958, for example, argued that the program would eliminate illiteracy in the region. Special teacher training courses were offered in Santiago, Chile; and São Paulo, Brazil, with the first class graduating in December 1958. The training of experts, it was believed, would have a trickle-down effect in spreading primary education for all throughout the region. Agriculture would improve because of an "educated mass population base"; industry would also thrive because of an "intelligent, literate and mobile" population. It was hoped that "a system of universal, free and compulsory primary education" for children between five and eleven in every Latin American country would eliminate illiteracy by 1968.[20]

In the postwar era, throughout the region, increased attention was paid to education issues. The proliferation of night schools offered opportunities for adult illiterates to better themselves, in keeping with a liberal, individualist model. Frequently, governments encouraged volunteers to teach reading and writing. They often employed the Laubach method, but they also frequently did not provide sufficient resources to guarantee success.

Historically, the Brazilian government had paid more attention to higher education and to the creation of a political class than to public education and the development of an educated citizenry.[21] A rural and slave society (slavery was abolished in 1888) with a dispersed population and a largely oral culture, Brazil's decentralized public school system was underfunded and undervalued. Even after the establishment of the republic in 1889, traditional patterns continued. Society was changing slowly and unequally. More than 80 percent of Brazil's population was living in the countryside at the turn of the twentieth century. Only slightly less than that percentage (roughly 75 percent) was illiterate. Migration to the cities (and, to a lesser extent, immigration) led to an increase in the urban population at a rate of roughly 5 percent a decade until the 1950s. From this point on, the rate of urbanization per decade was more than 9 percent. The constitution of 1891, following the Saraiva Law of 1882, had limited the right to vote to males who could read and write. The inadequacy of Brazil's educational system contributed greatly to the deprivation of large numbers of the population of their political rights as citizens. Brazil's oligarchical political system, a continuation to a large degree of that which had obtained during the years of the monarchy, from independence in 1822 to the establishment of a republic in 1889, had a space for regular elections but none for the active promulgation of citizenship. Brazil's large population of former slaves and their descendants were considered unfit for inclusion.[22]

Paulo Freire grew to maturity in an oligarchical Brazil on the verge of major changes. Brazil would no longer be the rural and even sleepy society it had been. Nor would the citizenry remain so relatively depoliticized and seemingly unconscious. Freire would share his century's, his nation's leaders' and, increasingly, his fellow countrymen's waking dreams of development. In these dreams, education would play a major, politically charged role. Cold War realities would create opportunities for dreamers and then shake them brutally awake. Freire's career would take him from a regional stage to a national one, and then, as a result of political difficulties, he would leave Brazil to make an international career and become influential in the First World as well as in the Third World. It is to his beginnings in the Brazilian northeast to which I now turn my attention.

Paulo Reglus Neves Freire was born on 19 September 1921 during the last years of the Old Republic (1889–1930) at a time in which greater attention was being paid to educational issues. Brazil is a country of 3.2 million square miles, and, at the time of Freire's birth, its population was roughly thirty million. It was, and is, a country of vast socioeconomic and regional inequalities. But it was a country that already in Freire's early years was beginning to move beyond its historic role as provider of sugar and coffee to a north Atlantic market. The beginnings of industrialization, though limited to the southern parts of the country, far from Freire's impoverished northeast, suggested a need to improve education. As Brazil underwent a protracted and incomplete transition from oligarchical to mass politics, educators and intellectuals like Freire sought to reform an educational system that had been implicated in perpetuating social inequality.

A generation of educators who became prominent in the 1920s, making up the so-called Escola Nova, or New School, movement, began to push for changes in the education system that would bring it more in line with evolving practices in the United States and Europe. They wanted to avoid overemphasizing literacy itself and to develop a more well-rounded education that would produce a modern Brazilian, characterized by hard work, health, and productivity. These reformers portrayed themselves as men of science, whose knowledge of the psychological and biological development of human beings, in particular, would help them bring about these changes in the ordinary Brazilian. Education, particularly a student-focused, active learning–based pedagogy, inspired by, among others, U.S. educator John Dewey, would bring about Brazil's salvation. The New School reformers' liberal individualism was put to the test when Getúlio Vargas, after coming to power in 1930, created the Ministry of Education and Public Health and employed many of these men as part of an effort to address educational issues on a national scale.[1]

The international crisis of the Great Depression ushered in a new era in Brazilian politics and a complex and contradictory figure who would dominate the nation's politics for the next quarter century. The rise of Vargas created the opportunity, it seemed, for a break in the traditional political system, not the least of which would be the introduction of the secret ballot and women's suffrage in 1932 and a turn toward the incorporation and manipulation of urban labor through the creation of an elaborate system of labor courts and laws. But these innovations seemed unlikely to lead Brazil toward a truer experience of democracy as Vargas took an increasingly authoritarian turn by the mid-1930s in response to the threat from both the Left and the Right. By 1937, Vargas seemed to have sided with the radical Right with his creation of a "New State," inspired, in part, by Italian and Portuguese models and established with the enthusiastic support of the military. Vargas courted the favor of traditionalists in the Catholic Church to help legitimize his turn to an authoritarian form of government in 1937 and encouraged a return to an emphasis on the church's role in education, blunting the effect of the New School reformers. Vargas established a regime that mixed paternalism, collectivism, nationalism, and statism. He promoted state-sponsored labor unions in order to achieve class harmony and encourage capitalist economic development. Although soon allied with the United States in the Second World War, even to the extent of sending troops to fight in Italy, he maintained a firm hold on government and society until the end of the war, when a new phase of democratization and labor mobilization began.[2]

In the early Vargas years, Brazil's low literacy levels had been increasingly recognized as a hindrance to national economic development. Adult illiteracy, however, only became an issue toward the end of Vargas's dictatorship. In 1944, Lourenço Filho, an educator who had helped give the name to the New School in a book he had written in 1929, and director of the Instituto Nacional de Estudos e Pesquisas Educacionais (National Institute of Pedagogical Studies, INEP), called on state governments to address the issue. Following Vargas's forced departure from power in 1945 and the establishment of an elected government, the Serviço de Educação de Adultos (Adult Education Service) was created in January 1947. In this national campaign, primary attention was given to providing night courses for adults. Although the states received federal grant money for this initiative (which was supposed to equal 25 percent of all national education funds), teachers often were volunteers. "The most enlightened part of the population understands its duty to cooperate in the recuperation of the large mass of illiterates," Lourenço Filho proclaimed. Borrowing from Frank Laubach the idea that one should establish a "minimum vocabulary for the average adult," the Adult Education Service prepared "reading guides" rather than "primers," to avoid making illiterate adults feel that they were being treated like children. Intended not to merely teach people to read and write but to help people "lead fuller lives," the material in the beginner guides focused on problems related to work, health, and daily life while the more advanced material focused on citizenship. A literacy hymn written for the campaign in 1949 promised that "we are now citizens, equal to all of our brothers." Its slogan was "For the love of the children, we should educate the adults." At its peak in 1953, the campaign may have reached 850,000 people. The campaign seems to have been a factor in the relatively rapid decline (11.2 percent) of illiteracy in the 1950s. Although this program faded out in 1954, there continued to be work done on literacy issues, primarily on the state level. One of the primary achievements of this program was to "raise interest in public education on all levels," according to scholar Celso de Rui Beiseigel. After Vargas was democratically elected president in 1950, his administration also sponsored a national rural education campaign.[3]

Brazil had begun to accelerate the transition to a more diversified and semi-industrial economy under Vargas. But the idea of economic development as a national, even popular, goal took hold in the late 1950s, particularly during the administration of Juscelino Kubitschek (1956–61), who promised "fifty years' development in five." By encouraging foreign investment and state-sponsored improvements to transportation and power capacity, he achieved economic growth rates "three times that of the rest of Latin America." The ultimate symbol of his "drive for development" was the building of a new capital in the heart of Brazil.[4] Surprisingly, perhaps, given its developmentalist orientation, Kubitschek's administration paid relatively little attention to education in its first years in office. A new campaign intended to "eradicate" illiteracy, as if it were a kind of disease, began in 1958 with a series of pilot programs in communities in each region of the country. Although the programs focused on both children and adults and recognized the need to connect adult education with improvements in people's working conditions, they seem to have had relatively little impact. By 1960, an estimated twenty million teenage and adult Brazilians out of a total population of roughly seventy million were illiterate.[5]

Having experienced a modernizing dictatorship under Getúlio Vargas in the 1930s and 1940s, which had begun to accelerate the process of social and economic change, Brazilians in the postwar period entered the most democratic phase in their history up to that point. The growth of a more urban and literate population made possible an expanding electorate, which grew from 16 percent of the population in 1945 to 25 percent by 1962. This made a return to traditional oligarchical arrangements difficult, at least in the more developed areas in the south. There, politicians often adopted a more populist persona and made direct appeals to urban workers for votes. Vargas had helped shape postwar politics by supporting the creation of two political parties. One, the Partido Trabalhista Brasileira (Brazilian Labor Party, PTB), was oriented toward the interests of urban workers, whose support Vargas had cultivated at the beginning and toward the end of his dictatorship. The PTB reflected Vargas's own inconsistencies but came to constitute the left of the mainstream political spectrum. Vargas also had strong support from the other party, the Partido Social Democrático (Social Democratic Party, PSD), which had the support of the more traditional sectors as well as newer industrial interests. (Vargas continued to have ties to both parties in the period prior to his election as president in 1950 as the candidate of the PTB and a small party linked to the populist politician Adhemar de Barros, but, once elected, he gave only one cabinet position to the PTB.) A third major party, professing classical liberal values but defining itself largely in opposition to Vargas, was the União Democrática Nacional (National Democratic Union, UDN).[6]

Other trends contributed to a more pluralistic and politically dynamic atmosphere. Despite its illegal status for much of the period under consideration here, the Communist Party continued to play a small but significant role. The growth of a reformist strain in the Catholic Church, notably the proliferation of various student movements, including the Juventude Universitária Católica (Catholic University Youth, JUC), was important as well. Generally, there was a more questioning attitude among certain intellectual sectors. Catholics in Recife who were active in Ação Popular (Popular Action, AP), the lay organization for adults and youths, were influenced by the example of French lay people who had begun faith-based work with the urban popular classes.[7]

Paulo Freire himself was a young man in the 1940s. Although he lived in a country that was beginning to dream of development, he was born and grew up in a part of the country that development seemed to have passed by. His parents had not been the poorest in the region, but the Great Depression and his father's ill health (due to arterial sclerosis) left its mark, forcing the family to relocate from Recife to the nearby town of Jaboatão, where the cost of living was lower. Years later, Freire recalled how his parents refused to sell the family piano, which marked their middle-class status during times of difficulty. Freire's father's death when the boy was only thirteen, however, left the family in even more difficult circumstances. Later in life, he often recalled the experience of hunger during those years as well as the friendships he made with people from the working class. While still in high school, he began his career as a teacher. Somewhat belatedly, at the age of twenty, he entered the University of Recife law school, which had trained the nation's leaders since the nineteenth century. His career, however, would follow a different path. He taught Portuguese on the high school level to help put himself through school and continued teaching even after he got the degree. He married another educator, Elza Maia Costa de Oliveira, in 1944.[8]

Freire abandoned the practice of law even before he accepted his first case to work for the Pernambuco branch of the Serviço Social de Indústria (Industrial Social Service, SESI), an industrialist-funded agency for the "improvement" of the popular classes created in June 1946, roughly a year before he finished his degree. The organization was founded in response to labor protests regarding the rising cost of living in Brazil as the Second World War progressed. The emerging Cold War exacerbated fears that the limited educational opportunities available to Brazil's working class made them likely to be led astray by left-wing leaders. The organization promised to deliver "social peace in Brazil." By eliminating class conflict, the organization would help further economic development. The organization employed social workers and educators, offered advice on personal and domestic problems, and provided adult literacy classes in which the cultivation of respectability and regular work habits, hygiene, and self-help were stressed.[9]

The first president of Pernambuco's branch of the new organization was Cid Sampaio, an owner of a sugar-processing plant. "His vision of service and his politics of action were actually liberal in orientation, but so much more open than the politics of half his industrial colleagues that they could be considered progressive," Freire recalled (although, as we shall see, Sampaio became a political enemy of some politicians with whom Freire later would be allied). Freire became the director of SESI's education and culture division. He was by now once again a member of the middle class, with a maid

Paulo Freire speaking as director of the education sector of the Pernambuco branch of SESI, 1949. Photo courtesy of Lutgardes Costa Freire.

(as was common among the Brazilian middle class) and a driver (which was not), but his work, as he later recalled, "made possible [his] reencounter with working-class reality."[10]

In eight years as director of education and two as superintendent of SESI-Pernambuco, he worked on "relations between the schools and families" and the "difficulties that families from popular areas would have in confronting problems with the implementation of their own educational activity." When liberal Rutgers economist and Latin Americanist Robert Alexander visited SESI in February 1956, Freire told him about the breakdown of traditional paternalistic bonds in Brazil due to the impact of industrialization and the consequent "dehumanization of labor." Freire said that he was skeptical that "social service" was an adequate replacement for the former paternalism, although, decades later, he would argue that SESI itself had been a paternalistic attempt to prevent workers' critical consciousness toward their working and living conditions and the organization of their society. The autonomy of the various branches of SESI, however, allowed Freire to experiment with new ideas and new ways of prompting workers, particularly in Recife itself, to think about and address what they themselves considered common problems. In keeping with the larger SESI interest in education as a means to promote active citizenship, Freire sought ways to encourage workers to become more involved with and informed about the electoral process. Accused even at this early date of being a communist, Freire told Alexander that he had no sympathy for communism and wanted to address Brazil's problems by using "Christian methods." Throughout his career with SESI, Freire tried to promote dialogue between officials and members of the urban and rural working classes and to encourage workers to get more involved in their children's education (to instill what he called a "pedagogical consciousness"). He later claimed that he had tried to progress from his own "discourse about the reading of the world to them" to motivate and challenge them "to speak of their own reading of the world." During these years, he also studied popular language, an endeavor that would help supply the foundation for his literacy training techniques, which used the language that adult illiterates actually employed in their daily life.[11]

In 1956, populist mayor Pelópidas Silveira named Freire to Recife's Conselho Consultivo de Educação (Consultative Education Council). Freire became well-known in educational circles nationally after presenting a paper on teaching the "marginal population" of the mocambos (improvised shantytowns) at the second national congress on adult education in July 1958 in Rio de Janeiro. At the meeting he argued that students should participate in the making of their own work plans and that teachers could learn from the illiterate.[12]

In the postwar era in Brazil, a new ideology known as "developmental nationalism" had taken hold, and it shaped Freire's understanding of the world. Much of the language and the worldview that many outside Brazil have tended to see as uniquely Freirean comes from the writers and thinkers associated with this school of thought, whose works dominated the first personal library Freire maintained in Recife. These authors were most often affiliated with the Instituto Superior de Estudos Brasileiros (Higher Institute of Brazilian Studies, ISEB). For these largely non-Marxist thinkers, it was possible through statist and nationalist policies of economic development to produce harmony among the classes, along with a transition to a new phase in Brazil's history. Freire and the isebianos (those affiliated with the ISEB) emphasized class over race (and over gender, an emphasis of later generations). Class for Freire and many at this time in Brazil was an imprecise concept, and so it continued to be throughout his career. Freire's vision remained throughout his career fairly inclusively nationalistic and oriented toward the poor. The cultivation of a critical consciousness, indeed, the idea of an awakening of consciousness so frequently attributed to Freire, was a central concern of these thinkers. It was this emphasis on consciousness-raising that separated him from previous generations of educational reformers.[13]

The isebianos saw the Brazil of Freire's young adulthood as a country in transition, experiencing the possibility of a truer experience of democracy, in which as an increasing number of people took part in elections, either traditional patterns of patron-client relations would be reinforced or Brazilians of the popular classes would develop a larger awareness of their changing social realities. The proliferation of mass media created a greater understanding of differing economic and social levels in Brazil and the world at large. And yet illiterates, unable to vote since the reform of 1882, were denied the opportunity to have the crucial learning experiences provided by participation in the electoral process.[14]

The dream of economic development, according to the isebianos, required that Brazil move beyond its traditional emphasis on the elite manipulation of ornamental language. The traditional elite, distant from Brazil's social realities, had shown that it could no longer lead. Anísio Teixeira, an author associated with the New School of educational reform but also linked to the developmental nationalists, spoke of the "civilization of engineers" as "the civilization of our time." He and others thought Brazil needed to adopt an educational system more in accordance with its aspirations rather than continue with a system designed for leisure and the "parasitism" of "office holders." Illiteracy, as one isebiano wrote, would only be eliminated when Brazil's economy and society had become truly industrial and urban.[15]

While Freire was heavily influenced by the isebianos, it would be wrong to ignore those influences Freire received from existentialist and Catholic thinkers of the postwar period, not least of all in the ways they informed the idealism that he frequently denied but that also drew others to him. He worked extensively in his free time with Catholic lay groups. French Catholic thinker Jacques Maritain's call for Catholics to address the problems of modern society led many to a deeper engagement with matters of this world. (Freire's debt to Maritain undoubtedly played a part in the second half of the 1960s in his willingness to work in the administration of the Latin American politician most deeply influenced by Maritain, the Chilean president Eduardo Frei.) As Vanilda Paiva notes, Catholic humanists and existentialists emphasized dialogue with "the other." And dialogue was to be a constant in Freirean practice throughout his career. The Hegelian distinction between nature and culture, the emphasis on authenticity and a process of humanization, and the actions of human beings as subjects of their own history all became central building blocks in Freire's theory and action.[16]

But to understand Freire we have to understand not only the national and international intellectual contexts but also the local political context. In the late 1950s, Recife was in many ways the radiating center of new and more adventurous political forces (which will be discussed more in depth in Chapter 2).[17] The city, Brazil's third largest in the early 1960s, was growing rapidly during this time period, as some people were being pushed off the land and others were choosing to make new lives in the city. The urban revolution that was transforming Brazil generally was changing the political dynamics in the northeast. Even more than was typical for cities in the south, the growth of Pernambuco's capital had far outstripped the growth in industry and infrastructure that provided employment and services to the newly urban population, and many of those Freire would work with were more often employed in domestic service than in industrial labor.[18] Recife experienced its first truly democratic elections in 1955, after decades in which the mayor had been appointed. From 1958 on, labor laws on the books through decades of incomplete implementation even in the more industrialized regions to the south began to be applied to some degree in the northeast.[19] But it was not just in the city that new dynamics were at work. The "peasant leagues" had begun to develop, first in 1955 in Galiléia, forty miles west of Recife. After an initial focus on issues such as creating a communal fund to help pay for burial expenses for their members, these organizations gradually became more oriented to larger issues of social and political transformation. In many ways, as Francisco de Oliveira has argued, the northeastern "peace" was eroding.[20]

State party politics could hardly remain immune to these social changes and increasing mobilization. In postwar Recife, as politician Etelvino Lins remarked, "One [couldn't] win elections . . . without the support of the left."[21] The 1958 election of Governor Cid Sampaio, an engineer, UDN dissident, and Freire's former boss at SESI, with 60 percent of the vote and the election of Recife's mayor (and Sampaio's then brother-in-law) Miguel Arraes in the following year were accomplished through the creation of a broad coalition of forces, including the Partido Comunista Brasileira (Brazilian Communist Party, PCB). Such coalitions were, necessarily, unwieldy and often short-lived.[22] Although Sampaio distanced himself from the Left after the election, these new political forces created a more dynamic era in Pernambuco politics, particularly in the city of Recife itself.

Emblematic of this was the new Movimento de Cultura Popular (Popular Culture Movement, MCP), founded in the city on 13 May 1960. The timing of the organization of the movement by Arraes's associates to coincide with the date of the abolition of slavery in Brazil less than a century before was intentional, since Germano Coelho and other leaders of the movement claimed to be trying to liberate the popular classes. Inspired by the French magazine *Esprit* and the writings of Emmanuel Mounier, Coelho saw an opportunity, as he put it, to renovate Christianity. Coelho was further influenced by the "people and culture" movement in France. The MCP, which involved popular theater as well as educational activities on the primary and (and, increasingly) adult levels, brought together, as Coelho recalled, "Catholics and communists, evangelicals and spiritists, students and professors, artists and the popular classes." The local archbishop even urged Catholics to work with communists. The movement relied on local businesses for funding, however, and the program was, in the beginning, quite uncontroversial. Faculty members and administrators from the University of Recife and the Catholic University of Pernambuco got involved. Freire, who had been increasingly drawn to work with the popular classes at this time in his nonworking hours, coordinated the research for the movement as a whole, as well as for the adult education program specifically. He began to experiment with cultural circles, in which members of a community joined together to discuss common interests and concerns and to work together; these "circles," which were built on his previous experience with SESI, became central to his work for the rest of his life. He began focusing increasingly on adult illiteracy and developing what in time would become known as the Paulo Freire method.[23]

It was at this time that Freire's northeast gained renewed attention nationally and internationally with the drought of 1958, the worst in decades. Journalist Antônio Callado in a series of articles for the Rio de Janeiro newspaper *Correio da Manha* created national interest in the problems of the sertão, the northeastern backlands in the interior, and the failure of previous government efforts to solve them. The United States rather gingerly offered assistance for the relief efforts but found President Kubitschek reluctant to accept its aid, presumably because of a sense of national pride, but also because of a belief that this was a problem with which the government was quite familiar already.[24] Despite his administration's emphasis on development, however, Kubitschek had paid relatively little attention to the region's problems in his first two years in office.[25] The authorization in 1959 of the creation of the Superintendência do Desenvolvimento do Nordeste

(Northeastern Development Agency, SUDENE), a development agency for the northeast, however, demonstrated that the federal government was going to devote more resources to the region. Recife's importance to the region was further enhanced after SUDENE began operating there in 1961.[26]

In that year, one rather anxious U.S. State Department official remarked, "This part of Brazil is presently making history."[27] The northeast had now become more than just a chronic problem area, with its high levels of poverty and unemployment. Through the Popular Culture Movement and the peasant leagues, it was also offering a range of possible solutions to some of the nation's long-standing problems, including illiteracy and the lack of political integration of a large portion of its population.

With an understanding of the local political context and the national intellectual context, one must also turn to Freire's neglected writings of the time period to see how his ideas were developing. The most important of these writings is a paper titled "Education and Brazilian Actuality," which he wrote for a competition for a chair in the history and philosophy of education department at the Escola de Belas Artes de Pernambuco (Pernambuco School of Fine Arts). Drawing heavily on the developmental nationalists already discussed, this manuscript of a little more than 100 pages introduced many of the major themes that would preoccupy him for the rest of this life. Education, Freire contended, had become a subject of increasing importance in the "national problematic"; it was necessary to adopt an ever more critical consciousness toward it. Human beings, who are able to analyze and to recognize themselves as historical actors and creators of culture, need to be "integrated into their reality" and to be able to act and change that reality. Brazil's overly verbal and verbose education, which was a reflection of the country's authoritarian traditions, was not helping achieve that goal. Since education was not aiding in the country's "political and cultural democratization," it was "inorganic" and "inoperative." In his work with SESI, Freire had become aware of the need for a "democratic education," the "work of man with man" and not "for man." Influenced by French Catholic Simone Weil, Freire saw that Brazilian workers needed to have more opportunities to participate actively in their working and community lives and in the schools of their children. Drawing on the work of Romanian psychologist Zevedei Barbu on dictatorship and democracy, Freire insisted on the centrality of dialogue in the making of a democracy and of citizens capable of being active members of their society. Freire believed that through his work with SESI he had really gotten to know workers and had developed a way of talking to them about their problems by using the language they used in their daily lives.[28]

Freire situated his analysis within a historical context in which Brazilian's "democratic inexperience" was in conflict with the new "immersion of people in national public life," which had resulted from the country's industrial development. People were "emerging" and "demanding solutions" to their problems but were being held back by authoritarian habits, the tendency to defer to authority ("Do you know whom you are talking to?") and to put personal loyalties over the common good ("To our friends everything, to our enemies, the law."), as well as the tendency to be passive and to remain silent. Without active participation, economic development would always be limited. People who were still accepting magical explanations for natural events and who were becoming "massified" could not contribute. Despite his fears of what Djacir Menezes called "a democracy without people," Freire still saw evidence of what he called an opposition to quietism on the national level. Brazil needed to provide an education that gave students practice in solving problems and to seek solutions through a true understanding of the nation's authentic culture and needs. Brazil's "great challenge," he insisted, was not just the elimination of illiteracy; it was the eradication of "democratic inexperience" and the "creation of education for democracy," as well as an education that suited the country's economic goals.[29]

As the 1950s ended, Freire was deeply engaged in educational issues and the role that education could play in helping address Brazil's social, economic, and political problems. He was not limiting himself to the problem of illiteracy. To understand the next turn in his life, which would make him first a regional, then quickly a national, then a hemispheric, and finally an international figure, we must turn to global trends that made illiteracy a defining issue of this stage of the Cold War and of his career.

Beginning in 1960, the United Nations and UNESCO sought to place greater emphasis on educational issues. With a series of meetings of ministers of education, the first being the World Conference on Adult Education held in Montreal in 1960, UNESCO brought more attention to education issues and sought to spur more attention to educational planning by national governments. In 1961, the UN General Assembly "asked UNESCO for a report on world illiteracy and recommendations for action." UNESCO's response was that it planned to wage a "worldwide frontal assault on illiteracy."[30] The rapid decolonization of Africa, in particular, gave more weight to poorer countries in both the United Nations and UNESCO and transformed these organizations, increasingly, from First World to Third World institutions.[31] In the early 1960s, while primary education was not neglected, adult illiteracy became a central international issue. Literacy and education generally were now linked as key to ever more urgent economic development. Beginning in 1960, there would be calls and plans for eliminating illiteracy during the course of the decade. The UN General Assembly soon called for its complete eradication. In 1961, UNESCO called a meeting at which experts in the field urged governments to address the issue. The fact that so many African countries were becoming independent in these years played a role in bringing questions of nation-building to the fore. Illiteracy rates between 80 and 85 percent on the continent became an urgent social and economic issue.[32]

Oscar Vera, the Chilean coordinator of UNESCO's major project, noted that while illiteracy in Latin America had been cut in half since 1900 (from 80 percent to 40 percent), the seventy million illiterates in the region still represented "one of the gravest obstacles to social and economic development." UNESCO took perhaps unwarranted credit for the increase in primary education in Latin America since it had initiated its "Major Project for the Extension and Improvement of Primary Education in Latin America" in 1957 (discussed in the Introduction). One skeptical UNESCO employee working in Santiago in 1962 noted that "the effort and impact may well be classified as minor—rather than major." Others noted that the primary achievement of the major project had been the "broadening" of "the horizons of the participants," both teachers and educational administrators, enabling them to analyze the problems of their native countries. Students in the program also got a better understanding of "social, political and economic phenomena in education." As UNESCO officials often felt obliged to remark on numerous occasions, the most important thing that UNESCO achieved was to make countries aware of their own responsibilities in the area of education and to help prevent them from making errors.[33] Looking back after the program had ended some years later, Juan José Arévalo, an educator and former president of Guatemala, noted that "Latin America needs specialists and that is what is easiest to provide." Critics of the program, however, argued that after starting out with a common curriculum, the students in the program over the course of the years had become overly specialized. (Of the students in the Brazilian program, 110 had focused on teacher education, 86 on school administration, 92 on methodology, and 21 in investigation techniques.)[34] The elite focus of the project, some UNESCO critics contended, was already being superseded, due to events in Cuba.

In a speech before the UN General Assembly on 20 September 1960, Cuban leader Fidel Castro made a vow to "eliminate illiteracy in one year." By the standards of most developing countries, Cuba already had a relatively low illiteracy rate, roughly 23 percent. Cuba ranked the fifth lowest regionally in Latin America on the eve of the revolution. Castro had announced plans for an intensive campaign against illiteracy while the armed struggle against Fulgencio Batista was still in its infancy in mid-1957. Following the departure of Batista, the new government established literacy programs in the revolutionary army and in the police force. Illiteracy was also being addressed in Cuba's cities and, to some extent, as part of Cuba's agrarian reform program over the course of 1959. Castro, however, wanted to create a program that would reach all corners of the island. Model primers from around the world were evaluated. A study was made of the working vocabulary of rural Cubans. In a country of roughly seven million, around 300,000 youth and adult volunteers were enlisted in the campaign, which lasted from April through December of 1961. The timing of Cuba's "Year of Education" itself is significant, since the campaign began around the time of the defeat of the U.S.-sponsored Bay of Pigs invasion and ended around the time that Castro announced that he was a Marxist-Leninist. Following Castro's speech at the UN, a national census was taken and teachers were recruited. As the campaign began, schools were closed so that Cubans ages thirteen and older could participate in a mass volunteer effort focused on a single goal, which would come to characterize the Cuban revolutionary government's idealism. Posters containing slogans such as "If you can teach, teach; if you can't teach, learn" were posted around the country. To facilitate social leveling and integration, as well as a broader understanding of the nation's economic and social problems, the government encouraged youths, who were key to the revolutionary process, to teach willing peasants. Children in sixth-grade and higher were organized into "Conrado Benitez brigades" (in memory of a literacy teacher employed by the agrarian reform institute who was killed by opponents of the revolution). A smaller group of factory workers became teachers in the "Fatherland or Death" brigades. Ideally, each teacher would have one or two students (although this was less often achieved in practice). Primers were intended to foster revolutionary values, a "sense of self-worth," and a faith in Castro as a leader. Photographs depicting typical Cuban daily activities were included. Teachers were supposed to encourage discussion of Cuban realities, some of which urbanites new to rural settings were just now learning. Teaching and learning were conceived of as being part of the larger revolutionary struggle that was transforming Cubans into "new men." By the time the triumphant brigadistas returned to Havana in late December to celebrate after an intensified effort in the final four months of the campaign, an estimated 707,212 Cubans had been taught to read and write, reducing the illiteracy rate to 4 percent (271,995 students remained illiterate).[35]

Castro promised those involved in the literacy campaign that its effects would "be felt all over the world."[36] Governments, indeed, did engage in discussion over whether they should replicate the kind of mass campaigns Cuba had undertaken. Many argued that these campaigns only provided temporary results and that the emphasis instead should be on education for production.[37] Nevertheless, the seeming success of the Cuban model helped create a more politicized environment for addressing literacy issues in the 1960s.

Castro's leftward turn led the new U.S. president, John F. Kennedy, in March 1961 to announce the creation of the Alliance for Progress, which greatly resembled President Kubitschek's call for a hemispheric aid program in 1958. The alliance, the more idealistic component of the Kennedy administration's Latin America policy, represented a large-scale effort to promote internal reforms in the region in an attempt to lessen the appeal (and the perceived threat) of revolution. Drawing on Kennedy aide Walt Rostow's understanding of economic development, the administration believed it could help Latin American nations achieve economic "take-off" and become modern. The United States was seeking to promote what Arthur Schlesinger Jr., Kennedy's special assistant, called a "middle-class revolution." Included in the ambitious program of economic growth and improvements in health, sanitation, and transportation was a promise to eliminate illiteracy by the end of the decade, since, like UNESCO, the United States understood that education was a central component in political and economic development. As scholars Christina Luhn, Michael Latham, and others have argued, U.S. experts rooted in Progressivism believed they had mastered the art of modernization and could replicate the successes of both U.S. long-term development and the more immediate experience of the Marshall Plan in western Europe.[38]

The Alliance for Progress, as well as the indirect influence of the Cuban Revolution, led to a greater emphasis on Freire's northeast. With 15 percent of Brazil's territory and one-third of its population, the region "had the lowest per capita income in Latin America" and a significant portion of the nation's illiterates.[39] By 1960, *New York Times* reporter Tad Szulc was already noting "the makings of a revolutionary situation" in the "poverty-stricken and drought-plagued Brazilian Northeast." The Kennedy administration began to focus on the northeast more directly. By early February of 1961, even before the Alliance for Progress was announced, the United States was already interested in providing aid for the region through "the new Social Development Program." Close Kennedy aides visited the region at this time.[40] By midyear U.S. anxieties regarding the region were quite pronounced. "The area contains many influential communist or pro-communist leaders," one U.S. official in Recife warned, "and efforts to subvert the area, already serious, may be expected to become more intensive and extensive during the immediate future." The region was "undoubtedly the priority area of Brazil, and possibly, Latin America." Officials in the region requested more personnel to handle "political reporting" and related responsibilities. "The eyes of the world are on Recife," one State Department official remarked, noting that it had only recently been considered "a third-class outpost." In July of 1961, President Kennedy announced a plan for the northeast, noting that "[n]o area in this hemisphere is in greater or more urgent need of attention than Brazil's vast Northeast." The region as a whole would have its own U.S. Agency for International Development (USAID) mission, which was not true for any other region in the world.[41]

President Kennedy also called for a global "decade of development" in a speech before the UN General Assembly in September of 1961. In response, UN Resolution 1710 (XVI) in December pledged united efforts by countries to "intensify their efforts to mobilize and to sustain support for the measures required on the part of both developed and developing countries to accelerate progress toward self-sustaining growth of the economy of the individual nations and their social advancement." Education was to be a central component in the UN's planning.[42]

It was in this international context that Freire's rise to prominence must be understood. Without the decolonization in the Third World and its impact on the UN and UNESCO support for development through education, and without the larger challenge posed by Fidel Castro to the United States generally and specifically on the issue of adult literacy, there would have been no urgent need for the new techniques that Freire was developing in the Popular Culture Movement. Freire himself had known very little even of his own country, let alone of the world, in 1960.[43] Local, regional, national, and international developments all came together in the 1960s to provide a space and time for Freire to become identified with the issue of adult literacy and with the process of consciousness-raising, first in the northeast and then nationally. Intergovernmental organizations and other foreign aid providers promoting development and inspired by a faith in state planning; a Cold War environment of fear and competition; an urbanizing, industrializing, and democratizing nation and society; and an evolving Catholic Church in the 1960s together propelled Freire into history.

Two / The Revolution that Wasn't & the Revolution that Was in Brazil, 1961–1964

With the accession to power of João Goulart following the unexpected resignation of President Jânio Quadros in August 1961, regional, national, and international dynamics turned illiteracy into a national issue of great political import and Paulo Freire himself into a major figure in political and educational circles. The northeast continued to be a center of dynamic and creative political impulses, as this chapter demonstrates, but state and local government activities now combined with the power and resources of a national government that was in the process of trying to define itself and an expanding student political movement that sought to have an impact nationally. It was in this time period that the idea of learning to read and write in forty hours of class time took hold, exemplifying the impatience of a wide variety of political actors in an anxious time. For many, like Freire's soon-to-be boss in the Ministry of Education, Paulo de Tarso Santos, it was "a revolutionary time . . . of profound and irreversible social change." Pernambuco politician Miguel Arraes and others often spoke of a "Brazilian Revolution."[1] But the constant references to revolution obscured disagreements over what the term meant, whether it was the rapid economic and social changes that were taking place, the impact of an ever expanding electorate, or a deliberate attempt by political forces to transform the political system, whether through peaceful or violent means. It also was a revolution, many insisted, that might come about through the dramatic expansion of educational opportunities for adult illiterates.[2] The sense of a changing historical reality is ever present in the rhetoric of this period, and not least of all in Freire's writings, in which the passage from a closed to an open society is paramount, as well as the dangers of this process being "distorted."[3] The talk of revolution, which some took to be merely descriptive and others predictive or prescriptive, raised alarm bells in some quarters. New and old forms of paternalism, however, combined with the promise of mobilization and empowerment, raised the possibility of, and inhibited the potential for, a transformation of Brazil into a more profoundly democratic country. Paulo Freire's rise to national prominence from 1961 to 1964 needs to be understood within the complex interplay of local, state, regional, national, and international forces in this time period. As João Francisco de Souza has argued, education became "the axis of a struggle polarized between a social project of popular tendencies and another modernizing one."[4] U.S. intervention, both in the northeast and throughout Brazil, also sought to shape internal political developments. In the end, however, a politically awakened military, supported by both the United States and more traditional civilian politicians, would cut short the state and national projects of Governor Arraes, President Goulart, and many others, as well as the dreams of Freire himself.[5]

Had Kubitschek's successor, Quadros, not resigned in August 1961, after less than seven full months in office, it is hard to imagine that literacy would have come to play quite as important a role as it did in defining the complex political dynamics of the period. Although Quadros himself was a former teacher and not uninterested in literacy, the fact that he was replaced by a man who had gained a reputation among the Brazilian military and traditional civilian politicians as dangerous was critical here. And the fact that the United States tended to take its political cues on Brazilian politics from these two groups, and, consequently, to provide covert aid to Goulart's enemies, contributed to further political polarization in Brazil. The United States, as demonstrated in the previous chapter, was already concerned about the example of Cuba and the restiveness of the Brazilian northeast. The U.S. emphasis on the region and the fact that aid agreements were being made with individual governors within the region made the United States more involved in Brazilian state politics than ever before or since. Some of these politicians were allied with the federal government, as we shall see, while others looked to the United States for patronage. Freire himself worked for a wide variety of them during this time period. President Goulart, for his part, needed to find reliable allies. Freire's hiring by the Ministry of Education coincided in 1963 with a shift to the left in President Goulart's political calculations. And the Ministry of Education itself also came to symbolize what many feared most about Goulart's administration.[6]

The central focus of Freire's activities from 1961 to early 1963 was still the northeast, where his influence was increasing. Northeastern reformist and nationalist politicians alike made mass literacy campaigns important components in their political projects. At the same time, as part of the Alliance for Progress, a "Special Northeast Agreement" was signed on the 13 April 1962. In a letter to President Goulart, President Kennedy promised that this agreement would "change the face of Northeast Brazil" (a phrase that U.S. ambassador to Brazil Lincoln Gordon had hoped would be stricken from the final text). The agreement envisioned a five-year development program, overseen by "the largest and only regional U.S.A.I.D. Mission in the world located outside of an embassy." The overall goal of the United States at that time was to provide an "action program of sufficient magnitude to impress upon the aspiring, democratic people of Brazil the willingness of the Alliance for Progress to join with them in seeking a lasting improvement in their way of life." Part of the appeal of the Freire method, overemphasized during the early 1960s and, fortunately, less central later, as we shall see, was the promise of providing "basic literacy in forty hours using minimal resources." But the United States also shared the explicit goals of those who wanted to "make [Brazilians] capable of being citizens." Christina Luhn argues that along with the sense of urgency so typical of this time period, "the unshakeable faith in the ameliorative powers of education clouded the U.S. officials' ability to understand the truly 'subversive' nature of Freire's program." One could argue, though Luhn does not, that U.S. officials' belief in a "middle-class revolution" that educational opportunities could create blinded them to the more popular revolution that many in Brazil anticipated.[7]

U.S. interest in the region was nowhere more visible than in Recife, where the number of U.S. advisers tripled over the course of 1962. The "huge AID mission," U.S. vice consul in Recife Lowell C. Kilday warned Ambassador Gordon, was an "easy target" for anti-U.S. politicians. It was certainly clear by 1962 that the Alliance for Progress was being used for political purposes. President Kennedy had urged USAID to "institute such programs as may be possible on an urgent basis in order to attempt to influence the 1962 elections in Brazil." Negotiations with the state of Pernambuco were conducted separately, in part inspired by U.S. interest in preventing the election of Recife mayor Arraes as governor in October. Former Freire boss and current Pernambuco governor Cid Sampaio had been urging the United States since at least June 1961 to provide aid that would produce visible results in time to influence the election. USAID signed an agreement that included support for a literacy campaign. Sampaio belatedly followed his own advice only weeks before the election by signing an agreement in September 1962 with a group that planned to employ the Laubach literacy method. Meanwhile, the rhetoric surrounding the Recife Popular Culture Movement heated up. While Arraes himself made the literacy component of the Popular Culture Movement one of the cornerstones of his campaign for governor, his opponents on the city council and elsewhere focused on the movement as a whole as "a nest of cobras." But despite U.S. support for many candidates who opposed Goulart, many on the Left, including Arraes, were elected. Arraes's victory and his frequent denunciations of the Alliance for Progress, both before and after the election, led the United States to distance itself from the most important state in the region. For his part, Freire, despite his strong ties to Arraes and whatever his own misgivings about the Alliance were, continued to work with governments closely allied with the United States, as well as some who were somewhat skeptical of U.S. motivations, and still others who were outspoken in their opposition to U.S. "intervention."[8]

U.S. officials' anxieties regarding the potential, in particular, of the Brazilian northeast were somewhat offset by analyses that suggested that the ignorance, fatalism, and passivity of the Brazilian peasantry mitigated against revolutionary agitation. "Most did not think they could help themselves," a U.S. Information Service study concluded. Few of the northeastern peasants were familiar either with Castro or the Alliance for Progress; moreover, the Brazilian peasantry were extremely difficult to organize.[9] The diffusion and success of Freire's programs in changing people's consciousness to offset these disadvantages, in urban as well as rural environments, would be critical.

From 1962 through 1964, the influence of Freire undoubtedly spread wider and deeper. Even within his own state of Pernambuco, his ideas and techniques became more broadly diffused. Arraes's election as governor extended the activities of the Popular Culture Movement into the interior. Arraes thought that by supporting campesinos' demands for respect for their rights, he could promote modernization in the countryside.[10] As Arraes argued, "The consciousness which Brazilian man is rapidly acquiring of his necessities and possibilities is one of the most important new elements of our process of change."[11] Germano Coelho, the movement's founder and a man U.S. undersecretary of state George Ball feared was a "communist or crypto-communist," was named the state minister of education. The United States certainly was quite concerned about the Popular Culture Movement by this point. U.S. officials considered the movement, "charged with the mission of politicizing Pernambuco's masses," to be "a vehicle for expansion of PCB influence," noting that the president of the organization in March 1964 was Governor Arraes's cousin, Newton Arraes, a Communist Party member. U.S. minister consul general Edward Rowell considered the "adult literacy program of the MCP as the program with the greatest potential for mass politicization." Although he himself had not seen the materials the MCP was using, Rowell felt confident that the course taught "class separation" and furthered "class antagonism" and "support for a 'popular' government." MCP teachers, for their part, told U.S. officials that the literacy campaign would prevent the election of a "reactionary" government.[12] Under Arraes, Pernambuco largely resisted any attempts to be drawn into the new patron-client relations that were being developed in the region under the Alliance for Progress. In a report prepared for the Arraes government, intellectuals closely associated with the movement rejected U.S. aid for education in Pernambuco, which they considered a violation of Brazilian national sovereignty.[13]

The MCP, however, was not without its own internal conflicts. Freire refused to put together a primer, but, according to his close associate Anita Paes Barreto, more left-leaning members of the MCP produced one without his input, and, to some degree, by working around him. Paes Barreto maintained that this reflected fundamental conflict at the time between the Catholic Left and the communists.[14] And it is certainly true that the Communist Party in Pernambuco and elsewhere saw opportunities for furthering its own interests through the literacy campaign.

The textbook produced by the MCP focused on issues of citizenship. "The vote is of the people" was the first lesson, and the fact that the vote itself was secret was emphasized in the initial class exercises. (Students were also encouraged to look for opportunities to make their wishes known through plebiscites.) Attention was paid both to individual and collective action. Students were urged to continue to study, making use of educational opportunities available on radio. "Through study," the primer read, "he will be in reality a free citizen." Map lessons were intended to help students to "think globally," as well as to "act locally." Attention was paid to regional difficulties, such as drought and illiteracy, as well as reasons for regional pride, such as the participation of northeasterners in Brazilian history (from the expulsion of the Dutch in the seventeenth century to the building of Brasília in recent years). The materials emphasized that students should support peasant unions and other forms of mass organization. Although exercises frequently emphasized the recognition of class distinctions, they also encouraged students to recognize which politicians were "friends of the people." (Indeed, they provided examples of "the people" cheering and not booing an imaginary people's deputy named Adam, who fought alongside them.) Repeatedly, as well, the book lauded the activities of the MCP itself and encouraged students to get further involved in the movement.[15]

Criticism mounted as the MCP moved into the countryside. Plans were announced in February 1963 to use the Freire method to teach 100,000 in the state to read and write. By January 1964, plans were launched to teach 200,000, including many in the rural interior. That there was a real need for education in the Pernambuco interior there can be no doubt. The greater activity there, combined with the ever expanding peasant leagues, presented a direct challenge, as Tia Malkin-Fontecchio and others have argued, to the rural landowners' traditional control of the vote.[16] These developments together with a push from above to organize rural workers with the passage in March 1963 of a national rural workers law meant that a broad array of forces, including the Communist Party, the Catholic Church, the federal government, and people with links to the Central Intelligence Agency, were trying to organize rural workers in Pernambuco. The result was more conflict and frequent acts of violence in the state toward the end of the Goulart years.[17]

The expansion of the MCP under Governor Arraes was significant, but Freire's association with the University of Recife had an even broader regional impact. In February 1962, the university's rector, João Alfredo Gonçalves da Costa Lima, appointed Freire as head of the university's new extension services division, which was intended to help bring the "people" into the process of the "improvement of socioeconomic conditions" as part of the larger drive for "common progress." The rector had been a friend of Freire's since the former had worked as SESI's health division director. Since taking office in 1959 he had wanted to see a university more engaged with the problems of the northeast and of Pernambuco and Recife in particular. As Freire had written in 1961 in a work intended to develop not only his own ideas but also those of the rector, Brazilian elites believed that they were now abandoning their inauthentic and alienated posture of the past and integrating themselves into their own world, rejecting both utopian optimism and despair and becoming critical "interpreters of the anxieties of the people." The people themselves, leaving behind their role as spectator, were to engage in a "vast work of education." Educational institutions themselves, Freire argued, needed to abandon their age-old patterns of elitism and irrelevance and devote themselves to the task of helping Brazilians become more active participants in their societies. Building on his thesis of two years before, Freire called for an "eradication of [Brazilians'] democratic inexperience" and not just illiteracy. Universities had to engage directly with problems of popular education. Given the state of Brazilian development, Freire suggested, university students would also be called on to engage in discussion and activities that in more developed countries they would not have had to engage in. (The extension service employed forty university students in a literacy program that was intended to reach 800 young people in Recife.) Attuned to the changing society they were a part of, Freire argued, students were becoming more rebellious than those of previous generations, who were accustomed to a static and closed society. Rector, faculty, and students were to engage in frequent discussions of Brazil's problems.[18]

At the same time, what became known as "the Freire method" (and that his colleagues in the extension service called his "system") was consolidated during this time period, following work with a small group (four men, one woman) in a poor neighborhood in Recife from January through March 1962.[19] Words common to the particular social environs in which he was operating were chosen both for their simple illustration of syllabic sound patterns and their ability to generate discussion about the learners' lives. His method was flexible enough to adapt what came to be called "generating words" to quite different social and economic environments. An important part of Freire's early work was the contribution of artist Francisco Brennand, who was an aide in the Arraes state government beginning in 1963. For Freire's literacy programs Brennand drew typical scenes of northeastern urban and rural life, and the drawings were then made into slides. The artist sought to illustrate the distinction between nature and culture (discussed in the previous chapter) to help students recognize that they themselves created culture and could have an impact on their world. Freire and his colleagues expected that people who up to this point knew neither the name of the governor of the state nor the name of the president of their country would become aware of their social and political responsibilities and become true citizens. According to Freire, the debate in which students were to engage as part of their literacy training could not end in "demagogic solutions."[20]

As head of the university extension services division, Freire's influence soon extended to other states in the region. Freire's methods were employed in the northeastern state of Paraíba, where roughly two-thirds of the state's population at the time was illiterate and the peasant leagues were extremely active. Reformist governor Pedro Gondim had been elected in 1960 by a coalition of dissident elements of mainstream parties, but he also received financial support from ultraconservative groups in the interior. He wanted to see rural modernization and a greater degree of industrialization in the cities, and he considered the creation of a movement for basic education an important step in the state's economic and social development. Over the course of three months' worth of Saturdays, Freire and his associates from the university extension service provided training on Freire's methods for the Campanha de Educação Popular da Paraíba (Popular Education Campaign of Paraíba, CEPLAR). CEPLAR, which brought together people from the state and municipal governments, the archdiocese, student organizations on the university and high school levels, the state press association, and various unions, was overseen by Ronald Queiroz, the state development council director, as part of his obligations with SUDENE. Left-wing Catholic students, as elsewhere, also played a major role in the campaign. Initial efforts were directed toward poor neighborhoods of the state capital of João Pessoa, where illiteracy rates reached 80 percent. CEPLAR also worked with unions and sports clubs. CEPLAR officials soon decided that they needed not only a short literacy training course but also one which was intended to provide two years of basic primary education. This course emphasized civic education and a focus on ways to resolve issues of particular concern in the neighborhoods, which would lead to what historian Afonso Celso Scocuglia has called a "permanent socio-political mobilization" (although not with partisan ends in mind). As the program became more controversial, Governor Gondim tried to keep his distance.[21]

In Rio Grande do Norte, the politics of literacy involved a complex blend of local, state, regional, federal, and international forces. The U.S. consul in Recife considered Rio Grande do Norte "the number two state in political volatility" (after Pernambuco).[22] Freire advised two adult literacy programs in the early 1960s, one sponsored by Aluizio Alves, the governor, and one by Djalma Maranhão, the mayor of the state's capital, Natal. Rio Grande do Norte had a particularly low-income level, even by regional standards. According to government sources, only the states of Maranhão and Piaui were poorer. The average life-span was only forty years, and the infant mortality rate in the capital was 420 in 1,000. The majority of the population was employed in subsistence agriculture in a state that is 92 percent semi-arid, and the economy was stagnant even as the population was increasing. Rio Grande do Norte officials considered the education system "one of the major obstacles to economic and social development." The state lagged behind a number of the newly independent African countries in terms of school attendance rates. Officials estimated that the literacy rate in the early 1960s was only 20 percent, and state and local administrations placed many of their hopes on education. As the state's top education official proclaimed, "Only the education of the people and progressive consciousness-raising can bring the indispensable change in mentality that will give the state the primary conditions to change [this] picture" and move the state toward the process of industrialization that offered the only way out of the state's precarious situation.[23]

In Natal, a city of only 160,000 in the early 1960s, 30,000 were illiterate. Djalma Maranhão, who had been expelled from the Communist Party during its brief period of legal existence after the war and then had become a member of the small Partido Social Progressista under João Café Filho, had been elected mayor with 66 percent of the vote. He was far less popular in U.S. circles than the state's governor Alves. Maranhão represented an alternative to traditional, oligarchical politics, despite his willingness in the 1950s to work with the cotton and ranching elites represented by Dinarte Mariz. He broke with Mariz in 1958 and became a federal deputy on the Partido Trabalhista Nacional ticket. Alves and Maranhão were allies during their respective campaigns; the mayoral candidate found Alves to be more sympathetic to his plans for "social advancement" than Governor Mariz. Alves, however, was more of a modernizing reformist and Maranhão was a left-wing nationalist.[24] Once they were in office, their paths began to diverge.[25]

The fact that Maranhão was Natal's first elected mayor was further evidence of the continuing process of democratization in Brazil. When Maranhão made education a primary concern of his administration, he was responding to pressure from the neighborhood organization called "Nationalist Committees," which had helped get him elected and had participated in discussions regarding the priorities of a Maranhão administration. His adult and child education program, called "With One's Feet on the Ground, One Also Learns How to Read," was launched in February 1961. "To have one's feet on the ground," the top education official in Natal later explained, "signified that you knew the reality and the magnitude of the problem." But it also meant that education was no longer going to be for just the privileged few but for even those without shoes. The program not only provided 2,000 makeshift schools made out of coconut trees in poorer neighborhoods but also funded popular libraries and a wide variety of other cultural activities. Although the primary focus was on educating children, there was also a concerted effort to teach illiterate adults, particularly the parents of children who attended the newly constructed schools during the day. As the program developed in 1962, local educators began training in Freire's methods. By 1963, roughly 3,000 adult students were involved.[26] The ideological content of Natal's textbooks was more clearly leftist than that of other literacy programs in Brazil. For example, Cuba was described as the "first country to achieve success in the great drive for national liberation" and popular culture was treated as a "political means, the work of preparing the masses for the conquest of power."[27]

The combative mayor proudly proclaimed that his own literacy programs, unlike those of the state's governor, were being supported with Brazilian and not U.S. funds. Edward Rowell, the U.S. minister consul general in Recife, grudgingly conceded that the program had been "partially successful in bringing a degree of literacy to Natal's uneducated" but was also "somewhat successful as an instrument of politicizing the masses and orienting them in Maranhão's favor." The city's education program had "enhanced the mayor's popularity noticeably." In early March 1964, Maranhão hosted a meeting of forty mayors from the state's interior to form the Municipal Popular Education Front. Natal would aid the mayors in setting up their own programs, but the mayors hoped to get support as well from the federal government. Rowell suggested, not unreasonably, that the program was an attempt to expand Maranhão's popularity throughout the state and make him a more attractive candidate for governor in 1965.[28]

The state of Rio Grande do Norte itself, although a much less significant one economically and politically than Pernambuco, became central to U.S. goals. The governor became the United States' man in the northeast. Like Mayor Maranhão, Governor Aluizio Alves was extremely popular. He had been elected in 1960 with 68 percent of the vote, having gained the support of parts of all three major parties, as well as a wide variety of smaller parties, including the communist and integralist (fascist) parties. Alves had belonged to the liberal UDN since it was founded and had served as a federal deputy since his election to that post in 1946 (he was only twenty-two at the time). However, as Alves himself later argued, since the UDN had long defined itself against Getúlio Vargas, the party nationally had lost its direction following Vargas's suicide in 1954. In his run for governor, Alves created a broad-based coalition, including many elements opposed to the traditional domination of large landowners in the state. Alves gained the support of the urban population in his "Crusade of Hope," as well as "some factions of the agrarian oligarchy." Alves ran a more broadly populist campaign, encouraging people, as he later recalled, to lose their fear and to believe in the possibility of significant social and political change through the ballot box. His government further changed the dynamics in the state by eliminating the political police. Alves promised "education for everyone" and attempted to "mobilize the people against ignorance."[29]

Alves was also keenly aware of the regional dynamics at work. "The Northeast," he argued in July 1963, "is already in motion. It is beginning to advance, defeating the residual resistance of consciousness formed in the past and numbed by centuries of immutability." Alves himself claimed to "have no commitments either with the past or with its inadequate traditional structures." Alves "repudiated equally immobility and subversion." The traditional order and Brazilian democracy itself, which kept the majority of the population from receiving an education and then excluded the illiterate from voting, were unrepresentative. The beginnings of the "awakening of consciousness" were increasing the "inquietude" in the interior and the impatience in the cities, particularly among the young, who "are skeptical in the face of the slowness of democracy."[30]

Alves was becoming one of the most prominent northeastern politicians, second only to Arraes, and was considered to be a likely vice presidential candidate in 1965. Moreover, he was astute enough to see the opportunities created by an attentive foreign power. U.S. State Department officials considered Alves "a welcome relief . . . because of his constructive talk about the problems of the northeast. His words are low in political, ideological, and demagogic content." Alves, who also praised the United States frequently, argued that he could be a pragmatic nationalist "without any elements of class ideology." Alves was the first Brazilian governor to sign an agreement with USAID, and he was a vocal supporter of the Alliance for Progress, which U.S. officials clearly appreciated. If little had been done by the Alliance for Progress, he argued, it was "already considerable in a region of such scarce resources." The United States, in turn, encouraged his attempt to extend his influence throughout the region.[31]

The state's literacy efforts began in January 1963 with an inaugural class of a special pilot program in Angicos. The governor's hometown was located in the hot, arid center of the state; it had a population of roughly 1,550, 75 percent of whom were illiterate or only partially literate. USAID funding for the literacy program prompted quite a polemic among the Brazilian Left and even among those who agreed to participate in the program. Marcos Guerra, a law student at the recently created Universidade Federal do Rio Grande do Norte, was put in charge of the program. The son of an influential Catholic intellectual who was involved in the ongoing reforms of the Catholic Church now popularly known as Vatican II, Guerra had worked with church literacy programs and was the president of the state branch of the União Nacional de Estudantes (National Students Union, une). Freire and other instructors from the extension service of the University of Recife, with Arraes's permission and following assurances from Alves that Freire could keep working with his rival in the state capital, taught Guerra and fifteen other student colleagues Freire's new literacy training methods. Teachers went door to door in Angicos looking for people who did not know how to read and write. They used a loudspeaker mounted on a jeep to make the town's inhabitants aware of the educational opportunities available to them. As one of those involved in the program later remarked, the traditional night school of earlier Brazilian literacy campaigns "was replaced by culture circles." Teachers were now "dialogue coordinators," and students were "small group participants." After spending time in the local community and interviewing the local population, the Guerra team created a "vocabulary universe, roughly 400 words related to their students' daily activities." Beginning in January 1963, 299 students (156 men and 143 women), most between the ages of fourteen and twenty-nine, began the course. (The oldest student was seventy-two years old.) The single largest occupation represented was domestic workers (94). (There were also classes taught in the local prisons).[32]

The students viewed slides depicting their daily lives and discussed what they saw, as they learned to write words such as "fair," "goalie," "vote," and "people." One of the slides chosen for discussion portrayed a man from the northeast voting. Teachers and administrators sought to combat what they saw as the "accommodating, conformist, indifferent, and fatalistic" attitudes of their malnourished and prematurely old students who could not see anyway to improve their lives. Freire argued at the time that Brazil was undergoing a fundamental transition and in search of new values and attitudes. The students were challenged to adopt "more critical positions" through dialogue and debate. Class monitors posed questions that were intended to promote discussion, and although debates were generally lively, teachers lamented the fact that women and younger students participated less frequently. Students learned the difference between "masses" and "people." The "masses" were illiterate; "people" were those who were conscious of themselves as citizens. As one student remarked, "People is what we are at election time." At the end of the course, a newly literate thirty-two-year-old washerwomen named Francisca Andrade wrote to President Goulart, proclaiming, "Now I am no longer part of the 'masses,' I am 'people' and I can demand my rights." One of Guerra's own classes began with the notion of work as culture and continued with a discussion of constitutional rights, the eight-hour day, and the minimum wage. The students then discussed the possibility that foreign owners of local plantations and salt businesses be thrown out of the country. Even discussions of sports turned political, as monitors compared soccer teams to rural workers' unions; both required unity for victory.[33]

President Goulart attended the last class on 2 April (General Humberto Castello Branco, the man who would be Brazil's president in a little more than a year, also attended.) At the closing ceremony, a fifty-one-year-old student named Antônio da Silva declared that, whereas years before Vargas had come to satisfy their stomach's hunger, now Goulart had come to fill their "head's" needs. Also speaking at the closing ceremony, Freire, for his part, noted that while his "eclectic method" seemed to have produced "magical results," it was actually "grounded in scientific, philosophical principles." He praised the University of Recife, which was aware of its social obligations to the Brazilian people and had renounced "esoteric and alienated knowledge." He promised that education would no longer be "timid" but would raise the consciousness of the people so that they could help make the reforms that could not be delayed. Brazilians, he continued, needed to be more aware of the development work of SUDENE. He noted that now the Brazilian poor would no longer vote for godfathers or large landowners but rather vote for those who would truly serve the people. There "exists today," Freire said, addressing himself to President Goulart, "a people who decides, a people that is rising up, a people that has begun to become aware of its destiny and has begun to take part in the Brazilian historical process irreversibly." Impressed by what he had seen, Goulart expressed his wish that hundreds of these courses be taught throughout Brazil, so that people could "participate and integrate themselves in the life of the nation," as the students in Angicos were now able to do, and demand their rights and make sure that laws on the books were borne out in practice. U.S. ambassador Gordon, for his part, after a visit to Rio Grande do Norte, recommended that other northeastern states that had signed agreements with USAID adopt Freire's method. In a letter to the governor, Gordon invoked the cooperation of Rio Grande do Norte in the Second World War (when an American air base was built near Natal) and suggested that the governor's programs as a whole constituted a new "trampoline for victory" against hunger, illness, and illiteracy. Following the success of the initial education program in Angicos, the state promised to provide the students with more classes that would focus on educating the newly literate on their role as active citizens in a democracy. As Guerra, the student director of the Angicos program, expressed it, "We don't consider it enough to teach people to read and write alone . . . without making it possible for him to became a conscious and true participant in Brazilian democracy, paying attention to the needs of the historic moment we are living."[34]

This was, in many ways, the turning point in Freire's career. With its claim of having taught people to read and write in only forty hours of class time, the literacy program drew national and international journalists to Angicos. The emphasis on the limited amount of time the program required was, to say the least, excessive and detrimental to serious thought in a hasty time. Nevertheless, Governor Alves gained acclaim throughout Brazil, and Freire, too, became a national figure with some, albeit still limited, international impact. Freire's unconventional and relatively inexpensive method and the rapidity with which it achieved its goals inspired the Rio Grande do Norte secretary of education to dream of eliminating "illiteracy in the state [thereby] permitting the integration of a greater number of adults into the rights and conquests of social and economic development of their communities." "We like to say," Governor Alves noted in 1963, "that we are realizing in our little state, a revolution through education: the beginning of revolutions." In the short term, working in five other cities (including Natal), the state hoped to teach 12,000 adults to read and write. By 1965, state officials hoped to reach at least 100,000. They promised "to do in three years what has not been done in three centuries." Alliance for Progress money via SUDENE and USAID continued to support Alves's government's efforts in this area in 1963.[35]

In private, however, Alves was increasingly disturbed by his UDN colleague and Guanabara governor Carlos Lacerda's accusations that Freire and his associates were communists and their methods suspect. An editorial writer for the Rio daily *Jornal do Brasil* warned that Alves was "liberating social forces that he did not know how to control." The first strike on record to occur in Angicos took place shortly after the class ended. Despite some mixed feeling within the Alves administration, the state government declared the strike to be based on legitimate demands by the workers. Alves was increasingly attacked by the Right and by leftists who resented the U.S. funding for the Angicos program. Meanwhile, the United States, Governor Alves's anxious foreign patron worried that the governor would find it politically advantageous to criticize the Alliance for Progress as other more left-leaning north-eastern politicians already had. The governor did criticize the Alliance, but when he did so, it was largely to lament the tendency, in both Washington and Latin American circles, to turn it into a bilateral aid program rather than a multilateral and dynamic program in which Brazilians as well as other Latin Americans would be involved in correcting problems. By August 1963, more-over, he was asking President Goulart to define the federal government's po-sition on the Alliance for Progress: to either cooperate with it fully so that the country would develop economically or to forthrightly reject it as an "instrument of imperialism." Soon Governor Alves himself was increasingly leaning toward the right-wing conspirators active in the UDN and working throughout Brazil against the Goulart administration. Secretary of Education Francisco Calazans Fernandes resigned in December 1963. A U.S. official ex-pressed regret that this had taken place; Fernandes was judged to be "com-petent and hard-working." "Much of the past success of the [Rio Grande do Norte] education program was directly due to his leadership," it was argued. Another U.S. official wondered whether Fernandes thought Alves was using education as a political instrument or whether it was Alves himself who sus-pected that Fernandes "was building his own little empire."[36]

Freire himself did not escape criticism for his part in the Angicos program. As would be true throughout his career, the only criticism that mattered to him was that which came from the Left. Many Brazilian leftists were un-happy that he had participated in a program that received financial support from the Alliance for Progress. Freire said at the time that it did not mat-ter where the money came from; what mattered was the education that was being offered by people independent of any partisan political agendas to help people "liberate themselves from the exploitation to which they are submit-ted." He noted his opposition to the ways in which aid could contribute to the domestication of the people and impede "the process of democratization in the country."[37]

The seeming success of the USAID-supported program in Angicos earned Freire a role in the government of President Goulart, a man whose virtues and defects Freire himself never analyzed in print. The son of a wealthy landown-ing family in Rio Grande do Sul, Goulart was a protégé of Getúlio Vargas. By 1952, he was the head of the PTB, the party that represented the urban labor system Vargas had constructed. He served briefly as Vargas's labor minister. He had been Juscelino Kubitschek's vice president, and, because of the quirks of the Brazilian electoral system that allowed separate votes to be cast for president and vice president, he was the successor to his political opponent Jânio Quadros when the latter resigned in August 1961. Quadros had hoped that the Brazilian people would clamor for his return and that politicians and military officers who feared Goulart would be willing to give him a free hand in running the government. The price for Goulart's accession to power was a reduction in his authority through the addition of a prime minister. After more than a year in office with his powers dramatically reduced, he finally could claim presidential authority following a plebiscite on 6 January 1963. He was often praised for his political acuity, but every step he took seems to have been wrong in the months leading up to his overthrow. He was rejected by the Right and much of the center for his association with Vargas and labor, and he was distrusted by the Left (not least of all by Pernambuco governor Arraes). Meanwhile, the military and others on the Right conspired against him with the anxious and attentive aid of the United States.[38]

Goulart appears at times to have been no more than a ward party boss in search of one more vote. He had focused for a time on the issue of giving illiterates the right to vote, as part of a larger process of mobilization that would provide support for the "basic reforms" that he hoped would be his political legacy.[39] His 1962 Development Council had envisioned a literacy campaign to enable "the civic recuperation" of those over fourteen who were illiterate. The recent expansion and diversification of the Brazilian economy had also made the need for a more educated populace palpable. The council members argued that Brazil was a "society in transformation, produced by the collective will to surpass the stage of a poor and underdeveloped country" (although it contradicted itself on the question of how much Brazilians already possessed this will and whether they had an awareness "of their dynamic socio-economic context"). Brazil needed to move beyond "an antiquated education system, organized in terms of education for leisurely consumption" by a privileged few. In the first few months of 1963, Goulart moved toward the center and took positions more in line with U.S. advisers' on economic issues. But despite U.S. support for the Angicos literacy campaign, Goulart's incorporation of Freire into the Ministry of Education accompanied a perceived turn to the Left by the middle of the year. Unfortunately for Goulart, it was a Left divided and mistrustful, particularly when it became clear in October 1963 that the president wanted to remove Pernambuco governor Arraes and rightist Guanabara governor Lacerda from office. The national literacy campaign, inspired by the experience in Angicos, became a central part of the last phase of his presidency, although he continued to press on the issue of granting the illiterate the right to vote, arguing that the diffusion of mass media (most particularly, at this stage, the radio) informed illiterate citizens in a way they never had been before. In his final presidential message, Goulart promised to transform Brazil "from an archaic society into a truly modern, free and democratic nation" through the "creative impulse of a people, conscious, after all of its backward condition, [and] no longer accepting of ignorance and misery."[40]

If Goulart was less consistent and in control than his political enemies maintained, then and later, it was certainly in the Ministry of Education, as we shall see, that the Left was strongest. Officials in the Ministry of Education argued that illiteracy was a way to keep "the majority of the people out of the electoral system." "The struggle against illiteracy," they argued, was "a political struggle in the sphere of power."[41] In June 1963, a popular culture commission was created in Brasília to employ Freire's methods. By July 1963, Freire had been named the head of the federal government's national commission on popular culture, which was intended to reach those who had not been "reached by the benefits of education." Research was to be conducted in order to create appropriate educational programs for the populations in particular regions. Regional commissions building on the work of existing popular culture organizations or university groups were also to be instituted.[42] Culture circles were inaugurated in Brasília in August. Freire demonstrated his methods in the Chamber of Deputies in October 1963.

A key and polarizing, if short-term, player in the national literacy campaign that never was, was Paulo de Tarso Santos, a member of Brazil's small Christian Democratic Party and the first mayor of Brasília. Santos had represented the state of São Paulo in the Chamber of Deputies before becoming Goulart's minister of education in June 1963. Goulart, who had never met Santos before, hoped that he would be a bridge to the Catholic student Left. (Indeed, a student activist later claimed that Santos had been chosen in consultation with the student Left.) Santos, for his part, expressed a "profound confidence" in Brazilian students. As he later testified, there were no strikes by students during his time as minister, in part because students "identified with the ministry." He also belonged to the group of self-identified nationalists within Congress. In his inaugural address he discussed at length the problem of illiteracy.[43]

U.S. officials, who feared that the young man represented "the extreme left, anti-U.S., pro-Castro wing" of his party, considered "his presence in the cabinet" to be "bad news."[44] U.S. ambassador Gordon told Goulart that Santos was so "advanced" that Gordon "doubted" he was a "good representative of" the Catholic Church. For his part, the minister quoted Pope John XXIII when criticizing those powerful countries that he claimed used financial and technical aid as a means to dominate developing countries.[45]

The Catholic Church in Brazil, in any case, was already changing in ways that the young man did represent. The reformist Catholic action groups inspired by European (largely Italian and French) models had gotten involved in community organizing and leadership training in the postwar era. Bishops had met in 1959 to call for greater attention to the social problems of Brazil, in particular those of the northeast. Under Goulart's predecessor, President Quadros, the church had run a national program of radio schools in what was called the Basic Education Movement. Through the Basic Education Movement, the church was, at the same time as Freire, developing its own methods of consciousness-raising to encourage people, primarily in rural areas, to get more involved in solving their own communities' problems. Its primer, *To Live Is to Struggle*, developed in 1963 and published in early 1964, began with the conjugation of the verbs in the title. It placed emphasis on people's right to schools and land and described the process by which an Everyman named Pedro became aware of social injustice and exploitation and begin to discuss the need to do something about it with his friend Xavier. "Pedro's struggle is our struggle," so concluded one of the last lessons. The textbook was criticized as vehemently by the Right as anything associated directly with Freire and was seized by Governor Lacerda's political police in Guanabara in early 1964.[46]

For his part, Santos had always stressed his own religious convictions and repeatedly disavowed any connections to communists. He even said that he felt uncomfortable with communists. Speaking at various conferences in his role as minister, Santos said that the literacy campaign, "through the Paulo Freire method," "was our revolutionary instrument" to "change the political correlation of forces in the country." These claims for the method and the campaign, he later ruefully noted, alarmed the Brazilian Right.[47]

Santos and Freire certainly found valuable allies for their literacy campaign among members of the student Left, some of whom were affiliated with the Communist Party but most of whom were part of an independent Left that was new in Brazil. The Brazilian student Left in the early 1960s considered politicizing and raising the consciousness of the Brazilian popular classes to be a central part of their political activity. They hoped to reach them through their own "popular culture centers" (inspired, in part, by the Recife MCP) and through a traveling group called the UNE—Volante (National University Students—Flying).[48] Although the student Left (and other members of the Brazilian left more generally) did not always approve of the Goulart administration's policies and doubted President Goulart's commitment to major social and political change, many members of AP, which was founded in 1962, and the UNE saw the national literacy campaign as a natural extension of their other ongoing activities. Herbert José de Sousa, an influential member of AP, became an important figure in the national popular culture commission and a Santos aide. Like Santos and (to some extent) Goulart himself, the student Left hoped to add millions of Brazilians to the electorate through the literacy campaign, which seemed to offer such "revolutionary" possibilities.[49]

Meanwhile, Freire began planning for the national literacy campaign, as well as working in the nation's new capital. He inaugurated culture circles in July with the help of his Recife team in the three-year-old capital of Brasília. The planned city had no room for the many poor people from the northeast, Minas Gerais, and Goiás who had come to build the capital in the late 1950s. They largely settled in a series of "satellite" cities, often constructing makeshift shantytowns after staging land invasions, even of local country clubs. As had happened in other cities in which Freire's techniques were employed, to attract students, vehicles with loudspeakers traversed the satellite cities broadcasting messages like "An illiterate people is an enslaved people." Words chosen for the classes in Taguatinga, Sobradinho, Gama, and other cities were taken from surveys done in hospitals and bus stations.[50] Speaking before teachers of a pilot program in September 1963, President Goulart reiterated the claim that his campaign would result in an additional five million voters in the 1965 presidential election. "With the culture they have been receiving, they won't be selling their votes to [presumed CIA front group] IBAD [Instituto Brasileiro de Ação Democrático (Brazilian Institute of Democratic Action)] or trading them for a pair of shoes." By that time, ninety-six culture circles were already in operation in the area. Goulart praised the miraculous results that Freire's method had already produced.[51]

Literacy and popular culture groups proliferated throughout Brazil, as demonstrated by a national meeting in September 1963 in Recife. A diverse group, including evangelical and Catholic organizations, as well as socialists and communists, were in attendance. At the conference, Miguel Newton Arraes, head of the Pernambuco state Popular Culture Movement, spoke of the lack of an "established order" in Brazil. "The people" needed to replace the "institutionalized disorder" now at the service of the enemies of the people with a "legitimate order" that satisfied popular needs. He noted that his remarks may have surprised many since they reflected a harsher social reality in which peasants were assassinated and against which the new state government had organized. Representatives of Natal's literacy campaign spoke out against "external domination" masking itself as "'alliances,' 'cooperation' and 'help.'"[52]

Meanwhile, Paulo de Tarso Santos resigned as minister of education in October 1963. He offered his resignation because he believed that Goulart was not fulfilling his role as a president from an ostensible labor party. Goulart reportedly told him, "Your position, which is that of the revolutionary Christians, corresponds more or less to the direction in which Brazil is heading. I think, however, that these things must be done gradually." Santos warned that those who were conspiring against the government should not be appeased and that Goulart needed to stand firm in his support for the new Brazil that was in the process of being born. U.S. officials believed that before he left the ministry, Santos had provided "communist-controlled student and labor organizations . . . three to six million cruzeiros . . . in the form of grants for adult literacy campaigns."[53] Santos was replaced on an interim basis by a veteran of state and national education bureaucracies, Júlio Sambaqui, who remained in office until the coup. He was hardly the polarizing figure that Santos had been, but the planning for the literacy campaign continued under Sambaqui as it had begun, and the new minister's public rhetoric differed little from that of his predecessor. If anything, the rhythm of organization picked up.[54]

With or without Santos in the government, the Goulart administration's enemies were more anxious than ever. Traditional politicians by late 1963 were convinced that "an extremely grave process of institutional subversion [was] underway in Brazil."[55] These fears were shared by U.S. ambassador Gordon, who, in October 1963, warned U.S. assistant secretary of state Edwin Martin that the "major threat to Brazilian democracy comes from Goulart himself." "Brazilian realities," he suggested, "might require removal of threat through military action."[56] These fears extended to the campaign itself, which Carlos Lacerda, a veteran conspirator against all governments in the previous decade, said represented a kind of "brainwashing." U.S. officials shared the concerns of many traditional Brazilian politicians like Lacerda. More to the point, U.S. officials concluded, the "primary short-range intent of the literacy program is to add substantial numbers of newly-literate and 'suitably' indoctrinated voters of the electorate. . . . In longer-range terms, a campaign of this nature could grow into an important instrument for the political organization of a major and previously untapped segment of the population." At least one U.S. official assumed that the primary beneficiary of the literacy campaign would be Goulart's party, the PTB (and not, as it was later claimed, the communists).[57]

Freire and his associates in the Ministry of Education began planning pilot programs in the states of Rio de Janeiro (which in the 1960s and early 1970s did not include the city of Rio de Janeiro) and Sergipe. They began to research the "vocabulary universes" of Rio de Janeiro in twelve municipalities in poor towns like Itagui and Duque de Caxias. Once again, the largest single occupational group involved in the culture circles was domestic workers (seventy-five in Itagui), with the second largest group being farmers (nineteen). To test their ability to think critically, students were asked if they believed in werewolves (in Itagui, 47 did and 159 did not). Political opinions within the groups ranged from conformist ("One should accept what God gives") to revolutionary ("I believe in revolution; one has to come"). Some felt that agrarian reform would not change anything, while others supported the closing of Congress. While some thought President Goulart to be the man to complete the reforms begun by that "great Brazilian," Getúlio Vargas, others expressed distrust of Goulart ("only he lives well") and of politicians in general. One person suggested that illiterates should only be allowed to vote until after a medical examination had confirmed that they were not mentally ill.[58]

In January 1964, Goulart announced the creation of the national literacy campaign. Noting the inadequacies of previous attempts to teach large numbers of people to read and write, Goulart promised to unite "all the classes of the Brazilian people." The advantages of the Freire method for making people literate in a short period of time having been demonstrated, the Ministry of Education planned to mobilize a wide variety of student and professional organizations, sports clubs, neighborhood organizations, religious and civic groups nationwide.[59] In the short term, however, the emphasis continued to be on the states of Rio de Janeiro and Sergipe.

The planning for the pilot program in the small northeastern state of Sergipe illustrates the dynamics at work in the last stage of the Goulart government. Unlike in Pernambuco, where literacy programs were primarily run by local officials, or in Rio Grande do Norte, where municipal, state, regional and international actors played a role, in Sergipe the federal government was primarily responsible for the program. The campaign was intended to teach 400,000 residents to read and write in three years. Sergipe was evidently chosen for the pilot program because of its small size and ease of communication.[60] Only a third of Sergipe's total population of 760,000 was literate in 1950.[61] The populist project in the more industrialized parts of Brazil had limited influence in the state prior to the mid-1950s, according to Sergipe's premier political historian. Like other northeastern states, Sergipe had experienced little in the way of industrialization, and the popular classes had not yet been brought into the political arena. The UDN was the largest political party, but it had not captured the governor's office. The decline of the PSD in much of the northeast in the latter half of the 1950s created opportunities for other political parties to gain ground. Unlike in many southern states, the northeastern UDN was more "open to populist policies." A nationalist front that included students, intellectuals, Catholics, and communists was formed in March 1958 in Sergipe.[62] As in the case of Rio Grande do Norte, one of the principal political figures was federal deputy João de Seixas Dória, a dissident member of the UDN who had played an important role in the Quadros presidential campaign in 1960, representing the nationalist wing of the party.[63] A split in the Sergipe UDN over the choice of a gubernatorial candidate led him to form a coalition in 1962 with the PSD *and* the PTB; his campaign manager in the governor's race was trabalhista José Conrado de Araújo. His victory, with 47 percent of the vote (due largely to support in more urban areas of the state) over his closest competitor's 40 percent, upset the traditional party blocs within the state.[64]

Following his inauguration in January 1963, however, Seixas Dòria discovered how precarious the state's finances were. He spent much of his short time in office traveling, trying to bring federal funds to the state. He was criticized in September 1963 for visiting the United States, but he argued that he had made it clear in his talks with U.S. officials that he was only interested in Alliance for Progress funds under certain conditions. He said that he would accept U.S. aid if it was intended to help transform Brazil's archaic economic structure. "But if the Alliance intends to strengthen the status quo," he said he added, "we will refuse and repudiate" that aid. He claimed to have spoken to U.S. officials as "equal to equal" and that the North Americans seemed receptive to his frank way of speaking (although he admitted that perhaps they were just being diplomatic).[65]

Despite his ties to Quadros and membership in the party that historically had opposed both Vargas and Goulart, Seixas Dòria came to admire Goulart (although he acknowledged that Goulart had little interest in administration). Although considered by some to be merely an opportunist, Seixas Dòria clearly had made his mark as a strong supporter of nationalist measures; as governor, he embraced Goulart's attempts to promote basic reforms in Brazilian society. The governor promised new agrarian reform measures and refused to move against peasants who had occupied abandoned federal property in the state. This created conflict within the state government, and in February 1964, the state secretary of agriculture resigned.[66]

Luiz Rabello Leite, Sergipe's secretary of education, was one of the founders of the state's branch of the nationalist front and the governor's "principal supporter in reform moves." The U.S. consul in Salvador did not consider him to be as far left as Seixas Dòria but noted that he "interprets Pope John XXIII's encyclicals liberally, as an authority on the social doctrine of the Church, and has strong views on basic institutional reforms needed to modernize Brazil." In an "impassioned speech" to teachers, Leite argued for the "necessity of making citizens aware of the 'Brazilian reality' and of having them become 'politically conscious.'" The secretary's most cogent statement of the aims of his educational activities in the state and of the literacy campaign was that he hoped to make people "the subject—and not the object of history." In the next election, he predicted, the people "will not be led to the ballot box like sheep by a political boss."[67]

Freire visited the state frequently during the second half of 1963 and early 1964, a period in which there was an unusual level of political mobilization in the state.[68] Local nationalist newspapers in Aracaju gave ample coverage to the planned literacy program and commended Freire's previous activities in Pernambuco and Rio Grande do Norte. There were heightened expectations regarding the political impact of the literacy program in Sergipe. Freire, "that intelligent Pernambucano [and] patriotic idealist," was praised for his interest in transforming education and making people more critically aware and bringing the previously marginal into active life in "this nation of privileged people." Where previously Sergipanos had only known how to sign their name so that they could vote for their patron, now they would not only know how to spell the word "latifundia" but also understand why it was an unproductive form of agricultural production. Accompanying Freire on his visits in January 1964 was Minister Sambaqui, who decried accusations that the literacy program represented an attempt to "Cubanize" Brazil and accused "reactionary" forces of trying to hold back the "economic development" that would accompany the success of a large-scale literacy program.[69]

In Sergipe, however, the literacy program did not have a chance to move beyond the initial training of teachers. The tide had begun to turn against Freire's literacy programs. In January, USAID withdrew its support for literacy programs in Brazil, allegedly because of administrative inadequacies within the program, not least of all "Freire's failure to produce [an] agreed upon written curriculum," although critics of the U.S. move argued that it was motivated by the same fears of subversion that were animating the right-wing conspiracy against the Goulart government. Christine Luhn, who has done the most comprehensive study of U.S. aid for education, has found no direct discussion of this issue, and my own research in USAID records has come up empty.[70] The United States was certainly more than a little worried about what it viewed as "Communist strength" in the education ministry.[71] In a 1987 interview, Ambassador Gordon suggested that concerns about the program's promotion of class consciousness were the primary issue, although I have found no contemporary evidence to suggest that he personally had such concerns in 1964. In Washington, Undersecretary of State George Ball did express concern that U.S.-trained educators were "disseminating anti-U.S. or Marxist doctrine in adult education programs." By March, the U.S. consulate in Recife, for its part, assured the U.S. secretary of state Dean Rusk that "no U.S.A.I.D. funds" were being "used in Pernambuco for adult literacy programs."[72]

In some northeastern states around the same time, the tide was turning against some of Freire's allies, despite evidence of growing strength in the education programs themselves. In Paraíba, it is clear that the Left had gained control of the literacy program CEPLAR. Domestic workers had become a central focus of early efforts because of student activists' frustrations in trying to organize them into unions when they could not read the materials they provided to try to convince them to form unions. An ever larger group of university and high school students were recruited to get involved. In the recruitment process, they were questioned regarding their attitude toward the illiterates themselves and the peasant leagues and whether they thought elected officials "really represented the Brazilian people," since the Congress was "in the majority" made up of "reactionaries." In 1963, buoyed by encouragement and financial support from the federal minister of education, CEPLAR extended its activities into the interior in Campina Grande and also in areas fraught with intense conflict between the peasant leagues and landowners. By late 1963 and early 1964, there were 135 cultural circles with roughly 4,000 people learning to read and write in the region, with expectations that up to 3,600 could be taught every two months. CEPLAR hoped to teach 80 percent of the state's peasant league members to read and write. The national popular culture commission sought to build on these activities and provide more aid and guidance. But many of the rural schools were destroyed by their political opponents. And CEPLAR's enthusiasm was tempered somewhat by the realization that many of the students, exhausted following their day of work, skipped classes or were inattentive in class. According to historian Afonso Celso Scocuglia, CEPLAR was increasingly dominated by student leftists and tied to the Goulart government more than to the state government. Its lesson plans included criticism of the United States and praise of Cuba, but, as teachers later recalled, the students were more interested in learning to read and write than in the political content of the courses in any case. The program become overextended and factionalized, and found itself short of funds. Worse still, students' gains in learning to read and write were not being sustained. Governor Gondim, for his part, began to move away from the populist leanings of the first several years of his administration. Criticized by both the Left and the Right and moved by what one historian has called "the pragmatic sense of political survival," he began to distance himself from the program. By the beginning of 1964, he had moved definitively to the Right and had begun to take action against peasant movements in the state.[73]

Even as the United States and domestic supporters of the literacy campaigns began to turn against them, they continued to proliferate nationally, accompanied by a general overconfidence on the Left that history was moving in their direction. Plans for the national campaign accelerated in January 1964. Despite many problems that were holding the program back, one Ministry of Education official asserted that the progress that had been made was due to the "Unity of the lefts in the national literacy program" and "the identity of [their] objectives."[74] In February 1964, a national gathering of popular culture and literacy groups inspired the education ministry to reorganize its popular culture commission.[75] At the same time, there was a concern at the national level that the literacy campaign was not organized sufficiently and that many of those involved in the campaign lacked "political perspective." The campaign was designed to "attend to the formation of a nationalist and democratic government" but, up to this point, had "developed in a spontaneous way, with a lack of political planning and centralized direction," which threatened to compromise its "revolutionary content." This could be resolved by more communication, more regular meetings, and standardization of methods.[76] Claims of unity notwithstanding, there continued to be conflicts between members of the Catholic Left and communists that threatened the program in what one journalist called the "deaf struggle."[77] While members of the student group AP became active in the national campaign in January 1964, there was soon conflict and distrust between them and members of the Communist Party as well.[78] Members of the AP thought that members of the PCB were using the campaign to increase their political party's membership.[79]

The student Left did play a significant supportive role in the national literacy campaign that was being planned, as they themselves were the first to admit, but to jump to the conclusion, reached by the military and its allies and historians like Thomas Skidmore, that they were in control of the campaign would be a gross overstatement.[80] Where Freire stood at this point regarding the internal conflicts and the ends of the campaign is not clear. As education minister Sambaqui testified before a military court, Freire told him that he would have to quit if he had learned that his methods were being used for ideological ends. And Freire even surprised some at the time when he told them that he did not mind if his students became followers of Carlos Lacerda, if they could explain why they were his followers.[81] Freire was certainly not interested in working to further partisan ends, so the emphasis on the PCB and the PTB by campaign critics seems equally misplaced. But clearly Freire shared a rather vaguely defined ideology with many in the Goulart administration. There certainly was a large degree of "directivity" on issues of land reform and economic nationalism. That he and his associates thought that most people, when they became "aware" or developed a critical consciousness, would reach the same conclusions they did on most issues, seems more than likely. In that regard, they, regrettably perhaps, were hardly different from other fallible mortals, then and now, who think that other thoughtful people must necessarily reach the same conclusions they have. In local communities, in soccer clubs, and in other organizations in which the literacy campaign was beginning to make its presence known, however, political conflicts and competing agendas already were starting to threaten the success of the program. Local leaders often were distrustful of what they saw as the ideological bent of the campaign.[82] What seems likely based on the evidence that we have is that these ideological conflicts would have become more and not less important the longer the campaign had lasted.

Certainly there was increasing concern about the campaign in early 1964 as examinations were held to determine who would take part as teachers.

Rightist Carlos Lacerda and others argued that the questions on the test proved that the Ministry of Education was engaging in the equivalent of the brainwashing associated with Communist Chinese programs. U.S. official John Kessel wondered whether Goulart had given up on his idea of giving illiterates the right to vote or whether the program would make peasants aware of the rights currently unavailable to them under the constitution. In any case, he believed that the new voters would be "suitably indoctrinated" and that this would lead to the "political organization of a major and un-tapped segment of the population."[83]

We cannot know what would have happened because by early 1964 the military itself was politically conscious and acting in a more direct way. A conspiracy long in the making was accelerated by Goulart's call for an im-mediate passage of his basic reforms, including giving illiterates the right to vote, in a rally in Rio de Janeiro on 13 March. (This move clearly indicated that the president himself was not placing all of his hopes on the literacy campaign.) Many found Goulart's tone more alarming than the substance of his proposals. His support for insubordinate members of the armed forces became the final precipitating factor in the military coup itself, which began on 31 March. Following the coup, most of those associated with the literacy programs in Paraíba, Pernambuco (including the MCP), Rio Grande do Norte, Sergipe, and other states either fled or were put in prison. The University of Recife and its rector were accused of subversion. Literacy program materi-als were destroyed, and even some of the school buildings themselves were burned. The coup took many of these people by complete surprise; some even later recalled that they thought there might be a left-wing coup but not a right-wing one.[84]

Some of the governors in whose states literacy campaigns were operat-ing, particularly those most usefully described as reformists and sometime electoral populists, survived the coup and, like Paraíba's Pedro Gondim, oversaw the elimination of programs they had created and now criticized as subversive. Gondim and other northeastern governors generally supported the new military government's Operation Clean-Up that targeted the region. Although he had not been involved in the planning of the coup, Gondim justified his support for it as being necessary to achieve "the tranquil climate indispensable to development."[85] Arraes and Seixas Dória were two of only three governors deposed and arrested following the coup, the other being Rio's governor, Badger Silviera, of the PTB, who, like the other two, had also participated in the 13 March rally (and in whose state another literacy program was planned).[86] In Rio Grande do Norte, onetime political allies ended up on opposite sides of the line dividing acceptable and unacceptable behavior under the new military regime. Natal mayor Maranhão denounced the coup and was imprisoned on 2 April. Libraries connected with his "Feet on the Ground" program were raided and closed, and educational materials were seized. Those associated with the program remained in prison for months afterward.[87] Rio Grande do Norte governor Alves, who had not been involved directly in the planning of the military coup, was one of the few individuals identified with the literacy campaigns to remain in office. Despite his close ties to the United States and to the conspirators, Alves was not as enthusiastic initially about the coup as expected. His "statement of support for the revolution was the most hedged of any made in the northeast," one U.S. official noted, obviously forgetting the lack of enthusiasm among those governors who had been deposed and imprisoned.[88] Nevertheless, although he later claimed that he prevented those involved in his state program from being imprisoned and tortured, Alves soon supported the investigation into "subversion and corruption" in Rio Grande do Norte.[89] Maranhão, who called his education program his "greatest crime," would die in exile in July 1971 in Uruguay. Marcos Guerra and others were imprisoned and interrogated numerous times, as was Sergipe's secretary of education, Rabello Leite.[90]

The military found it difficult to determine whether many of those who were in training for the program in Sergipe were themselves subversives or even whether Freire's method was, in essence, subversive. The military did not recognize that it was on shaky ground on this point, having itself subverted a constitutional government. Some of the prospective teachers in Sergipe rejected the premises of their interrogators, noting that the word "subversion" was "used frequently by regimes of force." The military accused Paulo Pacheco, one of the leading figures in the Sergipe training program, of distorting Freire's method there and "turning it into a partisan instrument: of indoctrination." If Freire's method was used correctly, "it could have good effects," one investigator suggested.[91] Many of the teachers rejected their military interrogators' assertions that there was an attempt to "agitate" or to indoctrinate people in a partisan way. The issues that were discussed during the training sessions, one woman responded, were those that were being discussed widely in Goulart-era Brazil, such as votes for the illiterate, basic reforms, and unionism.[92] One teacher, perhaps more politically naive than many of the others, claimed that she had not considered the program subversive but that after the revolution of April she had come "to understand the truth."[93] The coup, in that sense, created its own transformed consciousness.[94] The military also tried to prove that the directors of the campaign in Sergipe and elsewhere were personally corrupt. They questioned the would-be instructors at length regarding Pacheco's use of a Volkswagen sedan, in part because he took it with him to go into hiding when the coup took place. Considering the fate of those involved in the literacy campaign generally, taking the car seems to have been a prudent move. (Over the next few years, the case against Pacheco bounced back and forth between civil and military courts as judges quarreled over who had jurisdiction. Ultimately, the case against Paulo Pacheco was dropped in 1981.)[95]

The military had fewer doubts about the national campaign and, particularly, about the role of the student Left in it, even as they consistently exaggerated the importance of the Communist Party itself. The Freire method, they charged, was being employed in an attempt to "communize" Brazil. The directors of the campaign were guilty of political crimes. Freire, it was suggested, had wanted to create "five million electoral robots for the populist parties, including the communists." Given the low salaries paid to the literacy workers, it was suggested, only someone interested in proselytizing would work in the campaign. Freire and his associates, the military charged, had been engaged in "the planning and the beginnings of the execution of the most subtle and efficient work of subversion yet realized in Brazil," turning the "illiterate masses into an instrument of the peaceful conquest of power by the Communist Party."[96] The distinctions between the "lefts," which leftists themselves emphasized even when they were ostensibly working together, meant nothing to the military, and in their investigations of the national campaign, they tended to ignore testimony that pointed to the conflicts between the various groups.[97] The military noted, with equal disdain, the strong influence of ISEB.[98]

Although the United States had supported Goulart's overthrow, not all U.S. officials were equally optimistic about the military government's plans for Brazil in the first few months following the coup. Even U.S. ambassador Gordon, for all of his suspicions regarding President Goulart's intentions, was concerned about the early actions of the military government. Nevertheless, Gordon confidently asserted in a telegram that the "greatest hope for avoidance of undemocratic excesses rests in character and convictions of Castello Branco."[99] But there were particular concerns about what the coup would mean for the northeast. Edward Rowell, U.S. minister consul general in Recife, warned in early April, "The economic and social problems which led

Pernambuco's voters to elect Arraes remain as real as they ever were. . . . The new administration will have to prove that it can do a better job than Arraes in promoting real reform and progress."[100]

By April 14, the national literacy program, which had been inaugurated only months before, had been extinguished by military decree, asserting that the "material to be employed" in such a literacy campaign did not "transmit democratic ideas or preserve the institutions and traditions of our people."[101] Freire was officially relieved of his duties on 20 April and imprisoned on 16 June. He would spend more than twenty days in a small prison cell in Recife and an additional fifty days in Olinda later. As Anita Paes Barreto, Freire's colleague in Pernambuco's MCP noted, he was "imprisoned because he talked too much" and was too open about what he had been doing. Former minister of education Paulo de Tarso Santos, who, like Sambaqui, lost his political rights, argued that Freire and his associates were targeted because the campaign was the weapon of a "peaceful revolution." Freire himself, under interrogation (which included an extended discussion in at least one case of a wide range of pedagogical methods adopted in the Western world), denied that he was an admirer of the Soviet Union or of Castro's Cuba. He expressed misgivings about Goulart, whose government had "some positive aspects" but was unstable and did not "inspire sufficient trust." (In contrast, he was forthright regarding his positive opinion of Arraes.) He rejected the notion that he was interested in indoctrinating anyone and categorically rejected the suggestion that his techniques were the same as those employed by Adolph Hitler, Benito Mussolini, Joseph Stalin, or Juan Perón. He emphasized the Catholic humanist roots of this thought and the way he sought to promote an "open mentality," unlike that which existed in the Soviet Union or China. He refused to criticize the military government itself. Freire later claimed that his prison experience transformed his thinking on political matters (although his experience in Chile, as we shall see in the next chapter, does not really bear that out). He was freed in September but interrogated repeatedly in Rio. He anticipated being imprisoned again and so sought asylum in the Bolivian embassy. After more than a month in the embassy, he left for Bolivia, expecting to work for the Bolivian Ministry of Education.[102] (As far as the military was concerned, the fact that he and others chose to go into exile proved that they knew that they were guilty.[103])

Decades later, some students were still wondering why the northeastern Brazilian literacy programs had been canceled. A former student named Maria Luíza da Silva from Angicos asked Paulo Freire why he had been imprisoned. He replied, "Because you learned too much."[104] But what exactly they learned was not assessed adequately until much later. We are fortunate that, in 1997, a Brazilian educational researcher made a serious attempt to assess the long-term impact of Freire's program on ten of his former students. None of them continued studying following the end of the "forty hours." Even the better students continued to have trouble reading, which is hardly surprising given the relatively limited opportunities they had to learn in the decades that followed. For some of the students, however, the classes had changed their way of thinking about themselves and their possibilities. Freire certainly took pride in the fact that one of the children of his students had learned to read and write with her parents and had made a career as a teacher. While Freire's impact on the inhabitants of Angicos may be exaggerated in the frequent myth-making that surrounds his career, there is no doubt that the establishment of the military government limited the educational possibilities of many participants in the programs, especially the programs established in the northeast. (Nilcéa Lemos Pelandré suggests that these students also suffered from reprisals and threats following the coup.)[105]

The military coup of 1964 transformed Freire's life and interrupted Brazil's unprecedented process of democratization that had begun in 1945. Given Brazil's relative lack of democratic experience, which Freire himself frequently noted, the dynamism and pluralism of these years made many in the Brazilian political arena and in the military barracks uncomfortable. Certainly one can imagine that these same qualities tended to mask the factionalism and divisiveness that would have, in the long run, damaged the literacy campaign itself. The literacy campaign could have created other polarizing tendencies. A conflict might have developed between middle-class employers and their newly educated domestic workers as the latter demanded an improvement in their working conditions that the former were unwilling to provide. Meanwhile, the changes in the popular class's consciousness brought about through their participation in the peasant leagues themselves might have altered Brazil's political dynamics still further.

Freire's own explanations for the coup varied over the years. Having traveled throughout much of the country from 1961 to 1964, he believed that people were ready for the basic reforms that President Goulart had promised. At the same time, he criticized the "verbal incontinence" of the Brazilian lefts that gave the "impression of a power they did not have."[106] As the minister of education Paulo de Tarso Santos noted, the Left's tendency to talk about imminent social transformation made the military and others fearful.[107]

Pernambuco governor Arraes's belief in the early 1960s that Brazil had changed fundamentally and that what he called the "Brazilian Revolution" was irreversible was clearly an illusion. The vast majority of Brazilians were not as active or conscious as the Left thought. As Sergipe historian Ibaré Dantas has argued, popular participation was uncoordinated and not institutionalized; the triumphalist rhetoric of many on the Left, moreover, blinded them to the fact that the powers of reaction, and the military in particular (which, for its part, claimed to have its own revolutionary agenda), were much stronger than the divided Left was.[108] As José Willington Germano has argued regarding Maranhão's program in Natal, participants' faith in the transforming power of education was overly optimistic.[109] But, more to the point, it is hardly surprising that the military and so many traditional Brazilian politicians were alarmed by the constant use of the word "revolution" and other rhetorical excesses of the Brazilian student Left and many associated with Freire in the Goulart administration.

The military coup of 1964 that called itself a revolution is as perfect an example of a counterrevolution as there ever has been. The military set to work immediately to guarantee that the on-going mobilization of the Brazilian population was halted and reversed, but it also guaranteed that the northeast as a region would continue to be defined more as a problem than as a generator of possible solutions. In early December 1964, Edward Rowell commented, "At the moment Northeastern Brazil is incapable of influencing Brazilian national political affairs to any significant extent, but it remains a socioeconomic problem area that may well prove to be another powder-keg in the future." The military largely replaced innovative leaders with those who had no connection to or understanding of the more dynamic trends in the region. Even U.S. officials had to admit that the replacement for Maranhão's "vigorous administration" (and for that of others like Seixas Dória) was, at best, "uninspired." "Somehow, the political system is going to have to come to terms with these newly self-conscious masses," Roswell warned.[110] The military sought to reinforce old habits of deference by employing repression more extensively in the northeast and targeting peasants and union members in particular, thus making plain the dangers of a heightened consciousness.[111] For much of the next twenty years, military rulers and their own "Brazilian Revolution" would count on greater political support in the northeast than in the center south. (Ultimately, the military government would seek to resolve its northeastern problem through migration more than transformation.)[112]

For Freire, the coup meant more than a decade and a half of exile, which pained him greatly and that he later regretted. But for all of the personal anguish that it caused him and his family, it also created new opportunities that made him into first a hemispheric and then an international figure. Ironically, perhaps the most productive period of his life was now about to begin, working not, as it turned out, in Bolivia, but in Chile for a reformist government that garnered more U.S. support than did any other government in the hemisphere.

Three / Reformist Chile, Peasant Consciousness, & the Meaning of Christian Democracy, 1964–1969

Paulo Freire had developed new techniques for training adults to read and write, but his hopes of employing them to transform his native land were frustrated by the military coup of 1964. The experience of exile that resulted from the coup, however, opened up new opportunities for him. In Chile, the recently inaugurated administration of Eduardo Frei made popular education part of a larger Christian Democratic state project of promoting land reform and the enlargement of what we now call civil society. Central to Frei's vision was a plan to eradicate illiteracy.[1] The Frei administration sought both to liberate and to control, and at its best and worst, it exemplified the promise and the contradictions of 1960s reformism. Freire, Frei, and others engaged in the process of encouraging social transformation wanted to change the consciousness of the Chilean campesinos. Given the strengths and weaknesses of the Chilean social and political system, this created the potential both for furthering a paternalistic relationship between the government and the governed and for promoting changes that went beyond the boundaries of the permissible. Moreover, it awakened the consciousness of more than those it specifically targeted, radicalizing, at times, the very state agents who took part in the program of social transformation, seemingly even Freire himself, while inspiring more conservative elements in Chilean society to regroup and challenge the Christian Democrats in the 1970 presidential election.

Chile, a country with a population of roughly 8.2 million at the time Freire arrived, is spread out across 2,600 miles, although the majority of its population lived in the central valley. More than 70 percent of the population in the

1960s was urban. Most of the population was white, roughly one-third was mestizo, and only about 3 percent was purely indigenous. Chilean social realities, or at least myths of racial homogeneity, did not force Freire to emphasize race in Chile. One-fifth of the population could usefully be described as middle class. Chilean democracy had evolved over time, with urban workers and miners becoming integrated into the political system, but not without occasional setbacks and perhaps at times at what must have seemed a glacial rate. Electoral changes beginning in 1958 had upset the traditional, to a large degree still oligarchical system and created opportunities for the Left and for adventurous reformists like those represented by the Partido Democrata Cristiana (Christian Democratic Party, PDC). Only the literate could vote, but the vast majority of the population (as opposed to only 60 percent of the population in Brazil at the time) was literate.[2]

Paulo Freire's experience in Chile in adult literacy education from 1964 to 1969 represents a fruitful period in his life. As important as Freire's previous work in Brazil had been, it was during his Chilean exile that he became a figure of importance throughout Latin America. To understand how Freire became so central to the international debate over the importance of literacy in social transformation, one must examine him and his work within the context of the larger Christian Democratic reformist project, which he aided and eventually came to criticize. The Frei administration not only could boast significant achievements in enhancing civil society, but it also created problematic political dynamics that would be exacerbated during Salvador Allende's abbreviated term in office. To place Freire within the Chilean political context, one has to look closely at his allies in the administration, most particularly Jacques Chonchol, Freire's boss in the Ministry of Agriculture's Instituto del Desarrollo Agropecuario (Institute of Farming and Livestock Development, INDAP) and a controversial figure inside and outside of the administration, and the much lesser known Waldemar Cortés Carabantes, who was in charge of the education ministry's adult literacy campaign. Chonchol, a technocrat and devout Catholic, had worked for the agriculture ministry in previous Chilean administrations before going to Cuba to work as a Food and Agriculture Organization (FAO) adviser on agrarian reform from 1959 to 1961. To understand the relationship between literacy training and the broader process of social transformation, one must examine the tensions within the PDC and in Chilean society as a whole regarding the direction and the pace of reform. One must also examine the question of the degree to which "consciousness" was being changed, and whose consciousness was being raised, not only because of the literacy training programs but also because of the larger social and political dynamics involved.[3]

Freire arrived in Chile toward the end of November 1964. After having been imprisoned by the military dictatorship and then released, he was given temporary refuge in October in the Bolivian embassy. The Bolivian government of Victor Paz Estenssoro had offered to employ him, but the overthrow of that government on 4 November soon after Freire's arrival in the country and his difficulties with adjusting to the country's high altitudes combined to make his stay there untenable, and he left after roughly two weeks. Fortunately for him, the influx of Brazilians into Chile that had begun following the overthrow of the Goulart government in late March created employment opportunities for him there as well. Paulo de Tarso Santos, deposed president Goulart's former minister of education, was a member of the small Brazilian PDC and had political ties to members of the new Frei administration, which was inaugurated in the same month that Freire arrived. The poet Thiago de Melo, who had been Goulart's cultural attaché in Chile, and the agronomist Steban Strauss were friends with Chonchol, who became Freire's chief ally within the administration. Within days of his arrival in his new country, Freire was working for Chonchol (he recalled having arrived in Chile on a Friday and being introduced to and employed by him on the following Monday). Years later, Freire remembered the feelings of "euphoria" that accompanied the "rise of the Christian Democratic Party to power," the openness with which he and other Brazilians were received, and the hopes the reformist government's "Revolution in Liberty" represented for a "Third Way" in Latin American politics.[4]

Freire had left behind a country with a historically weak democratic tradition. He was now operating in a country in which a much more inclusive and politicized political system had operated for decades, and in which traditional parties of the Left were strong. The indigenous population was larger than in Brazil but it was still a small portion of the population, and its needs were not addressed by the Frei administration's literacy campaign. Recent electoral changes had dramatically weakened the political power of the traditional elites. The Freire of this period eschewed partisan identifications but tended to ignore those to the right of the PDC. Freire was now employed by an administration that was criticized by many on the Left as being bourgeois and even rightist.[5] Many in the Frei government, however, considered the Chilean Right irrelevant, and Freire, for his part, seems to have only worried about the "right" in the Christian Democratic administration itself. Conservatives who had voted for the middle-class reformer Frei out of a perceived necessity (to prevent the election of Socialist senator Salvador Allende) would soon view Frei's programs as dangerous, not least of all because of the president's attempt to transform social relations in the countryside, a task to which Freire himself would dedicate his years in Chile. (Members of the Brazilian military government stirred up a controversy in the fall of 1965 inside of Chile when they warned of the dangers that Frei's "Goulartista" policies could lead to.)[6]

The United States was backing the Frei administration wholeheartedly during the early years (in contrast to how it had sought to undermine the efforts of a majority of the people Freire had worked with in Brazil on city, state, and national levels). No South American country received more aid per capita from the United States during the 1960s. If the Alliance for Progress's plan to prevent revolution by promoting reform still meant anything after the death of John F. Kennedy, it was in Chile under Frei. The United States had spent millions of dollars to help Frei defeat his rival in the 1964 presidential election, Socialist senator Salvador Allende, and it was now ready to back Frei's programs. And while I have found no evidence that the United States supported the literacy campaign itself, there is no doubt that U.S. ambassador Ralph Dungan, who identified so strongly with President Frei himself, supported, in theory at least, the idea of eliminating illiteracy among the Chilean peasantry. In a speech before the American Chamber of Commerce in Santiago, Ambassador Dungan asserted that an attempt to "rescue" illiterates was "an indispensable step in agricultural, industrial and commercial growth. Nowhere in the world is there an illiterate peasantry that is progressive. Nowhere is there a literate peasantry that is not."[7]

Freire was involved with a number of different governmental organizations almost from the beginning. Chonchol offered him work with INDAP's Social Development Division. INDAP, which had been focused on technical and financial aid in the agricultural sector during the previous administration of conservative president Jorge Alessandri, was now more interested in helping campesinos organize. For INDAP, Freire gave lectures and engaged in discussions and planning sessions regarding ways to accomplish this end. Freire eventually also worked with the Corporación de Reforma Agraria (Agrarian Reform Corporation, CORA), providing instruction in literacy training techniques for those working with campesinos on expropriated properties administered by the agency called asentamientos (settlements).[8] In his four and a half years in Chile, he traveled the length of Chile, helping organize literacy training and broader popular education programs. In Chile, adult literacy training became closely linked to the broader "social and economic changes in the countryside" that President Frei envisioned, and to the need to "obtain the active and creative incorporation [of campesinos] into the community" and their "conscious participation in the process of development."[9] Frei and his state project sought to transform Chilean society and politics. It had the strengths and weaknesses of any state-directed project, but it also was imbued with a profoundly Catholic humanism.[10]

Eduardo Frei's ideology and praxis were deeply rooted in his faith. As a young man traveling in Europe in the 1930s he had come under the influence of the French Catholic philosopher Jacques Maritain. The Social Christian strain of Catholicism during that time period offered a democratic and socially progressive alternative to fascism while still maintaining a strict loyalty to the structures and traditions of the Catholic Church. Frei had found in Maritain a justification for political activism by religious Catholics. His interest in tackling Chile's intractable social and economic problems made it difficult for him to remain in the Conservative Party, the traditional home of politically active Catholics in Chile. As a young man, he helped form the Falange, which eventually evolved into the PDC in 1957. Frei promised Chileans a society that was democratic but not individualistic, "communitarian but not collectivist." He rejected Marxism and liberalism, both of which he saw as being based on materialist conceptions of humanity. The Catholic humanism of the Christian Democratic administration provided a congenial environment for Freire, who underwent significant political changes himself during his years in Chile.[11]

One of the major weaknesses of Chilean democracy in 1964, according to Frei and his allies, was the lack of incorporation of the Chilean peasantry into the larger political process. Unlike many Latin American countries, including Freire's Brazil, Chile was already primarily urban, and had been since the 1940s, and its politics reflected that fact. A relatively inclusive political system had been built in part by explicitly excluding the peasantry, despite frequent attempts by campesinos to organize rural unions in the period prior to the rise of a reformist Catholic Church.[12] One of Eduardo Frei's central concerns as president was to change the marginal status of the roughly 20 percent of the population that belonged to the peasantry. Beginning with the introduction of the secret ballot in 1958, the rural population became more politically active than ever before. The Christian Democrats hoped to harness the potential of this part of the electorate by enacting reforms that appealed to them. Having been elected with 56 percent of the vote on 4 September 1964, Frei argued that there was a need to create a "new political regime" that would be "capable of surmounting the obstacles that inhibit economic development and the realization of social justice without sacrificing liberty." In congressional elections in the following March, his party gained control of the lower house, which it was never able to do in the Senate. Frei's vision of a transformed Chile included expanded participation in the political process and in social and economic life. The key to political and social development, according to Frei, was organization. To this end, he argued for what he called "promoción popular" (literally, popular promotion). Frei wanted to encourage the creation of political and social organizations of a wide variety of types. As he would later argue, "An organized people, with a rising cultural level, that enjoys expanded access to information and the free and secret exercise of suffrage is a people that demands that its voice be heard and that is respected in the dialogue of power." Frei lamented the fact that in 1965 only 10 percent of wage workers belonged to unions. There were too few "structures that authentically represent the aspirations" of workers, campesinos, and pobladores in urban slums. The creation of "mothers' centers" also became an important concern of the Frei administration; they became the "largest and most influential women's organizations in both rural and urban Chile."[13]

In words that would not have sounded at all odd coming from Freire, the Chilean president argued that people needed to be "*subjects* and not *objects* of their liberation." But the national government also had to be able to respond positively to popular organizations and provide them with the resources they needed to thrive. Critics of the program argued that the government was simply creating new cliental linkages. Frei was certainly aware of the dangers implicit in such an approach; promoción popular, he said, could easily degenerate into "paternalism, sectarianism, and statism."[14]

Frei also wanted to promote agrarian reform and proposed expropriating properties that, according to "normal levels of productivity," were poorly managed within any given region. Broad sectors of the Chilean population saw a need for reform in the countryside by 1964. Chilean agriculture had suffered from poor productivity since the 1930s; it had not kept up with the needs of a growing (and urbanizing) population. Frei and his associates hoped that by promoting land reform they could stimulate the peasantry to abandon subsistence production and help "feed the national market."[15] (Others in the administration argued, of course, that what was at stake was social justice.[16])

Frei also argued, however, that agrarian reform had to be more than just re-distribution of land; it was a form of "social and human investment."[17]

Peasants, in particular, needed to abandon traditional mentalities and re-alize that they were part of a larger process of national economic develop-ment.[18] Christian Democratic reformers like Chonchol, the most prominent Christian Democrat concerned with these issues, saw peasants as "exces-sively subject to forces of nature." Peasants needed to embrace an awareness of "modern man's capacity to dominate nature through science and technol-ogy." They needed to be receptive to new agricultural methods and the poten-tial benefits of commercialization, and to develop "new social aspirations" that drive "men to progress." (Chile was dependent on the "importation of over $100 million worth of food each year," despite "nearly ideal agricultural conditions" in its central valley.) Chonchol was concerned that agrarian reform would just turn the peasant into a "traditional landowner who will be a dead weight on the future economic progress of the country, or a petit bourgeoisie who will join with the most reactionary elements and sectors of society." The values that a transformed campesino would exhibit, in contrast, were dynamism, cooperation, and solidarity. Chonchol, like many Christian Democrats, particularly those on the party's Left, also wanted to promote what they defined as communitarian over individualistic values. The new campesino would have a less provincial vision of the world and a "dynamic vi-sion of the destiny of his country." Campesinos would become "habituated to assuming responsibilities and making decisions by themselves."[19] Generally, the campesino's new mentality would be characterized by "cooperation," a tendency to participate in "organized activity," "dedication to work," "social solidarity," a "rational attitude toward consumption," and a "confidence in his own abilities to create as subject in the world and as builder of his own world."[20] One of the drawings used in literacy instruction illustrated the word "compañero" by showing a student at a desk handing a fellow student a pen-cil to write with.[21] Peasants were expected to develop ways to define and solve their own problems, whether technical or social.[22] Moreover, peasants were being encouraged to break out of their isolation and form their own co-operatives and unions through INDAP. "Only organized campesinos can push forward and take in their hands the direction of the process of transforma-tion of rural society," Frei contended.[23]

An integral part of the social transformation of the countryside for Frei was the elimination of illiteracy. To help further this goal, Frei appointed Waldemar Cortés Carabantes to head a literacy program. Cortés Carabantes had been serving in the ministry of public education for roughly a decade already and had worked in programs in the poor shantytown neighborhoods in the capital city. In 1963, he had suggested that Chile needed to find more "dynamic" ways to address adult illiteracy. While three-quarters of Chile's population was already literate by 1930, decades before most other Latin American countries even approached that literacy level, illiteracy had not dropped sufficiently since then (perhaps by as little as 5 percent between 1930 and 1952). If those trends continued, it would take Chile sixty years to achieve what was considered an "acceptable rate of illiteracy of between four and five percent." Moreover, combined with the 20–25 percent of the population that was illiterate by any definition was an additional 20 percent that was either semiliterate and/or illiterate because they simply had neglected to cultivate their former abilities to read or write. Since the size of the Chilean population continued to increase, the absolute number of Chilean illiterates was increasing. This was in large part due to serious problems in the Chilean educational system, not least of all the inadequate numbers of schools and teachers, particularly in rural areas, as well as the poor condition of existing schools. In rural Chile, 36 percent of the population was illiterate. Although Cortés Carabantes had argued that a long-term solution required an improvement in the schools, a problem that Frei was also committed to addressing, he was also well aware of the urgency of addressing the problems of those who were well beyond school age. Previous campaigns, including the Cuerpo Cívico de Alfabetización Popular (Civic Body of Literacy Training), organized in 1944, had largely depended upon the efforts of volunteers, as well as the working assumption that those who knew how to read and write necessarily knew how to teach people how to read and write. (This idea continued to be prevalent in the Alessandri administration, which was in office at the time Cortés Carabantes was writing.) Those involved in adult education, Cortés Carabantes argued, had to have special training in the field, as well as material and technical support for their efforts. Literacy campaigns, according to UNESCO, worked best when they were combined with more comprehensive plans to transform social and economic conditions in the countryside. Chile, Cortés Carabantes had maintained prior to Frei's inauguration, needed a national campaign that reached into all areas of the country. The traditional night school was no longer sufficient, he insisted; instead, schools should be established at the workplace. Moreover, the practical benefits of education needed to become clear to adult students, otherwise they soon would abandon their studies. New trends in adult education focused on the education of the community and not just of the individual. While not denying the need to create opportunities for personal growth, he thought that it was even more important that workers and campesinos, in an educational context, develop their own organizations and sense of group identity, which would help them in their larger goal of improving the quality of life within their communities. Adult education, furthermore, could not simply be primary or secondary education taught at night; it had to take into account the special needs and interests of a mature student body, as well as the broader needs of Chilean society as a whole.[24]

Soon after being chosen to lead the kind of campaign he had called for, Cortés Carabantes learned that Freire had already been working with mass literacy campaigns in Brazil and had developed a new technique that involved the use of what Freire called generating words, words, as we have seen, that had a special meaning in the daily life of the student. In their first meeting, Freire agreed to work with the Ministry of Education and, with what Cortés Carabantes called his "fraternal and disinterested spirit," said he would not accept royalties for the use of his method.[25]

Beginning with his presidential message of May 1966, Frei noted the new learning techniques that had begun to be applied on a national basis. More than 2,500 primary school teachers were already employed in the literacy campaign. Early expectations were that 100,000 adults could learn how to read and write at an anticipated 2,600 local community education centers spread out throughout Chile.[26]

Freire and his associates traveled throughout Chile, but especially in the central zone, where land concentration was particularly high. Cortés Carabantes and Freire began to adapt the latter's methods and styles of presentation to the Chilean milieu, to the particular needs of the Chilean campesinos, and to the different linguistic demands of Spanish, as they formulated an intensive literacy campaign. In Chile, Freire's method became known as the psychosocial method. Primary school teachers were trained in Freire's philosophy and techniques. Unlike in previous Chilean literacy campaigns, the teachers working for Cortés Carabantes were paid a salary and were compensated during their training periods. In keeping with Frei's larger social vision and their own personal philosophies, Cortés Carabantes and Freire emphasized that the students were the subject, and not the object, of their own education, and encouraged them through the educational process to become integrated as active and creative contributing members of their communities, so that they could participate consciously in the development of Chile. Freire and his associates began to develop their ideas by gathering information from their campesino "sources" and students in order to understand their social reality and present material that reflected the substance of their daily lives.[27]

The adoption of Freire's method was crucial, because it represented more than just a selection of one technique over another. The method, as we have seen, involved an attempt to "produce a change in the consciousness" of the student. Learning how to read was only one element of the literacy program, according to Cortés Carabantes; the adult student would also begin to view himself and his own reality critically. While looking at slide images representing his life, his "customs, his beliefs, his social practices, [and] group attitudes," the student would begin to "discuss his reality" with his peers. The words he would be learning to read would be those related to his "concrete situation." As we have seen, the distinction between nature and culture was central to the Freirean understanding of the transformation of consciousness. Students would begin to understand themselves as makers of and participants in culture. They would learn to break up everyday words into their phonetic elements and make new words using those elements, taking part in their own "intellectual creation." The teacher's role would be merely to facilitate dialogue and to "stimulate the reaction" to be produced in their students' "innermost" consciousness. Those taught using Freire's method would learn not only to read and write quickly but also to value themselves more highly.[28]

In 1966 and 1967, the Jefatura de Planes Extraordinarios de Educación de Adultos (Headquarters for Extraordinary Plans in Adult Education) in the Ministry of Education produced textbooks that laid out the theoretical groundwork for the literacy training programs, as well as providing short readings as part of a three-month course. These books provide important insight into the ideology of that branch of the Frei administration. They are theoretically grounded in Freire's teachings regarding the need for adult students to became active agents in their own history and education and Frei's desire to incorporate the unincorporated and have them engage critically in modern society. Campesinos were now to engage in an examination of the most significant elements of their daily life while they also "awaken[ed]" to "the feeling of social cooperation and living together" and their "full integration into society."[29] As Cortés Carabantes argued, the newly literate were moving beyond their former position as minors and being elevated "to the condition of men and women conscious of the high value they have as human beings." Cortés Carabantes, Freire, and Chonchol were all interested in seeing students replace their "magical consciousness," in which they attributed supernatural causes to things that happen in their daily life, with critical consciousness. Cortés Carabantes provided an example of this kind of thinking when he discussed the fishermen of Dichato, near Concepción. These men believed that fish fled those who possessed an excessive desire for profit. Therefore, after a good catch, the fishermen took off work for a few days. "Their lack of reflection hurt them." Cortés Carabantes, following Freire, wanted Chilean illiterates to develop a critical consciousness and become aware of themselves as historical actors in the world, who could change their own reality.[30]

Freire's method went beyond a "pure memorization of words, disconnected from the existential experience of men." Man was a man because "he worked and in working transformed the world." Literacy could not be "dissociated from his work," because the "word with which one plays, if it is true, it is work, it is reflection, and it is action on the world."[31] Ideally, the newly literate would learn to "speak their own words."[32] Decades later, Freire remembered "the intensity of the peasants' involvement when they were analyzing their local and national reality." With the "culture of silence" that defined traditional agrarian relations in the Chilean countryside broken, words spilled out all over, and the discussions continued virtually unabated.[33]

For Freire, the process of agrarian reform with which his literacy training program was associated demanded "a permanent critical examination of the transforming actions and its results." It was necessary to go beyond a mechanical view of the process, and to recognize that a social reality created by men could only be transformed by men. It would not be enough to replace magical thinking with mechanical, "economistic" thinking. Neither mode of thinking was, from Freire's perspective, critical or dialectical, and both tended to minimize men, who became only "a mere object of change." One cannot impose changes *for* or *on* people, but only *with* them, as subjects, Freire argued. Any attempt by agronomists to introduce new techniques that would enhance production had to recognize not only the historical and cultural conditions in which the campesinos lived but also the historical and cultural conditions of the extension workers themselves. Extension agents had to recognize the knowledge that the campesinos already possessed, without thinking that campesinos "should remain in the state in which they were encountered" in terms of their relation to the natural world. Campesinos should not be treated as people in whom the extension agents were going to "deposit . . . knowledge." Nor could men simply be treated as a "mere instrument of production." Agrarian reform was not fundamentally about productivity but, instead, about transforming human beings. As long as government officials recognized the campesinos as people who "transform nature with their work," they would understand campesinos' resistance to more efficient means of production as a cultural issue. The campesino mentality had been formed in a particular rigid and dehumanizing social structure, a "culture of silence which was closed and opposed to dialogue," and campesinos were now having to address the new social reality of the asentamiento.[34]

There were inherent difficulties with Freire's method, as Cortés Carabantes himself recognized. It was critical, he argued, that the new "critical consciousness . . . not navigate in a vacuum." It had to "open people to concrete changes" in the way they lived their lives. If it did not, they felt bitter and profoundly frustrated. "We were conscious that to achieve this [greater openness] we needed large structural changes" in society, as well as concrete changes in people's working lives. If large structural changes were not made, newly literate people would lapse back into illiteracy, since they would discover that knowing how to read and write did not change their particular situation.[35]

Making it clear to the Chilean peasants that fundamental changes were taking place was a central goal of the textbooks produced for the campaign. Roughly 800,000 copies of the introductory reading manuals were distributed by CORA.[36] These books tried to inculcate Christian Democratic ideology, and they focused on issues of particular concern to the Frei administration. A story titled "The Griefs of an Illiterate," for example, made clear the difficulties faced by a man who had not yet learned to read or write. He could not read danger signs or employment ads. Nor could he read a letter written to him by the woman he loved. A friend had to read her letters to him and write his responses for him. His friend thereby became acquainted with intimate details of José's life.[37]

The textbooks provided a further opportunity for the Frei administration to promote goals such as agrarian reform. In an article on rural society, the author discussed the plan to give inquilinos (tenant farmers) land that they had never had before. Another article explained the reasons why the right to private property could be infringed upon when rural properties had been abandoned or were inadequately managed.[38] These books also focused on the campesinos' need to organize, in order to "unite their forces to those of the government and thereby improve their cultural, economic, and social conditions." The manuals described what each type of organization would do and provided a basic history of labor unions and their role in improving the quality of workers' lives. Moreover, they promoted the idea of Chile itself as the "national community"; they emphasized the unity of the Chilean people rather than competing class interests. "Pueblo," or people, quite literally, was the last word in one of the manuals. There also was a call for the general need for "profound change in attitudes of Chileans" regarding ways they could improve their quality of life, including by adopting more mechanized forms of cultivation in the countryside. The manuals urged the campesinos to "accept technical help from the Ministry of Agriculture and CORA" and assured them that the problem of unequal distribution of land was "being corrected." Chile, the campesinos were reminded, was "*in a process of development.*" The Chilean people should "support honest governments" that were directing their "destiny." Photos depicted previous conditions in which peasants worked unhappily to emphasize that now they owned their own houses and had schools for the children. They had begun to work for themselves and their country to achieve economic liberation, "the ultimate goal of agrarian reform." The final photograph in one manual portrayed a couple dancing; the accompanying caption read, "For the campesino, new horizons are opening up."[39]

The manuals focused on social issues as well. They preached the virtue of temperance and the dangers of alcoholism. According to government sources, 250,000 Chileans were alcoholics. The manuals discussed the damage alcohol posed to heart and liver. The distinction between human beings and animals being central to Christian Democratic humanism, the manuals noted that alcohol had a brutalizing effect on men and led to a "low level of moral life."[40] The manuals promoted female domesticity to a certain degree, noting what they called women's special duties in keeping houses clean, and they emphasized the man's role as head of the household, as well as the need to prevent the disintegration of the nuclear family. In the advanced reading book, however, there was an emphasis on recognizing the fact that women now performed many different kinds of work in Chile and, by law, had equal rights. (Women had played a key role in Frei's election.)[41]

The manuals' inevitable tendency to standardize content for discussion conflicted with Freire's theories about following campesinos' lead in educating them. More generally, they blurred the distinction between developing a critical consciousness and developing a Christian Democratic consciousness. The readings clearly tended to celebrate what the Christian Democrats were trying to achieve, as much as to push the campesinos themselves to define their own path toward liberation.

By late 1967, the Chilean literacy programs had begun to be recognized internationally. In September, on the first International Literacy Day, UNESCO listed Chile as one of the five countries doing the most to eliminate illiteracy and awarded the Jefatura an honorable mention for the Pahlevi Prize for best overall literacy program. The citation praised the "new teaching methodology," the textbooks and audiovisual material, the training of 6,000 teachers and coordinators, and the integration of the program in "the tasks of community development" that other public and private institutions were undertaking.[42] Freire himself had now become an international figure in educational circles.

Despite this international recognition, those engaged in the Chilean campaign were aware not only of its potential but also of the difficulties inherent in the relationship between government officials and those they wanted to transform. This is made clear in a series of recordings made in October of 1968 by a "Circle of Thematic Investigation" in an asentamiento. Following the Freire model, groups of asentados were asked to look at slides illustrating aspects of their daily lives and to discuss what they saw. They clearly recognized their own reality in the images. "There are many fundos around here in which you work with a man on horseback behind," one campesino remarked. In the traditional agrarian system, people who just watched others work received "ill-earned gains." Now, the participants contended, they could work without an overseer.[43] They also saw images of strikes and asserted that things were changing, and they now felt free. They had more enthusiasm these days to work more, to learn more, and to be more productive.[44] One may wonder whether campesinos were simply saying what they thought the government officials wanted to hear; in any case, the officials, as we shall see, were not as reassured as one might expect them to have been.

The "Circle of Thematic Investigation" transcripts reveal certain tensions between the officials and the campesinos. Teachers who quite explicitly defined themselves as urban expressed an earnest desire to get to know rural people initially in order to lay the groundwork for future courses defined by campesinos' needs and interests.[45] But when asked what kinds of courses they needed, a campesino replied, "Rapid ones." In the short term, in any case, it was often difficult to schedule times to meet, given work and family obligations. On reviewing the transcripts, moreover, government officials expressed concern that discussion coordinators sometimes "intervened too quickly and didn't accept the group's initial silence."[46]

Freire, for his part, tended to see the positive side of what was taking place in Chile. He later recalled the enthusiasm with which the newly literate "wrote words with their tools on the dirt roads where they were working." When Freire and others asked why they were learning to read and write then and had not previously, one man replied, "Before the agrarian reform . . . I didn't even think. Neither did my friends . . . it wasn't possible. We lived under orders. We only had to carry out orders. We had nothing to say." Or, as another remarked, "When all this land belonged to one latifundio, there was no reason to read and write. We weren't responsible for anything." Now he knew he could go to the city of Santiago by himself and buy supplies for the asentamiento.[47]

At the time, however, many government officials expressed skepticism that significant change was in fact taking place. They tried to reinforce the idea that the asentados, by definition, no longer had *patróns*.[48] Officials feared that CORA itself represented a reality only glimpsed to a limited degree. Even where campesinos demonstrated an interest in rebelling, they still feared the patrón. In one instance, officials noted, asentados continued to refer to their former boss, Vicente Iñiquez (whose land had been partially expropriated to create the asentamiento), as the "true patrón." Don Vicente remained the "central figure" in their understanding of the world. But what government officials failed to see was that the asentados also criticized their boss, whom they portrayed as immoral and unnatural; Don Vicente, it was claimed, had sold his soul to the devil and had "both sexes." Government officials also were concerned that the people who had already become leaders in the asentados were more likely than the rank and file to participate in discussions. Government officials, many of whom were women, also were concerned that the rural women were reluctant to talk (and, for that matter, that coordinators intervened more during their discussions with the women than during those with men). Women also did not even recognize what was meant to be conveyed by a drawing depicting a meeting in which problems of the asentamiento were discussed. ("There are only men there; it must be a sports club.") Women in the asentamientos even argued that they did not "have a right to give an opinion." Asentado husbands, for their part, did not always allow women to take part in meetings. Women and the young, it was clear, were often marginalized under the asentamiento system. Moreover, the literacy training courses themselves sometimes seemed to have been less successful with women.[49]

To understand the complex dynamics at work as Freire and his associates sought to teach people how to read and write and how to transform their own consciousness and as campesinos were given more access to land, one must step back and consider the larger social and political picture.

President Frei himself had recognized the pitfalls of paternalism, and so had many of his administration's officials. Cortés Carabantes had feared that the new organizations being formed would be seen as just a "present from the elite."[50] Freire made the need to avoid paternalistic attitudes the cornerstone of his own discussions with government officials. He warned against the customary "feeling of superiority [and] domination with which agronomists encounter campesinos in traditional agrarian structures." Freire wanted officials to reconceptualize the relationship between agronomists and campesinos. Freire wanted agents to see themselves not as "extension" agents, a term that suggested a social and intellectual superior offering a hand in a godlike or messianic way, but as engaged in communication, whereby they would come to understand how the peasants saw the world. Agronomists and campesinos were to be engaged in a project of mutual transformation.[51] Peasants would incorporate themselves and not be manipulated, as Freire felt occurred under populist leaders.[52]

The Freire model at its most idealistic and empowering was exemplified by efforts made in areas such as the province of Colchagua, where rates of illiteracy were as high as 57 percent and in which literacy education became the "total responsibility of rural unions." There, one of Freire's associates reported, the campesinos took literacy training extremely seriously and had "absolute confidence in their capacity to realize it. They [were] firmly convinced that learning to read and write" would be the "key" that would "open up the door to a new world for all the peasants." "Only a campesino can teach another campesino," they argued. "You functionaries," one campesino said, "are in a different world than ours and cannot communicate with us because you are part of that culture."[53]

Freire hoped to extend his system throughout Chile, with 60 campesinos learning his method and in turn teaching an additional 500, and those 500 teaching 5,000, and so on.[54] This clearly had the potential to go beyond the traditional paternalistic dynamic, even as it, to some degree, challenged the way Cortés Carabantes had envisioned the literacy campaign, as an activity to be directed by professionals.

Some Christian Democrats seemed convinced that the days of paternalism and deference were already over. "The 'new man of Chile,'" according to one Christian Democratic leader, "no longer bows his head but meets all men as equals."[55] As one asentado remarked in a discussion with government officials, now one could talk without tipping one's hat and asking permission from the patrón.[56] A North American observer agreed that "in the countryside, the patrón-inquilino relationship never again will return to the status quo ante. Education once given an individual cannot be taken away. Aspirations have been aroused more than they had been previously." Underprivileged members of society now had "a sense of participation greater than ever existed before." For the first time in history, a Chilean government was "consulting and listening to campesinos."[57] Yet, at the same time, Freire saw the need to confront the "marks of old structures colliding with the new forms of behavior demanded by recently installed structures" like the asentamiento.[58]

But paternalism was not just a problem of old structures; it also was woven deeply into the fabric of Frei administration reforms.[59] The state-managed asentamientos, for example, which had been envisioned as transitional institutions, came to be seen as a permanent solution to problems in the countryside. As President Frei had suggested, agrarian reform was intended to "turn the campesino into his own patrón," but CORA, the owner of the asentamientos, often seemed to have taken the place of the old patrón, even though many campesinos clearly would have preferred owning their own land. But asentamientos, for their part, also hired seasonal workers who did not receive the same rights and benefits as the asentados did.[60] In addition, even where unions had pushed for the expropriation of land, once asentamientos had been established, unions tended to decline in importance, in part, it was suggested, because CORA officials themselves considered them disruptive to the asentamientos' operations.[61] And CORA officials were not the only ones in the Frei administration who were sending mixed messages regarding the growth of unions in the countryside.

Frei's emphasis on the countryside, in any case, had hardly been apolitical. The Christian Democrats lagged behind the Marxist parties in organizing the industrial and mining sectors. The unorganized countryside, therefore, offered an opportunity for the Christian Democrats. INDAP already had employed 505 people to promote union organizing, long before the law legalizing unions was passed in April 1967. Unions affiliated with the Christian Democrats may have been successful in organizing the campesinos, but rival Christian Democratic rural unions themselves were soon feuding. The Christian Democratic unions resented the fact that INDAP was organizing its own unions as well. The leaders of unions that were aligned with the PDC and yet institutionally independent considered Chonchol in particular to be unsympathetic to their unions, which he feared would work against the party and the government. Chonchol, in fact, was seen by some as more controlling and was even accused of trying to eliminate the independent unions.) INDAP-affiliated unions, in any case, grew faster than any other in the year following the legalization of rural unions. U.S. embassy officials suspected that Chonchol was "trying to construct a personal political base" in the INDAP unions. And generally by 1967, the embassy was looking for "indications, if any, of a political cutting-edge to the INDAP efforts in the campo." But some of the other "independent unions" had themselves received help from the International Development Foundation, the Agency for International Development, and, it was presumed, the Central Intelligence Agency. One INDAP organizer in Nuble province argued that the "'sheep-like' mentality of [local campesinos] underscores the problems of nurturing a flourishing, independent campesino movement." Frei, who had warned of the dangers of sectarianism, tried to stand above the fray and not "specifically endorse any particular union," but these conflicts continued to be serious ones, not least of all because, as David Lehmann has argued, unlike the land reform program, the unionization drive involved more people and was, ultimately, less under the government's control. Nevertheless, it is undoubtedly true that the Christian Democrats were able to make gains in the countryside at the expense of the Marxist parties.[62]

In any case, there were certain economic and social realities that were making it difficult for the Frei administration's goals to be accomplished. Inflation that had declined in the early years of the Frei administration soon climbed back over 30 percent, and this led Frei to push for a curb on strikes, as well as for a general austerity program.[63] In addition, the worst drought in 100 years of record keeping in Chile was wreaking havoc in the countryside.[64] Rural union leaders accused landowners of using the drought as a pretext to get rid of workers active in unions. Some in the administration, like Chonchol, hoped that the drought would provide an "ideal opportunity to accelerate agrarian reform."[65] Campesinos, for their part, had their own understanding of the drought; it was the "revenge of Saint Peter," because his day was no longer "kept holy."[66]

There were political problems, as well, both within and outside of the party. Factions within the administration and the PDC were extremely diverse in ideological terms. Some party and administration members like Chonchol historically had argued not only for a "third way" between communism and capitalism but also for the "total abolition of the capitalist way of life."[67] To some degree, governmental agencies were themselves divided politically, with CORA being more "reformist" and Chonchol's INDAP more "progressive."[68] Conflicts between factions in the PDC were becoming more acute by the halfway point in the Frei administration in 1967. Some even claimed that the party was already ideologically bankrupt.[69]

Certainly, not all members of the Frei administration were equally committed to Freire's ideas. Representatives of CORA were primarily interested in increasing production and thought that the hour-long meetings involved in generating critical consciousness distracted from this goal. A more practical consideration was the fact that the party had failed to win substantial support in municipal elections in April 1967. This created further splits within the party between those who argued for the need to consolidate and those who wanted to accelerate the process of reform. By this time, political analysts argued, the Christian Democrats were losing support from the middle class, particularly in the cities of Santiago and Valparaíso, due to the priority the administration had given to issues concerning the poor in the city and countryside. Small farmers, too, an estimated 15 percent of Chilean voters, were particularly resentful of INDAP policies, which farmers considered antagonistic toward the "capitalistic, selfish individualism" said to be typical of them; they decried the general "politicization" of the countryside and had become increasingly disaffected and withdrew their support for the party. Frei himself began to draw back from the more revolutionary aspects of his programs.[70] And yet Frei was convinced that because of his administration's initiatives, the campesino was already "more of a person and more realized in his human capacities."[71]

By 1967, Frei had begun to be concerned about the fulfillment of his dreams of a "dynamic national and popular society." He believed his congressional opponents were trying to promote the failure of his government and that others were actively promoting "subversion." Frei's talk of a "revolution" had begun to backfire. Frei claimed that he had never promised a "revolution in six years." He acknowledged the difficulty of achieving democratically in such a short time the social transformations that even violent and totalitarian regimes could not accomplish quickly.[72] Agrarian reform, Frei argued, was "advancing but not so precipitously that it would compromise its fortunes, but also without fear of its critics." Frei praised the campesinos' maturity and responsibility, but he also feared the "enemies of agrarian reform" who "agitate the countryside to hinder it or take it to impossible extremes."[73] In any case, it was already clear by 1967 that, "because of financial and technical stringencies," the Frei administration would not be able to reach its 1964 goal of 100,000 new landowners by 1970.[74] In the meantime, Frei began to focus more on the "need for commercializing and modernizing Chilean agriculture than on redistribution of land" and now praised Chilean landowners who were open to technological advances and making productive use of their land.[75] Frei also had amended his goal of eradicating illiteracy. He now hoped that illiteracy could be reduced from the 16 percent noted in the 1960 census to 7 percent by the end of his term in 1970.[76] U.S. ambassador Edward Korry noted in early 1968 that "the end of the noble and necessary Frei experiment in 'Revolution in Liberty'" had arrived.[77]

Freire later recalled that he "witnessed, sometimes with surprise, retreats in the area of political ideology by persons who had proclaimed their support for the transformation of society, then became frightened and repentant, and made a fearful about-face in mid-course and turned into hidebound reactionaries."[78] Others, he said, perhaps thinking of his friend Chonchol, advanced "by walking in a consistent direction, refusing to run from history."[79] Frei and Freire had shared an interest in organizing the unorganized, and both men were pleased with the results of their efforts. Frei's skeptical and critical attitude toward capitalism, however, was now less prominent as he embraced more of the modernizing elements of the Alliance for Progress, while Freire himself had come to define himself as anticapitalist.

In general terms, although trying to steer clear of any involvement in partisan disputes in a country not his own, Freire undoubtedly had more in common with those in the party who backed the so-called Chonchol Report, which argued that the poor showing in the elections of 1967 indicated the need for a deepening of the process of social transformation and that Chile needed to adopt a "non-capitalist" road to development. This report was highly controversial within the party and revealed the party's increasing divisions. By early 1968, there were even indications that some PDC members, including the presumed presidential candidate in the 1970 elections, Radomiro Tomic, proposed forming an alliance with parties to their left, including the Communist Party. (Frei himself, not surprisingly, was opposed to this idea.)[80]

Meanwhile, the youth organization Juventud Democrata Cristiana (Christian Democratic Youth, JDC), a small but important faction within the PDC was pressing for more "revolutionary" change. Since 1963, the JDC had been one of the factions that were most critical of capitalism and individualism. They had argued that a Christian Democratic government would represent the Chilean poor and create an "authentically human society." By the second half of the Frei administration, members of the JDC were encouraging land invasions. In November 1968, they enthusiastically supported the idea of creating a "popular force capable of constructing socialism." U.S. ambassador Korry saw them as viewing Chile "through a Marxist optic with revolutionary Christian overtones." The PDC, from this perspective and from that of Chonchol (with whom many of the party's youth were aligned), needed to rid itself of more conservative figures like interior minister Edmundo Pérez Zújovic. Although elder statesmen in the party disagreed with the younger Christian Democrats' diagnosis and methods, they did not want to lose what they considered the "most vital elements" of the party.[81]

Many of those involved in literacy training programs and others who worked in the countryside had themselves had their own consciousness transformed, as Freire had presumed would take place. "Their idealism and close contact with the people have not rendered them charitable towards the government's efforts," Robert Dean, a U.S. embassy official, noted. "Nor do they excuse the [PDC's] quashing of the revolutionaries' assaults." Christian Democrats active in the countryside, Dean continued, complained that

> the present bureaucracy does not understand the importance of a grass-roots movement. According to their liturgy, little time remains to effect a non-violent revolution and by its 'lack of faith in the Chilean people' is letting the opportunity pass. They see an embryonic revolution in the campo, with the campesinos being politicized to the left. In their view it should not be taken for grant that these people—'their people'—will lock step with the PDC. Indeed, unless the PDC-cum-government unleashes an ideological movement, FRAP [Frente de Acción Popular (Popular Action Front), the coalition led by Allende], by their reasoning would be the major beneficiary."

While these young people remained highly motivated, they were also increasingly frustrated with the pace of change and the general slackening of interest in the revolutionary aspects of the Frei program.[82]

We have more direct evidence regarding Freire's impact on the consciousness of his younger colleagues than of that he may have had on the campesinos. Freire had argued that professionals who were engaged in the work of social transformation needed to constantly reflect on what they were doing, and to see themselves historically, as the campesinos were being encouraged to do. Through dialogue and solidarity with the campesinos, they were themselves to be transformed.[83] As Rolando Pinto, one of Freire's students and colleagues, recalled in a 1991 interview, "Paulo Freire produced an enormous impression on those of us who were young college students." Freire's ideas were accepted immediately by students who saw themselves as progressive or revolutionary. "We thought that we had found in his philosophy one of the paths for the liberation of the oppressed classes," Pinto said. "In communication with our people, we were reborn as organic educators of the people." By the end of 1967 or early 1968, according to some of Freire's young colleagues, like Marcela Gajardo, there was a process of radicalization that had begun within the PDC, particularly among the younger members who at the same time contended that Frei's "Revolution in Liberty" had taken a turn to the right. Freire "defended the whole process of structural transformation, inspired not by Marxist ideology, but using Marxist categories for the analysis of reality."[84] Pinto and others argued that the utopianism of the presidential campaign and the early years of the Frei administration lasted until the middle of 1967. Frei's young critics argued that change was now no longer under the administration's control; popular forces were now taking charge, leaving the reformists to try to find a way to somehow halt the forward momentum.[85]

In the second half of Frei's tenure in office, there was a move away from "promotional action" in INDAP, and consciousness-raising was no longer part of the Ministry of Education's tasks. CORA, some complained, was no longer "studying the reality of the countryside." Some Brazilians who had been working with the Frei administration from the beginning now felt uncomfortable as the more conservative members of the PDC viewed them more suspiciously.[86] Fortunately for Freire, new opportunities presented themselves at the Instituto de Capacitación e Investigación (Institute of Training and Investigation, ICIRA), an arm of the Food and Agriculture Organization of the United Nations (FAO), and he became a consultant for UNESCO. Although ICIRA was a Chilean government–affiliated organization and Freire continued to work with Chilean government agencies, his involvement with FAO gave him a degree of independence and more time to reflect on and write about what he and his associates were doing. He worked for ICIRA from January 1968 to April 1969. Many of those who had worked with him in other organizations joined him there. Much of the remainder of his time in Chile would be spent putting more of his ideas on paper. Stung by criticism from within the Frei administration and the PDC generally, Freire tried to make clear that he had never felt himself to be an "educator" of Chile but that he had tried to establish a dialogue with Chileans (indeed, his whole theory of education was based on dialogue).[87]

But Freire himself had turned to the left, as well. He was ever more critical of the idea of treating illiterate people as "marginal" and not acknowledging that they may have been placed at the margins by others. Rather, he believed that illiterates were within the social structure as "the oppressed" and had internalized their oppression and thus were fearful of freedom. But whether the idea of "the oppressed" would be an improvement on the much-criticized idea of "the people" as an analytical category and whether "liberation" was a more realistic option than the Frei administration's hopes for inclusion remained to be seen.[88]

By late 1968, at least, the Frei administration had begun to modify its policies. It began to take strong measures against campesinos who staged land invasions and asked the government to expropriate the land. INDAP officials in Nuble province, in particular, were accused of encouraging such actions. Interior minister Pérez Zújovic sent in 500 carabineros to remove campesinos from the land.[89] Generally, Pérez Zújovic promised to "maintain order in the countryside."[90] One of Freire's closest Chilean associates, Marcela Gajardo, argued that something fundamental was at stake at this point. "The masses demanded more participation in the process of reform" that Chile was undergoing. "The government refused, and parts of the population took extreme attitudes" and "were suffocated by the authorities."[91]

INDAP official Chonchol, who had been expected to resign earlier in the year, finally left the government on 11 November 1968.[92] He refrained from criticizing Frei and sought publicly to maintain party unity, even though his own preference would have been to have those on the right of the Christian Democratic political spectrum leave the party. Chonchol was among those who supported the uniting of "popular forces," with or without the support of the leadership of the Marxist parties.[93]

It is important to keep in mind not only the politics of the Christian Democratic administration with which Freire had been associated but also the larger social and political context. The impetus the government had provided peasants and urban workers to organize had clearly borne fruit. By 1968, Frei took credit for the growth of unions and the greater use of petitions and collective bargaining.[94] Generally, Frei saw (or claimed to see) that Chilean society was entering an "era of dialogue, respect, and participation."[95] Frei expected the unions to, in their own ways, educate and even civilize the campesinos and make them into citizens.[96] By the end of Frei's term in office, union membership had almost doubled from 270,542 members in 1964 to 533,713 in 1969. Robert Alexander has argued that, under Frei, "the peasants increasingly spoke for themselves as citizens, and not for their employers as agents of their employers, as in the past." The number of strikes also almost doubled between 1964 and 1968 (476 to 901), although it declined after that (only 771 in 1969). A full 18 percent of the Chilean population now belonged to unions. The growth in organization among the rural population was particularly impressive; with union membership increasing from 1,658 members in 1964 to 104,666 in 1969, "surpassing," as Frei noted, "the most optimistic expectations." By 1970, "roughly half of the entire rural labor force" belonged to a union.[97] As historian Heidi Tinsman has argued, "Unions became the single most important conduit connecting the rural poor to what became the Agrarian Reform process. They fostered a new sense of citizenship among a historically disenfranchised population and nurtured campesinos' confidence that poor people were taken seriously by the state and political parties."[98] But as Chilean social scientist Eduardo Hamuy contended at the time, "Inert masses," once "pushed and placed in movement," naturally "sharpened conflicts" and also created a crisis in the legitimacy of the representative system. At the same time, the Frei administrations' initiatives in the countryside were losing support among urban Chileans.[99]

Ethnographic studies conducted late in the Frei years suggest that new forms of consciousness were developing, if not necessarily the ones that Christian Democratic leaders claimed they sought. Peasants continued to be cynical about politicians, yet they were aware of their own increasing dependence on them. Whereas previously their ties had been limited largely to the landowner himself, as David Lehmann has argued, "the growing incapacity of the patrons . . . to live up to their [traditional] obligations . . . [set] the scene for the rise of opposition consciousness," largely because of the actions of the government itself in promoting land reform and rural unionization. The Frei administration's reforms clearly led to increased conflict in the countryside between organized peasants and landowners. "Opposition consciousness," however, should not be confused with a peasant's growing sense of himself or herself as an independent political actor; the unions themselves provided whatever degree of newfound political strength the peasants had. Meanwhile, even if peasants now felt more integrated into Chile's social and economic system, the political reality was that peasants now had to court the patronage of powerful politicians. Partisan rivalries in the new unions in turn weakened larger class solidarity.[100]

On a fundamental level, the Frei government had tried to make significant changes and, in the process, attacked the interests of "privileged groups" in Chilean society. Chile's conservative political forces deeply resented Frei himself and the PDC generally for this reason.[101] Meanwhile, since rightist candidates had received only one-eighth of the vote in 1965, the Christian Democrats had felt that the Right no longer needed to be taken into consideration.[102] The Chilean Right, including former president Alessandri, for its part, was concerned that Chile had become an "over-politicized nation accelerating its plunge towards chaos, ruin, and inevitable military intervention."[103] The conservative daily newspaper *El Mercurio* had criticized Frei's attempts to "organize the discontented without a controlling mechanism."[104] A complicating factor was that not only were the rural and urban poor organizing; so were the employers.[105] These new developments clearly generated conflict in the countryside and within society at large. Eight squatters had been killed in March 1969, in an action for which the interior secretary bore some responsibility.[106] (In May of that year, many young Christian Democrats, as well as Chonchol, broke with the party and formed the Movimiento de Acción Popular Unitario [Movement for Popular Unity, MAPU] to help make the "Chilean Revolution.") In 1970, there were 368 land seizures, and a Frei administration agrarian reform official was murdered by an angry landowner.[107]

The changing political climate was one of the reasons that, by early 1969, it was time for Freire to move on. Criticism from the Right were partly responsible. The Frei administration was also attempting to distance itself from Freire, as illustrated by the fact that between June 1968, when the first draft of Cortés Carabantes's report on the literacy campaign was published in the *Revista de Educación*, and May 1969, when the final version was issued, Freire's name had disappeared from the report. Freire, for his part, was also getting invitations from abroad. The purely Latin American phase of Freire's life was now over. Cortés Carabantes himself left for Mexico in the same year to work for UNESCO in an adult education program called the Centro de Cooperación Regional para la Educación de Adultos en América Latina y el Caribe (Center for Regional Cooperation for Adult Education in Latin America and the Caribbean, CREFAL).[108]

The international context that had helped make Frei administration reforms possible was changing as well. Some observers on the Left were convinced that U.S. ambassador Korry was not as committed to the Frei administration as the previous ambassador, Ralph Dungan, had been.[109] Moreover, Richard Nixon, the Republican presidential candidate in 1968, was calling for a return to the Truman/Eisenhower Latin America policies of "trade instead of aid."[110] During a visit to Chile in the year prior to his election, Nixon "seemed to have developed an intense dislike for the Christian Democratic Party."[111] U.S. commitment to the Alliance for Progress was declining as well. "[P]roposed slashes in the Alliance are so large," one U.S. official complained, "as to call into question the entire United States commitment in this hemisphere." The problems Chile was confronting, including not only the decline in foreign aid but also the aforementioned drought, it was feared, could have an impact on the 1970 elections. (The United States remained concerned, as it had been in 1964, that a candidate of the Left would win.)[112]

Any assessment of Frei's reforms must take into account the inevitable fact that there had been winners and losers during these years. Under Frei, real wages in the countryside had increased by 40 percent, a much higher rate than for other sectors in the economy.[113] Although agrarian reform had been somewhat "diluted" by the Chilean Congress and the pace had been much slower than Frei anticipated, the Frei government had expropriated "about 12 percent of all irrigated land," with 20,000 families on asentamientos and 2,000 families getting land outright.[114] Naturally, only a "privileged minority," most obviously the asentados themselves, benefited from the agrarian reform process, leaving a majority unaffected. Some government officials were concerned that a new oligarchy was being created, one that was tied not to the union movement but to organizations that represented the traditional landowners. Surprisingly perhaps, while Christian Democrats dominated the new peasant organizations, they did not "gain a corresponding proportion of the rural vote in the 1970 presidential elections." While the asentados were themselves often depoliticized devotees of the official line, in general terms, the rest of the rural population was even less loyal to the party than it had once been to the landed elite.[115]

In his final presidential message, Frei dwelled at some length on the accomplishments of his administration in the area of adult literacy training, drawing heavily on the report written by Cortés Carabantes and, again, choosing to ignore the central role played by Freire himself (even when he explicitly described the Brazilian's methods). Government statistics indicated that illiteracy had declined significantly, from 16.4 percent in 1964 to 11 percent by 1969, with expectations that it would decline still further to 9 percent in the following year. In some rural areas, literacy rates more than doubled. Illiteracy had not been eradicated, although a CORA report suggested that it had been eliminated in most of the asentamientos themselves, suggesting again the marked differences between winners and losers during these years but calling into question the extent to which literacy training had contributed to a more critical consciousness.

Nevertheless, perhaps in any other era other than the impatient 1960s, the 5 percent increase in the percentage of the population that could read and write during the Frei years would have been recognized as a major accomplishment.[116] Cortés Carabantes himself clearly recognized that the momentum that he and Freire and others had generated needed to be sustained, no matter which party's president would succeed Frei.[117]

Chonchol, for his part, contended that the overall program of social transformation had not gone far enough. While other observers at the time thought that the growth of the union movement should put an end to the image of the Chilean campesino as passive, Chonchol argued that the consciousness of those involved in the rural organizations was limited. The campesinos were still not aware of the potential power they had. The organizational structures and functions were still "excessively informal," and there was little connection between the various organizations. Some of the new organizations in the countryside included latifundistas as well as campesinos. The union leaders still knew too little about the "social and economic reality of the country," although both their aspirations and their abilities were improving. "The campesinos still lacked confidence in themselves and in their ability to acquire what would benefit them," and were too fearful of change. This feeling of inferiority manifested itself in particular in relation to their former employers; the legacies of a paternalistic social system and habits of "passive acceptance of traditional domination and dependency" could not be overcome overnight. Generally, critics argued, the campesinos were still relatively marginalized. In some cases, those who had received land under the land reform process had become "new aristocrats," generating new tensions in the countryside. The "most dynamic elements" ended up migrating to the city. Nevertheless, to some extent, new "aspirations had been created."[118]

Chonchol, for a time, became a serious candidate for president, with some arguing that he was "capable of uniting" Chile's "progressive forces." Chilean poet and Communist Pablo Neruda in late 1969 referred to him as "a young man with ardent vital juices." While speaking in the United States at the University of Wisconsin–Madison's Land Tenure Center, Chonchol asserted that he wanted to make Chile's political system "more democratic by organizing more voters to participate in political process and bring pressure on elected officials." Chonchol, according to a U.S. embassy official, was a "complicated man" with a "burning anger at the injustices of Chilean society." Chonchol had a "vision of a new and more perfect order for the Chilean nation." Chonchol, it was said, did not "approach these problems with the spirit of a reformist; rather he hope[d] to attack them as would a revolutionary." He proposed and thought possible "a total break with the continuity of his nation's history." And he argued that a people could "be educated" to make a new noncapitalist, nonsocialist order work. Had Chonchol ended up being the candidate of a coalition of Chile's left-wing parties (admittedly, a big if) and had he won (an even bigger one), it seems likely that Freire would have heavily influenced his administration.[119]

By 1970, the Christians Democrats had accomplished much, but they had also alienated many of their former supporters. The 1970 election was disappointing for a party that had enjoyed increasing success since its founding, but the election did not provide a mandate for anyone. The party's presidential candidate, Radomiro Tomic, running on a platform promising more social transformation, won the support of only slightly less than 28 percent of the voters. While the Marxist-dominated Popular Unity coalition won, it received only 40,000 votes more than the conservatives who united behind the new National Party (and old) candidate Jorge Alessandri (the Left had also received a smaller percentage of the total than it had earned when it lost in 1964). Chonchol, who had briefly been MAPU's presidential candidate, had chosen to support Allende's candidacy and would be, for a time, his minister of agriculture, overseeing the fulfillment of his hopes for a "massive, rapid and drastic" land reform.[120]

The "Revolution in Liberty" represented an unusually dynamic, if problematic, period in Chilean and, more broadly, Latin American history. In almost any other South American country during the Cold War era, the degree of social change and political polarization that took place during the Frei years would have resulted in a military coup.[121] As I have demonstrated, the Christian Democratic dream of social transformation undoubtedly had its contradictory elements, not least of all in the Frei administration's sometimes inconsistent attempt to encourage people in the countryside to form unions. Freire's own vision for literacy training and popular education had profound ramifications for personal and collective change, yet its critique of campesino consciousness had its own limitations as well. Campesinos' consciousness was not merely magical; it was, in its own ways, critical. The campesinos' critique of social relations is exemplified by their tale of the hermaphroditic patrón who sold his soul to the devil. That critique was a product of history. It may have reflected a "false consciousness," but the Chilean popular class's mentalities also had their own strengths, as in Cortés Carabantes's story of the fishermen who resisted the temptation to exhaust the local supply of fish. Moreover, while many in the Frei administration hoped that education would enable the peasants to produce more in an increasingly commercialized countryside, campesinos hoped that education would make it possible for their children to be freed from the burdens of a life spent working in the fields. Their children would work in the cities and, it was hoped, in an office.[122] Literacy training would make possible the social mobility that peasants could only envision as an escape from rural restrictions. The true "Revolution in Liberty" would involve the free choice of so many to join the ongoing migration to the cities that was transforming Latin America as a whole.

For Freire, his participation in the Frei administration marked the last time he would advise a reformist government. His efforts on behalf of these kind of governments had been productive, and he had furthered the democratization of both Brazil and Chile, if, in the end, only temporarily. Over the course of the 1960s, he, as much as his allies, had moved to the left. As he later recalled, his time in exile, particularly his time in Chile, politicized him greatly. In a letter written from Geneva in 1970, he suggested that the Christian Democrats had been "playing at thinking with the people." But he believed that Chonchol's INDAP had taken this idea seriously. Freire was part of a new Left that was suspicious of the old Left, including the Soviet bloc, and of the United States, but supportive, and increasingly uncritically so, of a Third World Left. If, in later years, he complained of "rightist" critiques of his work in Chile, he seems to have taken more to heart the critiques of the Left, in which he was attacked for participating in the Frei government and for failing to emphasize class conflict in his literacy training programs in Chile. The Christian Democrats themselves were blamed at the time and later not only for ignoring those to their right who helped them win election in 1964 but also for simply writing conservatives out of the political equation altogether. Freire himself increasingly only engaged those to his left. Moreover, the United States, throughout the 1960s, moved steadily away from its ambivalent support for democratic reform in Latin America and increasingly relied upon the Latin American military, its historic ally in the region. Freire's exile was not going to end soon.[123] As options narrowed, opinions hardened. As the next two chapters demonstrate, Freire now saw himself as a revolutionary and, particularly in the late 1970s, preferred to help design literacy campaigns for one-party states.

Four / Paulo Freire & the World Council of Churches in the First & Third Worlds, 1969–1980

In the 1970s, Paulo Freire became an international figure. He traveled endlessly, mostly on behalf of the World Council of Churches (WCC), though not tirelessly. His ideas traveled even more widely and spread more rapidly around the world. If his Chilean experience had given him a broader Latin American perspective, he now increasingly spoke as a representative of the Third World. He began to have an impact in industrialized nations as well as in other developing countries beyond Latin America, often in ways that seemed to contradict his theories. It was a heady and, for Freire, in many ways, satisfying time. His activities during this decade have received less sustained scholarly attention, and there has been little effort made to distinguish even between the endeavors that took a great deal of his intellectual and emotional energies and those that received considerably less. His writings were translated into many languages, but as his ideas on literacy and consciousness-raising spread, his impact became more diffuse. His influence seemed to be everywhere but too often nowhere in as concrete a fashion as he might have wished, particularly between 1969 and 1975. His opportunities in Latin America decreased as more countries fell under military rule. In the second half of the decade, he concentrated his energies more and worked with a number of national literacy campaigns, primarily in newly independent countries in Africa, as well as Nicaragua, which is the subject of Chapter 5. Even as he received international recognition, he experienced failures, although they were only minimally recognized as such at the time. He also had changed political direction somewhat. Whereas in the 1960s he had worked in multiparty democracies, he now frequently was working with one-party states, whose educational practices often seemed to disregard Freire's theories.

In 1969, at a time when his situation in Chile was becoming more uncomfortable for him, Freire received almost simultaneous offers from Harvard University and the WCC. Development theorist Denis Goulet took credit for arranging his affiliation with Harvard. Freire later somewhat ruefully described his decision to go to the United States: "I thought that it was very important for me as a Brazilian intellectual in exile to pass through, albeit rapidly, the center of capitalist power. . . . I needed to see the animal close on its home territory." His stay in Cambridge was, indeed, relatively brief, in large part because he wanted a more active life than that of a professor. "[T]he Council was offering me more than any university," he later recalled.[1]

His publication of two articles in the *Harvard Educational Review* helped spread his name in broader educational circles. Even during his short stint as a research associate at Harvard's Center for Studies in Education and Development and despite his struggles with the English language, he began to have an impact on the intellectual life of politically minded academics in the United States. (The main difference between Freire before and after Harvard, one might say, was in his appearance; Freire grew a beard to ward off the Cambridge cold and kept it on for the rest of his life. If it may seem to fit with the revolutionary mantle he now claimed, it increasingly if gradually gave him the look of the "guru" he was becoming.) As many in the United States were themselves increasingly critical of their country's role in the world and concerned about social and racial divisions at home, Freire found a welcome audience. "Like you we perhaps are more utopian," James Lamb of the Center for the Study of Development and Social Change wrote to Freire after he departed in early 1970, "and we continue to draw on the strength of your friendship, message and spirit."[2]

The teacher and author most strongly influenced by Freire in the United States was Jonathan Kozol. His meeting with Freire in 1969 had been a transformative moment, as he later wrote. Their ensuing dialogue over many successive Sunday afternoons defined in large measure Kozol's intellectual journey. He told Freire in 1975 of the "upheaval (and the past five years of struggle within myself) since I first met you." "It has not been easy to be faced with painful choices of the kind you pose for me," he continued. "No other author, teacher, friend, ally—has left my life so different."[3]

Despite the impact Freire was having in his brief time in the United States, he was soon drawn to Europe. The WCC, an ecumenical organization based in

Geneva, Switzerland, founded in 1948, was undergoing dramatic changes in the 1960s. The fact that they hired Freire at the end of the decade certainly is evidence of that. The council, however, had always been interested in social issues. At its first conference, held in Amsterdam, the idea of a "responsible society" was introduced; by the time of the 1954 assembly in Evanston, Illinois, the council had linked this idea to the "increasing power of the state in economic and social affairs." The council was devoting increasing attention to what were called "areas of rapid social change." Its growing commitment reflected the fact that by the 1960s, the council had more representatives in Third World churches than any other ecumenical organization. In 1962, the Central Committee authorized the World Conference on Church and Society to help "develop a body of theological and ethical insights which will assist the churches in their witness in contemporary history" and to assess how God was "at work in the revolutionary changes taking place in the world." Martin Luther King Jr. was the most internationally prominent person to speak at the conference, which was held in 1966. This meeting, at which laypeople predominated, certainly was a turning point. A new emphasis was placed on "international economic justice" and, after the Uppsala assembly two years later, a "responsible world society." In 1968, one of the top council leaders concerned with international affairs asserted that "[t]he World Council of Churches will continue to keep development high on the list of priorities. We are very much aware of the fact that only the widest cooperation will help all peoples of good will to catch the train of history, in this particular hour."[4] Churches were encouraged to contribute 2 percent of annual income to support local and international efforts to promote social justice and development.

The interest in development continued to expand throughout this first "decade of development," culminating with the creation of the Commission on Churches' Participation in Development (CCPD) in 1970. Rather than focusing on economic growth alone, as the modernization theorists had proposed, the new thinking represented at the 1970 Montreaux Consultation conceived of development "as a process of people's struggle for social justice, self-reliance, and economic growth." There would be a significant cross-fertilization between the CCPD and the WCC's Office of Education created at the same time. In the next few years, there would be an increasing emphasis in the CCPD on a Freirean understanding of the poor becoming "agents (rather than objects)" of their own development. At the same time, the council hoped that those in the First World would become more aware of development issues and what the council believed was their responsibility to address them.[5]

The council's commitment to development came at a troubled time, however. The United Nations had declared the 1970s to be the second decade of development, but the optimism that had marked the initial declaration ten years before was less evident the second time around.[6] There had not been the economic "takeoff" that modernization theorists had proposed, and an economic weakening in the First World that was already evident did not bode well for those in the Third. At the same time, many in the council called for more structural change, support for liberation movements, and an expanding role for government.[7] The WCC was following trends in the Catholic Church, especially those connected with what was becoming known as liberation theology (which will be discussed further below).[8] The council's stances in the 1970s, particularly those in support of African revolutionary movements, were increasingly controversial.

The council's new focus on education, which Freire's hiring exemplified, reflected not only this concern with social transformation but also a sense of crisis in the larger world order, a conviction that "all traditional mechanisms of education have either broken down" or are "breaking down," and a belief that the churches had a responsibility to help societies address these problems. At the Uppsala assembly in 1968, the decision was reached to create a new office on education to help guide the churches in their work in this area. In the following year, discussions were held on ways to address issues such as racism, development, and education as a means "to bring about change." William B. Kennedy was appointed general secretary, and Freire was hired in February 1970 to take charge of general education. "The Council," he later recalled, "was offering me a worldwide chair . . . , the largest possible environment, its various experiences, a vision of some of its tragedies, its situations of poverty, its disasters, but also some of its most beautiful moments." In an introductory statement, the WCC declared that the office could not and would "not deal with education in a vacuum or in a merely theoretical way— it will have to take into account the situation of a world in need of peace, in need of justice, in need of development, in need of change."[9]

In May of that year, a consultation in Bergen, Holland, was held to help give the new Office of Education guidance in deciding which educational activities to pursue, given the rather general instructions laid out at the meeting in Uppsala.[10] In his address to the meeting, Raymond Poignant, director of UNESCO's International Institute of Educational Planning, emphasized the "quantitative inadequacy of primary education in Africa," pointing out that only 40 percent of Africa's children attended school. Although educational opportunities had increased in many parts of the developing world, he asserted, the absolute number of illiterates continued to increase. He spoke of the need to adopt economic models and increase educational efficiency in developing "human capital." Poignant did not think that social and economic preconditions existed in many countries for mass literacy campaigns to have the long-term effects desired.[11]

Freire's influence was already evident by this time. Many at the conference, which included not only the council's usual constituency of Protestants but also Catholics and non-Christians, took exception to Poignant's remarks and expressed support for Freire's ideas regarding education as liberation, to help people "think and act on their own."[12] Freire's ideas carried the day. The council's Office of Education was going to "concentrate its efforts on working toward education for freedom. . . . Everything we do and say should contribute towards that education which frees men from being domesticated into lives of repression or mere routine and which liberates them into living creatively and abundantly in societies whose structures support education for freedom."[13]

In the first few years of Freire's tenure, the use of the word "liberation" caused some concern among those who associated it with the discourse of communist countries. It was suggested that the council use the rather banal phrase "education for humanity." Critics charged that the education office was "preaching political liberation as a panacea for all the world's ills without taking seriously enough human sinfulness." The word "liberation," however, remained.[14]

It was not only the council's word choices, however, that were causing concern. There was a general belief in the early years of the Office of Education that Freire's ideas needed to be tested in social and political contexts other than Latin America. Charles Granston Richards, the director of Christian literature development for the Christian Literature Fund in Lausanne and a former UNESCO consultant, asked, "[B]efore too much time is spent on these ideas, should there not be more dialogue between [Freire] and others engaged in this work?"[15]

In order to acquaint fellow council members in other offices with Freire's theories, a colloquium was held in mid-December 1970. Participants were asked to read several of Freire's writings, including not only *Pedagogy of the*

Oppressed but also some short articles on "humanization" and "the political literacy process." In these articles, Freire made clear his belief in the need to abandon a pretense of neutrality and to engage with the subjects of one's educational activities in an attempt to modify existing socioeconomic structures. He spoke out against the attempt to create docile students, quoting the Tom Paxton song popularized by Pete Seeger, "What did you learn in school today?," which exemplified evolving notions of education as indoctrination. He spoke in favor of those educators who lived "the deep significance of Easter" by dying as bourgeoisie and being raised from the dead as liberating educators.[16]

Not all of those invited to participate found the presentation of Freire's ideas to their liking. "Quite honestly," one council member noted, "I experienced this as more of a 'repressive' educational process than any I ever had during my school or college days! On its own theory, should not such a group take more seriously (I don't mean, just listen politely to) points made by 'non-conformists' to the general line being taken?" This council member argued that anyone who disagreed with the notion that all educational systems are repressive and that the world needs its consciousness raised would be dismissed as either "blind or self-centered." Another rewrote the pop-folk song "Little Boxes" (also popularized by Pete Seeger) about conformity to fit what he saw as an attempt to make everyone into a Freirean clone. Still another attendee expressed concern that it was too easy to adopt (and that the council was too prone to adopting) a particular "vocabulary" before going deeply into a subject. One could later find that the language had gone "out of fashion" (as she suggested development already had). Once that happened, the fundamental issue itself could get lost.[17]

Despite these concerns, Freirean language quickly became the accepted language of the wcc's Office of Education, and Freirean goals became its goals. By 1972, Freire's ideas had become not only the guiding force within the Office of Education but also an important factor in the council's work as a whole. According to William Kennedy, head of the education office in the first half of the 1970s, "A significant thrust in all work has come from the thinking of Paulo Freire. . . . His work in 'conscientization' in Latin America and his books are challenging other cultures and situations to probe more deeply into the meaning and direction of their educational efforts." Freire's work offered a new approach to the question, "In the light of Christian faith, what should education be for in the lives of men?"[18] The education office sought to aid churches in becoming "increasingly active in . . . analyzing theologically the societies and structures, educational and church systems, policies and processes of education that shape human beings" in challenging those that "domesticate human beings" and helping those that liberate them.[19] At the same time, Freire himself wanted the office to avoid the dangers he saw inherent in other international work, that is, paternalistically defining other people's tasks. "Ours," he noted, "is an accessory task, not a prescribing task or determining task."[20]

Freire's activities in the first year seem largely, although certainly not exclusively, to have been dedicated to spreading his ideas in the First World by participating in meetings in many countries in Western Europe and in the United States. The publication of *Pedagogy of the Oppressed* in English in 1970 opened many doors for him, and in the following four years, editions of the book were published in Italian, French, German, Dutch, and Swedish. The English edition circulated widely in Africa and Asia. He found a "ready response in North America" and had particularly intense encounters during the 1970s with "sincere, studious, and thoughtful German university students."[21] He also developed working relationships with a wide variety of international organizations, including the International Labor Organization (also based in Geneva), as well as "groups and movements engaged in cultural action for liberation."[22] The education office was both responding to interest from the First World and in a savvy manner trying to engage with the council's "central constituencies."[23] Freire's impact on many in the First World during his years with the council was also profound. He received many letters from students, activists, and professionals in Western Europe and the United States. Many of the young people who wrote to Freire were critical of those who avidly took part in "consumer civilization." Freire responded with sympathy and encouraged these people to seek out others who were dedicated to making a different world.[24]

Throughout the 1970s, Freire continued to visit the United States, holding conferences with people like peace activist and priest Daniel Berrigan and meeting with community workers, church groups, and academics. Many of the people in the United States who identified with Freire were practitioners of what would become known as "identity politics," with which the Brazilian had a somewhat limited measure of sympathy. Freire argued that the emphasis on membership in a particular group hindered people from working together against the wealthy minority who had so much to gain from their divisions. At a meeting in Chicago in early 1973, his suggestions were dismissed by a "young black leader" as "white talk."[25] In general, after meeting with "groups of negroes [*sic*], indians [*sic*], chicanos [*sic*], puerto ricans [*sic*] and whites" during the course of a forty-day visit in 1973, Freire came away with a critical perspective on what he saw as the "lack of ideological and political clarity, the paroquial [*sic*] vision of reality [and] the lack of dialectical thought" among those considered progressive in the U.S. context.[26]

For his part, William Kennedy hoped that in the United States there would develop "adult education action-study groups to concentrate on the economic system which underlies and perpetuates these other forms of oppression."[27] He wrote in 1972 that the council was trying to "develop research in the levels of consciousness about which Freire talks in his books. We are concerned to discover more about the domestication which affects people growing up in industrialized countries. The process by which a culture of silence has been imposed on peasants in a rural area is fairly clear; much less obvious is the process by which middle class and lower middle class persons in urban industrial areas of the affluence world have been robbed of their humanity by the systems of society[,] including the educational system."[28]

In Freire's work in many First World countries he often focused on a nation's outsiders. He became engaged with what he called the "Third World in the First World," such as Spanish workers in West Germany. A social worker employed by a large chemistry firm near Frankfurt approached Werner Simpfendörfer, one of Freire's associates in the education office, about the possibility of holding a seminar there. In a document prepared for this seminar was the self-reflection: "I am a Spaniard. Why am I here? Why have I come to Germany to work? Because we have no money, the banks have it, and the capitalists."[29] In Geneva, he was contacted by Spanish resident workers who wanted to establish alternative schools that could encourage their children to reflect critically on what they saw as the conformist education they were receiving in the Swiss schools.[30]

During his years in Geneva, Freire also created an important organization to help diffuse and test his ideas and techniques. The Institute for Cultural Action (Institut d'Action Culturelle, IDAC) was established as a nonprofit organization under Swiss law in September of 1971. William Kennedy asserted that "a program like this would be an excellent opportunity for the work of Paulo Freire to be extended beyond the direct channels available to us in the World Council of Churches." "The more cross-cultural engagement we can stimulate in research and experiments in conscientization," he continued, "the more quickly we gain the advantages of such reappraisal." IDAC was to be independent of the council (although other staff members also served on the board of directors), and a time limit was placed on Freire's commitment to the organization. The Institute, like many of Freire's activities during these years, would require the aid of liberal institutions and individuals in the First World, and this aid was, to some degree, even more problematic for Freire and his associates than U.S. support for the Alliance for Progress and the Frei administration had been in the previous decade. A letter from Brazilian Claudius Ceccon, IDAC's top man, to Freire in early 1971 suggests the IDAC members' attitudes toward liberals. Writing about Len Clough of the World Student Christian Federation, Ceccon noted, "[H]e is a typical liberal American who thinks that the solution of problems can be found within institutions, that all is a question of 'good will' [in English in the original]. He isn't properly reactionary, but he is certainly apolitical in the sense that he doesn't feel comfortable in any essentially political conversation. That doesn't mean that he is totally naive or alienated. He is sophisticated enough to know, for example, that there is a fish beneath our soup, even if he doesn't want to know exactly what kind of fish it is." He recommended that Freire focus on "technical" issues in his discussions with Clough since that was how Clough conceived of education, and because Clough had faith in Freire as an "authority" on education.[31]

Freire's colleagues at the institute included several Brazilians who had been involved in the planning stages of the national literacy campaign, such as architect Ceccon and journalist and educator Rosiska Ribeiro, former Brazilian diplomat Miguel Darcy de Oliveira, and theologian and sociologist John Coutinho, a professor at the Center for the Study of Development and Social Change in Cambridge.

The institute directed "its efforts to the use of conscientization as a liberating tool in the process of education and development." It trained people to use Freire's techniques and also helped the groups engaged in applying them to share information with each other about what methods worked and what did not in particular situations, thereby creating "a worldwide conversation." Defining consciousness-raising as a tool for increasing awareness and developing a critical understanding in order that people might "through acting together . . . regain control over the creation of their own destiny and the shaping of a more human society," IDAC worked to support "development processes based on [a society's] real needs and cultural identities," largely in the Third World, while criticizing economic models promoted in the First World. Its programs were also aimed at the "sophisticated repressive societies" of the United States and Western Europe, which, it believed, were "becoming more and more repressive, reducing the entire individual, body and spirit, into a simple instrument." In the First World, IDAC focused on tearing away "the mysteries that surround the function of the school." At the same time, IDAC was committed to the women's liberation movement, "perhaps the most significant example of the new forms of politicizing activity that are being developed in the highly industrialized societies." As "militant observers," IDAC members combined action and research in "long-term commitments to oppressed groups . . . combining theoretical reflection with concrete involvement." The institute held seminars and workshops in the early 1970s in the United States (including those for Chicano groups), Italy (particularly in the first year and a half, often for urban workers' groups), and Denmark, and began to publish a series of annual publications.

IDAC struggled in the first year of its existence. By early 1973, the organization was forced to turn down some invitations to travel because of lack of funding. The institute tried to model democratic behavior in its own organization and structure, for example, "learning to work together without a leader," and "creating free spaces and alternative contexts." They were slow to develop fund-raising skills, but by the mid-1970s, IDAC was more stable economically, receiving funding from the council's CCPD for work on alternative models of aid and on the uses of technology as means of social control, as well as from the United Presbyterian Church (U.S.), the Rountree Trust (London), the United Church Women (New York City), and the X–Y Group (Hague). IDAC hoped to help dissenting groups "link their demands for immediate personal growth to a broader movement for social transformation."[32]

At the heart of Freire's activities with the World Council of Churches and the IDAC, however, was a contradiction that he rarely acknowledged. As he wrote to a woman working on issues of rural development in Malaysia in 1975, "We cannot expect the ruling classes to commit suicide. . . . They cannot really permit us to put into practice a kind of education that will lay them waste, once the raison d'être of the oppressive reality is revealed."[33] At the same time, this was, to some degree, what both Freire and his allies in the CCPD were proposing: "the possibility of conscientizing the rich, utilizing part of their resources for the struggle of the poor and eventually striking at the enemy from within." Fearful that the church leadership would be "agents of the status quo," the CCPD argued that either the leadership of the organized churches must become "conscientized" itself or the CCPD must somehow "prevent it from standing in the way of the development struggle."[34] And yet Freire's work with the council always received the vast majority of its funding from people in the First World, not just European social democrats from countries like Sweden but also often liberals who were members of mainline Protestant churches in the United States. U.S. church agencies provided the bulk of the funding for the Office of Education, with West German church agencies a distant, but nevertheless significant, second.[35] Although controversies over council funding during this time period led some groups to cut off aid, the fact remained that the Office of Education continued to rely upon the First World ruling classes throughout the 1970s.

In the first half of the 1970s, Freire still worked in Latin America. His influence there had increased dramatically during the years he worked for the Frei administration. Undoubtedly, it helped that he had been working in Spanish and not in Portuguese. As Jesuit priest James F. McShane wrote to Freire from Honduras in 1971, "I am sure that you are proud of the way in which your ideas and techniques are used all over Latin America" to help poor farmers "better their self-image and overcome feelings of timidity and inferiority."[36] By 1971, Freire had already become a kind of "myth" in many parts of Latin America; Susanne Korsukewitz, a German who had traveled throughout Latin America, informed him that he was seen as "a mix of 'revolutionary activist' and 'deep Catholic.'"[37] In 1974, Colombian Jaime Diaz urged Freire to discuss publicly which of those working in the area of "conscientization" had distorted his work. Referring to Freire's "spiritual sons [whom] you don't recognize," he suggested that Freire "say which are the legitimate ones and which are not."[38] At the same time, however, by moving to Geneva, Freire was accused by some of having "lost contact with the Latin American reality." For his part, Freire was critical of Latin Americans who claimed to be revolutionaries and put their faith in military activities, those who would "accomplish a hundred dangerous activities, even though they be void of political significance," rather than engage in "dialogue with a group of peasants for ten minutes."[39]

Freire's colleagues from the Chilean years were also making important contributions to the diffusion of his ideas, particularly following the coup in 1973. Waldemar Cortés Carabantes had left his native Chile in the same year that Freire left for Harvard. He continued Freire's work with CREFAL in Mexico beginning in November 1969. Sixty-one scholarship students from nineteen countries took part in the first Freire-tinged functional literacy course there.[40] Other local and regional education centers throughout Latin America made use of his techniques, particularly as liberation theology was being developed.

For Freire, the transformation of the Catholic Church in Latin America was more than welcome, for it represented a step beyond what he called the traditional church and the modernizing church toward the "prophetic church," which was "as old as Christianity itself, without being traditional; as new as Christianity without being modernizing." He welcomed the statements of the Second General Conference of Latin American Bishops in Medellín in 1968 that "denounced a Latin American context and announced a path to liberation." Rather than providing an emotional refuge, the church now challenged Christians.[41] In Medellín, the bishops had shown an interest in Freire's methods of consciousness-raising (and sometimes seemed unaware that the church itself had already been working in this same vein). Over the next few years, church groups hoped to use them "as a viable means of releasing the power for change which the masses of people in the Latin American countries possess but do not consciously recognize." The development of the Christian Base Communities and the increasing emphasis on Bible reading in Spanish also aided in the process.[42]

Liberation theology demonstrated intellectual and political dynamism at a time when ideological options were narrowing, democratic governments were falling, and the revolutionary option was declining following the death of Che Guevara in 1967. (The relative attractiveness of the Cuban model was also declining following the perceived failure of Cuban volunteerism in the sugar harvest of 1970.) The military dictatorships being established were increasingly brutally effective, as the use of torture and political murder by an increasingly hard-line government at home in Brazil itself demonstrated.

From 1970 to 1973, Chile was the one hopeful place in South America for Freire. Following the inauguration of Socialist president Salvador Allende in 1970, Freire became curious about what was happening in the country he had left a little more than a year before. The WCC also viewed the Allende administration positively. Allende, who had been interested in the issue of illiteracy since the late 1930s when he was a congressman, envisioned functional literacy programs centered around the workplace, with a special role to be played by student volunteers who had finished middle school. In this sense, he hoped to build on the Cuban model while using the momentum already built up during the Frei years.[43] Eugene Carson Blake, secretary general of the council, met with Allende in late July 1971 and assured the president that "we believe in the effort of liberation" that he was "heading up."[44]

It is important not to overstate Freire's own activities in Chile during the Allende years, however (as has so often been done in English-language publications on Freire), especially in comparison to what he did during the Frei years. But many of Freire's younger colleagues from the Frei years, like Marcela Gajardo and Rolando Pinto, were involved in Freire-inspired programs from 1970 until 1973, particularly through ICIRA.[45] Freire himself was more of an observer than a participant in the Popular Unity experiment.

Freire visited Chile in 1971 and 1972 and expressed admiration for the "beautiful historical process Chile is experiencing at the moment." In 1972, the stated purpose of his visit was to look at the "whole contribution of Christians to [the] structure of socialism." In addition, he reestablished his relationship with ICIRA. In the summer of 1973, he took "home leave" in order to study the "class struggle" and the revolutionary experience that Chile was experiencing.[46]

At the same time, he was not certain that the more mainstream left-wing parties in Allende's coalition had the requisite enthusiasm for popular education. He criticized an authoritarian poster from the Allende literacy program that depicted "a strong, determined hand" showering words over the "passive head" of a "middle-aged workman" and "sowing letters and syllables in the purely recipient head of the worker." He admired the Movimiento de Izquierda Revolucionario (Movement of the Revolutionary Left, MIR), founded in 1965 by students at the university in Concepción and associated with more radical political strategies than those favored by the Socialists and the Communists; Freire believed that "miristas" were more willing to engage in dialogue with the popular classes than were many members of the Socialist and Communist parties.[47]

But Latin America was changing, and opportunities for consciousness-raising in the region (outside of programs run directly by the Catholic Church) were diminishing even as Freire's intellectual influence was increasing. The overthrow of Allende on 11 September 1973 and its brutal aftermath marked not only the death of democracy in Chile but also the continuation of a trend that had been evident since the establishment of military rule in Brazil in 1964, the further narrowing of ideological options in the region. U.S. support for reform in the region had long since been abandoned; the Alliance for Progress had died a painfully prolonged death in some countries (while being strangled in its cradle in others), even before its definitive abandonment by President Richard Nixon following his inauguration in 1969. Freire's correspondence files from his council years after 1973 are filled with letters from exiled Chileans seeking advice on finding a secure place to establish a new life and help in finding a job. Having been forced to leave his native country and now not being able to return to Chile, Freire was exiled twice over. His increasing prestige could not make up for the limits placed on his activities in countries in which he felt most comfortable. (The military government of Brazil also occasionally put pressure on UNESCO to keep Freire from working as a consultant for that organization.[48])

Freire still occasionally received invitations from Latin American countries after the fall of Allende. Perhaps the most promising came from Panama. Xavier Gorostiaga from the Ministry of Foreign Relations dangled the possibility of a personal invitation from the populist dictator General Omar Torrijos, noting that the "the situation in Panama is very interesting." But Freire's health problems in 1974 and a new focus beginning in 1975 on Africa kept any significant literacy programs from materializing there. (One has to wonder how interested Freire really was in Panama, although the existing correspondence is not helpful in answering this question.)[49]

By the middle of the decade, things were changing globally as well. There was much less of a sense of a common, joint, global enterprise. Developing countries began to press for a reorganization of the global economy.[50] The First World, however, was too focused on the collapse of the postwar economic order to respond enthusiastically to discussions of economic equity. Loans were available, in large part due to profits earned by oil price increases and deposited in Western banks, but loans were hardly the ideal solution for Third World development needs (and, indeed, paved the way for the Latin American debt crisis of the 1980s).

By 1975, Freire was the most visible person working for the council and had come under increasing attack in the United States and, to some degree, in West Germany. Liberal Catholic priest and sociologist Andrew Greeley, for example, wrote in the *National Catholic Reporter* about Freire's "evil genius." William Kennedy was concerned about these attacks and urged friends in the executive council of the Episcopal Church in New York City to respond to them.[51] The personal criticism of Freire came at a time when the council itself was under attack from conservatives in the United States like columnist George Will, who complained that the council was "a carrier" of "a familiar but endlessly fascinating virus," liberation theology.[52]

The global economic crisis, including problems derived from fluctuating currency values, was beginning to have a direct effect on the council. The Swedish International Development Authority (SIDA) provided funding in the form of a three-year grant for Freire's projects, but there was serious concern about finding ways to fund even an extremely small office of only three staff members and their secretarial support staff.[53]

Freire and Kennedy both began to experience a crisis of confidence. Critics and supporters of the Office of Education's work recognized that there had been a general lack of direction to its activities. While the office served to help spread Freire's ideas throughout the world, the ideas themselves had relatively little impact on any particular place in any discernible way. By 1975, questions began to arise over what, if anything, the education office was accomplishing. "One of my regrets," Kennedy remarked in April, "is that we have not been able to do more specific work in literacy programs." In a symposium held in West Germany, Kennedy noted, "all agreed that work in education in the WCC needs sharper focus." "These exploratory years since Uppsala have had their frustrations for us all," Kennedy wrote in October. Expectations were that the upcoming assembly in Nairobi would help give renewed forward momentum and direction to the office. "The problem," Kennedy continued, "is how to help the Assembly direct us toward that focus so the committee and staff next year can develop sharp program priorities." In particular, it was believed that Freire needed to be used "in [a] more planned way." Kennedy remarked that he himself was "deeply frustrated about the relative shallowness of most of our activities."[54] Kennedy himself decided to move on. After his departure, his position was not filled until March of 1977.

Freire, for his part, seems to have been suffering from physical and emotional exhaustion after years of globe-trotting. He made frequent references to being "existentially tired" when declining invitations from various groups. (There were also family difficulties that had to be addressed at this time.) Early in the year, he had even planned to stay in Geneva "for the whole of this year, having just one or two trips around Europe."[55]

Nevertheless, despite many discouraging signs, 1975 was to be a year of confirmation and renewal for Freire. The Nairobi assembly held from 23 November to 10 December formalized the WCC's commitment to Freire's ideas of education as being "for liberation and community."[56] The "development of critical consciousness," a process whereby those "who sense their oppression enough to change it," was considered "directly related to God's work in the world." Regional church councils were encouraged to "engage in a process of expanding and deepening their own critical consciousness" while, at the local level, "youth, lay leaders, theological communities, cadres, religious orders, institutions in local grass-root situations" should "identify and analyze . . . contradictions and oppressive forces," "identify and develop strategies for action," and "mobilize power to bring about change."[57] And yet many who attended the Nairobi assembly once again expressed frustration with the way Freire's ideas were introduced and discussed. Participants had to both engage in discussion and produce a report in too short a period of time. This led "advisers and staff at times . . . to take the lead, and this increased the feeling of manipulation."[58]

With Latin America to a large extent off-limits in the second half of the 1970s, Freire increasingly turned his attention to Africa. Relatively soon after he arrived at the World Council of Churches Freire had developed a great deal of interest in Julius Nyerere's Tanzania. As he was about to leave for that country in September of 1971, he wrote a member of UNESCO's International Commission on the Development of Education that he was going to Africa for the first time. "As a Brazilian," he said, he felt himself to be "also . . . an African."[59]

Freire was deeply impressed by what he saw Nyerere trying to achieve in Tanzania, particularly with the villages of Ujamaa. Nyerere was one of two African leaders to influence his thinking during this decade (although he did not have an opportunity to meet the other one, Amílcar Cabral of Guinea-Bissau, who is discussed below). Freire admired Nyerere's emphasis on self-reliance and his belief in the need to find African models for development and not simply imitate European ones. In Nyerere's Tanzania, Freire embraced a one-party state that claimed to be democratic and in the 1970s was trying to relocate millions of Tanzanians into Ujamaa villages.[60] In responding to a letter from a Nicaraguan seminarian regarding his experience in Tanzania, Freire remarked that the concept of Ujamaa had "a fantastic richness of signification: communion, participation, fraternity." "Ujamaa," he explained further, was "a word used to translate socialism into Swahili"; it described an "eminently democratic model, in which popular participation is considered indispensable." In his conversations with Tanzanian peasants, Freire wrote, "[t]hey all spoke of their difficulties, of the obstacles to defeat, and of the poverty to overcome. But in all of them I perceived a profound sense of hope." The Tanzanians had hope, Freire continued, because they understood their past, were changing their world in the present, and saw a future to construct. Only in Cuba (which he had not yet visited) and in Chile before the coup did any Latin American peasants have any comparable feeling, according to Freire. Freire's visits over the course of the decade left their mark on Tanzania as well, according to his correspondents. Although he did not directly advise a literacy program per se, he did have an impact on Tanzanian understandings of community development. As Jane Vella, who worked with Community Education for Development, remarked, "Our own lives have been so radically changed by meeting you." After observing one of her seminars in a village, Vella wrote Freire, President Nyerere asked her, "Does Paulo Freire know what you are doing in the Ujamaa villages?" When in 1973 the Tanzanian government made adult education compulsory, the wording of the directive, which emphasized the need to liberate people "economically, ideologically, and culturally, to teach them how to transform their environment," demonstrated Freire's influence. In June of 1976, Nyerere hosted an international conference on adult education and development.[61]

African opportunities expanded still further with the independence of a number of African countries from Portugal in the mid-1970s. Freire was able to regain his lost energy and enthusiasm and to dedicate himself to more concrete projects in national reconstruction. His ideas were adopted to some extent in Mozambique. He also visited Angola numerous times as an adviser on postliteracy programs, although his engagement with Angola was not particularly systematic. He was directly involved in literacy programs in only two Portuguese African countries, Guinea-Bissau and São Tomé and Príncipe. These experiences seem to have helped him overcome the "existential fatigue" that had begun to set in early in 1975 (although his doctor periodically tried to encourage him to cut back on travel dramatically in the following years[62]). His wife Elza worked with him in these countries, and that certainly was a source of great personal satisfaction to him. Although neither experience was as successful as it was made out to be at the time, Freire clearly was acting more directly than he had in years in support of governments he admired. He told several of his correspondents in 1977 that it was important for him "to work with people who are trying to become themselves."[63]

The World Council of Churches had long supported the independence struggle in Guinea-Bissau. The Portuguese colony had received far less attention from the mother country than either Angola or Mozambique; it had attracted no Portuguese settlers. Guinea-Bissau gained worldwide attention for what between 1964 and 1974 became the most effective and united anticolonial movement for independence in Africa, led by the Partido Africano de Independência da Guiné e Cabo Verde (African Party for the Independence of Guinea-Bissau and Cape Verde, PAIGC).[64] Guinea-Bissau's independence having been formally conceded by Portugal in 1974, the PAIGC government approached Freire and IDAC in May 1975 and invited them to help them design a mass literacy training program for the new nation. Freire worked with IDAC on this project, as he would on that in São Tomé. The CCPD funded these activities and, in other ways, worked more closely with the Office of Education and IDAC in these campaigns in Africa than they ever had before.[65]

At the time of its independence, Guinea-Bissau had a population of roughly 800,000 people. Like other former Portuguese colonies, it had relatively little to build on in the way of educational infrastructure. Freire was excited by the prospect of working with a newly independent country, and he and his associates at IDAC began to immerse themselves in the writings of the late Guinean independence leader Amílcar Cabral. As many outsiders were then and have been since, he was impressed by Cabral's success in staging a war of liberation against Portuguese colonialism, a war that had played a major role in convincing Portuguese officers to overthrow the decades-old, neofascist Estado Novo regime in the mother country. Freire saw Cabral as a kindred spirit. Both men had a faith in dialogue and in the possibilities of participatory democracy. In working with the government of Guinea-Bissau, Freire and his associates did not want to be considered outside experts or "foreign technicians with a mission" but fellow militants engaged as "true collaborators" in the reconstruction of the country. Freire promised that he would not provide any "prefabricated" solutions to the nation's problems. He claimed not to consider his previous experiences to have any "universal validity." Perhaps for this reason, he relied heavily upon Cabral's writings for his understanding of Guinean reality, and his views of postindependence social realities were filtered through the prism of the experience of a unifying national war of liberation. In Guinea-Bissau, Freire and his associates counted on what Freire understood to be an unusually high level of political consciousness forged in the revolutionary struggle. While 90 percent of Guinea-Bissau's population at the time of independence could neither read nor write, Freire believed that the population was "highly politically literate."[66]

Freire's misreading of Guinean reality was grounded in incorrect assumptions concerning Portuguese colonial policy (again, largely based on his reading of Cabral). Since the Portuguese had devalued African culture and believed that only by learning the Portuguese language and way of life could Africans become civilized, the goal of a new nation was to "re-Africanize" the population and to "de-colonize" their "mentality." Freire was most concerned about the urban Guineans who had not been "touched in any direct way by the war" and who were "deeply influenced by the colonialist ideology." According to Cabral, the (admittedly small) Guinean middle class needed to divest itself of its worldview and commit "middle-class suicide." Freire wanted the urban youth to be reeducated by the people themselves. His distrust of Guinean middle-class youth is itself quite striking, considering the important role that members of the urban middle class had played in the literacy campaigns in Brazil and Chile. Freire also seems to have neglected the crucial role that newly urban young had played in the liberation struggle in Guinea-Bissau. Cabral had spoken of the awakening of consciousness that came about as Guinean youth compared their new environment with their rural homes. Had Guinea-Bissau had more educated youth, they undoubtedly could have served a valuable role as teachers in the literacy campaign (as they would in Nicaragua). (Although several hundred Guinean high school students did go into the interior to teach, their activities were largely restricted to the months during which classes were not in session.) Freire should have known that during many of those campaigns, the privileged youth themselves were frequently transformed politically, as they had been in both Brazil and Chile while working with him.[67]

In late 1975 and early 1976 Freire visited some of the country's first "liberated zones" and had his first contact with Guinean peasants. Although he had been based in Switzerland since 1970, Freire saw himself as "a man from the Third World." Guinea-Bissau reminded him of northeastern Brazil, and the similar climate and many of the same foods, sights, and sounds, as well as the "joy in living," filled him with a "deep nostalgia for Brazil." (He playfully wrote of having a "solemn meeting with mangoes and cashews.") From 1975 to 1976, Freire and his associates in IDAC continued to engage in dialogue with officials of the education ministry in Guinea-Bissau, whether in person, in Europe as well as in Africa, or through correspondence, but communication was often slow and intermittent.[68]

Freire viewed the Guinean peasantry positively, if somewhat sentimentally, but he had a particularly high opinion of the Guinean military, the Forças Armadas Revolucionários do Povo (Armed Forces of the People, FARP). Freire's faith in the military is noteworthy given that he himself was barred from returning to his native country by a military dictatorship. No single group benefited more from independence than FARP.[69] During the liberation struggle there were significant attempts to provide popular education. Africanist Basil Davidson reported having met teenaged soldiers who were learning to read. "They spelt their letters and formed words with a quiet astonishment."[70] As IDAC's Rosiska Darcy de Oliveira and Miguel Darcy de Oliveira remarked, "The best educational context was the liberation movement itself." FARP members, according to Freire, had already developed a highly "critical approach to reading and writing," based largely on the fact that they had already made history and were not forced to "read alienating stories" about other people's struggles. They already understood the "significance of national reconstruction." The fact is, there had already been a concerted effort to eliminate illiteracy among the military before Freire had even arrived in Guinea-Bissau. By late October 1978, illiteracy had been reduced from 41 percent to 4 percent in the military, a major victory for the government with potentially troubling ramifications, as we shall see.[71]

Although the coverage of the literacy campaign in 1976 and early 1977 in Guinea-Bissau's official newspaper, *Nô Pintcha*, is positive and supportive, by the middle of 1977, the problems with the campaign were clearly evident.[72] The most careful study of the literacy campaign in Guinea-Bissau, an unfortunately never published doctoral dissertation by Linda Harasim, concludes, in fact, that it was a complete and utter failure. Indeed, as the country's Department of Adult Education itself reported in November 1980, "Of the 26,000 civilian Guineans reached by the literacy campaign practically none had learned to read and write." As Harasim argues, this was due to a number of factors, some of which were largely technical. Despite funding from outside sources like the World Council of Churches, there was often a lack of material support for the campaign. There were never enough people who completed the basic training course in Freire's techniques. There was a lack of consistent commitment from higher authorities. As Harasim suggests, these problems were clear from the beginning but were never addressed sufficiently. Some of them were undoubtedly insurmountable.[73]

But there were other reasons for the failure that related to overall socioeconomic development. As Harasim suggests, the "Freire method was not relevant to the real conditions of Guinea Bissau." Although the city of Bissau itself had been growing before independence, the nation as a whole was predominantly rural, with 80 percent of the population engaged in subsistence agriculture. This situation contrasted sharply with the Brazilian and Chilean examples. Chile had been a largely urban nation since the 1940s. Brazil had been urbanizing rapidly during the late 1950s, even in the underdeveloped northeast. An urbanizing population had aspirations that were more in keeping with the goals of a national literacy campaign. To the degree that agriculture was modernizing, as well, as it was in Chile in connection with the agrarian reform campaign, it created a need to read and write that the 80 percent of the Guinean population that were peasants did not possess. The lack of a market economy, with such a high percentage of the population engaged in subsistence agriculture, was an inhibiting factor, as well. Literacy rates, as has been noted, were higher among members of the FARP (and illiteracy in the armed forces was officially eliminated by late 1978). Unlike Guinean peasants, however, Guinean soldiers had practical reasons for learning how to read and write. Among the civilian population, as Harasim notes, the literacy campaign remained "sporadic, spontaneous, and largely isolated experiences lacking in organized relationship to national economic or political objectives." Dropout rates were high. The motivation simply was not there, and the teachers had failed to establish a connection with the peasants that would have helped convince them that there was a need to learn to read and write in Portuguese.[74]

Undoubtedly, a large part of the problem stemmed from Freire's own historical experiences. Very few Guineans were motivated to or had practical reasons for wanting to teach others how to read and write. Brazil relied on teachers whose motivations were as much political as educational to accomplish what they could in the limited time available; Chile had a much more developed "educational infrastructure" and used it professionally and well. Plainly put, Brazil, Chile, and Guinea-Bissau all may have been considered "Third World" countries, even by Freire himself, but clearly the label obscured more than it clarified in terms of social and economic development.[75]

Furthermore, as Harasim suggests, the existence of a "revolutionary state" is "not in itself a sufficient condition for guaranteeing a successful literacy campaign."[76] Freire had never worked for a one-party state in Brazil or Chile. Brazil's political parties were marked by personalism and opportunism, but the political system was pluralistic prior to the coup of 1964. (Freire had largely shunned partisan politics on a personal level.) Chile's political parties covered a broad political spectrum and tended to be more ideologically consistent in their practices, but they took part in a competitive political system that accepted the existence of opposing political views. This is not to suggest that political parties in these two countries did not try to make use of the literacy campaign for partisan purposes. Nor is it to suggest that Freire was altogether out of place politically in Guinea-Bissau at this time. There is no doubt that by the 1970s, the PAIGC and Freire shared a certain number of what Harasim calls "ideological congruencies," such as "idealism and pedagogical populism." There also seems little doubt that PAIGC had the legitimacy to create the new nation-state. And the Freire of the 1970s had no reservations about working with a revolutionary one-party state.[77]

One must look back to the colonial experience that Freire misunderstood to explain some of the difficulties in Guinea-Bissau. Whatever one may think of Portuguese education policies and schooling practices, they certainly had a minimal impact on the majority of the Guinean population. The problem of "re-Africanization" was far less significant than either Freire or Cabral thought, with an estimated .5 percent of the population being "assimilado," or assimilated. Cabral's experience studying agronomy and his association with the Casa dos Estudantes do Império (Imperial Students' House) in Lisbon clearly shaped his vision, but while his experience in Lisbon helped him imagine a new nation and create a strong anticolonial movement, he did not see his countrymen themselves all that clearly. In the countryside, in particular, the European presence was virtually nonexistent and there was little interest in or necessity for learning to read and write in Portuguese.[78]

Undoubtedly, the decision to use the colonial language as the means of instruction was, ultimately, the major reason why the literacy program in Guinea-Bissau failed. As in most postcolonial African countries, leaders preferred to use the language of the colonizer as the new national language. Cabral himself had intended to use Portuguese as the unifying national language. During the liberation war, however, the "political work of explanation" had been "done in the local languages." Creole might have had somewhat more potential as a unifying force, as the use of it had spread during the war of liberation, but it was still only spoken by 45 percent of the population and had penetrated into the interior of the country to only a limited degree. The lack of written texts would not have been a significant factor had it been practical to adapt the Freire method in its entirety, since Freire himself had always advocated teaching the working vocabulary of the students themselves. In any case, the 5 percent of the population that actually spoke Portuguese was already literate. Freire's techniques could not work in teaching what was fundamentally for most of the students, and instructors, too, for that matter, a foreign language. Even Guinea-Bissau's president remarked to Freire once that speaking Portuguese for too long gave him a headache, even though he had attended colonial schools and spoke the language fluently. Although Freire later claimed that he had argued vehemently against using Portuguese, the Guinean leaders rejected his advice.[79] Ethnic divisions did not play the divisive role in Guinea-Bissau that they did in other parts of Lusophone Africa. Nevertheless, linguistic divisions were a significant factor in defeating the aims of the literacy campaign. Freire's experience had been in primarily monolingual countries since the indigenous population, comprising only roughly 1 percent of the population, was not much of a factor in Brazil; the Mapuche in southern Chile were marginalized, as well, and had no impact on the literacy campaign as a whole. Most African countries were too linguistically diverse and rural for Freire's techniques to be effective there.

The failure of the program in Guinea-Bissau was not widely publicized. Freire's book on the subject was published in 1978 and has remained in print in a number of countries, but later published writings (not to mention private correspondence) that analyzed the campaign's weaknesses have not received wide distribution.[80] The national commitment to literacy diminished dramatically, although there were attempts to engage UNESCO personnel to initiate small-scale functional literacy projects in conjunction with cotton and rice production.[81]

IDAC and Freire continued to work in the country in 1979 and 1980, not only trying to make up for their failure by following more closely the Tanzanian model and emphasizing mobilization over literacy training in later projects, but also encouraging the national government to abandon their attempts to impose Portuguese as the national language, which clearly the government itself had misgivings about. In the isolated village of Sedengal beginning in 1977, the acquisition of community development skills already preceded learning to read and write. Local leaders helped draw up the "verbal and thematic universe of the area," and greater consideration was paid to the irrelevance of Portuguese to the local inhabitants. Students began to use the technique of breaking words down into syllables in Creole and in local languages, as well. At the same time, an attempt was made to work directly with improving agricultural production in the area as these other skills were being developed. IDAC and its local collaborators began to discover that as the Sedengalese began to "write reality," they had more of an interest in learning (the reverse of previous Freirean expectations). "Before we didn't know we knew," one village inhabitant commented. "Now, we know that we knew and we can know more."[82] Despite the signs of progress that accompanied IDAC's new focus, Freire's later visits to the country in the final year of his employment by the council were shorter and less well publicized in the official Guinean press.[83] The government was moving on, and its own days were numbered.

A complete assessment of the politics of Freire's work in Guinea-Bissau must take into account the larger political context within the country after independence. The success of the PAIGC in leading a liberation struggle did not translate into successful state building.[84] Unlike Freire did, a historian must view this early period less through the writings of Amílcar Cabral and more through the actions of Amílcar's half-brother, Luiz. And one must view the failure of the literacy campaign within the larger context of the failure of the state project of President Luiz Cabral and the PAIGC. Luiz Cabral's experience certainly demonstrates how quickly political capital can be squandered. His economic mismanagement and overemphasis on the urban sector, as well as his increasingly repressive rule, clearly played a role in his relatively rapid downfall. It also could be argued that the emphasis on the urban population (which was so common in African countries after independence) might have encouraged the young to become literate, as required by a more urban society. The new government of João Bernardo Vieira, which replaced Cabral in November 1980, claimed to be following the path of Amílcar Cabral, but it would rely "entirely on the army as its base of power." Despite Amílcar Cabral's campaign against militarism during the liberation struggle, the process of independence had created an opportunity for the military to enhance its political importance. Literacy training had been most successful among those in whom political consciousness and indeed a national consciousness was already most highly developed. The literacy campaign benefited those who had already gained an enhanced political role through the independence process.[85] The Guinean peasants remained outside of the boundaries of the larger nation-state project, as they had been during the colonial period. In Brazil, the fear of an awakened consciousness among the peasants and the urban poor was one of the factors that increased the political consciousness of the military. In Guinea-Bissau, it was those who already had an expanded political consciousness who overthrew the Cabral regime, which Freire had tried to help strengthen.[86]

The literacy campaign that took place in São Tomé and Príncipe under Freire's guidance during the same period, differed in a number of significant ways from that in Guinea-Bissau, not least of all in a relative success rate that contradicted Freirean philosophy. With a population of roughly 75,000, the country was even smaller than Guinea-Bissau. An estimated 85 percent of the population was illiterate. São Tomé and Príncipe, a two-island nation, was, unlike Guinea-Bissau, wholly a colonial creation, uninhabited until the Portuguese arrived and peopled largely through the importation of enslaved Africans to work on plantations. During a second phase of colonialism in the late nineteenth century, new cash crops were introduced. Following the abolition of slavery in 1875, contract workers were brought in from other Portuguese African colonies. Like Guinea-Bissau, São Tomé also suffered from educational neglect, but the hybrid nature of its society guaranteed that much of the population spoke Portuguese. Unlike Guinea-Bissau, the country's path to independence did not include any significant armed conflict, let alone a unifying national war. Although São Tomeans created the Movimento de Libertação de São Tomé e Príncipe (Movement for the Liberation of São Tomé and Príncipe, MLSTP), the movement took part in little to no political action within the islands prior to the overthrow of the Portuguese dictatorship in 1974. It was, however, able to achieve some measure of popular support during the period of negotiations for independence with Portugal and won the elections for the constituent assembly in July 1975 prior to the creation of a one-party state.[87]

Freire, his wife Elza, and other members of IDAC began working in São Tomé and Príncipe in 1976.[88] Freire saw the country as "experiencing a face-to-face democracy in which one can perceive a strong hope in the people, in its avant-garde and in its government in the struggle for the reconstruction of the country." The reality was rather different. It was a one-party state in which members of the so-called National Popular Assembly were chosen by the party and "popular" organizations did not have much input. A secret police responsible for monitoring counter-revolutionary activities answered only to the "comrade" president, Manuel Pinto da Costa, and the atmosphere in the country was increasingly repressive.[89]

A national adult literacy seminar was held in late 1976 with representatives of various ministries, the armed forces, the "political office of the liberation movement," and youth. Following presentations by government officials and training in Freirean techniques, the thirty people involved in the seminar went to small fishing villages to form cultural circles.[90] As he did in all of his work with literacy programs, Freire sought to work with, rather than lecture at, people, frequently referring to "we," "us," and "our," as in "our society," "our Movement" (MLSTP), "our revolution," etc.[91] There is no evidence in Freire's writings that he was skeptical or critical of the government that he was advising. Nor does he seem, except in private conversations, to have made any distinctions between the background or political systems of that country and those of Guinea-Bissau or any other Portuguese African country.[92]

Freire and his IDAC colleagues took part in training seminars with ministries, the armed forces, and the party, and put together a series of textbooks that sought to undergird the MLSTP's political hegemony. "All these books," Freire's Chilean colleague Antonio Faundez wrote in the fifth textbook, "seek to help the students to practice a correct and critical form of thought."[93] Teachers were not supposed to give lectures but to help their students pose questions.[94] The "Comrade President" Manuel Pinto da Costa spoke fluent Freirean in his remarks to the national literacy seminar.[95] Yet the questioning attitude did not extend to the role of the party. Discussions were to emphasize "the role of the MLSTP in the conquest of our independence."[96] Students were taught to say, "I am a militant of the MLSTP, the revolutionary vanguard of our people," and to believe that "The People need the revolutionary vanguard."[97]

The textbooks encouraged "unity, discipline, [and] work."[98] The first word in the first textbook was "people"; an accompanying photo depicting an independence day rally demonstrated the unity of the São Tomean people.[99] (In that sense, Freire was returning to his roots in Brazil before he adopted the phrase "the oppressed.") Yet the texts emphasized the latter two "revolutionary duties." In a society with a legacy of various forms of forced labor, it was believed that the general population needed to develop reliable work habits. "We didn't achieve independence for everyone to do what he wants," a text warned.[100] Government officials were concerned that citizens would believe that since they were now free, they did not have to do anything.[101] Instead, they needed to be reminded that all work was important for the revolution; only if São Tomeans produced more would they live better.[102] Students were reminded that cacao was the "principal source of riches."[103] Following the departure of the Portuguese, the plantations had been nationalized. This meant that workers were no longer working for a minority, as they had been during the colonial era. While working for the reconstruction of their country, workers would also be involved in the larger process of creating a "society without exploited or exploiters."[104] The textbooks stressed developing practical problem-solving skills and suggested that study was a revolutionary duty as well.[105] The literacy programs also were intended to help address the nation's public health concerns, such as mosquitoes. "Taking care of health," students were reminded, also was "a revolutionary duty."[106] Students were told to abandon superstition and taught that treatable illnesses, not the evil eye, were to blame for many of their problems.[107]

Unlike the program in Guinea-Bissau, the programs in São Tomé and Príncipe seem to have been successful. According to government sources,

"55 percent of all those enrolled and . . . 72 percent of those who . . . finished the course" became literate.[108] Freire believed that had there not been a "the lack of available staff," it would have been possible "to overcome" illiteracy in a year. The failure of the literacy program in Guinea-Bissau and the success of the one in São Tomé suggests, indeed, that "political literacy" had little to do with acquiring the ability to read and write. São Tomé was a nation in which people had long spoken Portuguese, and this was far more important than the lack of a successful war of liberation or the creation of a democratic political system.[109]

In the short term, the São Tomean literacy program was a success; the World Council of Churches' Office of Education continued to support literacy activities in the early 1980s after Freire left the organization. Antonio Faundez, a philosopher who taught at the Institut Universitaire d'Etudes du Développement in Geneva and had begun working with Freire in São Tomé in 1979, took over his position and worked in São Tomé until severe economic problems forced the government to abandon its literacy programs in 1982.[110]

Freire's African experience had been a mixed one. He had thrown in his lot with revolutionary one-party states that were not committed to democracy. He had more success in a truly "colonial" society like São Tomé than in a country that had drawn worldwide praise for the revolutionary commitment of its people in the struggle against colonialism. More mundane considerations like whether the population actually spoke the national language mattered more than the level of its political development. Nevertheless, Freire's book on his experience in Guinea-Bissau remained influential in spite of the failure of the literacy program the book ostensibly described.

As Freire's time with the World Council of Churches was winding down, he had one more opportunity to return to Latin America to put his ideas into practice. His experience in revolutionary Nicaragua deserves a separate chapter of its own. He left the council in June of 1980 not because of his failures and contradictory successes but because of political changes in his native country of Brazil in 1979 and 1980. Although the military was still in power, an amnesty law had made it possible for political opponents of the military regime to return from long years of exile. Reflecting on his time with the council, Freire said that he had enjoyed "an atmosphere of seriousness, companionship and loyalty" for more than a decade. His memories of his time with the council were positive ones. As he was about to leave in 1980, he wrote a colleague that he had "never felt frustrated" and had "always been happy." His time at the council had widened "enormously the areas of and challenges to my action and reflection."[111] His work had not been thwarted by military action, as it had been in Brazil, nor was it subject to partisan conflicts, as it had been in Chile. His influence was broad, if not concentrated, and, following his departure, the education office hoped to be able to continue work along the same lines.[112] Freire's ideas had been enormously influential and had played a supportive role in a wide variety of countries during the 1970s. Ironically, perhaps, he also had become influential in the First World and even among elite members of First World societies. The support for his work by First World churches ought to have led to some greater complexity in his understanding of international politics, but there is no evidence that it did so. At the same time, as he recommitted himself to work in the Third World in the latter half of the decade (again with funding from many churches in the developed world), he failed on an unprecedented scale in a country that, according to his theory, should have been most receptive to his theories and succeeded in a country where the opposite should have been the case. Nicaragua would provide another model of a country remaking itself after a successful revolution and another country in which Freirean ideas and techniques were adapted to the needs of a one-party state.

The last major literacy campaign Paulo Freire advised while he was with the World Council of Churches took him back to Latin America, but not to South America, where he had developed his ideas and techniques in an era of reform, but to Central America in a time of revolution. He took the lessons he had learned working in Africa and applied them to Nicaragua, a nation that in 1979 was trying to rebuild following decades of economic mismanagement and dictatorship, not to mention a catastrophic earthquake and a destructive war of liberation. As in many of the African nations Freire had worked with in the 1970s, his methods were employed in establishing the hegemony of a one-party state, but one that professed its devotion to pluralism and contended that it was building a popular democracy. In the year following the overthrow of Anastasio Somoza Debayle, the Nicaraguan government undertook a massive five-month literacy campaign that was, in some ways, unprecedented in scale (comparable, in many ways, to the Cuban campaign of 1961) and that captured the world's attention to a degree that no other campaign Freire had been involved with had done.[1] For better and worse, the tiny Central American nation remained a central focus of the international community for the next ten years. But in that first pivotal year, the Sandinista literacy program embodied both the optimism and the contradictions of the Sandinista national project at a defining moment. Freire's enthusiasm for the Nicaraguan campaign helped legitimize it in the eyes of the international community, but he passed so quickly through Nicaragua that he failed to see how his campaign fit into the country's internal political dynamics. The character of the Sandinista government and the experience of the literacy campaign itself led to social polarization and a breakdown of national unity even before the onset of full-scale civil war.

Nicaragua was an undeveloped country with an authoritarian past. It had roughly 2.8 million people in 1980. It was integrated into the international economy in the late nineteenth century to a limited degree as a relatively minor player in the world coffee market. Society remained largely rural throughout the first half of the twentieth century, and educational opportunities remained limited among the dispersed Nicaraguan population. The Somoza family dynasty, which had come to power in 1936 through the control of the National Guard, and through U.S. action and inaction, had expanded its grip over the Nicaraguan polity and economy over the course of their four decades in power.[2] The Nicaraguan export economy began to shift its focus with the development of a new crop, cotton, in the early 1950s. Land concentration accelerated during this period, and a significant portion of the rural population was forced to move to the cities. The rate of illiteracy declined in the 1950s and 1960s, but the absolute number of illiterates continued to increase, a not unusual pattern in Latin America, as we have seen. As the society urbanized, the inadequacies of the educational system became more glaring, despite Somocista propaganda to the contrary, which claimed that an "efficient" public education system had been evolving gradually since independence, with schools "multiplying" and "modernizing," the teachers "improving constantly," and the buildings (less hyperbolically and more accurately) "more or less adequate." By the early 1960s, urban Nicaraguans had an average of only 2.5 years of formal schooling, while rural Nicaraguans had no more than 1.5 years (although overall trends in school attendance during the decade were somewhat encouraging). Economic problems in the 1970s led to a further rise in illiteracy rates. Of countries in the Western Hemisphere, only Haiti spent less on education. By 1980, only roughly 6 percent of the rural population had completed primary school.[3]

In Nicaragua, as in the rest of Latin America, verbal skills were highly prized. "Hola, poeta" was the way young men greeted each other in the 1940s, according to future Sandinista minister of culture (and poet) Ernesto Cardenal.[4] For a small country, Nicaragua has produced a disproportionately large number of major poets, starting with Ruben Darío, a truly international figure who is credited with modernizing Spanish as a literary language. Indeed, Nicaragua has been called "the country of poets." But poets, in Nicaragua as elsewhere in the region, had a political role to play. The first Somoza was assassinated by a poet, and numerous poets, including Cardenal and Gioconda Belli, aided the Sandinista revolutionary movement from the 1960s on.[5]

Given the global drive for development in the postwar period, particularly in Latin America, the Somoza regimes could hardly ignore literacy programs completely. In April of 1945, at a time during which the first Somoza regime was responding to democratizing trends in the region, a literacy campaign was decreed into existence. Given the fact that primary schooling had not "arrived in all parts" of the country with "the necessary intensity and efficiency," those Nicaraguans "of good will" over the age of fifteen who could read and write were enjoined to teach those who could not; promises were made to bring the "light of the written word" to the most remote parts of the country. This effort was to continue until there were no illiterates left. Although 25,000 copies of a training manual were printed, the campaign seems to have had little impact. The initial 1945 decree itself was not published in book form until September of 1951.[6] Ten Nicaraguan teachers trained by CREFAL in Mexico created a small-scale "fundamental education" project later in the 1950s in the isolated Rio Coco area in the northeastern part of the country.[7] But government efforts to promote literacy continued to be diffuse and inadequate.

The Catholic Church certainly made an effort to teach people to read and write during the Somoza years, and the private sector played a role as well. In the early 1960s, the publisher of the major opposition newspaper *La Prensa*, Pedro Joaquín Chamorro, initiated a literacy campaign. Since the postwar period, Chamorro had considered the nation's high illiteracy rates to be part of the reason for the longevity of dictatorship in his country. In September 1963, inspired in part by a Colombian program and with the participation of radio stations and funding from private businesses, including the newspaper itself, the program was launched with the slogan, "He who cannot read is like one who cannot see." More than 120,000 manuals, based, as were those of other programs of this type at the time, on the Laubach method, were published over the course of 1964. Daily reading lessons appeared in *La Prensa*. According to a government official, the literacy campaign unsettled then leader Luis Somoza and convinced him that the only way to destroy it was to have the national government take it over. By the following year, with aid and advice from the Venezuelan government, the government launched a new program that marginalized *La Prensa*'s participation, and soon the program fizzled out.[8]

An essential factor in the Sandinista literacy campaign of 1980 would be the active participation of high school and university students. Unlike in many Latin American countries, a student movement per se did not exist until toward the end of the Second World War, a time in which democratic rebellions against authoritarian governments were sweeping Central America. In Nicaragua, the student movement began organizing after Somoza announced that he would be running for "re-election." The dictator responded to the challenge of the student movement by closing the branch of the national university in the capital city of Managua temporarily in 1944 and permanently in 1946. By the 1950s, there were still fewer than 1,000 university students in a country with a university-age population of roughly 170,000. If most college students were apolitical, a significant restive minority remained a political problem that the Somoza regime had to confront periodically. A university autonomy movement, lagging decades behind even those in other Central American countries, began to have an impact, particularly after Mariano Fiallos Gil agreed to serve as rector of the Universidad Nacional de Nicaragua in León in 1957 and proceeded to run the university as if he lived in a free country. (Future Sandinista minister of education Carlos Tünnermann Bernheim also was one of the leading university officials at the time.) Anti-Somoza students became more vocal in the aftermath of the overthrow of Fulgencio Batista in Cuba. Luis Somoza tried a more direct approach to the problem of student protest in 1959. On 23 July, National Guardsmen killed four students and wounded roughly eighty on 23 July. In the 1960s, higher education expanded somewhat. Following congressional authorization, a Jesuit university, the Universidad Centroamericana (UCA), was founded in 1960, in part, it has been argued, to provide a counterweight to the increasingly politicized public Universidad Nacional in León. UCA, however, would be no less important a center of political activity for much of the next two decades.[9]

A new political force in Nicaragua was established following the Cuban Revolution, the Frente Sandinista de Liberación Nacional (Sandinista National Liberation Front, FSLN). Its founder, Carlos Fonseca Amador, drew inspiration not only from Fidel Castro and Ernesto "Che" Guevara but also from his analysis of Augusto César Sandino's struggle against U.S. occupation in the late 1920s and early 1930s. According to his biographer Matilde Zimmermann, Fonseca's writings from his high school years in Matagalpa reveal an interest in the issue of illiteracy and a confidence that Nicaraguan youth could play a critical role in eradicating it in the Nicaraguan countryside. As the Sandinistas, a small and frequently divided group in the 1960s and 1970s, sought to organize and to develop a political following and to wage armed struggle, they began to address the issue directly. From 1964 to 1966, "[t]hey gave literacy classes to workers, using phrases like 'Sandino was a great general' as their texts." Student revolutionaries in the movement often found it difficult to communicate with the workers in the cities and the campesinos in the countryside; one Sandinista criticized the FSLN's activities during this period as a kind of "paternalistic social work." The social distance between the Sandinistas and the popular classes lessened somewhat over time since some members of the FSLN lived in hiding in poor urban areas and others began organizing guerrilla bands in the countryside. Fonseca believed, as Che Guevara had, that a "new man" would be born in the revolutionary struggle. Fonseca urged his fellow Sandinistas to abandon middle-class "self-ishness" and undergo a process of "proletarianization" by "adopting a pro-letarian spirit: industriousness, humility, self-sacrifice, honesty." Personal transformation was a two-way street during the formative years of the move-ment. A story that became a central motivational tool in the literacy cam-paign of 1980 described how Fonseca, upon seeing his fellow revolutionaries Tomás Borge and Germán Pomares instructing peasants on how to "load and break down weapons," suggested that they "also teach them to read." Fonseca himself taught others who joined his movement to read and write and en-couraged many middle-class Sandinistas to do the same. Germán Pomares was one of the most noteworthy *guerrilleros* because he not only became lit-erate during the war of liberation; he also became a writer. Fonseca believed that although becoming literate was an important part of the process of self-transformation that defined the armed struggle, ultimately, a revolutionary state would have to devote significant attention and resources to solving the problem on a national scale.[10]

A literacy campaign of a rather different sort became a counterinsurgency tool of the Somoza regime. In order to counter the growth of a revolutionary movement in the countryside in the late 1970s, the government, under what was called the Plan Waslala, used 108 security agents as teachers "in the areas where guerrilla activity was greatest" in the northern Nicaraguan mountains. These agents taught literacy classes to local peasants to help ferret out FSLN members and sympathizers.[11]

The struggle against Somoza in the late 1970s unified Nicaragua. Although the Sandinistas themselves during much of this time had been a small group bitterly divided over the strategies and pace of revolutionary activity, their hand was forced as popular forces in 1978 staged spontaneous revolts following the assassination of newspaper publisher Chamorro. The FSLN had to follow these revolts if they were going to lead. As Zimmermann suggests, people increasingly identified themselves as Sandinistas because the FSLN had been willing to take up arms against Somoza. The Frente then tried to unify and direct the revolution, with the use of arms from neighboring countries, such as Venezuela and Panama, which wanted to see Somoza ousted. Although the Somozas had been able to co-opt and repress the economic elite for decades, the last of the Somozas, Anastasio Somoza Debayle, demonstrated less of an ability to ensure elite cohesion and a greater willingness to use force indiscriminately and (ultimately) ineffectively. Elite sectors that had supported Chamorro's reformist efforts and were frozen out of political power by Somoza had to accommodate themselves to a revolutionary process that they could not control.[12]

The extent to which the revolution represented a true cross-class alliance is not only a question for social scientists and historians, it was a vital question during the period of national reconstruction in which the literacy campaign played a significant part. Following Somoza's defeat, his former elite opponents pointed to actions they had taken in opposition to Somoza following the scandalous regime's response to the earthquake of 1972, which had allowed Somoza and his associates to profit handsomely from international aid. The Sandinistas, for their part, argued that urban workers and peasants had accepted the vanguard role of the FSLN in leading the revolution. The Tercerista faction of the Sandinistas, for its part, had actively courted representatives of the elite beginning in 1975. The businessmen and professionals who became known publicly as "Los Doce" (the twelve) in 1977 (among them the aforementioned university administrator Tünnermann Bernheim and Jesuit priest and professor Fernando Cardenal [Ernesto's brother] who would play leading roles in the literacy campaign) were members of the Nicaraguan elite who had already affiliated themselves, albeit covertly, with the FSLN. Many Sandinistas themselves had "bourgeois" backgrounds, particularly those who joined the movement as students. And when the governing junta of national reconstruction was formed in the weeks preceding the departure of Somoza, it was Pedro Joaquín Chamorro's widow, Violeta Barrios de Chamorro, a true representative of the bourgeoisie but never a member of the FSLN, who read the junta's proclamation of a national unity government.[13]

On 18 June 1979, the "government of national reconstruction" issued its first proclamation from "some place in Nicaragua." They promised a "profound reform in the objectives and content" of education. In phraseology reminiscent of Freirean programs of an earlier era, the junta promised to turn education into a "key factor in the process of humanistic transformation." Education in the new Nicaragua would be "critical and liberating." Illiteracy would be eradicated, and formerly illiterate adults would be "incorporated fully into the process of reconstruction and national development."[14]

A little more than a month later, the newly established government enthusiastically began to create a wide variety of new programs in the "difficult and jubilant [first] days, which will never return, but which we will never forget," as priest and minister of culture Ernesto Cardenal wrote at the time. As another poet, José Coronel Urtecho, wrote, "the past will not return." For many, there was a sense of limitless future possibilities; this was not the end of history, but its beginning. The Sandinistas and many other Nicaraguans, as well, saw themselves as being at the center of world developments, at a turning point, a new beginning in Nicaraguan history. As a phrase from the first draft of the literacy campaign primer stated, "The long and terrible night is over, the black nightmare dead. In each home will shine the Nicaraguan sun of flaming gold." From most accounts, it was an exhilarating time to be in Nicaragua. No program better reflected the utopian spirit in the first year than the Cruzada Nacional de Alfabetización (National Literacy Crusade) under the Ministry of Education headed by Carlos Tünnermann Bernheim. The year 1980 was declared to be the year of literacy training. The roughly 50 percent illiteracy rate (30 percent in the cities, 75 percent in the countryside) was to be dramatically reduced, if not reduced to zero, as roughly half a million people, it was hoped, would be touched by the campaign. This was to be no mere campaign but a crusade. Literacy became a priority of the new government even earlier than it had become in Cuba (where the revolutionary process had already advanced significantly before its campaign had been launched).[15] Tünnermann Bernheim had co-authored the proposal for a national literacy campaign even before Somoza was defeated. The literacy campaign was intended to make sure that people throughout the country recognize not only that the names of those in charge had changed but also that there had been a fundamental change in the kind of government Nicaragua had. The campaign, it was promised, would build on "the spirit of sacrifice and commitment that had been generated during the war."[16]

Roughly a fortnight following the overthrow of Somoza, on 2 August 1979, Fernando Cardenal was chosen to coordinate the campaign. Cardenal was a

Jesuit priest who had become politicized during the time he spent working in a poor neighborhood of Medellín, Colombia. There he discovered, he later recalled, that God wasn't neutral but that he took "sides with the poor." After returning to Nicaragua, he became vice rector of UCA but lost his job after only three days when he supported a student strike. He was also a chair of the philosophy department at the Autonomous University in León. In 1973, he founded the Revolutionary Christian Movement. He was recruited by the FSLN, and he joined them covertly. Like Tünnermann Bernheim, he had testified before the U.S. Congress on Somoza's human rights abuses against "peasant collaborators of the FSLN."[17]

Planning for the campaign began almost immediately. In September, in a meeting with representatives of the World Council of Churches, the junta requested Freire's help in designing their literacy program. During Freire's visit in October, popular organizations began to participate actively in the preparations. A national census, itself a task of monumental proportions, was initiated at the same time. The first teachers were recruited, and Marcos Arruda, who had worked with Freire in Guinea-Bissau, spent much of November working with the national staff of the crusade. In that same month, literacy programs were undertaken in the new revolutionary armed forces. Recruitment drives for teachers accelerated at the universities in mid-February of 1980. The campaign was to begin in late March and last through late August, a time in which campesinos were working in their home communities and not migrating to coffee plantations or cotton fields.[18]

Freire's time in Nicaragua was brief. He spent nine days in Nicaragua in late October and early November 1979. Sandinista planning was already fairly advanced by this time. Instead of using generating words based on an examination of local popular language, as was done in earlier Freirean campaigns, the Nicaraguan literacy manuals focused on revolutionary slogans. The Sandinistas also understood their campaign to involve consciousness-raising as part of the creation of the "new man." They employed the phraseology of the Chilean campaign (the "psychosocial method"), as had become common in many of the Spanish-speaking countries in Latin America. Words were broken down into syllables. Photographs were used to prompt discussion. The influence of Cabral and of the experience of the African one-party state in Guinea-Bissau and especially in São Tomé were significant here. Although some who have relied on Freire's own writings rather than an examination of his practices are surprised that Freire accepted the need for standardization in a national campaign bent on unifying the country, the Nicaraguan campaign, like so many dating back to the MCP in Pernambuco in the early 1960s, used prepared texts.[19]

Freire was profoundly moved by his experience in revolutionary Nicaragua. In his farewell letter to the WCC, he noted, "Hardly ever in my life had I experienced moments richer than or even comparable to this time spent in Managua, breathing a revolutionary air full of hope and genuine popular participation."[20] As he had in Guinea-Bissau, Freire expressed both his commitment to helping the government achieve its goals and his resistance to being seen as an expert with all of the answers, announcing that he had come to learn from the revolution. He was impressed by the "happiness that envelops the people of this country." The Nicaraguan people, having broken free of their chains, were now "singing joyfully, writing poems, painting." He praised the "political clarity," "militancy," and "competence" of those involved in designing the crusade. Only after a revolution could such a campaign take place, he suggested. Popular organizations, for their part, should take the lead in making sure that the crusade helped "deepen the revolution."[21]

While one should not deny the Freirean elements in the campaign, it might also be suggested that one of Freire's most significant achievements in Nicaragua was to legitimize the Sandinista campaign in the eyes of many in the international community. In reading speeches from before, during, and after the crusade, it is striking the extent to which foreigners invoke Freire. The Nicaraguans themselves, however, mentioned him less and less often after he left the country.[22] By the time the crusade got off the ground in March of 1980, Freire was preparing to leave the World Council of Churches and return to Brazil. Although at first it had seemed that he would be one of a small number of people who would not benefit from the new amnesty law allowing political exiles to return, in August of 1979 he returned briefly with members of his family, and in June of 1980 he returned to Brazil for good.[23]

Despite Freire's limited participation, the crusade had some of his spirit. The literacy campaign was intended to bring about "a great national dialogue," as Francisco Lacayo, one of the top campaign officials, suggested. The crusade was also designed to break down the boundaries between those who lived in the city and those who lived in the countryside (a theme discussed previously but particularly in Chapter 3).[24]

Education was to play a vital role in Nicaragua's process of national reconstruction. In the short term, the government hoped to promote production, not least of all by guaranteeing that the literacy campaign itself would not disrupt the normal rhythms of Nicaraguan economic life as people began to recover from war. In the longer term, people were to be trained to meet the technical needs of economic development. In an unfortunate choice of words, Bayardo Arce Castaño noted that Nicaraguan mentalities would be "reprogrammed" based on the "concrete needs and concrete necessities of our country and our Revolution." No longer should it be true that only "200 of 23,000 students at the National University" should be studying agriculture in a country in which the land was inadequately cultivated. Once workers and peasants had become literate, they would be able to acquire the technical skills the country needed, but they also would be ready to prepared to take power, to control production, and to run society. After reconstruction would come modernization.[25]

The political content of the literacy campaign would play an even more central role than economic concerns. As Sergio Ramírez noted in his speech to the departing brigadistas in March 1980, the "oppressed and humiliated" people of Nicaragua will now learn "with which letters . . . are written justice, dignity, liberation, revolution."[26] The crusade, it was hoped, would "elevate the political consciousness of the people."[27] Once educated, campesinos would not be able to be "tricked as before" by those who wanted to exploit them.[28] The campesinos, moreover, would develop a "collective vision," which peasants "working and dying alone" had not had.[29]

In order to "instill commitment and courage," the literacy campaign followed a military model, with teachers organized in a brigade for each municipality across six "battlefronts." Brigades were subdivided into columns with roughly 120 students in each. A column, in turn, was divided into four squadrons. Names of the brigades, columns, and squadrons were taken from martyrs and battles. Rural literacy teachers in the Ejército Popular de Alfabetizadores (Popular Army of Literacy Instructors, EPA) were known as brigadistas, and their urban counterparts were known as literacy guerrillas.[30] The literacy campaign was seen as a natural continuation of the struggle against Somoza. The unity, discipline, and organization required to win a war were expected to be the virtues of the new nation being constructed. Central to both struggles was what Fernando Cardenal frequently referred to as the revolutionary mystique. The Nicaraguan people should be confident that they could win the battle against illiteracy since they already had defeated a strong, well-armed enemy in the former dictator.[31]

Youth had played a role in all of the campaigns Freire had been associated with, but none was defined more in terms of youth participation than the crusade. "Without youth disposed to sacrifice," the slogan of the Juventud Sandinista 19 de Júlio (19 July Sandinista Youth) went, "there is no revolution." (The Sandinista Youth 19 July was an outgrowth of the Federation of Secondary and University Students.) But the reliance on students between the ages of twelve and twenty-three was due not only to youth's presumed idealism but also to the need not to disrupt production. High school and university students were chosen in part because they were not considered to be an essential part of the economy. Since students were, by definition, unproductive members of society, national production would not be damaged by their participation in the venture.[32] Teenagers and college students were also chosen because there had been such a high level of youth participation in the war of liberation itself. The campaign gave veterans a new way to focus their energies. At the same time in the early stages of the ongoing revolution, the National Directorate of the FSLN wanted to deepen ties not only with the youth who had fought but also with a larger number of Nicaraguan youth who had remained on the sidelines. As they had in Cuba, teenage volunteers played a central role as literacy teachers as part of an attempt to ensure their commitment to the revolution.[33] Youth were expected to develop the revolutionary virtues of the pantheon of heroes and martyrs who had died in the war against Somoza, to be transformed in the difficult conditions in which they would be forced to live as they shared in the lives of the poor. As the revolutionary slogan suggested, "En Cada Alfabetizador [in every literacy teacher], Carlos Fonseca Amador." They would leave behind the individualistic values of pampered youth and develop a sense of themselves as part of a larger collective whole, devoted to ideals of solidarity and fraternity. As Fonseca had hoped, they would become proletarianized.[34]

Members of the Juventud Sandinista played a critical role in encouraging high school and university students to volunteer for the EPA. Although many volunteers were committed Sandinistas when they began, the testimony of many others suggests that not all brigadistas were particularly politically aware or even interested in politics. The government certainly put pressure on the young to participate. Fernando Cardenal, attempting to induce feelings of guilt, argued that those who refused to either teach or learn during the campaign were betraying Nicaragua's martyred dead. University students who would not participate were also criticized; Sergio Ramirez, another top Sandinista official, suggested that a great majority of them "continued to act as if there had been no revolution, as if 50,000 people had not died." Besides this pressure from above, peer pressure helped the government achieve its purpose. Undoubtedly, the preparations for the campaign included a large measure of political "orientation," and the experience of the campaign itself had an impact on the political evolution of many brigadistas, as is discussed below, but it is important to recognize that many of the volunteers remained fundamentally disinterested in the political aspects of the campaign that its designers considered so essential.[35]

Parents also played a distinctive role in the crusade. Not all parents from middle- or upper-class homes wanted their sons or daughters to live in the countryside in what were feared to be, not all that unreasonably, unhealthy and unsafe environments. The government required brigadistas to get their parents' permission in order to participate (though some, as Ernesto Cardenal noted approvingly, simply ran away from home to take part in the campaign). The government made special appeals to the parents to embrace the campaign and the idea of their children as "combatants" in the fight against ignorance and not to take obstructionist positions that favored imperialism and social backwardness. Newspapers addressed parents' concerns, and not always were the answers to their liking. Parents asked, for example, whether their children would be allowed to study if they chose not to take part in the campaign. They were told that they could do so but that Nicaraguan high schools and universities would be closed for the duration of the campaign. Parents were assured that there would be no retaliation for those who did not volunteer or chose to leave the country to continue their studies.[36] Officials and official publications tried both to reassure some and to reason with others. Sergio Ramírez lamented the "conservative and paternalistic" ways in which fathers were judging teenagers, not acknowledging the changed historical circumstances, especially considering the fact that many of their children had already fought in a war. He suggested that parents talk with their children "democratically" about their interest in joining the crusade. But FSLN officials also took a more belligerent approach, threatening and deriding those who wanted to keep their children from participating. Students often joined in spite of parents' opposition, and then the parents had to accept their decision.[37]

In the teaching materials themselves, the Sandinistas sought to provide new unifying symbols around which the nation could rally. The role of heroes and martyrs was central to this nation-building effort. Sandino, the guerrilla leader who had fought the U.S. Marine Corps decades earlier and who had been killed on orders from the first Somoza in 1934, had been vilified officially as a "bandit" during the Somoza years, as he had been in life in most official sources. Intellectuals and other opposition figures throughout the period, however, had tried to present a heroic image of Sandino, beginning with student publications produced in conjunction with the protests of 1944 against the first Somoza's announcement that he wanted to remain in power. While Carlos Fonseca, for his part, had contributed greatly to an understanding of the leader's life and thought, Sandino had the advantage of being a somewhat ambiguous political figure. That he was a popular leader who had fought against the United States there was no doubt. Where he stood on particular questions of political and social organization was somewhat less clear, and critics of the FSLN during the campaign sought to discredit its exclusive claim to ownership of Sandino (and, indeed, an actual legal monopoly on the use of the word "Sandinista" through Decree 67/20 issued on 20 September 1979). The literacy campaign championed Sandino, the man in the big hat, as the new national hero and the "guide of the revolution." Although undoubtedly many in the Nicaraguan countryside would have known of Sandino, to others he must have been a somewhat obscure figure, a hero they did not know they had. To the extent that Somocista propaganda had penetrated into campesino consciousness over the years, the brigadistas had to work to overcome negative popular understandings of the man and his accomplishments.[38]

There was no cult of personality being created around the nine members of the National Directorate or the five members of the junta, but the campaign was dedicated to the memory of the heroes and martyrs of the recently concluded war. Students were taught to admire Carlos Fonseca, who had been killed in 1976. "Carlos" was one of the first words they were supposed to learn to write, a dramatic departure from Freirean practice of finding generating words that spoke directly to students' experience. In addition, Fonseca's role in reclaiming Sandino's significance and his "dream" of Nicaraguans becoming literate were emphasized in the textbooks. As one sixteen-year-old recalled, when you spoke to the peasants regarding their reality (demonstrating in this sense a fine understanding of Freirean methods) and then discussed the ideals of Sandino and Fonseca regarding the solution to their problems, they became more interested in learning about these men. (In the past, Freire, working toward partisan hegemony, had not emphasized the example of particular individuals, living or dead.)[39] To critics of the government's choice of official heroes, officials responded, "What do they want? [Do they want people to learn] the names of Adolfo Díaz and Emiliano Chamorro . . . names associated with the selling out of national interests to the United

States?"[40] Further lessons stressed both the popular agency involved in the war against Somoza and the importance of the FSLN in making liberation possible. Similarly, the training manuals stressed the continuing importance of popular organizations like the Sandinista Defense Committees in ensuring the revolution's success and the necessity for all Nicaraguans to participate in a number of these kinds of organizations.[41]

While promoting the adoption of new national heroes and seeking valida-tion of the role of the Frente as the popular vanguard, the Sandinistas were prudent in trying to lower expectations for what could be achieved in the short term, given the state of the nation over which they had recently as-sumed power. The manuals, not unreasonably, given how long the Somoza dictatorship had been in power, blamed it for the poverty and underdevelop-ment in the country. "We will share the little left by the Somocistas," they promised. At the same time, in the near term, they had to get Nicaraguans to accept austerity measures and to increase production. (The gross national product had declined in 1979 by 25 percent to 1962 levels, with $480 million in "damage directly due to the war.") "To spend little, to conserve resources, and to produce much is to make the revolution," they asserted. In the short term, as well, revolutionary enthusiasm could work together with visibly observed realities to keep expectations low. Nevertheless, students were in-formed that Somocista businesses would be nationalized in order to help the reconstruction effort.[42]

On 23 March, after months of planning, the crusade was launched with a massive rally in Managua. Roughly 50,000 high school and university stu-dents then left for the countryside with their knapsacks and canteens. They left on buses and on foot. At times, particularly in the Atlantic coast region, they had to take boats and canoes to reach their final destination. An addi-tional 30,000 went to work in poor urban areas. The official images from this time period are of idealistic young people ready for sacrifice and to experi-ence ways of life with which they were wholly unfamiliar. Such a massive commitment of volunteer energies is hard to imagine without the establish-ment of a revolutionary state. Although volunteers were involved in the other campaigns discussed in this book, the scale and the scope of this volunteer effort sets it apart.[43]

Although the coverage of the literacy campaign in all three major Nicara-guan newspapers suggests the depth of the commitment of the majority of the volunteers, there were clearly problems, and often ones one would expect when one is talking about high school students. Although outright desertion by brigadistas seems to have been fairly rare, absenteeism was not. "Some [brigadistas] were immature, some arrogant, others apathetic or resentful."[44] The brigadistas, being young, often lacked discipline and were sometimes even accused of robbing from the very campesinos they were supposed to teach.[45]

It is often difficult to tell to what extent the majority of brigadistas were committed to politicizing their students. They had professed loyalty to the revolution and to the ideas of Sandino and Fonseca. But since so many teachers had been required and since many had been recruited just weeks before they left the plaza in Managua, not all received adequate training or political preparation before they set off into the field.[46] Not all students were, by any means, equally committed to the political content of the course they were teaching, least of all those who cynically took part because it enabled them to receive passing grades for the school year.[47] It is also important to remember how young they were. As one North American volunteer recalled them, the brigadistas were "revolutionaries of high purpose one minute, rebellious cynics the next; half-guerrillas, half-children."[48] While some teachers were undoubtedly arrogant, it is also clear that many felt uncertain before a classroom of older people and that they did not feel comfortable telling them what to think. Some teachers remembered that political discussion occurred in daily interactions as often as or even more than in classes.[49] Moreover, these discussions did not always lead to simplistic answers. The discussions of photos that were in the textbooks often rubbed emotional wounds that were still raw. When shown pictures of National Guardsmen, campesinos often spoke of loved ones who had been killed not all that long ago. A fifteen-year-old brigadista named Katia, on the other hand, recalled a woman whose husband had joined the Guard to help pay for their family's meals and who had been killed by the Sandinistas.[50] And political matters often seemed less pressing to the literacy teachers themselves. During the course of the campaign, more practical matters had to be addressed. As the urgency to produce immediate results in teaching more people to read and write became apparent, political questions were often set aside, particularly during what was called the "final offensive," begun on 22 July.[51]

As with the Christian Democratic literacy campaign in Chile, it is often easier to see what impact the campaign had on the teachers than it is to gauge what effect it had on the students. Many brigadistas had never been on their own before, except to go to school and back. Volunteers who had left as children, it was said, came back men and women. Both male and female volunteers wanted a new relationship with their parents when they returned. There is no doubt that, for many, the experience helped them grow up. The relationship between teacher and student was, as it was intended to be, a critical component of the experience. Teachers had to overcome the campesinos' initial distrust of the brigadistas, distrust fueled by rumors about their ideology and their intentions. The hoped-for bonds between brigadistas and campesinos often did develop. The campaign changed interfamilial dynamics, but it also expanded the notion of family to include the larger society. The experience of living with families other than their own meant that Nicaraguan youth now had more than one "mama" and "papa."[52] In fact, one of the most moving aspects of the crusade was the evolution of the relationship between the brigadistas and their mostly campesino hosts. The evidence overwhelmingly shows that, whatever the initial (and quite natural) suspicions campesinos must have had about these young boys and girls from the city, over the course of the five-month campaign, many of them had developed strong emotional ties with the brigadistas.[53] Miguel Angel Aragón López, who has left one of the longer accounts of his experience with the campaign, wrote touchingly of his attachment to his students. Though there was a great need during the final offensive for brigadistas to move on to other areas and other responsibilities, he was reluctant to leave his students after they had learned how to read and write.[54]

Literacy workers also were now aware of social realities dramatically different from their own. "I tell you seriously, ma'am, your son has already learned how to read in our book," a campesino told a brigadista's mother.[55] The brigadistas were often shocked at the "isolation and poverty" they experienced in the countryside. They learned to appreciate how hard peasants had to work. They discovered that many families were going without food some days. They had to adjust to a variety of hazards, including heavy rains, contaminated water, mosquitoes, rats, and ticks. Although they were supposed to help their families in the field, often times their "help" was not needed or appreciated; nevertheless, many tried to master the intricacies of agricultural work. Nevertheless, the brigadistas also encountered a hunger for learning that sparked a greater enthusiasm for teaching. They began to appreciate the positive aspects to rural life and began to "identify" with the campesinos.[56] Moreover, some brigadistas' parents embraced their children's work. Despite the difficulties they experienced in getting to the places where their children were teaching, many parents visited their brigadista sons and daughters regularly on weekends, bringing food, medicine, and other supplies to help both the brigadistas and their host families.[57]

The literacy campaign held great promise for girls and women in particular. Sixty percent of the EPA was female, and the campaign that took them out of their sheltered lives at home and school offered new responsibilities and greater autonomy.[58] The literacy manual promised that the revolution would end women's historic exploitation. Female students, including many housewives, embraced the campaign as well. As one woman remembered, "I almost never left home" before the campaign. With the literacy campaign," she continued, "I felt like I was being liberated."[59] Women also were mobilized into "mothers' committees." All told, 161 committees were formed with a total of 1,597 members. They not only "mothered" the brigadistas and provided "logistical and moral support," but they also encouraged women to want to learn to read and write and to join Sandinista women's organizations.[60]

When the volunteers returned from their five-month campaign, they were not coming back as just any men (or women) but heroic New Men (or Women), some argued, "more noble, more revolutionary, more Nicaraguan." According to a study conducted several months following the end of the campaign by Jan Flora, John McFadden, and Ruth Warner, 32 percent of those surveyed considered the campaign "the determining factor in increasing their support of the revolutionary process."[61] As Sergio Ramírez had suggested halfway through the campaign, youths were expected to have developed a revolutionary consciousness after the campaign that would predispose them to dedicate themselves to whatever tasks "the Revolution" would indicate. Indeed, in August, at the rally that marked the end of the crusade, brigadistas made a vow to "continue in the fight." A banner flown at the rally proclaimed, "Comandante Carlos Fonseca, We Have Taught Them to Read. What Is the Next Task?" As Carlos Nuñez, FSLN National Directorate representative to the campaign, remarked, brigadistas had earned the right to be called "sons and daughters of Sandino." Having experienced the poverty of the countryside and the city firsthand, they were even more committed to working to address these social problems. Brigadistas returned with a greater sense of the nation. In the next few years, they disproportionately continued to volunteer to work at harvest time or in civil and military defense. Many, as was hoped, reevaluated their career goals, demonstrating, for example, a greater interest in issues related to health and rural life. In addition, according to the study cited above, those from the middle and upper classes who had a positive experience in the campaign were more likely to be more committed to the revolution than they had been before.[62] This change in attitude sometimes led to conflict between youths and their "bourgeois" parents, who had not gone through the same transformative process. As one fifteen-year-old son of a rich family said, quoted approvingly by Ernesto Cardenal, "After the Crusade, I discovered that my parents were my political enemies."[63]

The literacy campaign was not a wholly positive experience for a significant minority, however. As mentioned earlier, the commitment of many to the campaign even as they left in March, let alone their devotion to the revolution, was questionable. Moreover, participating in the campaign for some had a negative effect. Thirteen percent of the brigadistas surveyed for the study cited above considered the campaign "the determining factor in decreasing revolutionary support," and some went so far as to become active members of the opposition.[64] For some, the experience reinforced their prejudices against the peasantry.[65]

To place the crusade in its larger political context, one has to look beyond the brigadistas, their families, and the campesinos. The Sandinistas had relied upon aid from countries representing a wide political spectrum during the war and continued to do so as the campaign commenced, but the range of allies began to narrow considerably over the course of the five-month campaign. International aid, as Sandinista Guillermo Rothschuh-Tablada noted in a talk before CREFAL in Mexico, helped win the battle, and "similar forces will help us win the battle of science and culture and the war against the dictatorship of ignorance."[66]

By 1979, UNESCO had become more strongly identified with the concerns and interests of the Third World. Representatives of the organization helped prepare the national census of illiterates. Director Amadou-Mahtar M'Bow visited Nicaragua from the 16th to the 19th of December and issued a plea for financial support from the international community for the campaign. Following his return to Paris, he was said to be so moved as he described what he had seen in Nicaragua that he began to cry.[67] And many foreign countries responded to his appeal.[68]

Perhaps no single international organization played a more important role in supporting Nicaragua in 1980 than the World Council of Churches. Representatives of the council had arrived as early as the 25 July 1979 to meet with churches and to discuss emergency and reconstruction aid. The council soon issued an appeal to churches around the world for $5 million. By November, roughly $1.5 million had already been disbursed, with an additional $1.2 million already pledged. In the first eighteen months that the Sandinistas were in power, the new government received $3.3 million of WCC aid, which was funneled through the Comité Evangélico Pro-Ayuda al Desarrollo (Evangelical Committee for Aid to Development). During its first visit, the council team met with Carlos Tünnermann Bernheim. The WCC also provided significant funding for the literacy crusade. Of the $2.3 million the Sandinista government requested for the campaign, the council provided $500,000, which, one council official proudly noted, "was the largest contribution to the National Literacy Campaign." Funding came from churches in the United States, Canada, Switzerland, Australia, New Zealand, Denmark, Sweden, Chile, and Argentina. Although the ideological character of the Nicaraguan government remained a bit unclear to representatives of some church agencies, there was widespread support for the idea of helping the government out at this time.[69]

There is no doubt, however, that the government welcomed aid from some sources more than from others. No country contributed to the campaign more as a model and in terms of numbers of volunteers than Cuba. The FSLN had been created in response to the Cuban Revolution, and the Cubans had provided military training, ideological guidance, and (to a much lesser extent) arms during the revolution. The ties between the two countries were strong, and given the perceived success of the Cuban education programs, the Cubans could provide valuable pedagogical (as well as medical and logistical) assistance prior to, during, and after the campaign. The revolutionary dedication of Cuban volunteers had been a significant factor in Cuban foreign policy since the 1960s. A week after Somoza's overthrow, Fidel Castro promised the Nicaraguans that if they did not have enough teachers, Cuba was ready to send as many as were needed. Raul Ferrer, Cuba's vice minister of education, took an active interest in the crusade and visited frequently as a representative of UNESCO. Cuban volunteers had begun to arrive as early as the beginning of August 1979. Crusade officials visited Cuba in late September to talk to the volunteers who had taken part in the 1961 campaign and to examine materials in the national literacy museum. More Cuban volunteers provided advice on the crusade primer in November. The Cuban government paid their volunteers a salary of around $20 a month. Roughly 2,000 Cubans took part, and most of them stayed on after the campaign was over to continue working as primary school teachers. Most of these returned to Cuba after two years. The Sandinista victory and the literacy campaign had come at an opportune time for Cubans, when the success of their own revolution was being called into question by the eagerness of many to leave during the Mariel boat-lift crisis. Living in the countryside with Nicaraguan campesinos helped Cubans "deepen their revolutionary consciousness" as well. One twenty-year-old Cuban volunteer was shocked to see a newborn baby die. Having grown up enjoying the "fruits" of a revolutionary state, he attributed the child's death to the "marks of capitalism." Education minister Tünnermann Bernheim praised the dedication of the volunteers (he estimated that Cubans had taught 131,947 students during their time in the country). Junta member Daniel Ortega also praised the internationalists who came for once not to invade with guns but to bring "sentiments of revolutionary solidarity."[70]

Cuban participation did not come without political risks, of course.[71] Opponents of the Sandinistas exaggerated the degree to which the Cubans shaped the content and the conduct of the campaign. Even as the Sandinistas emulated the Cuban model in many ways, they also tried to stress the differences between the two countries' experiences. According to Ernesto Cardenal, Cuban teachers were strictly forbidden to engage in antireligious activities or to promote atheistic thought; those who treated popular devotion irreverently were repudiated strongly early on, and, according to Cardenal, this did not happen again.[72]

The crusade also received aid from European social democratic governments and countries. Swedish unions, for example, donated lamps, and the West German Ebert Foundation provided aid and advice. The Sandinistas had only limited interest in strong ties with these countries, however.[73] Several days before the campaign began, the Sandinistas and the Soviet Union signed an "ideology treaty." Nevertheless, Soviet aid in 1980 was relatively limited, and, unlike Cuba, the Soviet Union during this period was never put forth as a model for emulation.[74] The Soviet Union was never a subject of discussion during the literacy campaign, except to the extent that people like Alfonso Robelo (discussed below) brought it up.[75]

Costa Rican teachers also aided in the campaign as part of the Carlos Aguero brigade, which was named after a Costa Rican who had fought with the Sandinistas. Costa Rican president Rodrigo Carazo Odio praised the volunteers, who, he said, represented a country "which for 100 years had fought for culture." Although Costa Rican volunteers believed that their country's education practices were better, they were convinced that the Nicaraguan method was effective. They suggested that in the long term there would not be such a need to emphasize criticism of the previous regime and praise of the revolution. Once the government was consolidated, they suggested, there should be an attempt to consider other (unnamed) pedagogical methods, presumably ones more similar to those employed in Costa Rica.[76]

Materially, however, no country contributed more to the campaign than the United States.[77] This fact needs to be emphasized, given the amount the United States spent trying to overthrow the Sandinistas during President Ronald Reagan's administration. U.S.-Nicaraguan relations during the period from the fall of Somoza to the inauguration of President Jimmy Carter's successor were neither easy nor well-defined.[78] The Carter administration had wanted to keep the Sandinistas from coming to power. It had been inconsistent in pushing Somoza toward eliminating human rights abuses, in part because of a conflict between foreign service officers, who were more comfortable with traditional approaches to handling Latin American dictators, and Carter's handpicked people, most of whom tended to be more aggressive on this issue.[79] As opposition to Somoza increased in 1978, the administration was reluctant to intervene to force him out. By the time the administration began to work to forge an agreement with more moderate elements to prevent a Sandinista victory, even as Somoza still believed he could ride out the storm, the popular rebellion already had progressed too far. By early July 1979, the United States was expecting Somoza to leave; administration officials hoped that the National Guard could be "reconstituted" following a "purge of those involved in flagrant corruption and repression." They also hoped that moderate factions of the FSLN could be encouraged to split from the rest and form a broad-based coalition government. Panamanian president Omar Torrijos (who had been supplying the Sandinistas with guns) assured U.S. officials that the U.S. emphasis on Sandinista ties to Cuba was misguided and that Torrijos's nationalist "boys . . . ultimately will prevail." The U.S. feared that Torrijos's influence over the Sandinistas would decline once they were in power.[80]

Following the Sandinista victory, Robert Pastor, director of Latin American and Caribbean affairs on the National Security Council, wrote to national security adviser Zbigniew Brzezinski to suggest that the central question was, "How can we keep Nicaragua from becoming another Cuba, and how do we keep the rest of Central America from becoming another Nicaragua?" The Carter administration needed to decide how much reconstruction aid to provide. Pastor recommended giving "them the benefit of the doubt." The United States should "give them relief and later reconstruction assistance" and "hold them to their assurances." The United States could "tolerate their trespasses for a while," while crossing its fingers.[81] The CIA, for its part, predicted that there were "significant forces at work to constrain the radical impulses of the Sandinista movement," though "in the inherently unstable first phase of the Nicaraguan revolution, Communist and pro-Cuban elements" might "be irresistibly tempted to bid for dominance and try to overcome pressures for moderation."[82]

The Sandinistas certainly had resented U.S. efforts to keep them from attaining the power they believed was rightfully theirs, and opposition to the United States was an essential component of their ideology. The literacy training manual featured the words to the FSLN anthem, which referred to "the Yankee" as "the enemy of humanity." Once in power, the Sandinistas veered back and forth between strident critiques of Carter's policy as consistent with that of all previous U.S. presidents, and maladroit attempts to gain U.S. respect for what it claimed was a policy of nonalignment. The Carter administration after 19 July 1979 intended to keep the Sandinistas from following too closely the Cuban example by promising aid for reconstruction and not overreacting to Sandinista policies, as they believed the Eisenhower and Kennedy administrations had done regarding Castro's policies in 1959–61. U.S. emergency relief aid arrived as early as 28 July. Repeatedly, Sandinistas proclaimed that they would not be bought by U.S. aid. Whereas some private U.S. citizens were allowed to take part in the crusade, Peace Corps volunteers were barred from the country during this time period (because of the long-held belief among the Latin American Left that they were actually working for the CIA).

The Nicaraguan press closely watched congressional votes regarding aid. Funding for the Nicaraguan government was politically problematic for the Carter administration, given U.S. domestic political considerations as the 1980 presidential election approached and suspicions regarding the nature of the regime heightened. When aid was agreed to in late February 1980, its dispersal was conditioned on the Carter administration's assurances that the government was not itself supporting revolution as Cuba had so frequently done. The Carter administration's public affirmations of support for the Nicaraguan government belied even the more optimistic members' private misgivings, even given their hopes of preventing more radical outcomes of what one Carter administration official called "a political identity crisis."[83] On the eve of the literacy campaign, the CIA contended that the Sandinistas were "in a transitional stage of the revolution . . . and are attempting to consolidate their rule in order to achieve a final 'hegemony.'" Their goals for achieving "some sort of Marxist society" notwithstanding, the Sandinistas needed foreign aid and had demonstrated both pragmatism and "some ambivalence on how to proceed."[84]

All that being said, aid did arrive, including food for literacy workers in July 1980. Midyear, the pro-government newspaper *El Nuevo Diario* could opine that Nicaragua had gained the respect of the world with its "clear non-aligned policy and international fraternity," as proven by a recent letter from Carter. When Fidel Castro visited Nicaragua to celebrate the first anniversary of Somoza's overthrow later that month, he reportedly told U.S. ambassador Lawrence Pezzullo that the "U.S. attitude toward Nicaragua had not been negative in everything during the past year." Pezzullo responded, "I believe, Mr. President, that both the U.S. and Cuba should continue to work in Nicaragua for the benefit of the Nicaraguan people as we have been doing." At the end of July, *La Prensa* warned of the consequences for U.S.-Nicaraguan relations should Ronald Reagan be elected. As Hitler was born politically in Versailles, the newspaper asserted, Reagan was born in Iran. "It is important," it warned, "to safeguard the revolution from the spirals of hardening [of positions] both within and beyond our frontiers."[85] As the crusade came to a close, positions were hardening on many sides, but the U.S. position was still relatively soft.

UNESCO, which had aided the Nicaraguan government from the early stages of the crusade, gave its seal of approval by awarding the government the Nadezhda K. Krupskaya Award in September. The campaign was credited with having reduced the illiteracy rate to 13 percent, with 406,056 learning to read and taking into account the roughly 130,000 who the government determined to be "unteachable or learning impaired."[86] A 1983 UNESCO report concluded that, combined with other government programs in the early years, such as expanded health services, price controls on "basic foodstuffs," and a "subsidy for certain essential goods and services, the far-reaching effects of the National Literacy Crusade stimulated improvement in the living standards of the working classes."[87]

As some sympathetic observers have suggested, the Nicaraguan revolution was a "nationalist revolution moving toward a class-based revolution."[88] As it was doing so, even during the course of the campaign, it began to gain new enemies internally and externally, even among those who had been the revolution's essential allies but who had a different understanding of the revolution. Although the Sandinistas had not completely split from and other prominent political and social actors by the end of the campaign, the lines had clearly been drawn, and hopes for preventing further conflict and polarization were fading even as the enthusiasm for the crusade was at its peak.

The Catholic Church in Nicaragua, which, as elsewhere, had been a major factor in the privately funded literacy programs that had existed during the postwar years, also contributed significantly to the success of the crusade. Pope John Paul II indicated his support for the campaign early on. Many of those involved in the Sandinista government were themselves, of course, clergymen, and many of the top officials in the crusade were priests. Freire noted "the remarkable, quite extraordinary presence of Christians, who though committed to the revolution, have not renounced their Christian standpoint." According to Ernesto Cardenal, Nicaragua was "the only country in which liberation theology was in power." Sandinistas during the literacy campaign spoke of bringing the "good news" of the revolution to the Nicaraguan people. The campaign was called a crusade, after all, and invoked the spirit of martyrs. Many Christians had joined the FSLN in the previous decade and a half because of their commitment to the "preferential option for the poor." Crusade coordinator Fernando Cardenal spoke of his enthusiasm for the prospect of creating in Nicaragua, "for the first time in history, a revolution [that] might establish a socialism that wouldn't be anti-Christian or anti-clerical." "It is not in spite of but because I am a Christian that I am working in the new government," he added. He hoped, in turn, "that the church wouldn't turn away from it and be its adversary." Indeed, many deeply religious lay Catholics were equally committed to the goals of the Sandinista government. Brigadistas, for their part, sought to reassure campesinos that, whatever they might have heard to the contrary, they were "very Catholic, as much as they were." Many campesinos were happy to have the brigadistas read the Bible to them, and some brigadistas spent time during the campaign teaching catechism. In Nicaragua in 1980, the language of revolution and the language of the church blended together. Fernando Cardenal spoke of the experience of the brigadista as one of conversion. His brother Ernesto considered Christianity and revolution to be one and the same. The attitude of the church hierarchy toward the campaign and even toward the government in 1980 was complicated. In the beginning, the hierarchy supported the crusade. In January, church officials suggested that those participating in the crusade also give "testimony of Christian life" to those they were teaching to read and write. Even the language they used was not all that different from that employed by the Sandinistas. Church officials and Sandinistas alike called for Christian love for one's fellow human beings, and that one should find "Christ in the face of each man who suffers." One of the official posters of the crusade, in fact, portrayed an image of Jesus Christ under the slogan, "Love your neighbors as yourself; teach them to read." At the same time, the church hierarchy wanted to maintain the distinctions between revolution and religion. The literacy training manual promised to respect "freedom of religion for all churches which defend the interests of the people," but, in fact, the popular church and the official church were increasingly at odds. As the campaign commenced, the church began to criticize the participation of clergy in the government. On 13 May, the Nicaraguan bishops asked the clergy to leave the government.[89] Nevertheless, although Archbishop Obando y Bravo was becoming one of the most vocal critics of the Sandinistas, he regularly praised the literacy campaign and held a mass in honor of the literacy campaign workers at the conclusion of the campaign in August.[90]

The church was an important internal actor, with whom reconciliation was still possible in August 1980. Relations with other Nicaraguans began to worsen even as the campaign began and the political direction of the government became clearer. The original Government of National Reconstruction contained two moderate members. One was Pedro Joaquín Chamorro's widow, Violeta Barrios de Chamorro. An unidentified photo of her appeared in literacy campaign materials, but, as so frequently happened during her tenure in government, she was seen but not often heard. The other moderate member, Alfonso Robelo, became the leading Nicaraguan critic of the literacy campaign in 1980. He had made millions during the Somoza years through his cooking oil business, but in the early months after the fall of Somoza he had supported many Sandinista policies, including the nationalization of banking.[91]

Both Robelo and Chamorro stepped down in late April following the expansion of the Council of State to guarantee Sandinista-linked organizations a majority. At the time of her resignation, Doña Violeta consistently rejected claims that she was leaving the government because of political disagreements, pointing out consistently that it was her chronic health problems that had prompted her decision. Her memoirs indicate that she was distrustful of the Sandinistas from the beginning and that she thought she was being used to project a more centrist image at home and abroad when it was really the FSLN directorate making all the decisions. Nevertheless, she was not a public critic of the FSLN in 1980.[92]

Robelo, on the other hand, had already begun to mount a series of attacks on the political direction of the Nicaraguan government beginning in

February. He had particularly harsh words for the crusade itself, even before the students left the Plaza; as early as 11 March 1980 he had already charged that the campaign was an attempt to "domesticate" the Nicaraguan poor. He encouraged peasants to boycott the literacy classes. Robelo increasingly warned of a "totalitarian threat" in Nicaragua.[93]

Representatives of the National Directorate accused Robelo and others of undermining the literacy campaign in an attempt to create a democracy in which "dignified sons of the people like [the martyr] Georgino Andrade Rivera" would be silenced.[94] Junta member Daniel Ortega labeled Robelo a "leader of the confiscated" with an egoistic consciousness, who, unlike other junta members whose children were working in the campaign, had sent his children to the United States, despite their own enthusiasm for joining it. Carlos Nuñez accused Robelo of trying to create a "carefully pre-fabricated crisis and destroy national unity." Robelo's use of the phrase "domestication" was frequently criticized; he was accused of calling campesinos animals, "because only animals are domesticated" (thereby demonstrating an ignorance of Freirean theory). Many blamed Robelo for the deaths of brigadistas, particularly in Matiguás, where he had spoken against "Cuban-Soviet penetration" shortly before attacks on brigadistas took place. One Sandinista official, arguing that the campaign was promoting critical, independent thinking and "opening the door to scientific knowledge," charged that "no honest Nicaraguan" with a "drop of patriotic blood" could oppose the crusade.[95]

Robelo's words and actions notwithstanding, it is wrong to suggest that the Nicaraguan bourgeoisie was already opposed to all government initiatives, least of all to the campaign itself. One only has to read La Prensa from this period to see that the Sandinistas were hypersensitive to criticism. Despite accusations to the contrary, the coverage of the crusade in La Prensa was consistently laudatory from beginning to end. In January, the newspaper encouraged parents to reject the "social egoism" that led them to keep their children from taking part in the campaign.[96] There were, in fact, internal conflicts over the political direction of the newspaper that led to the removal of pro-Sandinista Xavier Chamorro as director. A strike by newspaper workers that followed, Doña Violeta believes, was encouraged by "Sandinista party bosses." But even after La Prensa began to publish again in late May, the paper continued to support the campaign and to criticize in no uncertain terms the murder of literacy campaign workers. (Xavier Chamorro, at that point, it should be noted, created a new pro-government newspaper, the aforementioned El Nuevo Diario.)[97] "To oppose literacy training," a late-May article in

La Prensa suggested, is "to betray the future of Nicaragua." La Prensa director Pablo Antonio Cuadra argued in July, "We want to identify with the transformations our country and our people are undergoing." Cuadra contended that the paper was offering constructive criticism and that it was on the same path as an "organ of pluralist expression WITHIN the Revolution." The government was not criticizing errors that the paper was making, he insisted, but rather what the government called the paper's "intentions." Cuadra pleaded with the government "not to make an enemy where there is none."[98]

While there is no doubting the national appeal of the campaign, even among the bourgeoisie, there was also significant internal resistance. Rural landowners, for example, sometimes refused to help the campesinos pay for the "costs of sustaining extra mouths."[99] Certainly, as noted, there was a degree of suspicion and unwillingness to cooperate on the part of campesinos. But there is also evidence that the literacy campaign prompted some campesinos to turn against the revolution. A supporter of the contras interviewed by Timothy Brown for his book The Real Contra War has said that her family's refusal to provide lodging for the brigadistas led to their being labeled "Somocistas." Her father and a brother were jailed, and an entire group of her relatives was said to have been murdered "by a Sandinista mob." Brown suggests that the peasants, who were "eager to learn to read and write," resented the arrogant, even contemptuous, urban revolutionaries with their attacks on the church and praise for Cuba. Many resented having to feed and house the brigadistas. The crusade, according to Brown, had altered the peasants' consciousness, but not in favor of the revolution.[100]

The Nicaraguan campaign certainly encountered armed resistance to a degree no other literacy campaign discussed in this book experienced outside of Cuba in 1961. Following the fall of Somoza in July of 1979, many former members of and officers in his private army, the National Guard, resettled in other Central American nations, some merely in search of refuge, others to prepare for armed struggle against the government that the Sandinistas were trying to establish. Those who were to become known internationally as contras in the 1980s were not yet receiving international aid, not even, it seems, from Argentina, their first international patron. But, again according to Brown, there was popular resistance to the revolution from the beginning. For many of those engaged in the counter-revolution, the literacy campaign was among the most visible symbols of the new Nicaragua they were committed to defeating.[101]

Soon after the crusade began, women teachers were raped "in the name of the counter-revolution." Brigadistas demanded to know whether the government was committed to protecting them. Although the government could not guarantee that similar acts of violence would not occur again, two brigadista squadrons returned to work in the area in northern Nicaragua where the women had been raped. Spokesmen for the squadrons said that they did not want to abandon "their" campesinos. But the threat of violence continued. From the earliest days of the crusade, in areas near contra strongholds, particularly in the border region near Honduras in northern Nicaragua, armed men began threatening brigadistas. Brown suggests that peasants even asked guerrillas to target the brigadistas.[102]

The first person involved in the campaign to be murdered was the aforementioned Georgino Andrade Rivera, who, in May 1980, was captured and tortured for five hours (his fingernails were torn out) before being killed. His alleged killer, Pedro Rafael Pavon, confessed that he had killed him because Andrade Rivera was a communist, although he also admitted that he wasn't sure what it meant to be a communist. Others killed during the course of the campaign were also brutalized before they died. Those involved in the murder of Marta Lorena Vargas in Yalí, Jonetega, on 21 July reportedly warned that "the same would happen to all who refused to go back to their homes." Following the death of Georgino Andrade Rivera, the Juventud Sandinista and the Association of Nicaraguan Mothers demanded "popular justice." Special legislation requiring maximum penalties for murderers of brigadistas was passed. Pavon, who was sentenced to thirty years in prison in late August, was killed while trying to escape during a routine transfer in a military vehicle. A total of fifty-six people were attacked during the course of the campaign.[103]

The crusade, which itself invoked martyrs, now had martyrs of its own, seven of whom died during the campaign. At the opening ceremonies of the congress held to assess the progress of the campaign at its halfway point, Georgino Andrade Rivera was honored with a moment of silence and the revolutionary invocation, "Georgino Andrade Rivera, Presente." The martyrs of the crusade were now "indissolubly linked to the history of the great cultural epic of the Nicaraguan people." Rivera's death, moreover, reinforced the brigadistas' commitment to the campaign, as only a small number actually ended up abandoning their duties.[104]

The Sandinistas, meanwhile, were contributing in their own way to increasing divisiveness that would damage their hopes for success. The Sandinistas could never resolve the contradiction of seeking national unity while employing language that emphasized class struggle. Throughout 1980, Sandinista officials and the official Frente newspaper, *Barricada*, could not resist the temptation to lambaste those whom they called the bourgeoisie. Many who wrote for *La Prensa*, the proponent, it might be said, of bourgeois interests, criticized the use of language that they considered to be polarizing and counterproductive in what they believed was a distinctively Nicaraguan multi-class revolution. They also rejected restrictive definitions of "the people.". As one editorial asserted, "The worker is people. The peasant is people. The businessman is people. The bourgeois is people." And the thousands of children of businessmen and workers who were teaching people to read and write were people. The newspaper also pointed out the role of the bourgeoisie in resisting Somoza. While the Sandinistas argued that the extent of bourgeois involvement in resisting the dictatorship was overstated in retrospect, they could hardly deny that many members in their own ranks and leadership were themselves products of bourgeois backgrounds.[105] Most disturbing for many members of the bourgeoisie who were not Sandinistas must have been the frequent coupling of the word "bourgeoisie" with the phrase "vende patria" (to sell the country).[106] As Sandinista poet Belli later suggested, "Those [of us] who had come from the bourgeoisie but had identified ourselves with Sandinismo felt inhibited about calling attention to exclusionary tendencies and to the necessity of respecting agreements that had been reached with some of these sectors during the period of armed struggle."[107]

A literacy campaign that sought to achieve national unity might have more fully availed itself of Nicaraguan heroes of the bourgeoisie, not least of all Pedro Joaquín Chamorro. While the late scion of a family long prominent in Nicaraguan politics was no Sandinista, he had participated in anti-Somoza activities throughout his life, including engaging in armed rebellion in 1959, had been tortured in Somoza's prisons, and continued to write vigorously against the Somoza regime when *La Prensa* was allowed to operate.[108] Not only had he tried to promote mass literacy in the 1960s, as mentioned above, but his death in early 1978 at the hands of Somoza cronies had helped spawn the series of popular rebellions that ultimately brought Somoza down. He had been a unifying symbolic figure during the struggle against Somoza and honored by Los Doce. Considered by some "the father of Nicaraguan political pluralism," Chamorro became known as the "martyr of civil liberties." The anniversary of his death was celebrated as National Unity Day in early 1980, with Sandinista officials taking part and singing his praises. By taking the next step and including him among the pantheon of official heroes depicted in the literacy manuals, they might have undercut the idea that they were the sole guiding force of the ongoing revolutionary process, but it would have strengthened the national unity that the Sandinistas instead were undermining.[109]

The Sandinistas also could not overcome the contradiction of both espousing pluralism and promoting themselves as the vanguard. Not yet a party, as Belli recalls, "they [formed] a movement with which all the people felt identified."[110] They claimed that the government was pluralistic by pointing to the moderate members of the junta who replaced Chamorro and Robelo and to other parties that belonged to the Council of State, yet all decisions were made by the National Directorate of the Frente Sandinista. Moreover, the Council of State was expanded in April to make sure that Sandinista-affiliated organizations were in the majority. They refused to establish a party per se, because they felt that if they did so it would diminish their role as the representative of the people and the popular will. Their pluralism did not extend so far as to allow criticism of the revolutionary process, however, and they reserved the right to define who was in or outside of the revolution.[111]

Over the course of the literacy campaign, certain sectors of Nicaraguan society began to focus on the question of elections and when they would be held. Members of the business community claimed that promises regarding the timing of elections had yet to be fulfilled. The pressure mounted after the anniversary of the victory over Somoza had passed and no decision had been announced as members of the business group Consejo Superior de la Empresa Privada (High Council of Private Enterprise, COSEP) believed had been agreed upon.[112]

Many Sandinista officials at this point began to make clear how distinctly their visions of democracy diverged from many of those who were part of the bourgeoisie. During the discussion over elections, the Sandinistas offered a slap in the faces of two countries that had provided valuable aid during the liberation struggle. Costa Rica had served as a place of refuge for the Sandinistas, and arms had frequently flowed to Nicaragua through the country. Venezuela had provided economic aid and, according to most accounts, was the first to give military aid for the armed struggle. Venezuela under Carlos Andrés Pérez, flush with funds from the oil price shocks of the 1970s, had sought to increase its aid to countries in the Caribbean Basin and to engage with Castro to counter his attempts to spread his influence. The Venezuelan president also had encouraged the shift away from East-West issues and toward a sympathetic treatment of North-South issues. These efforts continued under his successor, Luis Herrera Campins, who continued to offer petroleum at lower prices to countries in Central America.[113] Nevertheless, neither Costa Rica nor Venezuela, one Sandinista official announced, would be the model for elections under the new government. After only a year in power, the Sandinistas were alienating some of their most significant allies in Latin America.[114]

Junta member Moises Hassan argued in July that there would be elections only when the Popular Sandinista Revolution wanted them and in the form in which it wanted them. As an editorial in the pro-government newspaper *El Nuevo Diario* put it, there could be no elections in which parties that wanted to put an end to the revolution could participate, and it ridiculed the notion that the Nicaraguan people should have the "democratic alternative of voting for their enemies." Omar Cabezas, a veteran Sandinista guerrilla who had toured Europe to raise money for the crusade, argued that the Nicaraguan people had won "the right to vote if they want to vote and not vote if they don't want to vote" (implying that they currently did not want to) and that the Nicaraguan people did not intend to vote away what they had won in the armed struggle.[115] *Barricada*, the Sandinista newspaper, defined democracy as a government whose programs were intended for the "benefit of the great majority."[116] Ernesto Cardenal suggests in his memoirs that the Somoza dictatorship had discredited words like "president" and "deputy," which Nicaraguans hated, and that no one wanted elections, which were associated with the old corrupt system. As a literacy worker argued midcampaign, the FSLN "did not in any way resemble the old and corrupt" parties of the past. Moises Hassan argued that Nicaraguan society was not ready for elections, particularly when people like Robelo and members of organizations like COSEP, as well as the United States, might try to buy votes.[117] Moreover, Sandinistas insisted that public turnout at rallies such as that at anniversary celebrations of the victory over Somoza on 19 July themselves constituted a vote for the FSLN. Articles in the Frente newspaper *Barricada* suggested that newly literate and politically conscious campesinos had rejected attempts by members of opposition political groups to create "false expectations regarding the possibility of elections" (and were requesting copies of the newspaper instead).[118] A relatively recent moderate member of the junta, Rafael Córdoba Rivas, for his part, suggested that the literacy campaign was making free elections possible for the first time. In the final days before the campaign ended, the other moderate junta member, Arturo Cruz, insisted that the "leaders of the vanguard had expressed the idea that the people had won the right to vote and that nothing was going to stop that." The emergency state was transitory, and people could have confidence in the "profound honor of the Revolution."[119]

Meanwhile, the brigadistas returned to Managua after five months to another massive rally on 23 August. Emotions ran high as they were reunited with their friends and family. Generally, there was a sense that they had achieved a second liberation.[120] But interpretations of what the actual outcome of the campaign was varied dramatically. For *Barricada* it was a triumph for the Sandinistas, proof of FSLN hegemony and the validation of its vanguard role.[121] Sandinista officials saw the literacy campaign as proof of the unifying and efficacious policies of the FSLN, which was helping organize the Nicaraguan people to solve the problems confronting the nation. Some believed that the campaign had prepared the way for democracy. At the rally, members of the National Directorate (not of the ostensibly governing junta) announced that elections would be held in 1985 and that the junta would run the country until then. Despite the much-heralded success of the crusade, according to the National Directorate, the Nicaraguan people still needed to be better prepared for self-government. Elections would not be held, young professionals told *Barricada*, until the people were "politically clarified." As an editorial in *El Nuevo Diario* contended, by 1985, the people would be educated enough to guarantee that the elections would be the "most faithful expression of the will of the people." Moreover, it was suggested that only those who were part of the revolutionary process would be eligible to run for election.[122]

Although *La Prensa* viewed the campaign as a great national triumph and a patriotic (and non-partisan) act, the newspaper conveyed the popular discontent with the delay in the elections and lamented the ongoing employment of hostile and militant language, which "gratuitously makes enemies." It called for a language "of dialogue."[123] Members of other political factions, including Robelo's Movimiento Democrático Nicaragüense (Nicaraguan Democratic Movement, MDN), continued to press for elections in the shorter term. They asked for technical assistance from Costa Rica and Venezuela, and thus Sandino's dream of free elections monitored by Latin American observers would be fulfilled.[124]

For their part, the FSLN put their faith in a popular democracy (and not a "bourgeois democracy") embodied in the new mass organizations, representing campesinos or factory workers or women. These organizations, some of which had been formed during the revolution and some in its immediate aftermath, had played a major role in helping manage the campaign and making it run smoothly, as well as in aiding in the political education of the brigadistas.[125] At the same time, these mass organizations, described in literacy training manuals as "the base of our democracy," were also supposed to be strengthened as the newly literate came to understand the need to "get involved in the decisions that affected them."[126] The most important of these types of organizations were the Sandinista Defense Committees. Their critics then as now have portrayed them as internal policing and spying organizations to whom the Sandinistas gave "the right to apprehend and expropriate 'suspicious-looking elements.'"[127] All these organizations suffered from top-down supervision by members of the FSLN directorate during the 1980s.[128]

In the years following the literacy campaign, the Sandinistas continued to promote what was by then known as popular education. Throughout the 1980s, to a large extent, the government continued to rely upon volunteers, particularly the recently literate popular classes themselves.[129] Nevertheless, after the initial peak in the literacy rate at the end of 1980, the rate declined over the course of the decade. By 1985, illiteracy had already risen to 20 percent. If the volunteers had succeeded in convincing their students that they were living in a changed environment in which possibilities had improved, it clearly must have been less evident, sooner or later, that having learned to read and write, there was much value in continuing to do so, and the illiteracy rates began to rise again. In 1984, according to the minister of education, Tünnermann Bernheim, 194,800 Nicaraguans were enrolled in adult education courses; the number quickly declined to 83,797.[130]

Over the course of the 1980s, education could no longer be the priority it had been in 1980. The government had to devote an increasingly large percentage of national resources to fighting the contra war, which meant that more positive aspects of the Sandinista agenda were abandoned. We cannot know what the government would have looked like had it been allowed to develop without external interference. What we do know is that illiteracy rates remained high. In 2004, schools were unavailable to an estimated one million school-age children.[131]

In the period of self-criticism that followed the FSLN's defeat in the 1990 election, some of the more thoughtful members of the FSLN admitted that the party had demonstrated an "incredible lack of knowledge of the psychology of the Nicaraguan people, particularly of the peasantry," despite having designed the programs that had been devoted ostensibly to improving their condition.[132] In retrospect, the "consciousness-raising" they believed they had witnessed during the campaign seemed illusory. In 1991, Daniel Ortega went so far as to say that "we didn't lose the peasantry because we never had it."[133] It was the young people of Nicaragua who had been more receptive to their message. In fact, the coordinator of the literacy campaign, Fernando Cardenal, went on to work with the Sandinista youth, in charge of "political training and propaganda."[134]

Twenty-five years after the revolution, many former members of the Sandinista youth were bankers and businessmen, and, *La Prensa* reported, "[a]lmost all [had] advanced academic degrees." Most, according to *La Prensa*, were by then critical of the FSLN and, if they were still politically active, belonged to groups that had split off from the party in the 1990s. They remembered the dedication of those years and their belief that they were involved in making Nicaragua change for the better. The campaign was the most important experience they had during the years the Sandinistas were in power, and they still considered it something worth celebrating.[135] By 2004, Fernando Cardenal had broken with the party, too, but he still considered the mobilization of tens of thousands of young Nicaraguans to have been an impressive task, which no current political leader in his country could accomplish.[136]

In many ways, the literacy campaign represented the Sandinistas at their best. As a Nicaraguan remarked to me in 2004, "Sure, the Sandinistas were trying to politicize people, but who else was going to go into the countryside and teach the campesinos to learn to read and write?" Their attempt to jump-start national reconstruction through education was ambitious and well-conceived. One could argue that the revolutionary fervor of the campaign years could not have been sustained. Cuba, some might suggest, represents a good example of how difficult it is to maintain high levels of voluntary participation for years, but it is also important to note that its educational achievements seem to have been more long-lasting and sustainable than those of the Sandinistas. (Cuba's literacy rates had been historically higher than Nicaragua's, of course, but many of the best educated left the country in the first few years after Castro consolidated his power; on the other hand, Nicaragua did not receive the massive aid from the Soviet Union that Cuba did.)

Like Freire's campaigns in Africa in the 1980s, the Sandinista campaign, which used Freire's techniques as a take-off point, intended to promote the hegemony of a one-party state. It promised to use mass organizations to provide popular input and rejected electoral democracy as premature, but it did not use the mass organizations to develop a new generation of popular leaders. Had the Sandinistas been able to sustain their education efforts throughout the decade, however, Nicaragua's democratization process in the 1990s might have been more profound than it was. The "old and corrupt" parties that Sandinistas had assumed were a thing of the past returned in the 1990s, and the FSLN ceased being a vanguard party in a democracy lacking not only modifying adjectives but also transcendent goals.[137]

Freire himself remained proud and uncritical of what he thought the Sandinistas had achieved in 1980 using his method. In an interview in the mid-1980s Freire quoted Nicaraguan ambassador to Brazil Ernesto Gutierrez, who considered the literacy campaign a success due to two factors: "the Freire method and the passion of Nicaraguans." Freire also reiterated his enthusiasm for the Nicaraguan revolution; by that time, however, he had been working for years to help consolidate Brazil's transition to a pluralist democracy, in which a party he had helped found, a party of workers and intellectuals, played an essential role.[138]

Six / The Long, Slow Transition to Democracy in Brazil & the End(?) of Utopia, 1980–1997

Paulo Freire returned to a Brazil that was still run by the military but experiencing "a concrete opening." Freire felt that he had to "take advantage of the existence of this space." The amnesty law of 1979 had made it possible for him and his family to make a life once again in his native land. After his return, he found it necessary, as he frequently noted, to "relearn Brazil" while responding to abundant invitations to speak throughout the country.[1] Brazil had undergone significant social and economic change since his departure in 1964, but these changes were not yet reflected in the political system. Brazil's transition to democracy would take most of the following decade, and Freire would play a role in the democratization process, first through his involvement with a new political party the likes of which Brazil had never seen before, the Partidos dos Trabalhadores (Workers' Party, PT), and then though his employment as the secretary of education in a PT municipal government in São Paulo. In the last decade of his life, the end of the Cold War also changed the international context in which Freire thought and worked.

The Brazil that Freire returned to was new in more ways than one. Economic growth and social change had continued to be uneven under the military, but in the late 1960s and early 1970s, growth rates in the gross domestic product had reached double-digit levels, constituting what became known as the Brazilian miracle. Industrialization and urbanization continued to accelerate as a result of government policies that encouraged foreign investment but also maintained a strong role for the state in the economy. The military model of economic growth exacerbated historical patterns of vast inequalities of income distribution. The years of the "miracle" were also the years

Paulo Freire and his wife Elza after their return to Brazil from exile, 1980. Photo courtesy of Lutgardes Costa Freire.

in which torture was employed most heavily as a means of keeping political opposition in check.[2]

In the 1970s, the military had borrowed heavily from Freire's literacy training methods in a program called the Movimento Brasileiro de Alfabetização (Brazilian Literacy Training Movement, MOBRAL). The primary method was the use of key words, but not ones that were particular to a given community or social group but those that were used throughout the country, in keeping with the military's nation-building goals. Not surprisingly, the dictatorship had no interest in replicating the mobilizing aspects of the Freire method. MOBRAL claimed to be ideologically neutral and did not attempt to examine the worldviews of teacher and student. The military government, more perhaps than any other government since the establishment of the republic in 1889, wanted to promote "order and progress" as well as economic development. While focusing on "functional literacy" and the creation of a more skilled labor force, this national program also sought to eliminate subversion. There was naturally no interest in promoting critical thinking about the social and economic order and about the military's chosen model of economic development. There was also a general tendency, as Gilberta Januzzi has argued, to view education as "information" in a most un-Freirean way. Yet even a somewhat critical observer of the campaign like H. S. Bhola has argued that MOBRAL "strengthened community awareness and collective action and . . . created a demand for wider and more effective political participation." To assess MOBRAL's impact, however, one also has to take into account the larger socioeconomic context in which Brazilian urbanization, industrialization, and economic diversification accelerated rapidly and that led to sociopolitical developments that the military could not altogether control. Moreover, some critics of the campaign have noted that the general rate of decline in illiteracy in the 1970s was the same as in the previous decade. In any case, illiteracy had declined to 25 percent by the year of Freire's return (it had been 40 percent in 1960).[3]

The Brazil Freire returned to was new in another way as well. Employment opportunities in universities in Brazil's more industrialized south led him to settle in São Paulo rather than to his native Pernambuco. Literacy rates were significantly higher in the urban south, "varying from 73 to 82 percent." São Paulo was not only economically stronger; it was also the center of a wide variety of social and political movements that were at the cutting edge of a push for the return to democracy.[4]

The Brazilian military, in power since 1964, had constructed a hybrid political system that they could control; it included a rubber-stamp Congress and a mandated and therefore artificial two-party system with fairly regular elections (although not for the presidency or the most important political positions). An international economic crisis brought on largely by actions of the Organization of Petroleum Exporting Countries (OPEC) in 1973 had put an end to the "economic miracle" of the late 1960s and early 1970s because of Brazil's heavy dependence at the time on the importation of foreign oil. The military responded to the crisis by borrowing money from international banks and loosening some of its controls over the political system. The official opposition party had taken advantage of its new political opportunities to win elections and encourage actions like the passage of the amnesty law that enabled Freire to return.[5]

As the military eased up on some of its restrictive policies, the hardship engendered by their economic policies began to spur the growth of a new union movement, which took shape in the industrial heartland of São Paulo. Workers in 1977 responded angrily to news that the government had been manipulating official inflation data in order to keep down wage increases linked to the inflation rate. In 1978, this led to strikes by a relatively privileged group of metalworkers at a Saab-Scania truck manufacturing plant in São Bernardo in the industrial suburbs. The union was led by a man named Luís Inácio Lula da Silva. The military initially responded weakly to the strikes, and other workers in the area soon joined them. The workers won wage increases from the company and gained the support of a now less rigidly controlled press, the Catholic Church, and a burgeoning civil society. Strikes in the following year were met with repression, but they also led to labor actions involving ultimately more than 3.2 million workers from a broad range of occupations in fifteen Brazilian states. Workers' demands expanded to include not only specific workers' issues such as the right to strike and to engage in collective bargaining, union autonomy, and internal democracy, but also a return to political democracy. By 1980, "Lula" (as he was known) himself had been declared in violation of the National Security Law (although his conviction was overturned on appeal) and was removed from his position as union leader. But a new, more militant working class had been created, representing, finally, for some, the awakening of the industrial workers' consciousness, and a political leader's career was launched.[6]

The workers' actions were the most dramatic sign of a strengthened opposition to the military government, which would only become more vigorous with the collapse of the Brazilian economy in the early 1980s. (Growth rates dropped to zero and then even negative growth rates were recorded.) The debts Brazil accumulated in an attempt to maintain economic growth rose dramatically, and Brazil, like much of Latin America, was soon an economic pariah in international financial markets.[7]

In an effort to divide the opposition and maintain control of the political system, the military dismantled the two-party system it had created and allowed new political parties to be established. Workers and sympathetic intellectuals had been meeting since the late 1970s to discuss the possibility of creating a new Socialist Party. Many on the Left wanted to keep the opposition strong and ideologically heterogeneous, while many workers themselves increasingly believed that it was necessary to create a new party. The PT, therefore, was founded in February of 1980. Freire himself had only briefly been affiliated with a political party as a young man. Although he had occasionally worked for governments attempting to establish partisan hegemony, as we have seen, he had foresworn partisan definitions on the personal level. He would make an exception to his rule for the PT. The PT, of which Freire became a founding member, was a quite self-consciously new development in Brazilian history. Members and leaders argued that the PT was beyond the populist parties that had existed in Brazil before 1964 and was authentically popular. "In my youth," Freire remarked, "I never imagined that the Workers' Party would have developed, though I used to feel the need for its existence. I waited more than forty years for the Workers' Party to be created." It was a party in which workers were now toiling for their own "emancipation" as political actors in their own right, to "learn the art of politics, government, and administration." Workers would no longer be simply "called to vote"; they would become candidates and elected officials. At the same time, the PT intended to encourage popular organization and to "democratize society" while fighting "for power." The peculiarities of the military-dominated political system allowed this new political party and the larger social movements, including shantytown neighborhood associations, peasant organizations, church groups, and the new unions that surrounded and supported the party, to grow even while the government was still led by a four-star general. The party had to work on two fronts, both to encourage a transition to civilian rule and to shape the nature of the democracy they envisioned. The PT rejected the idea that democracy was a "bourgeois value," seeing it as a "universal ideal" that had been "taken by the working class from the hands of the bourgeoisie, and made a conquest of humanity." Moreover, the PT also had to become a national party, because it was far stronger in the state of São Paulo than it was in the rest of Brazil.[8]

An extremely active group of educators was tied to the PT; Freire was one of the most prominent. They began meeting in July of 1980, soon after Freire's definitive move to São Paulo from Geneva. The party's education commission, created a month later, was based in São Paulo. The commission intended to define educational policies that would be oriented toward workers' interests (instead of against them, as PT members argued had been traditionally the case in Brazil) and that would help to "contribute toward the building of a socialist society." As Freire's associate Moacir Gadotti argued, "The PT . . . is a popular educator of the masses in the way in which it raises consciousness in favor of and against those [the masses] struggle against." The party could not, according to Freire, "be the educator who already knows everything, which already has an untouchable truth, in front of popular masses that are [seen as] incompetent and in need of guidance and salvation."[9]

Freire and other PT leaders, like Carlos Rodrigues Brandao, emphasized the role that political parties had to play in educating their own party members and in making it possible for them to take part in political action. At the same time, the party had a specific role to play in criticizing existing educational systems and practices and to propose alternatives to them. Gadotti contended that while the current government had "bet on ignorance," a national mobilization under a PT administration could eliminate illiteracy in less then three years.[10]

Throughout the 1980s, Freire continued to teach (at the State University of Campinas and the Catholic University of São Paulo) and write about issues that had long interested him, but he also began to take part in the development of the PT's theoretical framework. Building on ideas Freire had begun working on with SESI in the 1950s in Pernambuco, the PT began to put forth ideas regarding the creation of a more democratic school system, with increased involvement of parents and community members from the popular classes in the decision-making process. Educators, often defining themselves as workers, also sought to organize themselves more effectively to represent their own interests. Education became a central theme in local elections in which the party put forth candidates. Central to the PT program, not surprisingly, was a vigorous defense of public education in a country in which private schools of higher quality prepared students from the middle and upper classes to pass the entrance examinations for the free public universities.[11]

Over the course of the 1980s, the shape of a postmilitary democratic order was defined. And while the military certainly had some control over the speed and timing of their departure from the nation's political life, a wide variety of political actors sought to take part in the creation of what became known as the "new republic." In 1982, direct elections were held for state governors for the first time in almost two decades. In 1984, a movement to restore direct elections for the presidency, in which the PT played a leading role, served, as Freire argued, its own educational purpose in countering the military's notion that the Brazilian people were not yet ready. The amendment was defeated in a Congress still controlled by allies of the military.[12] Divisions among the forces that hitherto had supported the military made it possible for the opposition candidate, Tancredo Neves, to be chosen as the first civilian president in more than twenty years. The elderly man's death prior to his inauguration prevented his taking office and ironically led a longtime supporter of military rule, his vice president José Sarney, to become president.

As civilians took control at all levels of government, a critical component in the democratization process was the drafting of a new constitution, which a constituent assembly began discussing in February of 1987. Since the 1982 elections, opposition politicians had been calling for the vote for illiterates, a measure that President Goulart had failed to get passed by Congress in the years before the 1964 coup.[13] Discussions continued through October 1988, with illiterates' right to vote written into the constitution. While for the rest of the population between the ages of eighteen and seventy, voting was mandatory, for illiterates, it was optional. The government also promised to establish a multi-year "national education plan" that promised, among other things, to eradicate illiteracy. The new constitution, according to PT leaders, included a few "small victories, a few small conquests, some minimum rights for workers."[14]

During the 1980s, as Brazil's internal evolution engaged much of his attention, Freire also continued to travel throughout the world. His most notable trip during this time period was to Cuba in 1987 for a psychologists' conference. This was his first and only trip to Cuba, where his work was little known. The invitation seems to have been motivated in part by an evolving interest on the island in liberation theology. He was moved by the experience, telling his Cuban hosts, "I believe you understand the emotion I feel setting foot on a soil where there is no child without a school, where there is no one who has not eaten today." He praised the Cuban and Nicaraguan literacy campaigns, and declared himself to be a progressive popular educator in a bourgeois country. If it were a merely a mechanical question, Freire said, he would help Lula make revolution in Brazil. "But it is not a mechanical process, but a historic one." Popular education in Brazil had to take place within the existing popular movements. He told his hosts that he did not expect to see the transformations take place in Brazil that had taken place in Cuba and Nicaragua. He praised Cuba for what he said were its "horizon of liberty [and] . . . creativity" and the willingness to admit errors.[15]

Around this time, Freire also received the most significant international recognition for his life's work. In 1986, UNESCO awarded him its prize for peace education. Director Amadou-Mahtar M'Bow noted Freire's "unflagging determination and devotion to provide literacy training and education for the neediest population groups—thereby enabling them to take an active part in the struggle against poverty, the eradication of which is one of the key preconditions for the establishment of a lasting peace."[16]

While Freire continued to teach and write, as well as travel and receive awards, the November 1988 election of the PT's Luiza Erundina as mayor of São Paulo made it possible for him to play a more active role in his nation's educational and political life. A northeasterner like Freire and a social worker, Erundina had been involved in Freirean literacy movements as a young woman and had worked on behalf of the homeless in the city.

A founding member of the PT, she had served on the city council and as a state representative. Her victory with 30 percent of the vote and by only a small margin over the longtime military ally Paulo Maluf was surprising. Mayor Erundina chose Freire to be her secretary of education in the municipal government beginning in January of 1989. Freire recalled that he "was overtaken with doubts, fear, joy, a sense of duty, hope, dreams, and my need for taking risks," and that he "felt the need to be coherent with all I had up to now spoken and written about in education." If it were not coherent, he said, he would have had to throw away all that he had written and never speak again. His new position enabled the educator and party militant to focus on a much broader range of issues than he had ever had to address before. Freire began to write a series of informal letters to educators in the municipality to begin a dialogue over common educational tasks. He proposed an education in which the child's own knowledge and cultural frames of reference would be respected and in which mutual help and working in groups rather than competition and individualism would be encouraged. He argued that many "dropouts" were actually expelled because of class-based assumptions about knowledge and behavior. Freire proposed a school that would be both "serious" and "happy" and would encourage communitywide participation in discussions of curricular issues. Freire brought in specialists in all areas of learning to help reform the curriculum. But he and his associates also prepared material to "open debate" and "revitalize discussion and reflection" regarding curricular issues. Beginning in 1990, it solicited more input from residents through what was called the "Citizen School" and created a program called "Would you accept a word of advice?" The attempt to move beyond authoritarian models of school organization and administration was built on plans initiated toward the end of the Mario Covas administration to provide not just a "word of advice" but also, as implied in the double meaning of the question, school councils, which had been held in abeyance by the Jânio Quadros administration that had succeeded it. The democratization of the schools placed extra demands on all involved. Teachers were now having to devote more of their evening hours not only to preparing classes but also to taking part in discussions over how to transform the public schools. There was also an attempt to move beyond the idea of students "as consumers" and parents as providers of financial support.[17]

Undoubtedly, as secretary, Freire found much that frustrated him. The dilapidated state of and indeed the often precarious and sometimes even dangerous conditions in the schools themselves was one of them. In some schools, rain flooded classrooms and "sewage systems [were] plugged up." "About fifty school buildings," Freire noted, "were in a deplorable state with ceilings failing, floors caving in, electrical wiring presenting real threats to life; fifteen thousand school desks were broken, and many schools were without any desks whatsoever." Many schools had to be closed for repairs, with apparently no money to fix them. The economic crisis in Brazil, with more than 30 percent monthly inflation, made it difficult to even begin to address these problems, particularly when the municipal government itself had inherited a debt of $1.5 billion in 1989. Official social spending increased from 33.5 percent under Quadros to 48 percent. In 1989, 20.8 percent of the city budget was to be devoted to education. Freire found it difficult to adjust to working with a bureaucracy, something he had never found appealing. In Brazil, it was "suffocating." In addition, as a participant in the "Would you accept a word of advice?" program suggested, there was a good deal of resistance among members of the education bureaucracy who saw their power threatened by attempts to decentralize the school system, as well as a general lack of trust in the ability of the popular classes to form an opinion and make decisions regarding school issues. Administrators and teachers did not often know how to talk to parents and students in a language "accessible to everyone." The Erundina administration also had to contend with striking public employees (many of whom were PT members), whose demands the city could not afford to meet. Her administration, having barely been elected with the support of less than a third of the electorate, suffered from low approval ratings and the lack of support from federal and state governments and the city council.[18]

UNESCO had declared 1990 to be the "international year of literacy training," and the Erundina administration, inevitably, focused on this issue. Official statistics indicated that there were more than 1.5 million illiterates in the metropolitan area; an additional 2.5 million had fewer than four years of education. Many of these illiterates had migrated to São Paulo from the northeast and from the rural parts of the state. Surprisingly, perhaps, Freire did not want to address the issue via a mass campaign that he feared would give "literacy work an emergency character." The municipal government encouraged the growth of community neighborhood literacy training programs through the Movimento de Alfabetização de Jovens e Adultos (Literacy Movement for Youth and Adults, MOVA). Erundina's "popular democratic" government, as Freire defined it, had the "indispensable political will" to launch an effective literacy campaign that had been lacking in the previous administration. Freire spoke of the illiterates' difficulties in "exercising fully their rights of citizenship." As he had in much of his career (albeit with exceptions already noted), he wanted to stimulate critical thinking and political consciousness. He predicted that with the cooperation of popular organizations and the decisive action of leaders, both of which were taking place during his tenure, illiteracy could be eliminated in ten years in the country as a whole. In São Paulo, local community groups were encouraged to choose whatever methodological approach best suited their needs. The relationship between these groups and the secretariat was both promising and problematic. "The Secretariat does not want to absorb the movements," Freire said, "but neither does it want to simply give away" money. Expectations were that an additional 180,000 people would know how to read and write by the end of Erundina's term in office. The MOVA program, first discussed several months after Erundina was inaugurated, did not get off the ground until late in the year. Funding itself did not become available until March of 1990. Although a large number of literacy training programs were launched in the next couple of years by roughly seventy grassroots groups, many of the groups themselves had virtually no experience in the area.

Freire did not work for partisan hegemony, as he had in various African countries and in Nicaragua. The pluralistic political system within which he operated made that impossible. Instead, he spoke once again of "the people" and of their achieving hegemony. Although Freire had been working with primers for years, despite the frequent criticisms he had made of them, MOVA did not produce one, and this prevented the type of partisan indoctrination that had made many question Freire's actual practice rather than his theory.[19]

Not surprisingly, given the impact of migration from the northeast to São Paulo, more than half of those who participated in the MOVA literacy programs were from Freire's own region. A little less than two-thirds of the students were women, a proportion that might have been even higher if many women had not had small children or husbands unsympathetic to their interest in enrolling in a literacy class. Nelly Stromquist, a North American education specialist who studied gender dynamics in MOVA, argues that many of the women who did participate became more self-confident and assertive as a result of their classes. She laments the fact that students liberated to read chose to "consume the messages produced by the upper classes," particularly those addressing "feminine" issues. As with previous Freirean programs, the impact on the teachers themselves was significant, although there was less of a class divide in the MOVA program than there had been in many of the other campaigns.[20]

Freire did not remain as secretary of education throughout Erundina's term in office. After two and a half years, he had missed teaching and reading too much to continue as an administrator. But administration officials believed that there had been substantial improvements in the school's education system during his tenure. An additional 120,358 students were enrolled in the public schools, an increase of 15.59 percent, in large part because an additional seventy-seven schools had been built, and in spite of the fact that less federal money was available for school construction than had been in the past. Student dropout and failure rates dropped substantially, as well. Freire's direct contact with large numbers of teachers, which was unusual for an administrator at this level, evidently had an impact on morale. Nevertheless, some of Freire's associates had doubts about how the school system was responding to their attempts at reform. Freire's chief of staff, Moacir Gadotti, for example, left the administration several months before, in large part because he felt that the grassroots movements had not been given sufficient autonomy. Some suggested that Freire left because of his problems with the lack of sympathy for his ideas among a preexisting and permanent bureaucracy. An unidentified member of the PT cited in Stromquist's book noted, "We won an election; we didn't make a revolution." In any case, the PT program of popular education ended when a conservative candidate won the mayoral race in the next election.[21]

The last decade of Freire's life roughly coincided with the end of the Cold War. The 1990s saw a general narrowing of ideological options throughout the world. There was no longer a "Third World," in part because there was no longer a second one, not only because the Soviet bloc and the Soviet Union itself collapsed, but also because the economic success of a number of Asian countries created increasing gaps between countries that previously had been seen as having much in common. Freire himself had never been an admirer of the Soviet Union or Eastern European communist countries, but he was certainly disappointed to see the Sandinistas, whom he had so much admired, voted out of office. More generally, some of the "winners" in the Cold War even went so far as to claim that history itself had ended since there were no longer any alternatives to capitalism or a rather narrowly defined democracy.[22]

Freire spent a great deal of intellectual energy in the last years of his life trying to combat the idea of the end of history (and, indeed, the notion that he himself was already a part of the past and not of the present or the future). He continued to emphasize the alternatives open to humanity and the unfinished quality of reality and to emphasize process over results. He continued to stress the difficulties of creating a democracy in a country such as Brazil with such vast social inequities and bad political habits. At the end of his life, a dynamic life filled with valuable contributions and unacknowledged failures, Freire clung to the idea of utopia, to possibility.[23]

Epilogue / Legacies of a Cold War Intellectual in a Post-Cold War World

Since his death on 2 May 1997, Paulo Freire's writings, ideas, and techniques have had a life of their own. They may, at times and in turn, create their own historical contexts. His influence remains strong, particularly among those involved in what is known as popular education and among those in the academic world who practice what they call critical pedagogy.[1] As the second decade of the twenty-first century begins, literacy campaigns as part of state projects are still often associated with the Left, whether in Húgo Chávez's Venezuela (where the teachers are often Cuban) or in Maoist Nepal. UNESCO, still given to naming years and even decades of literacy, has not given up hope that by 2015, "education for all" will be attained and the adult illiteracy rate will be cut in half.[2]

Illiteracy remains a global problem, with an estimated one in five adults (774 million people) illiterate. But the illiteracy of the present is both more and less of a problem in a world in which the majority of the population lives in cities than it was in the rural societies of the past. Urbanites may have more opportunities to become literate, and urban life often makes reading and writing skills more necessary, which can create a greater incentive to learn to read and write. In any case, literacy is no longer the urgent issue that it was during the Cold War. The global reach of the Cold War meant that all corners of the world could be perceived as being at risk of falling into the opposing group; superpowers had more reasons to compete for loyalty and to provide support for development. As we have seen, it was that perceived sense of urgency that helped make Freire's work even more important than it

In 1993, thirty years after the literacy campaign in Angicos, Rio Grande do Norte, which made Freire nationally renowned, a local public school honored Freire. He is pictured here with his students from the campaign. Photo courtesy of Lutgardes Costa Freire.

would have been otherwise.[3] As the Cold War ended, complacency settled in, and much of the world could safely be ignored. Or so it seemed.

Paulo Freire was not only a significant figure in intellectual and educational circles in his time but also an important political actor. It is a tribute to the power of his ideas that they could be employed in countries with formal democratic systems, as well as in countries recently emerging from colonial status or dictatorships. If his language often now seems time-bound, it is in part because we are living in a post–Cold War world. The Cold War shaped his career, and both limited and expanded his horizons. If the Cold War provided an impetus at times for a deepening and consolidation of democracy in parts of South America, in particular, and at least temporarily, it also distorted these political processes, often halting significant progress and reversing it at critical moments. The failure of the United States to stay true to its democratic principles undoubtedly had an impact on the thinking of many on the democratic Left in Latin America.

But the Latin American Left, as personified by Freire, had its own illusions, its own impatience, and its own inability to stay true to its democratic beliefs. And it is striking how some segments of the Latin American Left became more rigid even as their options narrowed and the chances of achieving power became extremely remote. It was the pluralism of the Brazil of the early 1960s and of Chile before 11 September 1973 that increased the democratic potential of Freire's ideas. Cold War realities could not allow this pluralism to survive, even in the "Free World." Freire's historical experiences suggest that he should have embraced political pluralism more readily and more consistently, but the Left's disdain for "bourgeois democracy" and enthusiasm for the one-party state were slow to wane.

And the Cold War transformed the context in which this man from the Brazilian northeast operated. Freire was purely a nationalist as long as he remained in Brazil, and yet even during his years as an internationalist he never truly abandoned the hope for a unifying nation-state, even one in the form of (and one might say compressed into) the Leninist one-party nation-state. Freire's career exemplifies the promise and failures of a generation that moved from dreams of development to ones of liberation. Without the Cold War, the drive for development would still have inspired many to try to change their societies, even if their efforts would not have attracted so much attention from the United States. But Freire's own political evolution would have been dramatically different had he not been a nationalist forced by political circumstances to work for a decade and a half in exile. He deeply regretted having to leave his native country, yet he would not have been quite the historical figure he became had he remained.

Had he not been forced to leave Brazil, the contradictions in his thought and practice perhaps would not have become so pronounced. He contributed to the deepening of democracy in countries with pluralistic traditions and aided the legitimation of one-party states in countries that lacked them. His successes, compromises, failures, and mistakes need to be examined closely because they reflect in so many ways the strengths and weaknesses of a Latin American new Left whose history is just beginning to be written. I believe that history will show that it was the Left's contributions to democratization that will be their most lasting. By the 1980s, as I have suggested, the Latin American Left learned its lesson when it embraced pluralism in political competition and other "bourgeois" ideals that it had previously dismissed.[4]

Freire's lifelong engagement in dialogue with the poor was admirable, and his faith in cross-class alliances never fundamentally disappeared, in part because however much he denied it, his vision was still profoundly shaped by the nationalism of his younger years. One may be less impressed by his relative lack of interest in engaging with people who were not poor and who were politically to his right.

Freire's ideals were often compromised in practice, as the previous chapters demonstrate. To some degree, it is hard to imagine how they could not have been, particularly when they were employed on the national level and, even more importantly, by one-party states. The temptation for states to use his techniques to foster loyalty to the state and to its programs and goals was always too great. And, undoubtedly, states generally prefer that people focus more on becoming productive workers than on becoming critical thinkers. (Educators, for their part, often become uncomfortable with overly critical, thoughtful students, but it is to be hoped that Freire's writings will continue to challenge teachers to examine their own practices.) And while it may dismay some to discover how much of Freire's efforts involved working for or advising states, it may also be said that his work was most effective in those places where at least one of the major goals of the government was to expand civil society. His techniques can still be employed to promote active citizenship. Encouraging people to participate in organizations of their own and helping them mobilize themselves in defense of their own interests, however, is vastly different from marching voters to the polls or to the plaza in support of government initiatives or inviting them to join organizations created by the state. (And historians should themselves make more of an effort to examine the processes through which people historically have become citizens.) To Freire's credit, even in the early 1960s, which are so often characterized as his populist years, he never encouraged (nor did those who employed his techniques) loyalty to the charismatic leaders that are so frequently seen as being the bane of populist political systems. Those interested in the relationship between classes and between states and their citizens, particularly in countries in the process of democratization (as well as "development"), will continue to profit from reading Freire's work. His endeavors were always most democratic when they emphasized process over results (witness the constant struggle over the use of primers in the literacy campaigns). Moreover, Freire recognized the difficulties in the relationship between teachers and students when it moved beyond paternalism, particularly when that relationship involved an attempt to communicate between classes, and even more so when it involved an attempt to change people. (The desire to improve others should always lead to the soul-searching and self-criticism that Freire insisted on, at least in theory.)

It is easy to understand why Freire was so drawn to work for newly independent countries and in revolutionary societies. He had already worked for a "Brazilian Revolution" and a "Revolution in Liberty" with results that were not to his liking. The desire to wipe the slate clean was strong on the Latin American Left, burdened as it was by so much antidemocratic history in the region. For that matter, while the desire to create political utopias in the twentieth century often had monstrous consequences around the world, the refusal to embrace dreams can also lead to stagnation and despair.

What would Freire have made of Luís Inácio Lula da Silva's presidency? Would he agree with Plínio de Arruda Sampaio, a fellow former exile and cofounder of the PT, who has criticized the administration for failing to promote the transformation of society? Indeed, Freire's former colleague maintains, the Lula administration has engaged not in "a dialogue with the popular sector [but rather in] a good dialogue with the dominant class, and in a fraternal way." Given the range of reactions of Freire's friends, family, and associates to the Lula government, however, one should not be tempted to commit the sin of putting words in the mouth of the dead.[5]

The language Freire employed, as mentioned, may often seem timebound. Relatively few now use such abstract terms as "the people," let alone "the oppressed." Freire's move from a humanist to a class perspective was never complete, and his imprecision and inclusiveness now seem more like strengths than weaknesses, which they were perceived to be at the time. The idea of the Third World itself, which he and others embraced, was similarly capacious, even though at times the idea was often sentimental and emotionally more than intellectually satisfying, and even intellectually misleading. It was the collapse of this idea, far more than the failure of the Soviet bloc, that made the post–Cold War world less hospitable to those who shared Freire's dreams. After the fall of the Berlin Wall, the Left's greatest strength remained its immunity to the overselling of the market as the solution to all problems, even as its faith in the state was somewhat tempered. But the decline of a common "Third World" project of development and economic liberation has had its costs. The poorer peoples of the world do not need to be encouraged to think that their condition is permanent, and Freire would have been the last person in the world who would have encouraged them to do so.[6]

Given the nature of Paulo Freire's theories, it should hardly be surprising that those who have remained most faithful to the best of them often are those who have been engaged in private and nongovernmental, often church- or community-based, educational activities as part of broader popular movements. The proliferation of these groups in recent decades has been an important factor in the development of Latin American democracy in particular. Much of the vitality of democratic practice in Latin America today is still derived from these groups. Freire certainly would have found some personal satisfaction in that.

Notes

Abbreviations

APE-PE	Arquivo Público Estadual de Pernambuco
APE-RGN	Arquivo Público Estadual de Rio Grande do Norte
BCNC	Biblioteca del Congreso Nacional de Chile, Santiago
Carter Library	Jimmy Carter Presidential Library, Atlanta, Georgia
CCIAF	Churches' Commission International Activities Files
CCPDF	Commission on Churches' Participation in Development Files
CPDOC	Centro de Pesquisa e Documentação de História Contemporânea do Brasil, Rio de Janeiro
DOPS	Departamento de Ordem Político e Social (Department of Political and Social Order), Pernambuco
FRUS	U.S. Department of State, *Foreign Relations of the United States* (Washington: Government Printing Office, 1958–68)
FUNESC	Fundação Espaço Cultural da Paraíba in João Pessoa (Cultural Space Foundation of Paraíba), Arquivo Histórico, João Pessoa, Paraíba
IP	Inquérito Policial
IPF	Instituto Paulo Freire (Paulo Freire Institute), São Paulo
JFK Library	John F. Kennedy Presidential Library, Boston, Massachusetts
PPPUS	*Public Papers of the Presidents of the United States* (Washington: Federal Register Division, National Archives and Records Service, General Services Administration, 1961–62)
RG 59	Record Group 59, Department of State, National Archives II, College Park, Maryland
RG 84	Record Group 84, Department of State, National Archives II, College Park, Maryland
RG 286	Record Group 286, U.S. Agency for International Development, National Archives II, College Park, Maryland
SECERN	Serviço Cooperativo de Educação (Cooperative Education Service)
Sergipe Inquérito	Poder Judiciário, Estado de Sergipe, Comarca de Aracaju—Segunda Vara Criminal, Forum Gumercindo Bessa, Auditória da Sexta Regiao Militar (Exército, Marinha, e Aeronautica) Bahia—Sergipe Number 27/65, 1965
STM	Superior Tribunal Militar (Military High Court), Brasília
UCA	Universidad Centroamericana, Instituto de Historia de Nicaragua y Centroamérica, Managua
WCCA	World Council of Churches, Archives, Geneva

Introduction

1. Freire's longtime associate Marcos Arruda plays with one of these images when he has President Luís Inácio Lula da Silva mistake St. Peter for Freire in "Crônica de Amanha," in *Cartas a Lula*, p. 228. See also the discussion of Freire as myth in Alípio Casali and Vera Barreto's preface in Ana Maria Araújo Freire, *Paulo Freire*, pp. 20–21.

2. See Westad, *Global Cold War*, particularly pp. 3–7, 32–38, 67–72, 86–109, and 396–404; and Cullather, "Miracles of Modernization," p. 231.

3. Graff, *Labyrinths of Literacy*, pp. 2–3. Graff argues that simple causal linkages between literacy and development are not sustained by historical evidence. See also Staples, *Birth of Development*, particularly pp. 1–12, although she does not address literacy itself. Nor does Arturo Escobar, *Encountering Development*, or Saldaña-Portillo, *Revolutionary Imagination*. For a recent discussion of the presumed link between literacy and development, see Bartlett, "Human Capital or Human Connections?," particularly pp. 1613–18 and 1628–30.

4. Cullather, "Miracles of Modernization," p. 227; Weinstein, "Developing Inequality."

5. Graff, *Labyrinths of Literacy*, p. 30.

6. Hobsbawm, *Age of Extremes*, pp. 96–97, 272–74, and 377–86. For a different perspective, which stresses a more mainstream European acceptance (and a more complicated etiology) of planning, see Judt, *Postwar*, particularly pp. 67–77. On the increasing acceptance in the United States of the idea of planning (and particularly how it played a role in the postwar transformation of Japan), see Westad, *Global Cold War*, p. 24. See also Arnove and Graff, *National Literacy Campaigns*, p. 3.

7. Graff, *Labyrinths of Literacy*, pp. 35 and 61; Arnove and Graff, *National Literacy Campaigns*, pp. 5, 6–8, and 10–17. Regarding "modernity," see Cooper, *Colonialism in Question*, particularly pp. 113–49.

8. Bhola, *Campaigning for Literacy*, pp. 39–57; Ben Ekloff, "Russian Literacy Campaigns, 1861–1939," in Arnove and Graff, eds., *National Literacy Campaigns*, pp. 127–29, 134–35, 138–41, and 144–45. See also Fitzpatrick, ed., *Cultural Revolution in Russia*, pp. 1–2 and 25–26; Fitzpatrick, *Education and Social Mobility in the Soviet Union*, pp. 9, 158–59, 161–64, and 171–72; Gail Warshofsky Lapidus, "Educational Strategies and Cultural Revolution: The Politics of Soviet Development," in Fitzpatrick, ed., *Cultural Revolution in Russia*, pp. 79–80; and Reese, *Stalin's Reluctant Soldiers*, pp. 80–82. Regarding the New Economic Policy phase, see Clark, *Uprooting Otherness*, pp. 15, 17–19, 32–33, 36–37, 72, 87–88, 93, 115–16, 170, and 178–80.

9. Charles W. Hayford, "Literacy Movements in Modern China," in Arnove and Graff, eds., *National Literacy Campaigns*, pp. 163–64 and 167; for an official perspective, see Wang Yanwei, "People's Participation and Mobilization: Characteristics of the Literacy Campaigns in China," in Carron and Bordia, eds., *Issues in Planning*, pp. 47–50; for a sympathetic treatment, see Bhola, *Campaigning for Literacy*, pp. 73–90.

10. For a discussion of the evolution of Marxist understandings of consciousness, see, for example, Kolakowski, *Main Currents of Marxism*, particularly pp. 105–7, 121–22, 128–30, 143–45, 148–49, 262–67, 278–84, 386–88, 420–24, 566–76, 664–74, 1010–13, and 1180–83. On the emphasis on state planning in the Third World, see, for example, Westad, *Global Cold War*, pp. 90–97; and Engerman, *Modernization from the Other Shore*, pp. 153–243.

11. For an admiring portrait of Laubach, see Medary, *Each One Teach One*, particularly pp. 4–6, 16–18, 21–27, 36–62, 81–109, and 116–22.

12. Kirkendall, *Class Mates*, particularly pp. 39–61, and "Student Culture and Nation-State Formation."

13. Szuchman, *Order, Family, and Community in Buenos Aires*, pp. 151–63.

14. Vaughan, *State, Education, and Social Class in Mexico*, pp. 14, 25, 33–35, 89, 113–15, 125, 144, 162, 189, 211, and 258–66. See also Vaughan, *Cultural Politics in Revolution*, pp. 5–6, 44, 65, 75, and 189–201. Regarding Torres Bodet, see Jones, *International Policies for Third World Education*, pp. 38–40.

15. Arthur Gillette, "The Experimental World Literacy Program: A Unique International Effort Revisited," in Arnove and Graff, eds., *National Literacy Campaigns*, p. 197. Phillip W. Jones calls "universal literacy" UNESCO's "most extensive and intensive single commitment" (Jones, *International Policies for Third World Education*, p. 1).

16. Kirpal, "UNESCO's Contribution to Development," in Pompei et al., *In the Minds of Men*, p. 117; Jones, *International Policies for Third World Education*, pp. 33–34. Jones's fine work aside, the history of UNESCO is just beginning to be written. See Droit, *Humanity in the Making*, particularly pp. 43, 50, 57–59, 62, and 66.

17. A good introduction to the subject can be found in Oman and Wignaraja, *Postwar Evolution of Development Thinking*, particularly pp. 1–2, 9–13, and 37–57. See also Love, *Crafting the Third World*, pp. 1–5 and 213–26; and Mallorquin, *Celso Furtado*, pp. 26–29, 32–46, and 51–81.

18. Regarding "fundamental education," see Jones, *International Policies for Third World Education*, pp. 22–23, 26, and 47–87; and UNESCO, *World Illiteracy at Mid-Century*, pp. 5, 16, and 190–93. See also Lionel Elvin, "Education," in Pompei et al., *In the Minds of Men*, pp. 55 and 58–59; Kirpal, "UNESCO's Contribution to Development," in Pompei et al., *In the Minds of Men*, p. 123; René Maheu, "Serving the Minds of Men," in Pompei et al., *In the Minds of Men*, pp. 301–3; Droit, *Humanity in the Making*, pp. 57–59; and Valderrama, *History of UNESCO*, pp. 47, 60, 66, 82, 104, and 124.

19. Westad, *Global Cold War*, pp. 106–9.

20. Adiseshiah's remarks in UNESCO Correspondence Files 372 (8) MP 01 A 63 (81), "Extension Primary Education LA Major Project No. 1," 17 March 1958, pp. 2, 12, and 14. For a general introduction to UNESCO's efforts in Latin America in the first twenty-five years of its existence, see Juan Goméz Millas, "Latin America," in Pompei et al., *In the Minds of Men*, pp. 177–99. See also *UNESCO Courier*, July/August 1966, p. 72.

21. I discuss this at some length in *Class Mates*.

22. Bomeny, *Os Intelectuais da Educação*, pp. 11–21. The history of voting in Brazil is traced in Letícia Bicalho Canêdo, "Aprendendo a Votar," in Pinsky and Pinsky, eds., *História da Cidadania*, pp. 517–43. See also Love, "Political Participation in Brazil." Regarding the frequent denial of the vote to illiterates in Latin America generally, see Sabato, "On Political Citizenship."

Chapter One

1. Regarding the history of Brazilian education, see Fernando de Azevedo, *Brazilian Culture*, pp. 325–99 and 415–40. His partisan participant's perspective on the New School can be found on pp. 440–86. See also Bomeny, *Os Intelectuais da Educação*, pp. 11–13, 16, 20–26, 31–33, 39–43, and 50–53; Cury, *Ideologia e Educação Brasileira*, particularly pp. 65–98 and

165–69; Reis Filho, *A Educação e a Ilusao Liberal em São Paulo*, pp. 178–79; and Monarcha, *A Reinvenção da Cidade e da Multidão*, pp. 14, 16–20, 43, and 97. Lourenço Filho attempted to make Brazilians aware of trends in pedagogy in Europe and the United States in *Introdução ao Estudo da Escola Nova*; regarding the philosophy of the New School, see particularly pp. 17–27, 34–115, 151–54, and 163–64. See also Dávila, *Diploma of Whiteness*.

2. Skidmore, *Politics in Brazil*, pp. 12–33, 39–41, and 48–53. See also French's thoughtful examination of the Vargas legacies in *Drowning in Laws*, particularly pp. 2–4, 10, 12–15, 24–39, and 64–67; and Fischer, *Poverty of Rights*, pp. 2–8.

3. Beiseigel, *Estado e Educação Popular*, pp. 8, 67–69, 78–96, 121, 128, 154, 157–58, and 170–72; Paiva, *Educação Popular e Educação de Adultos*, pp. 175–94 and 215–21. These are the best books available on the early part of Freire's career. Fischer (*Poverty of Rights*, p. 32) notes, "Illiteracy showed a strong inverse correlation with sewer service, water pipes, electricity, and pavement, and a modest negative correlation with public transportation routes."

4. For the economic changes under Vargas, see Skidmore, *Politics in Brazil*, pp. 41–47, 82–100, and 131–36. Regarding Kubitschek's economic policies, see ibid., pp. 164–70. For an analysis of Kubitschek's thinking, see Cardoso, *Ideologia do Desenvolvimento*, particularly pp. 77–104, 109–36, 157–82, and 203–30; and Alexander, *Juscelino Kubitschek*, particularly pp. 160–253.

5. See the official acts related to national campaigns and education programs in Bittencourt, org., *Fundos e Campanhas Educacionais*, pp. 90, 92, and 482–89. For a general introduction to this period, see Claudia Maria Moretzsohn, "Contribuição para o Debate: Meio Século de Descontinuidade e Dispersão de Recursos," in Seminário Internacional sobre Educação e Escolarização de Jovens e Adultos, Parlamento Latinoamericano São Paulo 1996, pp. 9–10, IPF. Moretzsohn says that the materials were little different from those used to teach children. See also Beiseigel, *Estado e Educação Popular*, pp. 8, 67–69, 78–96, 121, 128, 154, 157–58, and 170–72; Paiva, *Educação Popular e Educação de Adultos*, pp. 175–94 and 215–21. See also "Documentos Referentes a Campanha de Educação de Adultos," in Lourenço Filho Collection, CPDOC, roll 4, pp. 178–322, particularly p. 190; and Lourenço Filho's reports on the campaign at its beginning and at roughly its halfway point in "A Campanha de Educação de Adultos," in Lourenço Filho Collection, CPDOC, roll 2, pp. 414–19, 518–80. See also "The Adult Education Campaign in Brazil," UNESCO Correspondence Files 375 (81) A 63 CEA. Regarding the Laubach connection, see Medary, *Each One Teach One*, pp. 97–101, 116, and 119–20. See also Carmen Nava, "Pátria and Patriotism," p. 106. One could argue that it was Kubitschek's focus on short-term results that led him to neglect education, although, as the examples in this book suggest, it might have also led him to concentrate on adult education. See also Duarte, *Por Que Existem Analfabetos no Brasil?*, p. 29.

6. Skidmore, *Politics in Brazil*, pp. 51, 55–60, 67–69, and 74–82. The electorate percentages are available in Burns, *History of Brazil*, p. 396.

7. On Brazil's Communist Party, see Skidmore, *Politics in Brazil*, pp. 60–62, and 65–67. On the Catholic Left, see Paulo Rosas, "Depoimento I," in Freire, *Educação e Atualidade Brasileira*, pp. li–liv and lx–lxii.

8. A brief biographical sketch can be found in Gadotti, *Reading Paulo Freire*, pp. 1–5. See also Freire's memoir in the form of letters written to his niece, *Letters to Cristina*, particularly pp. 16–22, 25, 35, 39–44, 49–51, 56–57, and 75.

9. Weinstein, *For Social Peace in Brazil*, discusses SESI's activities in the more industrialized

southern part of Brazil. See particularly pp. 101–13, 148–65, 227–35, and 250. See also Luiz, *SESI: 50 Anos*, pp. 12, 14, 17, 50, and 53; and Betânia Gonçalves Figueiredo, "A Criação do SESI e SESC," particularly pp. 26, 29, 30, 51–52, and 68–74. Figueiredo emphasized the interest in controlling workers' use of their free time. Regarding the postwar repression under former general and now elected president Dutra, see French, *Drowning in Laws*, pp. 67–69, 78.

10. On Freire's tenure in SESI, see the (very limited) materials (primarily photographs) in SESI–Pernambuco, Centro de Ensino Supletivo, Virginia Correa de Oliveira—Biblioteca Paulo Freire. The photos show Freire attending meetings of various SESI clubs and handing out diplomas to graduates of SESI courses. (There is also a picture of his first driver, a Mr. Juarez.) See also Freire, *Letters to Cristina*, pp. 81–108.

11. See Alexander's notes from his interview with Freire in Robert Alexander Papers, Rutgers, The State University of New Jersey, Archibald S. Alexander Library, Special Collections and University Archives, Box 5, Folder 53, Brazil, State Economic Development Groups, 1959 and 1966. See also the various interviews Alexander conducted, in Robert Alexander Papers, Box 5, Folder 48, Brazil, 1956–65, particularly the interview with Olavo da Silva Virgilius. Freire, *Pedagogy of Hope*, contains more extended reflections on his experience with SESI; see pp. 17–31. See also his brief discussion in *Educação e Atualidade Brasileira*, p. 14. Regarding Freire's ideas on the relationship between the school and the community at the time, see his 7 August 1952 report in SESI–Pernambuco, Centro de Ensino Supletivo, Virginia Correa de Oliveira—Biblioteca Paulo Freire, particularly pp. 6 and 11. See also Rosas, *Papéis Avulsos*, pp. 55–59. For Freire's later, more critical stance on his work with SESI, see *Letters to Cristina*, pp. 81–82 and 88–108.

12. Regarding the 1958 conference, see the *Segundo Congreso Nacional de Educação de Adultos: Boletim Informativo No. 7*, p. 247, in Lourenço Filho Collection, CPDOC, roll 4,239; and Moretzsohn, "Contribuição para o Debate," p. 10. On the evolution of Freire's ideas, see Paiva, *Paulo Freire*. See also Ana Maria Araújo Freire, *Paulo Freire*, pp. 115–26.

13. Regarding ISEB, see Skidmore, *Politics in Brazil*, p. 170; and Paiva, *Paulo Freire*, pp. 34–35, 55–58, and 71. Like most of the best books on Freire, all so far written in Portuguese, Paiva's book focuses on his work prior to his departure from Brazil. See also José Eustáquio Romao, "Contextualização: Paulo Freire e o Pacto Populista," in Freire, *Educação e Atualidade Brasileira*, pp. xxix–xxxiii and xxxviii–xxxix. For a Marxist critique, see the works of Caio Navarro de Toledo, such as "ISEB Intellectuals, the Left and Marxism" and *ISEB: Fábrica de Ideologias*, particularly pp. 31–34, 43–48, 122–40, and 147–57. See also Pécaut, *Os Intelectuais e a Política no Brasil*, particularly pp. 5–12 and 107–41. The fullest treatment of the notions of consciousness written by an isebiano is the two-volume study by Álvaro Vieira Pinto, *Consciência e Realidade Nacional*. For an introduction to the thinking of Vieira Pinto, whom Freire called his "master," see Roux, *Alvaro Vieira Pinto*, particularly pp. 51–64, 80–145, and 193.

14. See Djacir Menezes, "Estrutura Social do Brasil," in ISEB, *Introdução aos Problemas do Brasil*, p. 121; Oliviera Junior, *Doze Ensaios sobre Educação e Tecnologia*, p. 11; and Ramos, *Condiçoes Sociais do Poder Nacional*, pp. 17–18. Regarding the media's role, see also Teixeira, *A Educação e a Crise Brasileira*, p. 143. Teixeira argued that because of the rise of mass media, illiteracy was no longer "the famous blindness of the nineteenth century." Illiteracy had less of a political importance than an economic one, in terms of its impact on people's means of employment.

15. See Roberto Campos's criticism of bacharelismo in "Cultura e Desenvolvimento," in

ISEB, *Introdução aos Problemas do Brasil*, pp. 230–31; and Anísio Teixeira's in *A Educação e a Crise Brasileira*, pp. xi–xii and xv, and *Educação Não é Privilégio*, pp. 20, 31, 35, 49, and 68. His reference to the "parasitism" of "officeholders" is in *A Educação e a Crise Brasileira*, p. xv. Regarding engineering, see his preface to Oliveira, *Doze Ensaios sobre Educação e Tecnologia*, pp. 5–6, as well as Oliveira's essays, particularly pp. 17–18, 45, and 82–83. See also Geraldo Bastos Silva, *Educação e Desenvolvimento Nacional*, pp. 32–33 and 41.

16. Paiva, *Paulo Freire*, pp. 35, 45–49, 58–59, 67–68, and 74–98. See also José Eustáquio Romao, "Contextualização: Paulo Freire e o Pacto Populista," in Freire, *Educação e Atualidade Brasileira*, pp. xviii–xxii; and Roland Corbisier, "Situação e Alternativas da Cultura Brasileira," in ISEB, *Introdução aos Problemas do Brasil*, pp. 190–91 and 193. I consulted this book in Freire's personal library. Regarding Freire's idealism, see, for example, Donald Macedo's introduction to Ana Maria Araújo Freire, *Chronicles of Love*, p. 2.

17. Callado, *Tempo de Arraes*; Page, *Revolution that Never Was*.

18. Page, *Revolution that Never Was*, pp. 52–53.

19. José Arlindo Soares, *A Frente do Recife*, p. 43.

20. Page, *Revolution that Never Was*, pp. 149–69; Francisco de Oliveira, *Elegia para uma Re(li)gião*, p. 80.

21. José Arlindo Soares, *A Frente do Recife*, p. 38.

22. For a sophisticated analysis of the complex forces at work in state politics, see Jaccoud, *Movimentos Sociais e Crise Política*, particularly pp. 9–10, 93–94, and 121. See also José Arlindo Soares, *Frente do Recife*, p. 97; and Francisco de Oliveira, *Elegia para uma Re(li)gião*, pp. 93–94.

23. Rosas, *Papéis Avulsos*, pp. 63–65; Germano Coelho, "Paulo Rosas e os Parques e Praças de Cultura do Recife," in Medeiros et al., eds., *Paulo Rosas*, pp. 27–36; Malkin-Fontecchio, "Citizens or Workers," pp. 100–112.

24. *FRUS, 1958–1960*, vol. 5, *American Republics*, pp. 683–84. The best available treatment of U.S. relations with Brazil during Kubitschek's presidency is W. Michael Weis, *Cold Warriors*, particularly pp. 113–39. For a historical critique of the evolution of discourse about the northeast, see, for example, Albuquerque, *A Invenção do Nordeste*, particularly pp. 22–36 and 66–172.

25. Bojunga, *JK: O Artista do Impossível*, pp. 517–24.

26. For an analysis of the creation of SUDENE, see Cohn, *Crise Regional e Planejamento*, particularly pp. 57–72, 108–10, 132–51, and 153–59. See also Francisco de Oliveira, *Elegia para uma Re(li)gião*, particularly pp. 22, 25, and 37; and Mallorquin, *Celso Furtado*, pp. 167–201.

27. Ernest S. Guaderrama, "Operations Memorandum: Request for Additional Personnel," 4 May 1961, p. 4, RG 84, Lot 66, F 121, Acc. no. 67A1450. Any U.S. government materials that were not consulted in presidential libraries were consulted in National Archives II in College Park, Maryland.

28. I first read a copy of the original "Education and Brazilian Actuality" in the IPF in 2001. The institute has since published it with useful accompanying materials. See *Educação e Atualidade Brasileira*, particularly pp. 9–18 and 22. In his work in a poor neighborhood in Recife, Freire believed he had helped awaken an awareness of the need to work together to solve common problems. See ibid., p. 115.

29. Freire, *Educação e Atualidade Brasileira*, pp. 26–45, 55–57, 78, 81–88, and 109–11.

30. Jones, *International Policies for Third World Education*, pp. 11–114 and 130–43; Arthur Gil-

lette, "The Experimental World Literacy Program: A Unique International Effort Revisited," in Arnove and Graff, eds., *National Literacy Campaigns*, p. 200; Lionel Elvin, "Education," in Pompei et al., *In the Minds of Men*, pp. 59–60.

31. Prem Kirpal, "UNESCO's Contribution to Development: Introduction," in Pompei et al., *In the Minds of Men*, pp. 117 and 119.

32. Sewell, *UNESCO and World Politics*, pp. 227–34; see also William A. Etecki-Mboumoua, "Africa," in Pompei et al., *In the Minds of Men*, p. 169.

33. Oscar Vera, "A Continental Challenge: 70 Million Illiterates," *UNESCO Courier*, June 1961, pp. 33–34. See also six-month report, addendum, p. 1, from E. J. Cain, education expert, Major Project—Chile, sent to G. Cruz Santos, UNESCO Bureau of Relations with Member States, 28 March 1962, in UNESCO Correspondence Files, Ext. Prim. Ed. Latin America M.P. 1—Associated Universities, Santiago 372 (8) MP 01 A63 (83). In the same files, see remarks on p. 3 of speech by Shannon McCune, director of UNESCO's Department of Education, and on p. 3 of "extractos del Discuros pronunciado por el Sr. Oscar Vera en el acto de Clasura del V Curso del Centro LatinoAmericano," 14 December 1963. See also A. D. Marquez, "Curso de Formación de Especialistas en Educación para América Latina, Proyecto Principal sobre Extensión y Mejoramiento de la Educación Primária en América Latina," UNESCO Mission Reports, no. 247/BMS.RD/EDS, São Paulo, 1958–66, pp. 3 and 9.

34. Juan José Arévalo, "Centro Latinamerica de Formación de Especialistas en Educación: Proyecto Principal sobre Extensión y Mejoramiento de la Educación Primária en América Latina," Santiago de Chile, 1963–76, UNESCO Mission Reports, no. 94/BMS.RD/ED, June 1967, p. 6; A. Oliveros, "Administración Escolar y Supervisión," UNESCO Mission Reports, no. 59/BMS.RD/EDS, May 1967, pp. 5–6; Marquez, "Curso de Formación," p. 8.

35. Jaime Canfux Gutiérrez, "Evolución de la Experiencia Cubana de Educación y Alfabetización," in UNESCO, *Alternativas de Alfabetización en América Latina y el Caribe*, pp. 185 and 190; Bhola, *Campaigning for Literacy*, pp. 91–105. A particularly thoughtful and sympathetic analysis of the Cuban experience is provided by Fagen, *Transformation of Political Culture in Cuba*. See particularly pp. 6–12, 16–18, 23, 33–68, and 145–47. See also McDonald, *Making a New People*, particularly pp. 54–72; Marvin Leiner, "The 1961 National Cuban Literacy Campaign," in Arnove and Graff, eds., *National Literacy Campaigns*, pp. 173–96; and UNESCO, *World Illiteracy at Mid-Century*.

36. "Castro's Speech on the Literacy Campaign," available in Fagen, *Transformation of Political Culture in Cuba*, p. 187. See also Arthur Gillette, "The Experimental World Literacy Program: A Unique International Effort Revisited," in Arnove and Graff, eds., *National Literacy Campaigns*, pp. 200 and 205–6.

37. Arthur Gillette, "The Experimental World Literacy Program: A Unique International Effort Revisited," in Arnove and Graff, eds., *National Literacy Campaigns*, p. 200; Lionel Elvin, "Education," in Pompei et al., *In the Minds of Men*, pp. 59–60. One of the most remarkable achievements of the Cuban Revolution was the virtual eradication of illiteracy, which seems to have been verified repeatedly and independently over the years. See McDonald, *Making a New People*, p. 55.

38. "Address at a White House Reception for Members of Congress and for the Diplomatic Corps of the Latin American Republics, 13 March 1961," in *PPPUS: John F. Kennedy, 1961*, pp. 170–75; "Memorandum from the President's Special Assistant (Schlesinger) to President Kennedy, 10 March 1961," in *FRUS, 1961–1963*, vol. 12, *American Republics*, pp. 10–18. For apprais-

als of the Alliance, see Levinson and Onís, *Alliance that Lost Its Way*, particularly 5–16 and 215–78; Rabe, *Most Dangerous Area in the World*, pp. 148–72; and Taffet, *Foreign Aid as Foreign Policy*. See also Luhn, "'Catechism of Development,'" pp. 2–54, 108–25, 172, and 175, in which she builds on the work of Latham, *Modernization as Ideology*; and Cullather, "Development?" and "Miracles of Modernization"; Ekbladh, "'Mr. TVA,'" 349–70; and Mark H. Haefele, "Rostow's Stages of Economic Growth," in Engerman et al., eds., *Staging Growth*, pp. 81–103.

39. Roett, *Politics of Foreign Aid*, pp. ix and 28–38.

40. "Paper by the Operations Coordinating Board," February 1, 1961, *FRUS, 1961–1963*, vol. 12, *American Republics*, p. 423. For an account of the trip by Arthur M. Schlesinger Jr. and others, see Schlesinger, *Thousand Days*, pp. 175–81.

41. Edward T. Walters, "Recommendation for Reestablishment of Consular Operations in Natal," 13 June 1961, RG 84, Lot 66, F 121, Acc. no. 67A1450; "Statement by the President Concerning a Plan for the Development of Northeast Brazil: 14 July 1961," *PPPUS: John F. Kennedy, 1961*, pp. 508–9. See also Francisco de Assis Lemos de Souza, *Nordeste*, p. 6.

42. John F. Kennedy, "Address in New York City before the General Assembly of the United Nations," 25 September 1961, *PPPUS: John F. Kennedy, 1961*, p. 623. See also Pompei et al., *In the Minds of Men*, pp. 302–3. For more general information on UN thinking on these issues, see Weiss et al., *UN Voices*, pp. 186–93; and Jolly et al., *UN Contributions*, pp. 50–89.

43. Freire, *À Sombra Desta Mangueira*, p. 50.

Chapter Two

1. Santos, "Educação e Desenvolvimento," delivered before a gathering of ministers of education in Bogotá, available in his *Os Cristãos e a Revolução Social*, p. 123. Regarding the U.S. response to this speech, see, for example, Lincoln Gordon to Rusk, 8 August 1963 telegram, RG 286, Entry 816, "Education 1963–1964" Folder. See also Arraes, *Pensamento e Ação Politica*, pp. 18–21 and 33. Regarding various interpretations of the "Brazilian Revolution," see Freitas, *Álvaro Vieira Pinto*, p. 31.

2. See, for example, Miguel Arraes, "Discurso de Saudação a João Goulart," in his *Pensamento e Ação Politica*, p. 37. The best guide to Freire's thinking and those of his associates at the university extension office at this time are the documents collected in Fávero, ed., *Cultura Popular Educação Popular*, pp. 99–172.

3. Freire, "Conscientização e Alfabetização: Uma Nova Visão de Processo," in Fávero, *Cultura Popular Educação Popular*, p. 103.

4. João Francisco de Souza, *Uma Pedagogia da Revolução*, p. 33.

5. It should be noted here that Arraes was one of the few politicians from these years whom Freire singled out for praise in later years. See, for example, Freire and Guimarães, *Aprendendo com a Própria História*, vol. 1, particularly pp. 16–22. He referred to Arraes's government as "a popular government in a national populist situation" (ibid., 16). He continued, "His dream was always much more serious and radical than the populist ambiguity" (ibid., 22). He also praised Natal mayor Djalma Maranhão, who is discussed below, in ibid, p. 25.

6. Moniz Bandeira, *O Governo João Goulart*, pp. 58, 81–86, 91–97, and 139–44. Regarding the unusually large numbers of U.S. officials in Brazil during these years, see ibid., pp. 136–38. See also Leacock, *Requiem for Revolution*, pp. 31, 43, 47, 55–58, 65, 72–73, and 135. Although U.S. concerns about President Goulart's abilities as an administrator were justified, U.S. fears about

whether Goulart's government was "reliably on the side of the Free World" were exaggerated. See USAID minister-director Leonard J. Saccio's 19 July 1962 message on "U.S. strategy for aid" to U.S. ambassador Lincoln Gordon, RG 286, Entry 1189, Box 5.

7. Rabe, *Most Dangerous Area in the World*, pp. 148–72, For information on education issues in the Alliance, see Levinson and Onís, *Alliance that Lost Its Way*, pp. 279–306. See also the *Evaluation Report on AID-Supported Programs to Improve Primary Education in Northeast Brazil 1962–1970* (Washington, D.C.: American Technical Assistance Corporation, 1971), particularly pp. 57–73. Kennedy's letter to Goulart is in *PPPUS: John F. Kennedy, 1962*, pp. 327–28. Gordon's concerns regarding the face-changing promise is available in a 17 April 1962 letter to J. W. Wilson, Office of East Coast Affairs, Bureau of Inter-American Affairs Department, RG 286, Entry 1189, Box 5. See Luhn, "'Catechism of Development,'" pp. xii–xv, 2–54, 172, and 175. Luhn quotes USAID education expert Philip Schwab on p. 170. See also *New York Times*, 2 June 1963. See also Malkin-Fontecchio, "Citizens or Workers," pp. 171–229.

8. For criticism of the MCP in the 1962 election year, see "Ministros Evangélicos em Defesa de MCP," *Jornal do Comércio*, 13 October 1962, APE-PE, DOPS, no. 29.841, MCP, "Material Didáctico" Folder. See also the "Nota Official" and the article on intellectuals supporting the MCP in the 30 September 1962 edition of *Jornal do Comércio* in the "Recorte de Jornais" envelope. Regarding Arraes's goals, see also "A Grande Orgia," *Jornal do Comércio*, 7 September 1962. Regarding Kennedy's wishes, see Harris P. Dawson Jr. to Leonard J. Saccio, 8 February 1962, RG 286, Entry 1189, Box 5. See also J. L. Haynes, "Memorandum of Conversation, Governor's Palace, Recife," 14 September 1961, RG 286, Entry 1189, Box 7. See also Albert A. Rabida's 13 September 1961 and 30 June 1961 reports in the same box, as well as various documents in RG 286, Entry 1148, Box 9, Education-Agreements Folder. Regarding the Sampaio plan to launch a literacy campaign, see Arthur F. Byrnes, Chief, Education Division, U.S.A.I.D., to Philip R. Schwab, 13 September 1962, RG 286, Entry 1208, Box 1. See also Roger Hilsman, State, Director of Intelligence and Research, to Mr. Martin, Chairman, Latin American Policy Committee, "Brazil and the Alliance for Progress," in National Security Files, Ralph A. Dungan Papers, Box 390, Brazil 3/62–9/62 Folder, JFK Library. Regarding the expanding U.S. presence, see Lowell C. Kilday to Lincoln Gordon, 3 December 1962, RG 286, Entry 1189, Box 5. Kilday warned that "the political effect of such a large AID mission would well nullify any benefits to the US the staff members could bring about." U.S. discussions of what to do about Arraes can be found in John Dieffenderfer, "Recommended Policy Towards Arraes Government in the State of Pernambuco," 24 October 1962, in RG 289, Entry 1189, Box 5, Northeast General Folder. Dieffenderfer noted the problems facing the United States when "economic assistance programs are carried out directly with state governments subject to political change." See Freire's thoughts on the Alliance in "Conscientização e Alfabetização," available in Fávero, *Cultura Popular Educação Popular*, p. 108. This was written after he took part in the Alliance-supported program in Angicos. That the Alliance was a response to the Cuban Revolution, as Freire notes, is undeniable. That it necessarily represented only the objectives of the United States may be questioned, especially given the original intention that it not be viewed as simply an aid program.

9. "Paper by the Operations Coordinating Board," February 1, 1961, *FRUS, 1961–1963*, vol. 12, *American Republics*, p. 423; Page, *Revolution that Never Was*, pp. 12–33; Albert A. Rabida, "Operations Memorandum to Department of State," RG 84, Lot 66, F 121, Acc. no. 67A1450; Edward T. Walters, "Recommendation for Reestablishment of Consular Operations in Natal,"

13 June 1961; and Ernest S. Guaderrama, "Operation Memorandum: Request for Additional Personnel," p. 3, both in RG 84, Lot 66, F 121, Acc. no. 67A1450; "U.S.I.S. Poll on Peasant Attitudes in Northeast Brazil," 22 July 1963, RG 59, Central Foreign Policy Files, 1963.

10. Jaccoud, *Movimentos Sociais e Crise Política em Pernambuco*, particularly pp. 9–10, 93–94, and 121.

11. Quoted in João Francisco de Souza, *Uma Pedagogia da Revolução*, p. 33.

12. See George Ball's 20 March 1964 telegram, RG 286, Entry 816, Box 2, Area Program—Northeast—1964 Folder. For U.S. officials' attitudes toward the Popular Culture Movement, see, for example, Edward J. Rowell, Minister Consul General, AmConGen Recife, 4 March 1964, RG 59, Central Foreign Policy Files, 1964–66, Box 1936; and D. Eugene Delgado-Arias, American Consul General, "Airgram Weekly Summary No. 37," 13 March 1963, RG 59, Central Foreign Policy Files, 1963, Box 3833.

13. Edward Rowell, "Pernambuco Education," 23 March 1964 telegram, RG 59, Central Foreign Policy Files; Grupo de Trabalho, Governo do Estado de Pernambuco, *Aliança para o Progresso*, pp. 21–26, 45–52, and 80. Regarding U.S. attitudes toward the Arraes government, see, for example, "U.S.A.I.D. Program and Policy in the State of Pernambuco, Brazil," in National Security Files, Ralph A. Dungan, Box 390A, Brazil 1/63–6/63 Folder, JFK Library. "Arraes is not believed to be controlled by Communists even though he does cooperate with them. It is not uncommon for Brazilian politicians of diverse political convictions to play along with communists and extreme leftists for political support. Where this happens the motivation often is political opportunism without appreciation of or ability to understand the dangers of communism." In early 1963, U.S. ambassador Lincoln Gordon believed it was still possible to "build a satisfactory relationship with Arraes." Loans to support the development of the "economic infra-structure" were the primary ones planned in early 1963. See also Roett, *Politics of Foreign Aid*, pp. 130–40.

14. Paes Barreto, "Depoimento," pp. 44 and 47, CPDOC. It is not clear, however, that Coelho was a communist. See Flávio Henrique Albert Brayner, "Alguns Aspectos da Relação entre o Partido Comunista e a Frente do Recife," in Rezende, ed., *Recife*, pp. 206–10. For further discussion, see Barbosa, *Movimento de Cultura Popular*, pp. 140–46, 203–4, and 225.

15. Godoy and Coelho, *Livro de Leitura para Adultos*, Lessons 1, 28–30, 35, 53, 54, 59, 63, 64, and 66. See also the materials available in APE-PE, DOPS, pontuário no. 29.841, Movimento Cultura Popular, exercises 1, 6, and 8, and lessons 10, 25, 29, as well as Doc. no. 1501-D, "Tijolo." Regarding Communist Party plans, see the undated party document, pp. 3 and 4, in APE-PE, DOPS, pontuário no. 12.385, Miguel Arraes de Alencar.

16. Malkin-Fontecchio, "Citizens or Workers," pp. 82–87, 98, 105, and 123–29.

17. Page, *Revolution that Never Was*, pp. 149–69.

18. Freire, *A Propósito de uma Administração*, pp. 4–6, 8–16, and 22–23. See also his comments regarding the role of the University of Recife at the closing ceremony of the Angicos literacy campaign discussed below. These comments are available in Textos Escolhidos, vol. 32, "Angicos," IPF. See also Jarbas Maciel, "Fundamentação Teórica do Sistema Paulo Freire de Educação," pp. 127–29, in Fávero, *Cultura Popular Educação Popular*. See Freire's reflections on his university extension office experience in *Letters to Cristina*, pp. 131–37. See also "UR Executa Programa para Difusão da Cultura Popular," *Diário de Pernambuco*, 30 December 1962; "Universidade do Recife Treinará Pessoal de Alagoas: Cursos," *Jornal do Comércio*, 3 March

1963; Rosas, *Papéis Avulsos*, p. 52; and his testimony in Ana Maria Araújo Freire, *Paulo Freire*, pp. 172–81.

19. Cunha and Góes, *O Golpe na Educação*, p. 20.

20. Freire, "Conscientização e Alfabetização," pp. 125–26, and Aurenice Cardoso, "Conscientização e Alfabetização: Uma Visão Prática do Sistema Paulo Freire," pp. 162 and 165–72, in Fávero, *Cultura Popular Educação Popular*.

21. Scoguglia, "Paulo Freire e a CEPLAR da Paraíba," pp. 3–5, 47–48, 50–51, 62, 67, and 70–71. This source includes oral history interviews with students from the period. The chapter "A História da Ceplar e o Movimento Social," in Guedes, ed., *O Jogo da Verdade*, pp. 291–300, provides much of the basic information. For reasons that are not altogether clear to me, the material available in the IPF is superior to the published version; see Scoguglia, *Educação Popular*, particularly pp. 59–147. See also Porto and Lage, *CEPLAR*, particularly pp. 12, 34–41, and 47. For material on Pedro Gondim's policies, consult the FUNESC. For the decrees that authorized state funding for the campaign, see Governos Estaduais Pedro Moreno Gondim, 1961–66, Caixa 73, Ano 1961, Decree no. 639, 5 April 1962, FUNESC. Gondim's opinions regarding the creation of CEPLAR can be found in his 13 February 1962 letter to the president of the state legislative assembly, Inácio Joel Freitas, in Caixa 84, Ano 1962, and in his 14 March 1962 letter to Freitas's successor, Clovis Bezarra Cavalcanti, in Caixa 93, Ano 1963. See also the coverage in "Tres Anos de Trabalho," *Correio da Paraíba*, 2 February 1964, p. 10, as well as "Os Dozes Meses de Cultura," in the same edition, p. 16; and Germano Vidal, "A Revolução Alcançou o Ensino," *A União*, 6 May 1962, p. 3. See also Hélio Zenaide, "Pedro Gondim: Ascensao e Declínio de uma Liderança Popular," in Pontes da Silva, ed., *Poder e Política na Paraíba*, particularly pp. 147–53; Nélson Coelho, "A Cronologia dos Fatos, na Visão de um Repórter," in Guedes, ed., *O Jogo da Verdade*, p. 49; and José Octavio, "Do Populismo Radical ao Desenlace na Paraíba," in Guedes, ed., *O Jogo da Verdade*, pp. 97–99.

22. Edward T. Walters, "Recommendation for Reestablishment of Consular Operations in Natal, RGN," 13 June 1961, RG 84, Lot 66, F 121, Acc. no. 67A1450.

23. "Plano de Aplicação dos Recursos dos Fundos de Ensino Primário e Médio, Destinado ao Estado do Rio Grande do Norte, por Cantado Plano Trienal de Educação," June 1963, pp. 1–2, APE-RGN, SECERN, 1963, "Secretaria de Educação e Cultura" Box.

24. Aluizio Alves, *Memória Viva*, p. 112; Germano, *Lendo e Aprendendo*, pp. 62–70.

25. See 6 June 1963 telegram the mayor sent to Goulart, reprinted in Aluizio Alves, *A Verdade que Não é Secreta*, pp. 168–69, in which the increasing tensions between the mayor and the governor are evident. The mayor resented the close ties that developed between the U.S. government and the governor.

26. Germano, *Lendo e Aprendendo*, pp. 71–72, 100, 102, and 108–9.

27. Quoted in ibid., pp. 142–43.

28. Edward Rowell, AmConGen Recife, "Interview with Djalma Maranhão," January 8, 1964, RG 59, Central Foreign Policy Files, Box 1941; Rowell, "Djalma Maranhão Extends His Popular Education Program to Interior Towns," 11 March 1964, RG 59, Central Foreign Policy Files, Box 1941. In July of 1962, the mayor had complained that the U.S. government had promised wheat in support of the literacy campaign but had cut the aid because of his "nationalist leadership." The United States denied that they had ever promised such aid. See Saccio to Gordon, 9 July 1962 telegram, RG 286, Entry 1189, Box 5.

29. Aluizio Alves, *O Que Eu Não Esqueci*, pp. 99–116; Aluizio Alves, *Memória Viva*, pp. 95, 112–16, 126, and 136–37; *Segundo Mensagem Anual Enviada a Assembléia Legislativa a 1 de Junho de 1962*, p. 38 and 42–43; "Bases da Lei Agrária Estadual," pp. 3 and 4, both in *Documentos Parlamentares*. Regarding his campaign, see Mariz and Suassuna, *História do Rio Grande do Norte Contemporânea*, pp. 80–83; and Trindade, *Uma Síntese da Abertura Política*, p. 21, as well as the *Album de Esperança*. I would argue that Alves, in some ways, lies somewhere between an electoral and a reformist populist, to use John French's formulation. He did have a larger vision of what he wanted to achieve, but his commitment to popular reform did not survive the 1964 coup, although he himself would. See John D. French, "Workers and the Rise of Adhemarista Populism," pp. 41–43.

30. 29 July 1963 speech, reprinted in Aluizio Alves, *Sem Ódio e Sem Medo*, pp. 155 and 170–71.

31. Daniel M. Braddock, Minister Consul General, São Paulo, "Weekly Summary No. 87, 30 August 1962," RG 59, Central Foreign Policy Files, Box 3834. See also D. Eugene Delgado-Arias, AmConGen Recife, "Aluisio [sic] Alves Bids for Regional Leadership," 2 September 1963, RG 59, Central Foreign Policy Files, Box 3312; and Aluizio Alves, *Sem Ódio e sem Medo*, p. 168. See parts of Alves's speech before SUDENE contained in Sousa, *Fascículos do Diário de Natal*, p. 233. Regarding U.S. support for the Alves government, see also Roett, *Politics of Foreign Aid*, pp. 111–12 and 118–26; and Alves, *O Que Eu Não Esqueci*, pp. 122–30. Alves continued to identify his own political project with that of the late president Kennedy. See his 7 May 1965 invitation to then senator Robert F. Kennedy to attend the inauguration of the President Kennedy Institute of Education in Natal in Robert F. Kennedy, Senate Papers, Trips, Box 1, Latin American Correspondence, JFK Library.

32. See Heinz Peter Gerhardt, "Angicos—Rio Grande do Norte—1962/63," pp. 10, 11, 14–15, 22, and 28; Francisco Calazans Fernandes, "Melhoramento e Ampliação do Sistema de Educação Primária e Básica no Estado do Rio Grande do Norte, do Nordeste Brazileira," pp. 37–38; Equipe Eduplan—São Paulo, "Projecto Campanha de Alfabetização de Adultos—Rio Grande do Norte, 1963," not paginated, all in "Programma de Ensino Primário do Estado do Rio Grande do Norte," APE-RGN, SECERN, "1964" Box. Regarding Marcos Guerra and student involvement in the Angicos program, see Justina Iva de A. Silva, *Estudantes e Politica*, pp. 87–88, 95, and 97–99. Two accounts by participants are Fernandes and Terra, *40 Horas de Esperança*, pp. 19, 99–100, 106, 147–53, and 192; and Lyra, *As Quarenta Horas de Angicos*, pp. 20, 22–31, 47–48, 63, and 95–97. See also Freire's discussion in *Letters to Cristina*, pp. 137–42.

33. Gerhardt, "Angicos—Rio Grande do Norte—1962/63," pp. 10, 11, 14–15, 22, and 28; Justina Iva de A. Silva, *Estudantes e Politica*, pp. 98–99; Fernandes and Terra, *40 Horas de Esperança*, pp. 168–191; Lyra, *As Quarenta Horas de Angicos*, pp. 51–103 and 119–45.

34. Gerhardt, "Angicos—Rio Grande do Norte—1962/63," pp. 10, 11, 14–15, 22, and 28; Lyra, *As Quarenta Horas de Angicos*, p. 61. A copy of the Gordon letter can be found in Fernandes and Terra, *40 Horas de Esperança*, p. 110. For the complete text of Freire's remarks, see the transcript in Textos Escolhidos, vol. 32, "Angicos," IPF. See also Freire's discussion in *Letters to Cristina*, pp. 137–42.

35. Francisco Calazans Fernandes, "Melhoramento e Ampliação do Sistema de Educação Primária e Básica no Estado do Rio Grande do Norte, do Nordeste Brazileira," 3 March 1963, p. 6, APE-RGN, SECERN, 1962–65, "Plano de Aplicação" Box. See also pp. 1–5 of his May 1963 report in the "Curso de Treinamentos para Professores Leigos" Folder in SECERN, 1963;

"Uma Aliança para o Progresso," pp. 8 and 13. See also Alves, *Sem Ódio e sem Medo*, p. 170; and Fernandes and Terra, *40 Horas de Esperança*, pp. 134–35.

36. Fernandes and Terra, *40 Horas de Esperança*, pp. 114, 116, 136–38, and 194. Regarding the care and handling of Alves, see, for example, U.S. ambassador Lincoln Gordon's 1 May 1963 telegram in the National Security Files, Countries, Box 14, Brazil 5/1/63–5/10/63 Folder, JFK Library. Regarding the fears that Alves would criticize the Alliance, see the 19 June 1963 CIA Information Report in the same folder and the 5 August 1963 telegram from Delgado-Arias, in the 8/1/63–8/20/63 folder, in the same box. The "declaration of northeast governors" can be found in Box 14, Brazil—General—8/1/63–8/20/63 Folder. The document clearly suggests Alves's important role in drafting it, given its pro-U.S. stance, its emphasis on the "revolution in education," and its rejection of the image of the northeast as being on the verge of a Cuban-style revolution.

37. See "Experiência Revolucionários em Angicos e Natal," *Ultima Hora*, 17 February 1963.

38. We are still lacking anything remotely resembling a definitive and fair-minded biography of Goulart. One of the more thoughtful, if highly polemical, studies is Moniz Bandeira, *O Governo João Goulart*. See particularly pp. 12–13, 47–57, 99–107, 111, 127–32, and 144–61. See also Leacock, *Requiem for Revolution*, pp. 113–36, 177–79, 182–84, and 191–92; Dulles, *Castelio Branco*, pp. 301–4 and 314–16; and Skidmore, *Politics in Brazil*, pp. 218, 224–26, 234–43, 263–67, and 276–84.

39. See Duarte, *Por Que Existem Anafabeltos no Brasil?*, pp. 58–60 and 66. Regarding the isebianos' support for these reforms, see Toledo, "ISEB Intellectuals," p. 129.

40. See "Programa Nacional de Desenvolvimento: Anteprojeto Preparados pelo Conselho do Desenvolvimento Agôsto 1962: Diretrizes para a Quinqüenia 1963/67," pp. 1–4, in Arquivo João Goulart, Série Presidência da República, Conselho de Desenvolvimento, CPDOC. See also March 1962 and March 1964 presidential messages in *Documentos Parlamentares 127 Mensagens Presidenciais, 1947–1964*, pp. 355, 357, 376, 394, 429, and 433; and João Goulart, "Plano Trienal para a Educação," 3–7. On polling data regarding giving illiterates the right to vote, see Herminio Augusto Faria, *Três Pesquisas*, particularly pp. 7 and 15.

41. See Programa Nacional de Alfabetização, "Documentos para Discussao," pp. 3 and 6, in STM, IP 1426/68, vol. 2.

42. Following the military coup of 1964, Freire and his associates were investigated by the government. Many of the documents which should be available in the Arquivo Nacional in Rio or COREG in Brasília were seized by the military in order to make their case that Freire and the Ministry of Education had been engaged in subversive activities. See, for example, the documents contained in STM, IP 1426/68, vol. 2, particularly the those from 28 June and 8 July in which Paulo de Tarso Santos instituted the popular culture commissions. See also Santos, "Da Educação e Cultura, no Uso de Suas Atribuiçoes," 23 July 1963, STM.

43. To understand his thinking in 1963, see Santos, *Os Cristãos e a Revolução Social*. This book was dedicated to Pope John XXXIII, whose encyclicals "Mater et Magistra" and "Pacem in Terris" he cited extensively. He was also influenced by the French Dominican priest and economic theorist Padre Lebret. Like Christian Democrats in Chile with whom Freire (and Santos himself) worked later, Santos wrote of moving beyond the "anti-human systems" of communism and capitalism. See ibid., particularly pp. 21–23, 96–100, and 110. He also cites approvingly various Chilean Christian Democrats like then senator and future president Eduardo Frei and Chilean senator and Eduardo Frei's future ambassador to the United States,

Radomiro Tomic. See ibid., pp. 48–49 and 66. Regarding his attitude toward students, see ibid., p. 128. See also Santos, "Educação e Desenvolvimento," p. 700. His testimony before a military inquiry can be found in "Têrmo de Perguntas ao Indiciado—Paulo de Tarso Santos," in STM, IP 1426/68, vol. 1. See also Freire and Guimarães, *Aprendendo com a Própria História*, 1:13–15; and *DC—Brasília*, 19 June 1963, pp. 1 and 4; and 27 June 1963, p. 1. See also Pernam-buco congressman José Carlos Guerra's praise for the invitation to Paulo Freire in *Diário de Congreso Nacional*, 3 July 1963, p. 17; and Ewaldo Pinto's similar enthusiasm in the same pub-lication, 6 July 1963, pp. 37–38.

44. See Jean Davis, "Memorandum for Mr. McGeorge Bundy: Subject: Analysis of New Brazilian Cabinet," in RG 59, Central Foreign Policy Files, Box 3837; and William H. Brubeck, "Memorandum for Mr. McGeorge Bundy," National Security Files, Countries, Box 14, Brazil General 6/63 Folder, JFK Library. Santos was said to believe communism "the lesser of two evils," although that is not evident from his writings. There is no doubt that he believed in the long-term victory of "Christianism, which he defines as a system of partially 'free' enterprise aimed solely at the common welfare." It was feared that he would "strengthen pro-Communist influence in student and teacher organizations where it was already substantial" (CIA, Office of Current Intelligence, "Current Intelligence Memorandum: Subject: The Brazilian Cabi-net," National Security Files, Countries, Box 14, Brazil General 7/16/63–7/31/63 Folder, JFK Library).

45. Lincoln Gordon, "17 July 1963 memo to Secretary of State," National Security Files, Countries, Box 14, Brazil General 7/16/63–7/31/63 Folder, JFK Library; Santos, *64 e Outros Anos*, p. 54. Regarding his selection as minister of education, see the interview with Marcello Cerqueira in Moraes, *A Esquerda e o Golpe de 64*, pp. 278–79. For further information on U.S. attitudes regarding the student Left, see Daniel M. Braddock, "Airgram, 16 August 1963: Com-munist-oriented students win national election," in National Security Files, Countries, Box 14, Brazil 8/1/63–8/20/63 Folder, JFK Library. Regarding the Alliance for Progress, as seen by its critics, see Santos, *Os Cristãos e a Revolução Social*, pp. 23–24, 127, and 133–35.

46. See Madeleine Adriance, *Opting for the Poor*, pp. 27, 45–46, and 48–52. See also Movi-mento de Educação de Base, *Viver é Lutar*, pp. 2, 8, 18, 20, 28, 32, 54, and 58. The best study of the Basic Education Movement is Wanderley, *Educar para Transformar*, particularly pp. 15, 16, 25, 26, 28, 44–45, 99–100, 110, 114, 158, 348, 351, and 404; regarding the influence or lack thereof of Paulo Freire on the movement, see pp. 431–32. An overview of the movement, based on secondary sources in Portuguese, can be found in Dawson, "Very Brazilian Experiment." See also "D. Távora 'Arrancou' Cartilhas do MEB Assaltadas Por Lacerda," *Gazeta de Sergipe*, 29 February 1964, p. 1.

47. Santos, *64 e Outros Anos*, pp. 60–61.

48. See "Apesar de Tudo—UNE Revista: Memorex: Elementos para uma História da UNE," São Paulo: Universidade de São Paulo, undated in Coleção Jean Mare, Folder 6, Arquivo Público do Estado do Rio de Janeiro. See also Berlinck, *O Centro Popular de Cultura da UNE*, particularly pp. 21–42 and 107–12; Ridenti, *Em Busca do Povo Brasileiro*, particularly pp. 107–13; and Barcellos, *CPC da UNE*. Documents by members of the student Left from this time period are also available in Fávero, *Cultura Popular Educação Popular*, pp. 15–70. Regarding the Communist Party, see Chilcote, *Brazilian Communist Party*, particularly pp. 78–81 and 160–61. A valuable sociological study of the Brazilian college student of this time period is Foracchi, *O Estudante e a Transformação da Sociedade Brasileira*. She argued that Brazilian students of

the petit bourgeoisie or rising middle class experienced most profoundly the transformations Brazilian society was undergoing. See, particularly, pp. 220–52.

49. See the interview with Herbert José de Souza, better known as Betinho, one of the organizers of AP, in Moraes, *Esquerda e o Golpe de 64*, p. 252. See also the history written by founding members Haroldo Lima and Aldo Arantes, *História da Ação Popular da JUC ao PC do B*, particularly pp. 13–15, 19–24, and 31–50; Berlinck, *O Centro Popular de Cultura da UNE*, p. 27; and UNE, *Alfabetização e Cultura Popular: Resoluçoes do primeiro encontro nacional*, particularly pp. 13–14. 25, and 36–43, in STM, processo 1426, 7 October 1968. Regarding UNE's participation in finding volunteers for a literacy campaign in Osasco, São Paulo, see Walter Garcia, "Planejamento de uma Campanha de Alfabetização para o Estado de São Paulo," p. 7; and Celso de Rui Beisiegel, "Estudo de um Processo de Alfabetização de Adultos," p. 12, in Centro de Informaçoes Bibliograficas em Educação/INEP, Ministério de Educação, Brasília, Caixa 8, Maço 80.

50. A brief introduction to Freire's work in Brasília can be found in "Paulo Freire: Fundamentos e Perspectives de Sua Concepção Educacional," in Caetano, *Paulo Freire e a Educação Brasileira*, n.p. See also José Leao Filho, "A Revolução dos Analfabetos," *Brasília* 7 (May 1962–September 1963): 73–77. Regarding the history of the satellite cities, see, for example, Vasconcelos, *Taguatinga*, pp. 17–18. See also "Taguatinga: 'Candangos' Consumaram a Invasão," *DC—Brasília*, 4 May 1963, p. 1; and "Country Club de Taguatinga Teves Suas Terras Invadidas," *DC—Brasília*, 6 May 1963, p. 1.

51. See "Jango: Mais 5 Milhoes de Eleitores em 1965," *DC—Brasília*, 6 September 1963, p. 3. See also "Em Marcha o Fim do Analfabetismo," *DC—Brasília*, 4 October 1963, p. 1. IBAD was an anti-Goulart political action committee.

52. Miguel Newton Arraes's closing speech on 21 September 1963, in STM, IP 1426/68, vol. 2. In the copy in the military archives someone (presumably one of the investigators) underlined the references to communists, subversion, and revolution. See also "Cultura Popular e Pé no Chão: Comunicação ao I Encontro de Alfabetização e Cultural Popular," STM, IP 1426/68, vol. 2.

53. "Tarso: Conspiradores Tramam a Deposição do Governo," *DC—Brasília*, 16 October 1963, p. 3; "Razoes da Renúncia do Ministro da Educação," *A União*, 17 October 1963, pp. 1 and 3; Robert W. Dean, Counselor of Embassy, Brasília, "Airgram: 18 October 1963: Frente de Mobilização Popular," RG 59, Central Foreign Policy Files, 1963, Box 3832; Daniel M. Braddock, Minister Consul General, São Paulo, "Airgram: 25 October 1963: Paulo de Tarso's Resignation," RG 59, Central Foreign Policy Files, 1963, Box 3833.

54. "Têrmo de Perguntas ao Indiciado—Julio Furquim Sambaquy [sic]," in STM, IP 1426/68, vol. 1.

55. See, for example, the text of a 19 September 1963 speech by Auro Moura Andrade, "Um Gravíssimo Process de Subversao Institucional está em Marcha no Brasil" (Brasília: Senado, 1963).

56. Lincoln Gordon to Edwin Martin, 18 October 1963, RG 59, Central Foreign Policy Files, 1963, Box 3312, AID 2/1/63 Brazil Folder.

57. See AmEmbassy Airgram, 16 January 1964, RG 59, Central Foreign Policy Files, 1964–66, Box 1932; see also Thomas J. Duffield, American Consul, Porto Alegre, "Weekly Summary, No. 101, 24 March 1964," RG 59, Central Foreign Policy Files, 1964–66, Box 1930, Political and Defense Folder.

58. See the Ministry of Education and Culture documents contained in Textos Escolhidos, vol. 32, "Angicos," IPF; and Aron Abend, "Para a Revista R. N: Exposição Sintética," in STM, IP 1426/68, vol. 2.

59. See Decree no. 53,464, 21 January 1964, signed by Goulart and Sambaqui, "Institui o Programa Nacional de Alfabetização do Ministério de Educação e dá Outras Providências," in STM, IP 1426/68, vol. 2.

60. Seixas Dória, Eu, Reu sem Crime, pp. 89.

61. Ibid., pp. 71–72.

62. Dantas, Os Partidos Politicos em Sergipe, pp. 208–9, 232–33, 243, 257, and 274; Ariosvaldo Figueiredo, História Política de Sergipe, pp. 178–79.

63. The best single source on Seixas Dória is his Recortes de uma Jornada. Regarding his ideas on economic nationalism, see particularly his 1957 speech "Nacionalismo e Desenvolvimento Econômico," pp. 27–46, in ibid.

64. Wynne, História de Sergipe, pp. 265–67; Dantas, A Tutela Militar em Sergipe, p. 6.

65. The governor referred to Sergipe's "calamitous financial situation" in a 10 September 1963 telegram to Paraná governor Ney Braga and in his 9 September 1963 and 25 October 1963 telegrams to SUDENE's Celso Furtado asking for funds for drought relief. Both telegrams are in Arquivo Público de Estado de Sergipe, G1 1881. See also "Seixas Dória na Casa Branca Reaffirma Posição Nacionalista," Gazeta de Sergipe, 27 September 1963; and Dantas, Os Partidos Politicos em Sergipe, p. 274. A notably sympathetic character sketch of the governor can be found in Benjamin R. Read, "Memo for McGeorge Bundy: Request for Presidential Appointment of Visiting Brazilian Governor," in National Security Files, Countries, Box 14, Brazil General 9/63 Folder, JFK Library. See also Read's 10 June 1963 letter to John Dieffenderfer, Director, USAID Northeast, in Arquivo Público de Estado de Sergipe, G1 1879.

66. Regarding Seixas Dòria's support for Goulart and rejection of movements that opposed him, see his 21 March 1963 telegram to Senator Heribaldo Vieira, among others, in Arquivo Público de Estado de Sergipe, G1 1879. Regarding a promise the federal government had made to supply cotton seeds and beans, see also 4 April 1963 letter to President Goulart, in Arquivo Público de Estado de Sergipe, G1 1879. See also Seixas Dória, Eu, Reu sem Crime, p. 24; "Seixas: 'Não Utilizarei a Policia Contra os Camponeses da "Bia,"'" Gazeta de Sergipe, 9 January 1964; Dantas, Os Partidos Politicos em Sergipe, p. 280; and American Consulate, Salvador airgram, "Visit to Sergipe, February 26–29, 1964," 12 March 1964, RG 59, Central Foreign Policy Files.

67. Dantas, Os Partidos Politicos em Sergipe, p. 265; American Consulate, Salvador airgram, "Visit to Sergipe, February 26–29, 1964," 12 March 1964, RG 59, Central Foreign Policy Files.

68. Dantas, Os Partidos Politicos em Sergipe, p. 287.

69. "Alfabetização do Povo," Gazeta de Sergipe, 18 January 1964; and Juarez Ribeiro, "ABC do Povo e Conscientição," Gazeta de Sergipe, 9 February 1964; "Método Paulo Freire: 200 Mil Pessoas Será Alfabetizadas," Gazeta de Sergipe, 15 December 1963; "Quinta Feira em Aracaju o Ministro de Educação," Gazeta de Sergipe, 14 January 1964; and "Sambaqui em Aracaju: Método Paulo Freire Não É Baléia," Gazeta de Sergipe, 17 January 1964.

70. Sergipe Inquérito, copy available in Instituto Paulo Freire, Interrogation of Jackson da Silva Lima; Germano, Lendo e Aprendendo, p. 60; Levinson and Onís, Alliance that Lost Its Way, p. 291–92; Luhn, "'Catechism of Development,'" pp. 169–71.

71. See, for example, Lincoln Gordon, "Telegram from the Embassy in Brazil to the Depart-

ment of State, 21 February 1964," *FRUS, 1964–1968*, vol. 31, *South and Central America; Mexico*, pp. 401–3.

72. See Charles Stuart Kennedy's 30 September 1987 interview with Gordon in the Foreign Affairs Oral History Collection, pp. 22–23, Association for Diplomatic Studies and Training, Arlington, Va. Gordon's memories do not seem particularly reliable on this point. See also George Ball's 20 March 1964 telegram, RG 286, Entry 816, Box 2, Area Program, Northeast, 1964 Folder; and Edward Rowell, "Pernambuco Education," 23 March 1964 telegram in same folder. Other documents from this era suggest that U.S. officials were not sure what to make of Freire. See, for example, Delgado-Arias, "U.S. Assistance—Pernambuco," 10 August 1963, RG 286, Entry 816, Box 2. He clearly thought that Freire's method was preferable to the "class conflict" preached by the MCP primer.

73. Scoguglia, "Paulo Freire e a CEPLAR da Paraíba," pp. 73–78, 82–88, 91–92, 100, 133–36, and 166–67; Porto and Lage, *CEPLAR*, pp. 41–46, 66–86, and 101–40; "CEPLAR vai Levar Cultura Popular á Campina Grande," *A União*, 21 April 1963, p. 1; "Alfabetização do Brasileiro," *A União*, 15 August 1963, p. 3; "MEC Vai Aplicar 138 Milhoes em Alfabetização em Paraíba," *A União*, 17 August 1963, p. 8; "Alfabetização em Massa pelo Método Paulo Freire: CEPLAR," *A União*, 22 August 1963, p. 8. Regarding the governor's turn to the Right, see Monique Cittadino, "A Política Paraibana e os Estado Autoritário (1964/1986)," in Cittadino et al., *Estrutura de Poder na Paraíba*, pp. 111–13;

74. See the 6 March 1964 telegram from Milton Veloso Borges to Gondim, which praises his "energetic and patriotic attitude in maintaining order and tranquility that is being threatened by a minority of disorderly marginal types and professional students who are agents in a foreign power interested in imposing its domination over the Brazilian people." This telegram can be found in Governos Estaduais Pedro Moreno Gondim, 1961–66, Caixa 111, Ano 1964, FUNESC; see a rather different opinion expressed in a 10 March 1964 letter from José Serra, then president of the National Students' Union, in Caixa 119, Ano 1964. Regarding the shift in policy that began in January 1964, see "Governador Destrói Acusações do Deputado," *A União*, 27 May 1964. See also the Ministry of Education's "Relatório da Paraíba," in STM, IP 1426/68, vol. 2. Regarding CEPLAR's activities in the interior, see Francisco de Assis Lemos de Souza, *Nordeste*, pp. 116–17. Regarding Gondim's support for actions taken against peasants during early 1964, see Francisco de Assis Lemos de Souza, *Nordeste*, pp. 171–82; Nélson Coelho, "Cronologia dos Fatos, na Visão de um Repórter," in Guedes, ed., *O Jogo da Verdade*, pp. 50–51; and José Octavio, "Do Populismo Radical ao Desenlace na Paraíba," in Guedes, ed., *O Jogo da Verdade*, p. 113.

75. See undated Ministry of Education document, "Esquema de Intervenção," in STM, IP 1426/68, vol. 2.

76. Decree no. 53,465, 21 January 1964, "Institui o Programa Nacional de Alfabetização do Ministério de Educação e dá Outras Providências"; and "Reformula a Comissao de Cultura Popular, Criada pela Portaria Numero 195, de 8/7/963," 16 March 1964, both in STM, IP 1426/68, vol. 2. See also Skidmore, *Politics in Brazil*, pp. 279–84.

77. "Contribuição Crítica dos Chefes de Seçoes do Serviço de Pessoal do Programa Nacional de Alfabetização," 29 February 1964, in STM, IP 1426/68, vol. 2.

78. See José Moura, "Periga o Plano de Alfabetização," *Ultima Hora*, and the many angry responses from those involved in the campaign in STM, IP 1426/68, vol. 2.

79. "Informe No., Fração do PNA," in STM, IP 1426/68; "Têrmo de Perguntas ao Indiciado—Marcus Machado de Alencar" and "Têrmo de Perguntas ao Indiciado—Ambrosino de Serpa Coutinho," in STM, IP 1426/68, vol. 1.

80. Skidmore, *Politics in Brazil*, pp. 279–80.

81. "Têrmo de Perguntas ao Indiciado—Julio Furquim Sambaquy," in STM, IP 1426/68, vol. 1. Regarding Lacerda, see Barbosa, *Movimento de Cultura Popular*, p. 204.

82. See, for example, the complaints about the "retrograde" treasurer of a soccer club in Niterói in "Relatório da Equipe de Mobilização—Niterói," 18 February 1964, in STM, IP 1426/68.

83. See John Keppel, Weeka 3, 16 January 1964, particularly p. 3, in RG 59, Central Foreign Policy Files, 1964–66, Box 1932, POL 2-1 "Joint Weekas 1/1/64."

84. Moniz Bandeira, *O Governo Joao Goulart*, pp. 163–84; Nélson Coelho, "Cronologia dos Fatos, na Visão de um Repórter," in Guedes, ed., *O Jogo da Verdade*, p. 53; Scoguglia, "Paulo Freire e a CEPLAR da Paraíba," pp. 114, 118, 120–21, and 126–33; Scoguglia, *Educação Popular*, pp. 139–47; Skidmore, *Politics in Brazil*, pp. 284–302. Regarding the charges against the University of Recife, see STM, Autos do IPM, "UNE/UBES/Pernambuco, Volumes IV and V, 1965." For an account of the coup in Natal, written by the coordinator of the Pé no Chao campaign, see Galvão, *1964, Aconteceu em Abril*. Regarding what happened to Marcos Guerra, see Galvão, *1964, Aconteceu em Abril*, pp. 72–76. Regarding the accusations against those involved in the campaign, see Galvão, *1964, Aconteceu em Abril*, pp. 172–80 and 193–98. Regarding the repression in Paraíba, see Márcio Moreira Alves, *O Cristo do Povo*, pp. 199–200; and Porto and Lage, *CEPLAR*, pp. 141–62.

85. Scoguglia, "Paulo Freire e a CEPLAR da Paraíba," p. 123. See also "Paraíba Atravessou Tranquila a Crise do Primeiro do Abril," *Correio da Paraíba*, 2 April 1964, p. 1; and "Editorial," *A União*, 2 April 1964, p. 3. Governor Gondim's 1 April statement can also be found in Hélio Zenaide, "De Como os Militares Passaram a Cassar e Caçar," in Guedes, ed., *O Jogo da Verdade*, pp. 82–83; and Zenaide, "Ascensao e Declínio," in Silva, ed., *Poder e Política na Paraíba*, p 160. Gondim made a distinction between reforms that were needed and that he had supported and the "grave rupture in discipline" exemplified by Goulart's support for insubordinate military men. Regarding his support for investigations into state and municipal officials who were acting against "national security and the democratic government," see "Operação Limpeza Começará Hoje na Paraíba," *Correio da Paraíba*, 17 April 1974, p. 8. Note how an article in July 1964 on education in Gondim's administration ignores CEPLAR completely. See "A Educação na Administração Governador Pedro Gondim," *A União* 14 July 1964, p. 8. This newspaper ran positive coverage of CEPLAR consistently in 1962 and 1963.

86. Dulles, *Castello Branco*, p. 350. Arraes was considered a "secret communist" and the "chief of subversion in the northeast." See the "Relatório do IPM do IV Exército," p. 78, in APE-PE, DOPS, pontuário no. 12.385, Miguel Arraes de Alencar. The MCP was considered one of his most serious "crimes."

87. Germano, *Lendo e Aprendendo*, pp. 150–53 and 158–60.

88. Edward J. Rowell, AmConGen Recife, "Weekly Summary No. 37," 8 April 1964, RG 59, Central Foreign Policy Files, Box 1930.

89. Germano, *Lendo e Aprendendo*, p. 66; see also Alves, *O Que Eu Não Esqueci*, p. 123.

90. Regarding Maranhão's "greatest crime," see his July 1965 message to the Brazilian people

in his posthumously published *Cartas de um Exilado*, pp. 69–71; Ariosvaldo Figueiredo, *História Política de Sergipe*, vol. 5, p. 84.

91. Sergipe Inquérito, Relatório, Jorge Henrique Leite Fontes, 4 September 1964.

92. Sergipe Inquérito, Interrogation of Tereinha Silva Ribeiro, 19 August 1964.

93. Sergipe Inquérito, Interrogation of Maria Auxiliadora da Silva, 20 August 1964.

94. For examples of "transformed consciousness" in another northeastern state, see "Mentalidade Nova Cria o Exéricito na Paraíba," *A União*, 14 June 1964, p. 1.

95. Sergipe Inquérito, Response to Report by Major Francisco Rodrigues da Silveira, September 1964. See also Ministério da Guerra, IV Exército, Sexta Região Military, Quartel General, Comissão Geral IPM/6, 3 December 1964, from Manoel Mandes Pereira, Sergipe Inquérito, Letter from Dr. Rinaldo Costa e Silva, Juiz de Direito da Segunda Vara Criminal da Comarca de Aracaju, 30 September 1981.

96. Celso dos Santos Meyer, "Relatório" and "Têrmo de Inquirição de Testemunha-Amado Menna Barreto Filho"; and Alcino de Paula Salazar, "Ação Penal 166," all in STM, IP 1426/68. Freire himself was said to have voted for every candidate supported by the Communist Party, with the exception of General Osvaldo Cordeiro de Farias in 1954. See Manoel Moreira Paz, "Relatório," 30 September 1964, in STM, Autos do IPM, "UNE/UBES/Pernambuco, Volumes IV and V, 1965."

97. See "Têrmo de Inquirição—Oscar Favero" and "Têrmo de Perguntas ao Indiciado-Marchus Machado de Alencar," in STM, IP 1426/68, vol. 1.

98. See, for example, Celso dos Santos Meyer, "Relatório," in STM, IP 1426/68.

99. Lincoln Gordon 10 April 1964 telegram, RG 59, Central Foreign Policy Files, 1964–66, Box 1939, p. 2.

100. Edward J. Rowell, AmConGen Recife, "Weekly Summary No 37," 8 April 1964, RG 59, Central Foreign Policy Files, Box 1930.

101. Cunha and Góes, *O Golpe na Educação*, p. 15. U.S. ambassador Gordon notes the extinction of the literacy campaign in Gordon to SecState, 16 April 1964, RG 59, Central Foreign Policy Files.

102. Rosas, *Papéis Avulsos*, pp. 28–30. For the transcript of Freire's interrogation, see Ana Maria Araújo Freire, *Paulo Freire*, pp. 182–98.

103. On the perceived admission of guilt, see, for example, Celso dos Santos Meyer, "Relatório," and "Têrmo de Inquirição de Testemunha-Amado Menna Barreto Filho," in STM, IP 1426/68. The military concluded that Freire was "one of the most responsible for subversion among the least favored." See also Ana Maria Araújo Freire, *Paulo Freire*, p. 199.

104. Lyra, *Quarenta Horas de Angicos*, pp. 12–14.

105. See Pelandré, *Ensinar e Aprender com Paulo Freire*, particularly pp. 38–39, 61–62, 134–35, 174–74, 180–83, 196–205, and 225–27.

106. Freire, *À Sombra Desta Mangueira*, p. 50.

107. Santos, *64 e Outros Anos*, pp. 60–61.

108. Dantas, *Os Partidos Politicos em Sergipe*, pp. 313–14; see also Skidmore, *Politics in Brazil*, p. 292.

109. Germano, *Lendo e Aprendendo*, p. 178.

110. Edward Rowell, AmConGen Recife, 2 December 1964, "Politics in Northeastern Brazil," RG 59, Central Foreign Policy Files, 1964–66, Box 1929. See also his 24 March 1965 report

in RG 59, Central Foreign Policy Files, 1964–66, Box 1941, Provincial, Municipal, and State Governments Folder, in which he notes that "signs announcing grand municipal achievements [in Natal] are limited to a few lauding the previous regime, which no one has gotten around to removing." See also Harold M. Midkiff, Consul (Salvador), "Aspects of the Current Situation in Sergipe," 13 May 1965, RG 59, Central Foreign Policy Files, 1964–66, Box 1941, Provincial, Municipal, and State Governments Folder. Midkiff notes that "the government is better organized than that of Seixas Dória, but lacks drive and enthusiasm." He also notes that "there was more enthusiasm under Dória than now, especially in the field of education" (p. 4).

111. Scoguglia, "Paulo Freire e a CEPLAR da Paraíba," p. 121.

112. Skidmore, *Politics of Military Rule*, pp. 24–25 and 144–49.

Chapter Three

1. Robert Austin refers to this period in Freire's life as "the engine room of Freirean intellectual history." See his *State, Literacy, and Popular Education*, p. 66. See also Eduardo Frei, "Primer Mensaje de Presidente de la República de Chile," 21 May 1965, p. 10, BCNC; and R. V. Fimbres, "National Plenary Council of Christian Democratic Party Meets to Consider National Political Campaign," 22 April 1964, RG 59, Central Foreign Policy Files, 1964–66, Box 2027, POL 12, "Political Parties, 1/1/64 Chile." In English, consult Frei, "Aims of Christian Democracy." The United States had hoped to encourage literacy programs that would combat "communist-dominated" literacy training programs during the previous conservative administration. See p. 5 of the 15 October 1962 memo from USAID/Chile economic adviser Otto H. Kerican to Ralph Dungan (special assistant to President Kennedy who then became President Johnson's ambassador to Chile) in National Security Files, Ralph A. Dungan, Chile General 10/6/62–11/30/62 Folder, JFK Library. Regarding the Left's hopes for a national literacy campaign in one year following a FRAP victory in 1964, see "Erradicación del Analfabetismo, Una Tarea de Honor," *El Siglo*, 5 April 1964, p. 14; and "La Educación en el Gobierno Popular: En Un Año Debe Terminarse con el Analfabetismo," *El Siglo*, 21 June 1964, p. 9. For a left-wing critique of the Frei administration, in particular its education policies, see Castro, *La Educación en Chile de Frei a Pinochet*, particularly pp. 45–89. He criticizes Freire for not including the concept of class conflict in the literacy training classes.

2. Gil, *Political System of Chile*, particularly pp. 1, 13–19, 23, 56–64, and 81–83. Regarding the "myth of race homogeneity," see ibid., p. 33.

3. One of the few significant attempts to view Freire's experience in Chile historically is Williamson Castro, *Paulo Freire*. A good introduction to Chilean Christian Democracy can be found in Lehmann, *Democracy and Development*, pp. 104–8. Regarding Jacques Chonchol, see, for example, Keith Wheelock, "Jacques Chonchol: The Legend, the Man, the Nexus," 8 January 1969, RG 59, Central Foreign Policy Files, 1967–69, Box 1978, POL 1 "1/1/69." For early conservative criticism of his alleged domination of more senior figures in agriculture in the Frei administration and what was believed to be his excessive influence on the agrarian reform program, see "Memorandum of Conversation with José Garrido N.," 25 March 1965, RG 59, Central Foreign Policy Files, 1964–66, Box 2027, POL 12-6 "Membership Leaders." When reflecting on his Chilean experience in interviews, Freire did not even mention President Frei himself, emphasizing instead that in Chile he had worked for "the former Minister of Agricul-

ture in the Allende Government." See "Freire Speaks on Freire," p. 7. For indications that the U.S. embassy was keeping its eye on Chonchol, see R. V. Fimbres, "Headquarters Structure of Frei Campaign," 4 April 1964, RG 59, Central Foreign Policy Files, 1964–66, Box 2027, POL 12-6 "Membership Leaders." Later sources indicate that the embassy had not kept in contact with him, as Ambassador Dungan thought it should. See 21 February 1967 memo to Bob Dean in Ralph Dungan Papers, Ambassador to Chile Files, Chronological Files, February 1967, Box 23, JFK Library. Left-wing newspaper *Punto Final* described Chonchol as "a man hated by the large landowners." See Leonardo Cáceres Castro, "El Fin de una Casta," *Punto Final*, February 1966, p. 16. Freire's relationship with Chonchol was also extremely close on a personal level. The fondness and admiration Freire felt for Chonchol was expressed in his presentation to him of the original handwritten copy of *Pedagogy of the Oppressed*, available in the IPF. In the dedication, he wrote that he "believed in" Chonchol (and his wife Maria Edy Ferreira) from the beginning. See Freire and Guimarães, *Aprendendo com a Própria História*, 1:99.

4. Freire and Guimarães, *Aprendendo com a Própria História*, 1:76–77, 80–81, and 85. The U.S. embassy in December of 1964 was planning to "follow the activities of these Brazilian exiles with particular interest in their possible contacts and influence" on the Christian Democratic youth groups. See Robert A. Stevenson, "Joint Weeka No. 51," 18 December 1964, RG 59, Central Foreign Policy Files, 1964–66, Box 2025, POL 2-1 "Joint Weekas Chile." Note that this document suggests that Paulo de Tarso Santos didn't arrive until mid-December.

5. For a critique of the Frei administration from the Left, see, for example, Roxborough, O'Brien, and Roddick, *Chile*, pp. 40–47 and 49–50. Barbara Stallings describes the Christian Democrats as "the only real multi-class party in Chile." See her *Class Conflict and Economic Development*, pp. 55 and 61–62. The bourgeoisie was represented by modern industrialists and the "petty bourgeois intelligentsia" (p. 55). Members of the popular classes were "real allies" in the "centrist alliance" (pp. 61–62). David Lehmann, however, refers to a "bourgeois leadership, a middle class membership and a working class and peasant clientele." See his "Political Incorporation versus Political Instability," p. 374. Robert Austin's stimulating work on Chilean literacy programs is weakened considerably by its ideologically driven misreadings of the Christian Democrats' complicated politics (and the prior Brazilian context, as well). It is not clear why he neglects the critical role of Jacques Chonchol, for example. He does, however, add to our understanding of the "contribution made by Chilean intellectuals to the development of Freirean philosophy of education." See *State, Literacy, and Popular Education*, pp. 65–123.

6. See the coverage of the Brazilian military government's comments on the nature of the Frei government in the Communist Party newspaper *El Siglo*, including the articles "Canciller de Brasil Amenaza a Frei," 2 September 1965, p. 1; "Indignación Causa Declaración Gorila," 3 September 1965, p. 1; "Repudio Nacional ante Amenazas Gorilistas: Parlamentarios de Todos los Partidos Expresan su Protesta ante Declaraciones de Canciller Brasileño," 5 September 1965, p. 9; as well as the editorial "Una Grosera Amenaza," 4 September 1965, p. 2; and the piece by Orlando Millas, "Sr. Leitao da Cunha: No es Fatal el Camino del Brasil," 5 September 1965, p. 2. The comparison of Frei and Goulart by the minister of foreign relations, Vasco Leitao da Cunha, was repeated a few weeks later by the minister of planning and development, Roberto Campos. See "Gorilas Brasileños Repiten la Amenaza al Gobierno Chileno," *El Siglo*, 21 September 1965, p. 1.

7. Regarding the U.S. support for the Frei administration, see Kirkendall, "Kennedy Men."

See also "Memorandum of Conversation: Mr. Mann's Second Meeting with the Mission of President-Elect Eduardo Frei, 17 Oct. 1964," p. 2, in RG 84, Box 144, American Embassy Santiago; Dungan, "The Government and the PDC: The Gap between Ideology and Reality," 12 July 1967, RG 84, Box 176, American Embassy, Santiago; and Dungan's 23 June 1966 speech to the American Chamber of Commerce in Santiago, p. 6, in Ralph Dungan Papers, Ambassador to Chile Files, Box 20, Speech Files Material 1966, JFK Library. Regarding U.S. policies in Brazil, see Rabe, *Most Dangerous Area in the World*, pp. 63–71. For policies in Chile, see Rabe, *Most Dangerous Area in the World*, pp. 109–16; and Sater, *Chile and the United States*, pp. 139–58. See also the fine study by Taffet, "Alliance for What?," particularly pp. 63–64, 151–83, and 214–24. Taffet's focus, however, is limited to economics. See also his *Foreign Aid as Foreign Policy*, pp. 67–93.

8. Williamson Castro, *Paulo Freire*, pp. 39 and 87–88; see also Ralph Dungan, "Visit to a CORA Project," Ralph Dungan Papers, Ambassador to Chile Files, Chronological Files, March 1966, Box 22, JFK Library; see the positive coverage of INDAP in *El Siglo*: "INDAP, Los Campesinos y la Reforma Agraria" and "Esto es INDAP," 31 December 1965, p. 11.

9. Frei, "Mensaje 1968," p. 259, and "Mensaje 1970," p. 30, BCNC; Williamson Castro, *Paulo Freire*, p. 75. Regarding the changing political dynamics in Chile, see Williamson Castro, *Paulo Freire*, pp. 9–10, 21–22, 29–30, and 68–69.

10. See James C. Scott's criticism of state-directed development in *Seeing Like a State*, particularly pp. 4–5 and 93–102.

11. The best introduction to this aspect of Frei's intellectual development in English is Ramos-Reyes, "Impact of Jacques Maritain"; see particularly pp. 15–16, 107–8, 148–49, 211, 260–62, and 274. A good, brief, and sympathetic introduction to his thought can be found in Jorrin and Martz, *Latin American Political Thought and Ideology*, pp. 411–15. For background on Christian Democratic parties in Latin America, see Lynch, *Latin America's Christian Democratic Parties*. Lynch provides a critical, antistatist perspective to explain the long-term failure of such parties in the region.

12. Loveman, *Struggle in the Countryside*, particularly pp. 144–44, 152–56, and 170–75.

13. Eduardo Frei, "Mensaje 1965," pp. 5–6, BCNC. Regarding the need for organization, see Frei, "Mensaje 1966," pp. 17–18, BCNC. For further information regarding the Christian Democratic understanding of the relationship between popular organization and the needs of Chilean society, see Ahumada, *La Crisis Integral de Chile*, pp. 21–23, 41, and 43–44. Regarding the Centros de Madre, see Frei, "Mensaje 1967," p. 6, BCNC. The longer quotation is from the presidential message of 1969. Regarding promoción popular, see Gazmuri, Arancibia, and Góngora, *Eduardo Frei y su Época*, pp. 609–12; and Riquelme, "Promoción Popular y la Educación para la Participación." Regarding the Centros de Madre, see Tinsman, *Partners in Conflict*, particularly pp. 146–56.

14. Frei, "Mensaje 1966," pp. 18–19, BCNC (emphasis in original); Lehmann, "Political Incorporation," p. 369. INDAP, for its part, claimed to be an "institution free of paternalism." See "Esto es INDAP: La Tarea del Campesino," *El Siglo*, 31 December 1965, p. 11. Regarding Frei's conviction that paternalism itself was dying in Chile, see Frei, "Aims of Christian Democracy," p. 65.

15. Frei, "Mensaje 1965," pp. 51–54, BCNC. From 1934 to 1964, according to government statistics, agricultural production increased 1.8 percent per year, while the Chilean population increased 2.5 percent per year during the same period. See also Frei, "Mensaje 1970," BCNC.

For a recent examination of the process of agrarian reform in Chile, see Tinsman, *Partners in Conflict*. For a conservative critique of Frei's agrarian reform, see Garrido, Guerrero, and Valdés, *Historia de la Reforma Agraria en Chile*, particularly pp. 97–133. To place thinking on land reform in a larger intellectual historical context, see Lehmann, *Democracy and Development*, pp. 9–10, 23, 33–34, and 44; and Roxborough, *Theories of Underdevelopment*, pp. 31–32 and 101–2. A good summary of the reform can be found in Joseph R. Thome, "Law, Conflict, and Change: Frei's Law and Allende's Agrarian Reform," in Thiesenhusen, ed., *Searching for Agrarian Reform*, pp. 191–201.

16. Chonchol, *El Desarrollo de America Latina*, p. 11.

17. Frei, "Mensaje 1965," p. 26, BCNC.

18. Frei, "Mensaje 1966," p. 331, BCNC. See also Chonchol, *Desarrollo de America Latina*, pp. 73–74.

19. Chonchol, *La Reforma Agraria como Proceso Dinámico*, pp. 10–11, 19, 23–24, 26, and 28. This was a lecture given at an INDAP course in 1967. Regarding Chilean agriculture, see Sigmund, *Overthrow of Allende*, p. 20. Stallings (*Class Conflict and Economic Development*, p. 100) notes, "The meaning of the term 'communitarian' was always very vague, but the basic idea seemed to be an emphasis on the common interests of workers and owners. In negative terms, it was the rejection of the process of the class struggle that the Marxist parties stressed." See also Loveman, *Struggle in the Countryside*, pp. 242–44. For a discussion of right-wing opposition to Chonchol, see Kaufman, *Politics of Land Reform in Chile*, pp. 163–65. Regarding the often age-based differences between the factions in the Christian Democratic Party, see Kaufman, *Politics of Land Reform in Chile*, pp. 84–93.

20. Santos, "Capacitación en Reforma Agraria," p. 11.

21. See Folder "25 Carteles" at the Instituto Paulo Freire.

22. Santos, "Educación Agrícola y Desarrollo Rural," p. 31.

23. Frei, "Mensaje 1970," p. 31, BCNC; for more on INDAP, see p. 33. Marcela Garjado, one of Freire's Chilean associates during these years, notes that, given the government's emphasis on rural unionization, "strike" inevitably was one of the generating words employed in the Chilean literacy program. See her "Educação Popular e Conscientização no Meio Rural Latino-Americano," in Wertheim and Díaz Bordenave, eds., *Educação Rural no Terceiro Mundo*, p. 117.

24. Cortés Carabantes, "Formas Muertas y Dinámicas en nuestra Educación de Adultos." See also Informe del Ministério de Educación, *La Educación de Adultos en Chile*, p. 9. Cortés Carabantes himself argued that the illiteracy rate was as high as 59 percent in rural Chile. Regarding literacy rates in the countryside on the eve of Frei's inauguration, see Joseph R. Thome, "Law, Conflict, and Change: Frei's Law and Allende's Agrarian Reform," in Thiesenhusen, ed., *Searching for Agrarian Reform*, p. 192. *El Mercurio* saw much to admire in the literacy program during the Alessandri administration. See, for example, "Realizaciones Educacionales Chilenas," *El Mercurio*, 27 June 1966, p. 31; and "Segundo Año de Alfabetización," *El Mercurio*, 20 October 1964, p. 3; as well as the news stories "Clausura de Espoción sobre la Campaña de Alfabetización," *El Mercurio*, 22 October 1964, p. 21; and "En Dos Años Aprendieron a Leer y Escribir 150,000," *El Mercurio*, 23 October 1964, p. 21. See also Oscar Herrera Palacios, "Futuro de la Campaña de Alfabetización," *El Mercurio*, 22 December 1964, p. 3. Cortés Carabantes's curriculum vitae is available in WCCA, Office of Education Files, Latin American Correspondence 1970–75.

25. Triviños and Andreola, "Da Opressão para a Esperança," pp. 5 and 18–19. This invaluable report, based largely on oral interviews, is available at the Instituto Paulo Freire.

26. Frei, "Mensaje 1966," pp. 189–90, BCNC.

27. Cortés Carabantes, "Los Planes Extraordinarios," pp. 30–31; Waldemar Cortés Carabantes, "Cursos para Educadores de Adultos," *El Mercurio*, 22 November 1965, p. 33.

28. Cortés Carbantes, "Los Planes Extraordinarios," pp. 30–31.

29. "Guia Didactica para el Professor," in Jefatura de Planes Extraordinarios de Educación de Adultos, *La Raiz y la Espiga*, pp. 1, 3, and 4; Lehmann, "Political Incorporation," pp. 367–70. See also Orrego Vicuña, *Soldiaridad o Violencia*, pp. 61–62 and 215–16; and "Material para La Educación," *El Mercurio*, 1 July 1967, p. 1. Austin offers his analysis in "Freire, Frei, and Literacy Texts in Chile" in Torres and Puiggrós, eds., *Latin American Education*, pp. 323–45.

30. Cortés Carabantes, "Introducción," in *Manual del Método Psico-Social para la Enseñanza de Adultos*, pp.1–3.

31. ICIRA, *La Alfabetización Funcional en Chile*, p. 6.

32. Ibid., pp. 7–10, 14, and 20.

33. Freire, *Pedagogy of Hope*, p. 38.

34. ICIRA, *La Alfabetización Funcional en Chile*, pp. 2–5.

35. Triviños and Andreola, "Da Opressão para a Esperança," pp. 143–48.

36. Informe del Ministério de Educación, *La Educación de Adultos en Chile*, p. 23.

37. "Los Apuros de un Analfabeto" in Jefatura de Planes Extraordinarios de Educación de Adultos, *Lectura para Adultos: Primer Nivel*, pp. 6–9.

38. "La Sociedad Rural," in Jefatura de Planes Extraordinarios de Educación de Adultos, *Comunidad*, p. 35. See also pp. 62–68.

39. "La Organización de la Comunidad," pp. 38–39; "La Patria," p. 43; "Hacia una Vida Mejor," p. 71; "Los Sindicatos," p. 82; "Los Cultivos," p. 87; "La Industria," pp. 92–93 (emphasis in original); "Chile: Un País en Marcha," p. 122; "La Vida del Campesino Chileno," pp. 123–28; and "Razones y Fines de la Reforma Agraria," pp. 128–30, all in Jefatura de Planes Extraordinarios de Educación de Adultos, *Comunidad*; Cortés Carabantes, *Manual del Método Psico-Social para la Enseñanza de Adultos*, p. 60.

40. "Alcohol," in Jefatura de Planes Extraordinarios de Educación de Adultos, *Lectura para Adultos: Primer Nivel*, pp. 35–36; Jefatura de Planes Extraordinarios de Educación de Adultos, *Comunidad*, p. 23. Regarding earlier Popular Front initiatives against alcoholism, see Rosemblatt, *Gendered Compromises*, pp. 162–66. Regarding Frei administration policies on alcohol, see "El Gobierno Tendrá Preocupación Fundamental por el Alcoholismo," *El Mercurio*, 14 November 1964, p. 29. See also Benjamin Viel, "Alcoholismo, una Enfermidad Nacional," *El Mercurio*, 17 June 1965, p. 3.

41. Jefatura de Planes Extraordinarios de Educación de Adultos, *Lectura para Adultos: Primer Nivel*, p. 49; Jefatura de Planes Extraordinarios de Educación de Adultos, *Lectura para Adultos: Segundo Nivel*, p. 29; Jefatura de Planes Extraordinarios de Educación de Adultos, *Comunidad*, pp. 13, 29, and 36.

42. "Distinción de UNESCO al Ministerio de Educación," *El Mercurio*, 3 September 1967, p. 45; see also letter from Juan Gomes Millas to Tor Gjesdal of UNESCO and the 9 October 1967 telegram noting the participation of Professor Cortés, in UNESCO Correspondence Files, Relations with Chile—Official X 07.21 (83). UNESCO in the 1960s had turned its attention to the concept of "functional literacy," a phrase that Freire also used more during his Chilean

tenure than at any other time. See Jones, *International Policies for Third World Education*, pp. 108 and 143–85. The phrase "work-oriented literacy," also in use at the time, better captures the spirit of much of the thinking at this time.

43. Transcript of recording of "Circulo de Investigación Temática," 3 October 1968, with men of asentamiento, El Recurso, pp. 1–3, 6, 14, and 15, IPF.

44. Transcript of recording of "Circulo de Investigación Temática," 13 November 1968, pp. 6–7, IPF.

45. Ibid., 20 November 1968, discussion with men, p. 1.

46. Ibid., p. 6.

47. Freire, "Adult Literacy Process," pp. 222–23.

48. Transcript of recording of "Circulo de Investigación Temática," 20 November 1968, discussion with men, p. 6, IPF.

49. Margarita Depetris, "Visita July 14, 1968," pp. 7 and 10, and "Breve Esquema Explicativo de los Principios Basicos de las Tecnicas Proyectacas," pp. 6–7, 9, and 11; and Maria Edy Ferreira, "Algunas Observaciones sobre el Asentamiento, El Recurso," accompanying transcript of recording of "Circulo Investigacion Tematica," IPF; Ferreira, *Tendencias del Poder*, p. 9; Clara Arce R., "Informe Socio-Cultural: El Recurso," 17 June 1968, accompanying transcript of "Circulo de Investigación Temática," p. 10, IPF.

50. Cortés Carabantes, "Introducción," in *Manual del Método Psico-Social para la Enseñanza de Adultos*, p. 4.

51. Paulo Freire, *Extensión o Comunicación*, pp. 12, 19, 34–35, and 48. (Chonchol wrote the introduction.)

52. Paulo Freire, "Actividades Desarrolladas en el Año de 1968," pp. 1–5, 7, and 19.

53. Maria Antonioneta Saa in *Alfabetización Funcional*; Julio Salgado Moya in *Alfabetización Funcional*.

54. Freire, "Actividades Desarrolladas en el Año de 1968," p. 11.

55. "Fuentealba Speech at PDC National Plenary Council, 28 Oct. 1968," p. 4, RG 84, Box 179, American Embassy, Santiago, Political Parties. One of the best studies of peasant attitudes and behavior in this period is Petras and Merino, *Peasants in Revolt*.

56. Transcript of recording of "Circulo de Investigación Temática," 13 November 1968, p. 9, IPF.

57. Weintraub, "Economic and Social Aspects of Parliamentary Elections," 13 March 1969, RG 59, Central Foreign Policy Files, 1967–69, Box 1980, POL 15-2 "Chile"; "First Colchagua Province Congress," 10 January 1967, RG 59, Central Foreign Policy Files, 1967–69, Box 1976, POL 2 "Chile."

58. Paulo Freire, "El Asentamiento como una Totalidad," pp. 2–5, 7–9, and 12.

59. See labor attaché Arthur P. Shankle Jr., "Marxist Activity in Rural Chile," RG 59, Central Foreign Policy Files, 1964–66, Box 2030, POL 23 "Internal Security. Counterinsurgency."

60. Frei's quotation from Tinsman, *Partners in Conflict*, p. 82. Regarding the complex relations in the asentamiento, see ibid., pp. 180–84; Loveman, *Struggle in the Countryside*, pp. 252–56 and 275; Lehmann, "Political Incorporation," pp. 380–83; Lehmann, "Peasant Consciousness," pp. 309 and 322–23; and Thome, "Law, Conflict, and Change," p. 200. For a more positive assessment of the asentamiento as a transitional structure, see Marion R. Brown, "Radical Reformism in Chile, 1964–1973," in Thiesenhusen, ed., *Searching for Agrarian Reform*, p. 237. See also Kaufman, *Politics of Land Tenure in Chile*, pp. 115–23; Ferreira, *Tendencias del*

Poder, p. 28; and Lynch, *Latin America's Christian Democratic Parties*, pp. 76–80. U.S. ambassador Dungan referred to "the new patron, that is CORA," in a 20 March 1967 memo to Sam Moskowitz and John Robinson, in Ralph Dungan Papers, Ambassador to Chile Files, Chronological Files, March 1967, Box 23, JFK Library.

61. Ferreira, *Tendencias del Poder*, pp. 7 and 10.

62. Dungan to Sam Moskowitz and John Robinson, "Reporting on INDAP and CORA," 20 March 1967, in Ralph Dungan Papers, Ambassador to Chile Files, Box 23, Chronological Files, March 1967, Box 23, JFK Library; Robert Dean, 23 January Report, "PDC: Party in Search of a Role," pp. 1, 3–5, and 8–9, and "The Government and the PDC: The Gap between Ideology and Reality," 12 July 1967, p. 8, both in RG 84, Box 176, American Embassy, Santiago; "Report on First Colchagua Province Campesino Conference," 10 January 1967, RG 84, Box 173, "Labor Management Relations" Folder; Ambassador Dungan letter, "Mercurio Editorial Economic Powers in Chile," 29 March 1967, pp. 1–5, RG 84, Box 173, "Economic Affairs (General)" Folder; "A View of the Campo," RG 84, Box 176, American Embassy, Santiago; K. A. Guenther, "Memorandum for the Files," 5 May 1967, RG 84, Box 177, American Embassy, Santiago; L. Spielman, "Pre-Election Peace Maneuvers in the Campesino Field," 17 May 1968, RG 84, Box 177, American Embassy, Santiago; Dungan, "Community Action in Otingue: Not Yet the Millennium," 29 March 1967, RG 84, Box 176, American Embassy, Santiago, "Political Affairs/Relations: Elections Municipal/Provincial" Folder; "CNC Sets up First Legal Chilean Campesino Federation," 30 December 1967, RG 84, Box 177, American Embassy, Santiago, "National Organizations Campesinos" Folder. Regarding funding for Christian Democratic trade unions, see Lester Spielman, "Recommendation on Continued Embassy Assistance to the CNC," 13 March 1967, RG 84, Box 173, American Embassy, Santiago, AID 1967. See also Roxborough, O'Brien, and Roddick, *Chile*, pp. 58–62; and Lehmann, "Political Incorporation," pp. 372 and 378. Lehmann refers to "promoción popular" generally as "paternalistic agitation." See p. 377. See also his "Peasant Consciousness," p. 300. Regarding the relationship between peasants and politicians, see Petras and Merino, *Peasants in Revolt*, pp. 40–43. For an analysis of the tensions between rural unions and government officials, see Kaufman, *Politics of Land Reform in Chile*, pp. 137–44; and Affonso et al., *Movimiento Campesino Chileno*, vol. 1, pp. 259 and 262; regarding INDAP organizing, see pp. 25 and 59. On Socialist Party understandings of Frei's intentions regarding unions "that escaped his paternalistic policies," see its pamphlet "1966: Año de la Organización y las Luchas Campesinas," p. 50. Lynch argues that "Catholic social thought insists on the genuine independence of social groups and warns against close ties to either a state or a political party" (*Latin America's Christian Democratic Parties*, pp. xi–xii and xv). See also the lead editorial "Catorce Años de Sindicalismo Política," *El Mercurio*, 16 February 1967, p. 3; and "INDAP y Pequeños Agricultores," *El Mercurio*, 12 October 1967, p. 3. For critiques of INDAP from people to the right of Chonchol on the political spectrum, see, for example, "Profesionales de INDAP Señalan Marginación de Planes Agropecuarios," *El Mercurio*, 5 August 1967, p. 31; and "Denuncia Contra INDAP por Crear Conflictos Campesinos," *El Mercurio*, 11 September 1968, p. 19.

63. Angell, "Chile since 1958," p. 150.

64. Collier and Sater, *History of Chile*, p. 315; Alexander, *Tragedy of Chile*, p. 107.

65. Edward Korry, "Politics of Drought," telegram, 9 September 1968, RG 84, Box 179, American Embassy, Santiago, "Social Conditions" Folder.

66. Paulo Freire, "Actividades Desarrolladas en el Año de 1968," p. 4.

67. Chonchol and Silva, *Hacia un Mundo Comunitario*, p. 5.

68. Williamson Castro, *Paulo Freire*, p. 35.

69. Robert Dean, 23 January Report, "PDC: Party in Search of a Role," p. 10, RG 84, Box 176, American Embassy, Santiago. Regarding Chonchol and the divisions in the party, see Gazmuri, Arancibia, and Góngora, *Frei y su Época*, pp. 593, 612, 654, 668, 686–87, 704, and 800. See also, for example, the lead editorials "Nueva Directiva Democratacristiana," *El Mercurio*, 18 July 1967, p. 3; "Partido de Gobierno y Régimen Presidencial," *El Mercurio*, 19 July 1967, p. 3; and "Gobierno y Democracia Cristiana," *El Mercurio*, 29 July 1967, p. 3.

70. "The Government and the PDC: The Gap between Ideology and Reality," pp. 1 and 3, 12 July 1967, RG 84, Box 176, American Embassy, Santiago; "The New PDC Directiva: A Moment of Truth for President Frei?," RG 84, Box 176, American Embassy, Santiago; Ralph Dungan, "Municipal Election Results Signal New Political Ball Game," pp. 1, 2, 9, 13, and 15, RG 84, Box 176, "Political Affairs and Relations: Elections Municipal/Provincial" Folder. Regarding small farmers, see "Chilean Small Farmer Disenchantment with the Frei Administration," 10 February 1968, RG 84, Box 177, American Embassy, Santiago, "National Labor Unions" Folder. For an analysis of the loss of support among urban groups in the 1967 elections, see Kaufman, *Politics of Land Reform in Chile*, pp. 123–25.

71. Frei, "Mensaje 1967," p. 342, BCNC.

72. Ibid., pp. 72–74.

73. Frei, "Mensaje 1968," pp. 32–34, BCNC.

74. Sidney Weintraub, "Land Use/Land Reforms," 9 May 1967, RG 84, Box 173, American Embassy, Santiago.

75. J. Norbury, "Telegram, 17 July 1967," RG 84, Box 175, American Embassy, Santiago, "Political Affairs and Relations" Folder.

76. Frei, "Mensaje 1967," p. 50, BCNC.

77. Edward Korry, "The End of the Revolution in Liberty," 29 March 1968, RG 59, Central Foreign Policy Files, 1967–69, Box 1980, POL 23 "Chile."

78. Freire, *Pedagogy of Hope*, p. 38.

79. Ibid.

80. U.S. ambassador Korry argued that by not openly rejecting such an alliance and maintaining good relations with Tomic, the U.S. would subtly direct the Communist Party toward a rejection of the alliance. See Korry's 30 April 1968 telegram, RG 84, Box 179, American Embassy, Santiago, "Political Parties" Folder. See Stallings's class analysis of the divisions in the governing party in *Class Conflict and Economic Development*, pp. 62, 108–15, and 229–30.

81. Edward Korry, "The JDC: Both Seen and Heard," 9 November 1968 telegram, RG 84, Box 179, American Embassy, Santiago, "Political Parties—PDC Youth" Folder. To understand the JDC's political hopes and expectations prior to Frei's inauguration, see "Segundo Congreso Nacional de la Juventud Democrata Cristiana—Informe" (Santiago: Oct./Nov. 1963), particularly pp. 5, 7, 10, 11, and 13. Regarding Chonchol's appeal to youth, see Roxborough, O'Brien, and Roddick, *Chile*, p. 66.

82. See Robert Dean, 23 January 1967 report, "The PDC: A Party in Search of a Role," p. 8, RG 84, Box 176, American Embassy, Santiago.

83. Paulo Freire, "El Compromiso del Profesional con la Sociedad," pp. 1, 3, 4, 5, 8, 9, 11, and 13. Freire was often quite critical of the young "petty bourgeois" students who engaged in literacy campaign efforts during their summer vacations. See the rather sad letter written by

Carlos Calvo on 8 August 1978 to Freire in WCCA, Office of Education Files, Correspondence Paulo Freire.

84. Triviños and Andreola, "Da Opressão para a Esperança," pp. 5–6 and 194.

85. Ibid., pp. 34–35. See also Williamson Castro, *Paulo Freire*, p. 42.

86. Rolando Pinto has argued that the Brazilians were viewed unsympathetically from the beginning by some members of the PDC. See Triviños and Andreola, "Da Opressão para a Esperança," pp. 38–40.

87. Ibid., pp. 196–98 and 203. I have been unable to find any criticism of Freire in *El Mercurio*. See, for example, the favorable coverage of the Freire method in "Alfabetización de Adultos, Inversión a Corto Plazo," *El Mercurio*, 17 June 1968, p. 34; and "Diminuye el Analfabetismo," *El Mercurio*, 30 October 1968, p. 27.

88. See Freire, "O Homem Analfabeto da América Latina como Marginado. Descrição Político-Social de sua Situação e Aspirações," which was presented at a "meeting of experts on the collaboration of Catholics in literacy training in Latin America" in Bogotá in July 1968. It can be found at INEP.

89. "The Moneda, the PDC, and a Man Called Tomic" and "Zukovic [*sic*] Heard From: Telegram 23 Oct. 1968," both in RG 84, Box 179, American Embassy, Santiago, "PDC Folder No. 2."

90. Edward Korry, "Politics of Drought," telegram, 9 September 1968, RG 84, Box 179, American Embassy, Santiago, "Social Conditions" Folder.

91. Triviños and Andreola, "Da Opressao para a Esperança," pp. 185–86.

92. "Frei's Compromise—Hobson's Choice?," pp. 2 and 3, RG 84, Box 179, American Embassy, Santiago, "Political Parties" Folder; Dean, "President Up and Chonchol Out," and T. Friedman, "Chonchol: Game and Set to Frei," RG 84, Box 179, American Embassy, Santiago, "PDC Folder No. 2"; "S. E. Aceptó Renuncia del Vicepresidente de INDAP," *El Mercurio*, 12 November 1968, p. 41. Frei had earlier asked for Chonchol's resignation, then withdrew the request. See "Frei Anuló su Petición de Renuncia a Chonchol," *El Mercurio*, 7 August 1968, p. 23. Chonchol was increasingly criticized in the pages of *El Mercurio*. See, for example, "Incógnitos de la Reforma Agraria," *El Mercurio*, 8 July 1968, p. 27.

93. Edward Korry, "Chonchol," telegram, 2 December 1968, RG 84, Box 179, American Embassy, Santiago, "PDC Folder No. 2." See "'El PDC debe Constituirse como un Partido de Izquierda no Marxista,'" *El Mercurio*, 28 March 1969, p. 37, regarding a meeting of Chonchol and others in his faction of the party.

94. Frei, "Mensaje 1968," p. 417, BCNC.

95. Frei, "Mensaje 1969," p. 92, BCNC.

96. Tinsman, *Partners in Conflict*, p. 85.

97. Frei, "Mensaje 1970," pp. 4, 9, 31, and 35, BCNC; Alexander, *Tragedy of Chile*, pp. 92–93. Regarding rural unions, see the editorial "Sindicación Campesina," *El Mercurio*, 16 September 1965, p. 3.

98. Tinsman, *Partners in Conflict*, p. 83.

99. Hamuy B., "Chile," pp. 24–25, 27, and 29–30. Regarding the increasing loss of support in the cities, see Kaufman, *Politics of Land Reform in Chile*, pp. 41, 223–26, and 235–55.

100. Lehmann, "Peasant Consciousness," pp. 306 and 309–24.

101. Sidney Weintraub, "Some Reflections on the Senate's Rejection of President Frei's Pro-

posed Trip to the United States," 11 February 1967, pp. 2, 6, and 9, RG 84, Box 175, "American Embassy Chile."

102. Collier and Sater, *History of Chile*, p. 310.

103. 21 December 1967 report by Korry, RG 84, Box 176, American Embassy, Santiago.

104. Quoted in Robert Dean, "GOC Gives up Plan to Legislate on Promoción Popular," 10 June 1967, RG 84, Box 176, American Embassy, Santiago.

105. Angell, "Chile since 1958," p. 153.

106. Regarding unrest in the countryside, see, for example, the lead editorials "Huelgas Revolucionarios en la Agricultura," *El Mercurio*, 10 February 1966; "La Subversión en la Agricultura," *El Mercurio*, 11 February 1966, p. 3; "Marxismo en el Campo," *El Mercurio*, 16 February 1966, p. 3; and "Autoridad para Progresar," *El Mercurio*, 8 March 1966, p. 3.

107. Angell, "Chile since 1958," p. 153; Collier and Sater, *History of Chile*, pp. 314 and 325. See also "Progresiva Desmembración en la Democracia Cristiana: Renuncias de Chonchol, Jerez, Silva, Sota y Dirigentes de la JDC," *El Mercurio*, 10 May 1969, pp. 1 and 16. Regarding the hopes MAPU had of creating a "pluralist, socialist and communitarian society . . . directed by the workers and functioning in the interest of the large national majority," see Jacques Chonchol, "Informe Político," mimeo, 1 August 1969, available in Land Tenure Center Library, University of Wisconsin, Madison. He noted the need to engage in a long period of "political pedagogy so that the Chilean people [could] become conscious of their actual situation" and to take steps toward active participation in society in permanent dialogue with the leaders of the movement. MAPU wanted a new education that prepared people to make changes and integrate into a new society with new values.

108. Gajardo, *Educación de Adultos*, particularly pp. 66–67.

109. Joseph Norbury, 14 January 1968 memorandum quoting the Communist newspaper *El Siglo*, RG 84, Box 175, American Embassy, Santiago, "Political Affairs and Relations," POL 2, "Country Situation Report." See also Kirkendall, "Kennedy Men."

110. Richard M. Nixon, "For a Productive Alliance, 15 Oct. 1968," p. 4, RG 84, Box 177, American Embassy, Santiago, "Aid (Gen)."

111. Sigmund, *United States and Democracy in Chile*, p. 34.

112. See, for example, "International Developments and Economic Defense Policy," "Letter from the Administrator of the Agency for International Development (Gaud) to the Director of the Bureau of the Budget, 25 Nov. 1968," *FRUS, 1967–1968*, 9:232–34.

113. Angell, "Chile since 1958," p. 150. Stallings (*Class Conflict and Economic Development*, p. 57) notes that white-collar workers benefitted most from Frei policies, although the "bourgeoisie . . . did not lose all that much." See also Kaufman, *Politics of Land Reform in Chile*, pp. 126–28.

114. Angell, "Chile since 1958," pp. 152–53.

115. Tinsman, *Partners in Conflict*, p. 206; Lehmann, "Peasant Consciousness," p. 318; Thome, "Law, Conflict, and Change," pp. 200–201; Kaufman, *Politics of Land Reform in Chile*, p. 131; Ferreira, *Tendencias del Poder*, pp. 25, 31, and 33.

116. Frei, "Mensaje 1970," pp. 29–31 and 54, BCNC. In 1965, Chonchol suggested that the problems of the peasantry had to be resolved in "at most five to ten years" (*Desarrollo de America Latina*, p. 74). See also Gajarda, *Educación de Adultos*, p. 21.

117. Gajarda, *Educación de Adultos*, p. 10; Williamson Castro, *Paulo Freire*, p. 76.

118. Chonchol, *Reforma Agraria como Proceso Dinámico*, pp. 16–19; Chonchol, "Poder y Reforma Agraria en la Experiencia Chilena," particularly 269, 272, and 310–13; Affonso et al., *Movimiento Campesino Chileno*, vol. 1, pp. 7 and 251.

119. Karkashian [first name unknown], "A Political Round-up: Ten Months before the Election," 19 October 1969, p. 3, RG 59, Central Foreign Policy Files, 1967–69, Box 1979. Karkashian argued that "[t]he threat of Chonchol's candidacy appears to have shaken the Socialists out of the lethargy induced by their internal differences over Allende's candidacy" (p. 4). See also "Popular Unity: The Joys of Toils," 18 September 1969, and "Chonchol Resignation Fallout," 13 November 1968, both in RG 59, Central Foreign Policy Files, 1967–69, Box 1977, POL 12. In Box 1977, Folder POL "1/1/68," see A. P. Shankle's 6 October 1969 telegram that discusses his trip to the United States. Townsend Friedman, "Chonchol: Some More Dimensions," 1 February 1969, and Keith Wheelock, "Jacques Chonchol: The Legend, the Man, the Nexus," 8 January 1969, both in RG 59, Central Foreign Policy Files, 1967–69, Box 1978, POL 1 "1/1/69."

120. Loveman, *Struggles in the Countryside*, pp. 280–301. For a summary of Allende's agrarian reform, see Thome, "Law, Conflict, and Change," pp. 201–15. "El MAPU Proclamó Candidato Presidencial a J. Chonchol," *EL Mercurio*, 28 September 1969, p. 43. For a sympathetic portrayal of Chonchol's policies under Allende, see Mallon, *Courage Tastes of Blood*, pp. 88 and 105–7.

121. Lehmann, "Political Incorporation." See also the lead editorial "Momento Prevolucionario," *El Mercurio*, 4 June 1968, p. 3.

122. Transcript of recording of "Circulo de Investigación Temática," 20 November 1968, discussion with women, pp. 7, 8, and 9; Santos, "Educación Agrícola y Desarrollo Rural," p. 21; Gould, *To Lead as Equals*, pp. 30–31; Taussig, *Devil and Commodity Fetishism*, pp. 7–11 and 94–97.

123. Freire and Guimarães, *Aprendendo com a Própria História*, 1:15. The letter written in Geneva is in Manuscritos de Paulo Freire, Textos Selecionados, vol. 3, IPF. Regarding the Nixon administration's support for regional "policemen" in the Third World, see Westad, *Global Cold War*, p. 197.

Chapter Four

1. Freire and Faundez, *Learning to Question*, pp. 11–12.

2. Denis A. Goulet to Leopoldo J. Niilus of the CCIA, 27 January 1970, in WCCA, CCIAF, Development, Correspondence, 1969 [sic]; James Lamb to Freire, in WCCA, Sub-Unit on Education, Office of Education Files, General Education 1970–71 Folder. Freire discusses his surprise at finding out that being able to read English and being able to live day to day in an English-speaking country were different things in Freire and Guimarães, *Aprendendo com a Própria História*, 2:51–56.

3. Jonathan Kozol to Freire, 20 June 1975, in WCCA, Office of Education Files, Paulo Freire Correspondence USA 1974–76. See also Kozol, *Night Is Dark*, pp. 193–94. Note how Kozol faults the Harvard School of Education for not offering Freire a permanent position.

4. Albert van den Heuvel to Gibson Parker, 20 October 1968, in WCCA, CCIAF, Development, 1951–65, 1966–68; WCC, *Handbook*, pp. 3, 4, 6, and 10. See also Bock, *In Search of a Responsible World Society*, pp. 24, 42–51, 201–3, 214–15, and 218–24. A conservative critique of the council's policies is advanced in Lefever, *Amsterdam to Nairobi*, pp. 14–15 and 18–29.

5. For background on WCC interest in development issues, see Robert S. Bilheimer, "Theological Bases for the Support of Programmes of Economic and Technical Assistance," 28 November 1958, in WCCA, CCIAF, Development, Economic Development, 1951–65, pp. 66–68; Draft of "Resource Sharing Book for the Commission on Churches' Participation in Development," in CCPD/EDF Budgets Folder, 1974–85; and CCPD, "Minutes of the Meeting on Development Education Strategy, 17–23 June 1972," p. 5, and 1975 Financial Report of the Commission and the Ecumenical Development Fund, both in WCCA, CCPDF. Freire took part in the "consultation on development education" in Geneva in late May of 1969. See the correspondence from this year in WCCA, CCIAF, Development. The debt to Freire becomes ever clearer as the decade progressed. See G. I. Itty, "The Role of the World Council of Churches in the Field of Development and its Relation to the United Nations and its Related Agencies," 17 January 1972, in WCCA, CCIAF, Development, Documents/Correspondence 1969–73. See also Appendix to 7 September 1976 memo from Manfred Drewes in "Minutes of the Officers' Meeting of the CCPD October 1976" and "Report of the CCPD, 1970–1976," p. 21, where it discusses the "guiding principle: conscientization approach." CCPD also worked closely with the Institute for Cultural Action itself. See "Toward a CCPD Strategy on Development Education," p. 2, in Appendix 3 to 1972 CCPD Minutes, CCPDF; and "Development Education—Review and Perspective," in WCCA, Working Group on Education 1979/80. For a retrospective view, see "The 2% Appeal Reassessed: Report of the Consultative Workshop on the 2% Appeal, Geneva 29–31 July 1982," in WCCA, CCPDF, EDF, 2% Appeal Papers 1977–87.

6. Indeed, many had become highly critical of the use of the word "development." See Gutiérrez, *Theology of Liberation*, pp. x–xi, 22–27, and 33–37. He preferred the word "liberation."

7. *International Development Strategy: Action Programme*, particularly pp. 2–5 and 16–17; "The 2 % Appeal Reassessed: Report of the Consultative Workshop on the 2% Appeal, Geneva 29–31 July 1982," in WCCA, CCPD, EDF, 2% Appeal Papers 1977–87.

8. Some suggest that the council had a hand in the advancement of liberation theology at the 1966 meeting, at which Princeton theologian Richard Shaull called for a "theology of revolution." See Sigmund, *Liberation Theology at the Crossroads*, p. 28. For more on Shaull, see Smith, *Emergence of Liberation Theology*, pp. 116–17. Regarding the origins of liberation theology, see Lernoux, *Cry of the People*, pp. 11–13 and 24–56. Mario Ramos-Reyes offers a critical view from a Christian Democratic perspective in "Impact of Jacques Maritain," pp. 215–19. He does not seem aware of Freire's link to both points of view.

9. For information on the background of the council's interest in education, see William B. Kennedy, "Education in the World Ecumenical Movement"; "Draft of Introductory Letter from the OE to Churches and Educational Agencies," in WCCA, Sub-Unit on Education, Office of Education Files; and Kipnow, "Alienation, Liberation, Community." Regarding Freire's retrospective view, see Freire and Faundez, *Learning to Question*, pp. 12–13.

10. See Van den Heuvel, ed., *Unity of Mankind*, p. 71, as well as Goodall, ed., *Uppsala Report 1968*, pp. 197–99. See also notes from a 9 September 1969 discussion "Education in the DEA," p. 2, and "The Background of the Office of Education: Notes from a Conversation with Ernest Lange," p. 1–2, in WCCA, Sub-Unit on Education, Office of Education Files, Background Folder.

11. Dr. Raymond Poignant, "Topics for Consideration on 'Educational Planning' in Developing Countries," in WCCA, Office of Education Files, Bergen Box, Doc. 21 Folder, pp. 2–4 and 10.

12. "WCC Consultation on Educational Programmes—Efficient Education or School for Freedom?—Different Situations and Christian Responsibilities"; and Document no. 44, "Report of the Committee on Non School Education," both in WCCA, Bergen Box, Publications on Bergen Folder.

13. See "Report of the Office of Education, Divisional Committee Meeting, Loccum, August 2–8, 1970," in WCCA, Sub-Unit on Education, Office of Education Files, Background Folder, pp. 2 and 3.

14. See Ralph Mould's concerns at the 15–16 October 1971 meeting in WCCA, Sub-Unit on Education, Staff Working Group on Education, November 1971; see also his 28 October 1971 memo regarding "Minutes of Foyer John Knox Meeting of October 15–16/71," pp. 1–2, in WCCA, Sub-Unit on Education, Ed. Staff Working Group 1970–73 Folder; and 4 July 1974 memo from Stephen Whittle to Freire in WCCA, Sub-Unit on Education, Correspondence Paulo Freire.

15. C. G. Richards to William Kennedy, 16 December 1970, WCCA, Sub-Unit on Education, Colloquium on Education, 14–18 December 1970 Folder.

16. See Freire, "Notes on Humanisation [sic] and Its Educational Implications," particularly pp. 2–4; and "The Political 'Literacy' Process: An Introduction," p. 9, both in WCCA, Sub-Unit on Education, Colloquium on Education, 14–18 December 1970 Folder.

17. Charles Granston Richards to Kennedy, 16 December 1970; Victor E. W. Hayward to W. B. Kennedy, 18 December 1970; and Tina Baggott to Kennedy and Freire, 29 March 1971, in WCCA, Sub-Unit on Education, Colloquium on Education, 14–18 December 1970 Folder.

18. Kennedy to Elizabeth O'Connor, author of a book on the Church of the Savior in Washington, D.C., 24 October 1972, in WCCA, Office of Education Files, Correspondence Paulo Freire 1972 (and 1971).

19. "Report of Education Staff Working Group: Plans for 1972–1972," in WCCA, Sub-Unit on Education, Unit III Minutes.

20. "Future Developments in the Educational Work of the Church (W. C. C. Staff)," p. 1, in WCCA, Office of Education Files, USA, USA visits Folder.

21. "Education Concerns for Unit III 1972," in WCCA, Sub-Unit on Education, Plans of Work 1969–74; Freire, Pedagogy of Hope, p. 120–22.

22. Freire, "Progress Report on the Work of Paulo Freire from March 1970 to October 1971," in WCCA, Sub-Unit on Education, Progress Reports 1970–74 Folder.

23. "Proposal for North American Workshops in 1972–73," 7 December 1971, in WCCA, Sub-Unit on Education, Ed. Staff Working Group 1970–73 Folder.

24. See, for example, Freire to Alexander Mittermair, 2 June 1975, in WCCA, Office of Education Files, Correspondence W. Kennedy/P. Freire 1975.

25. Freire, Pedagogy of Hope, pp. 150–54. Kennedy also addressed Freire's experience in his lectures to the Perkins School of Theology, 5–7 March 1974. See his second lecture, "Education for Unfreedom," p. 10, in WCCA, Office of Education Files, Will Kennedy's Correspondence 1973/1974/1975.

26. Freire to Idrian Resnick, 19 February 1973, in WCCA, Office of Education Files, Correspondence Paulo Freire 1972 (and 1971) [sic]. In her letter to Freire of 4 January 1973, Resnick referred to "Amerika."

27. See William Kennedy's lectures to the Perkins School of Theology, 5–7 March 1974,

Lecture Two: "Education for Unfreedom," pp. 10–11, in WCCA, Office of Education Files, Will Kennedy's Correspondence 1973/1974/1975.

28. Kennedy to Elizabeth O'Connor, 24 October 1972, in WCCA, Office of Education Files, Correspondence Paulo Freire 1972 (and 1971) [sic].

29. "Unsere Welt und Unser Leben," 9 October and 3 November 1970 memos from Werner Simpfendörfer to Freire and others, in WCCA, Sub-Unit on Education, "Seminar with P. F. Re: Migrant Workers 1970–1971, 22 December 1970" Folder.

30. Freire, *Pedagogy of Hope*, pp. 138–43.

31. Claudius S. P. Ceccon to Freire, 22 March 1971, in WCCA, Sub-Unit on Education, IDAC 1971–72 Folder. For the background of IDAC, see Freire et al., *Vivendo e aprendendo*, particularly pp. 9–14.

32. Institute for Cultural Action, *What Is IDAC?*; "Second Report of the Institute of Cultural Action (IDAC), Covering the Period July 1972 to June 1974," pp. 1–5, and 9–12, in WCCA, Sub-Unit on Education, IDAC 1971–72 Folder. See also the description of IDAC on pp. 10–12, as well as the attached personnel section in the founding document. Regarding difficulties in raising funds, see "Annual Report of the Institute of Cultural Action, September 1971–June 1972," in WCCA, Sub-Unit on Education, IDAC 1971–72 Folder. See also Kennedy to E. Weisser, Executive Secretary of Kirchlicher Entwicklungsdients in Stuttgart, 30 June 1971, and Kennedy to Ceccon, 3 September 1971 in WCCA, Sub-Unit on Education, IDAC 1971–72 Folder. Regarding the work with Italian workers' groups, see Freire et al., *Vivendo e aprendendo*, pp. 15–37; regarding work with the women's movement in Switzerland, see Freire et al., *Vivendo e aprendendo*, pp. 39–67.

33. See Freire to Judy Heath of Bukit Lan Methodist Rural Life of Malaysia, 4 June 1975, in WCCA, Office of Education Files, Correspondence W. Kennedy/P. Freire 1975.

34. See "Toward an Overall Strategy for the CCPD," 17–23 June 1972, in Appendix 2 to 1972 CCPD Minutes, p. 3, CCPDF.

35. See "Working Draft: 2 July 1972 OE/WCC Progress Report," in WCCA, Sub-Unit on Education, Office of Education Files, Progress Reports Folder.

36. James F. McShane to Freire, 28 October 1971, in WCCA, Office of Education Files.

37. Susanne Korsukewitz to Freire, August 1971, in WCCA, Office of Education Files.

38. Jaime Diaz to Freire, 25 October 1974, in WCCA, Office of Education Files, Latin American Correspondence.

39. IDAC, *Conscientization and Liberation*, pp. 3 and 12.

40. Waldemar Cortés Carabantes, "Significación del Primer Seminario Operacional para Centroamerica y Panama," *Carta Informativa del CREFAL*, March 1971, pp. 1–5; "Notas de Actualidad," *Carta Informativa del CREFAL*, no. 7, December 1969, pp. 8–9.

41. Freire's ideas on developments in Christianity during this time period can be found in "Education, Liberation and the Church," particularly pp. 13–15.

42. Roy G. Neehall, "The Study and Education Programme of SODEFAX in Relation to Development," Appendix 5 to 1970 CCPD Minutes, in WCCA, CCPDF, Commission Minutes 1970–79. See also the discussion of Freire's methods in Antonio Cechin, "Evangelizing Men as They Are," pp. 131–36. Regarding Christian Base Communities, see Smith, *Emergence of Liberation Theology*, pp. 130–32.

43. Austin, *State, Literacy, and Popular Education*, pp. 132–33, 138–49, 156–60, and 171–86.

Austin's partisan perspective tends to distort the picture somewhat. Regarding Allende's plans for education, see his presidential message of 1971, BCNC; and Austin, *State, Illiteracy, and Popular Education*, p. 42.

44. Eugene Carson Blake to President Salvador Allende, 1 September 1971, in WCCA, CCIAF, Country Files, South America, Chile; and Dwain Epps to Blake, 23 June 1971, in WCCA, CCIAF, Country Files, South America, Chile, 1960, 1972–73 [sic].

45. See Rolando Pinto, "La Participación de los Trabajadores y la Educación Popular, Elementos Essenciales de la Transformación Socialista en Chile," in "Education for Revolution" Folder, WCCA, Sub-Unit on Education. Inspired by Freire, Isabel Hernández designed a literacy campaign simultaneously in Spanish and Mapuche in 1973. See her *Educação e Sociedade Indígena*, particularly pp. 42–54 and 57–114.

46. Freire to Joe Holland of the Chicago Divinity School, 3 August 1972, in WCCA, Office of Education Files, Correspondence Paulo Freire 1972 (and 1971); see also the July 1972 memo from Will Kennedy to Office of Education Staff, p. 5, in WCCA, Sub-Unit on Education, Office of Education Files, Progress Reports 1971–79; and "Minutes of the EEC Staff Committee Meeting, 18 October 1972," in WCCA, Sub-Unit on Education, Ed. Staff Working Group 1970–73 Folder.

47. Freire, *Pedagogy of Hope*, pp. 36–37 and 188.

48. William Kennedy to Leo Niilus, 27 March 1972, in WCCA, Sub-Unit on Education, UNESCO Correspondence, 1969–77. For examples of letters from Chilean exiles, see Waldermar Cortés Carabantes and Hector Urrutia Quijada to Freire, 9 December 1975, WCCA, Office of Education Files, Latin America Correspondence 1970-1975; Susana Flores Martinez to Freire, 26 May 1976, in WCCA, Office of Education Files, Dossiers; and Carlos Calvo to Freire, 8 August 1978, in WCCA, Office of Education Files, Correspondence Paulo Freire.

49. See the letters in WCCA, Office of Education Files, Latin America Correspondence 1970–75, Panama Folder.

50. See Berger, "After the Third World?," pp. 23–24.

51. Andrew Greeley, "Catholic Social Activism—Real or Rad/Chic?," *National Catholic Reporter*, 7 February 1975, pp. 7–9 and 10–11. William Kennedy's letters to various people in response to Greeley's article are in WCCA, Office of Education Files, Will Kennedy's Correspondence with the USA, 1973/1974/1975. See also the 18 March 1975 memo from Kennedy to Philip Potter, in WCCA, Office of Education Files, Correspondence W. Kennedy/P. Freire 1975. Kennedy suggested that this attention to Freire "indicate[d] the fact that Paulo's work is being taken seriously in powerful areas of United States church life."

52. Lefever, *Amsterdam to Nairobi*, p. vii.

53. Kennedy to Ralph Mould, 18 March 1975, and Kennedy to Frank Wortham, 7 May 1975, in WCCA, Office of Education Files, Correspondence W. Kennedy/P. Freire 1975.

54. Kennedy to Marion Halvorson of Intermedia Regional Services in Nairobi, 22 April 1975, and Kennedy to Karl Ernest Kipnow, 17 October 1975, in WCCA, Office of Education Files, Correspondence W. Kennedy/P. Freire 1975; see also Kennedy, "Education in the World Ecumenical Movement," p. 154.

55. See, for example, Freire to Australian William Hanson, 13 January 1975, and Freire to J. P. Naik of New Delhi, 13 January 1975, in WCCA, Office of Education Files, Correspondence W. Kennedy/P. Freire 1975.

56. Paton, ed., *Breaking Barriers*, particularly pp. 85–97. See also Lefever's critique in *Amsterdam to Nairobi*, p. 41.

57. "The Formation of Critical Consciousness," p. 1, and summary chart in WCCA, Office of Education Files, Preparation for Section IV: Education for Liberation and Community.

58. "Minutes of Meeting of Section IV Staff Team 15 January 1975," in WCCA, Office of Education Files, Preparation for Section IV—Nairobi.

59. Freire to G. Deleon, 7 September 1971, in WCCA, Sub-Unit on Education.

60. Regarding the development of Nyerere's distinctive "African socialist" ideology, see Pratt, *Critical Phase in Tanzania*, particularly pp. 2, 4–7, 56, 63, 66–69, 77, 201–15, 228–37, and 243–64. Regarding the influence of Catholicism on his thinking, see Duggan and Civille, *Tanzania and Nyerere*, pp. 43–50 and 223–25. For a more critical perspective, see Scott, *Seeing Like a State*, pp. 223–47. The Tanzania that Scott describes bears no relation to the idealized one Freire saw or thought he saw.

61. Jane Vella to Freire, 11 May and 24 July 1975, in WCCA, Office of Education Files, Africa Correspondence Files; Freire to Abelino Conde, 2 June 1975, in WCCA, Office of Education Files, Latin America Correspondence 1970–75. See also Budd Hall of the Institute of Adult Education in Dar-es-Salaam to Freire, 19 July 1973, in WCCA, Office of Education Files, Correspondence Paulo Freire 1973 (and 1971) (an 11 July 1973 article from the *Daily News* was attached). To understand the thinking of Nyerere on education, see the 20 May 1974 opening address "Education and Liberation," in WCCA, Sub-Unit on Education, 1974, Dar-es-Salaam Seminar on Education and Training and Alternatives in Education in African Countries. See also "Paulo Freire's Trips to Africa 1976/76," 19 March 1976, in WCCA, Sub-Unit on Education, Correspondence 1976–77; "Document No. 5—Adult Literacy and Education Programmes," in WCCA, Working Group on Education 1979/80; and Unsicker, "Adult Education," particularly pp. 9–12, 17–26, 107–18, 128–36, 148–52, 156–63, 176–94, 208–21, and 242–54. Unsicker emphasizes Swedish influences on the Tanzanian model. Michaela von Freyhold opines that Freire's suggestions that Tanzanian primers be more "'problem-solving' and open" were rejected because officials thought they would undermine the authority of extension agents. See Freyhold's "Some Observations on Adult Education in Tanzania," in Hinzen and Hundsdorfer, eds., *Tanzanian Experience*, p. 166. See also S. Malaya, "Literacy—A Work-Oriented Literacy Project and a National Campaign," in Hinzen and Hundsdorfer, eds., *Tanzanian Experience*, pp. 141–52; and Y. O. Kassam, "Literacy and Development: What Is Missing in the Jigsaw Puzzle?," in Hinzen and Hundsdorfer, eds., *Tanzanian Experience*, pp. 153–55.

62. Irmela Köhler, Freire's secretary, to Johan Galtung, 13 March 1975, in WCCA, Sub-Unit on Education, Dossiers.

63. Freire to Reginald Connolly, 25 January 1977, in WCCA, Sub-Unit on Education, Correspondence 1976–77. See also "Programme Unit III: Education and Renewal: Sub-Unit on Education Working Group on Education Meeting July 17–22, 1977: Adult Basic Education (The Work of Paulo Freire)," in WCCA, Working Group on Education 1977/78. Elza's son Lutgardes Costa Freire noted that Elza had a particular gift for selecting the richest words to begin teaching people to read and write. See Lutgardes Costa Freire, "A Amorisadade do Método Paulo Freire," IPF.

64. See Chabal, "The End of Empire," in Chabal, ed., *History of Postcolonial Lusophone Africa*, particularly pp. 3–16. Regarding the limited impact of the Portuguese, see Chabal, "The Con-

struction of the Nation-State," in Chabal, ed., *History of Postcolonial Lusophone Africa*, p. 49. On the controversy surrounding council support for the independence struggle in Guinea-Bissau, see Lefever, *Amsterdam to Nairobi*, p. 32.

65. See "Development Education—Review and Perspective," in WCCA, Working Group on Education 1979/80. UNESCO paid the printing cost for the Guinea-Bissau textbooks.

66. Regarding trends in enrollment in Guinea-Bissau, see Najafizadeh and Mennerick, "Worldwide Educational Expansion," p. 344. The two best biographies of Cabral are Tomás, *O Fazedor de Utopias*, and Chabal, *Amílcar Cabral*. Regarding the inadequacies of education under the Portuguese, see Chabal, *Amílcar Cabral*, pp. 20–23. For a more critical view of the war itself, see Tomás, *O Fazedor de Utopias*, pp. 110–11, 126, 145–49, 161–64, 172–79, and 232–38. The main published source on Paulo Freire's thinking about his experience in Guinea-Bissau is his *Pedagogy in Process*; see particularly pp. 6, 8, 10–12, and 17–19. See also IDAC, *Guinea Bissau*. Regarding Cabral's social and political thought, see Chabal, *Amílcar Cabral*, particularly pp. 172–87.

67. See also "Campanha de Alfabetização," *Nô Pintcha*, 29 January 1977, p. 4; and "O que Pensa da Alfabetização?," *Nô Pintcha*, 8 September 1977, p. 2.

68. Gadotti, *Reading Paulo Freire*, pp. 45–47.

69. Dhada, *Warriors at Work*, pp. 97–112.

70. Davidson, *Liberation of Guiné*, pp. 70 and 82.

71. Freire, *Pedagogy in Process*, pp. 13–16, 23, and 25–31. Regarding the success of literacy efforts among the FARP, see IDAC, *Guinea Bissau*, pp. 22–24 and 50; "A Alfabetização das FARP Atinge Cada Vez Maior Nível," *Nô Pintcha*, 16 June 1977, p. 1; and "Eliminando o Analfabetismo no Seio das Forças Armadas," *Nô Pintcha*, 7 October 1978, p. 1.

72. See, for example, "Paulo Freire: Um Educador ao Serviço da Nova Escola: Um Centro Democrático com o Professor e o Aluno Engajado na Realização de Objetivos Sociais," *Nô Pintcha*, 21 October 1976, p. 4; and "Paulo Freire ao 'Nô Pintcha': Há uma Unidade Indissolúvel entre a Revolução e a Educação," *Nô Pintcha*, 9 April 1977, p. 5.

73. Harasim, "Literacy and National Reconstruction," abstract and pp. 335–37.

74. Ibid., pp. 69–70, 194, 239, 250, 254–55, 274, 280, and 296; see also IDAC, *Guinea Bissau*, pp. 25 and 49.

75. Harasim, "Literacy and National Reconstruction," p. 197. Regarding lack of time and motivation among Guineans, see "Dia Internacional de Alfabetização," *Nô Pintcha*, 8 September 1977, p. 4; and "Campanha de Alfabetização dos Trabalhadores de Bissau," *Nô Pintcha*, 13 March 1979, p. 4.

76. Harasim, "Literacy and National Reconstruction," p. 14.

77. Ibid., abstract.

78. Davidson, *Liberation of Guiné*, pp. 23–29; McCulloch, *In the Twilight of Revolution*, pp. 12–16; Lopes, *Guinea-Bissau*, pp. 18–24; Freire et al., *Vivendo e Aprendendo*, p. 99.

79. Harasim, "Literacy and National Reconstruction," pp. 174–75. Freire hoped that Creole would work in the long run in any case. See *Pedagogy in Process*, p. 127. For more on Freire's misgivings, however, see the unpublished letter he wrote on 15 July 1977, in WCCA, Sub-Unit on Education, Correspondence Paulo Freire 1976–77. This letter is reproduced in Freire, Guimarães, and Macedo, *Literacy*, pp. 160–67; see also pp. 108–11. Freire attributed the lack of knowledge of Portuguese not to the failure of Portuguese colonial education, however, but to the cultural resistance of the Guineans. See Freire and Faundez, *Learning to Question*, p. 108,

and Freire and Guimarães, *A África Ensinando a Gente*, pp. 32–33 and 42–48. See also the interview with minister of education Mário Cabral, in Freire and Guimarães, *A África Ensinando a Gente*, pp. 164–65 and 174–83. The language problem was also addressed in the official press. See, for example, "Dia Internacional de Alfabetização," *Nô Pintcha*, 8 September 1977, p. 4; "Camarada José Araújo ao 'Diário de Lisboa': 'Ninguem Quer Tirar ao Português a Função de Lingua Oficial,'" *Nô Pintcha*, 14 March 1978, p. 4; and "Campanha de Alfabetização dos Trabalhadores de Bissau," *Nô Pintcha*, 13 March 1979, p. 4. It is interesting to note that Creole seems to have its roots in the language brought to Guinea-Bissau by people from Cape Verde. See Tomás, *O Fazedor de Utopias*, p. 36.

80. The most sustained discussion by Freire himself is in Freire and Faundez, *Learning to Question*, pp. 107–17. See also his farewell letter, "Document No. 5—Adult Literacy and Education Programmes," in WCCA, Working Group on Education 1979/80, which was printed in the WCC Education Newsletter 1980, no. 2, pp. 6–8.

81. Harasim, "Literacy and National Reconstruction," pp. 275–78.

82. "Experiência Piloto em Sedengal: O Povo Adquire Novas Perspectivas para a Transformação da Sociedade Através do Movimento de Alfabetização," *Nô Pintcha*, 26 May 1977, p. 4; "Alfabetização em Sedengal: Criar nas Pessoas um Espírito de Comunidade Centralizada na Produção com Base na Agricultura," *Nô Pintcha*, 30 July 1977, p. 4; IDAC, *Guinea-Bissau '79*, pp. 31, 36–45, 49, and 51. See also Freire to Mario Cabral, in WCCA, Sub-Unit on Education, Correspondence Paulo Freire 1976–77.

83. See the rather short and uninformative "Paulo Freire no País em Visita de Trabalho," *Nô Pintcha*, 17 May 1979, p. 1.

84. See Chabal, "The Construction of the Nation-State," in Chabal, ed., *History of Postcolonial Lusophone Africa*, pp. 54, 56, and 70.

85. See Dhada, *Warriors at Work*, p. 112; Tomás, *O Fazedor de Utopias*, pp. 193–95, 209–11, 242–46, and 304–6. Regarding the stated goals of the new government, see "Fim às Injustiças e á Corrupção e Regresso à Linha de Cabral," *Nô Pintcha*, 14 November 1980, p. 1; and "Mensagem do Comandante Nino Vieira: Vamos Construir a Pátria de Cabral," *Nô Pintcha*, 31 December 1980, p. 1. Vieira stayed in power until 1999. After being elected president and returning to power in 2005, he was killed by soldiers on 2 March 2009.

86. Chabal, *Amílcar Cabral*, pp. 161–66; Joshua Forrest, "Guinea Bissau," in Chabal, ed., *History of Postcolonial Lusophone Africa*, pp. 250–51 and 261; Patrick Chabal, "Revolutionary Democracy in Africa: The Case of Guinea Bissau," in Chabal, ed., *Political Domination in Africa*, pp. 98–100; Lopes, *Guinea-Bissau*, pp. 91–92 and 137; McCulloch, *In the Twilight of Revolution*, pp. 33–34.

87. See Gerhard Seibert, "São Tomé e Príncipe," in Chabal, ed., *History of Postcolonial Lusophone Africa*, pp. 291–93.

88. Faundez, *Cultura Oral, Cultura Escrita*, p. 12.

89. Freire to Richard Harmston of the Canadian Council for International Cooperation, 5 January 1977, in WCCA, Sub-Unit on Education, Correspondence Paulo Freire 1976–77. See also Gerhard Seibert, "São Tomé e Príncipe," in Chabal, ed., *History of Postcolonial Lusophone Africa*, pp. 295–97.

90. Freire to Richard Harmston of the Canadian Council for Internatxional Cooperation, 5 January 1977, in WCCA, Sub-Unit on Education, Correspondence Paulo Freire 1976–77.

91. Freire, "Quatro Cartas aos Animadores," pp. 137 and 139.

92. Freire and Guimarães, *A África Ensinando a Gente*, p. 40.

93. "Document No. 5—Adult Literacy and Education Programmes," in WCCA, Working Group on Education 1979/80.

94. Freire, "Quatro Cartos aos Animadores," p. 154.

95. Ibid., p. 138.

96. Ibid., p. 159.

97. Ibid., p. 186; Ministério da Educação Nacional e Desporto, Departamento de Educação de Adultos e Alfabetização, República Democrático de São Tomé e Príncipe, *A Luta Continua: Segundo Caderno*, pp. 11 and 12.

98. See Freire, "Quatro Cartas aos Animadores," p. 160; and Ministério da Educação Nacional e Desporto, Departamento de Educação de Adultos e Alfabetização, República Democrático de São Tomé e Príncipe, *A Luta Continua: Primeiro Caderno*, pp. 17–19 and 25, as well as the comments by Pinto da Costa, pp. 76–77.

99. See Freire, "Quatro Cartas aos Animadores," p. 145; and Ministério da Educação Nacional e Desporto, Departamento de Educação de Adultos e Alfabetização, República Democrático de São Tomé e Príncipe, *A Luta Continua: Primeiro Caderno*, p. 3.

100. Ministério da Educação Nacional e Desporto, Departamento de Educação de Adultos e Alfabetização, República Democrático de São Tomé e Príncipe, *A Luta Continua: Primeiro Caderno*, p. 42.

101. Freire, "Quatro Cartas aos Animadores," p. 153.

102. Ministério da Educação Nacional e Desporto, Departamento de Educação de Adultos e Alfabetização, República Democrático de São Tomé e Príncipe, *A Luta Continua: Quinto Caderno*, pp. 25 and 32.

103. Freire, "Quatro Cartas aos Animadores," p. 162; Ministério da Educação Nacional e Desporto, Departamento de Educação de Adultos e Alfabetização, República Democrático de São Tomé e Príncipe, *A Luta Continua: Primeiro Caderno*, p. 55.

104. Freire, "Quatro Cartas aos Animadores," p. 163; Ministério da Educação Nacional e Desporto, Departamento de Educação de Adultos e Alfabetização, República Democrático de São Tomé e Príncipe, *A Luta Continua: Segundo Caderno*, pp. 18 and 23; Chabal, "Construction of the Nation-State," p. 72.

105. Ministério da Educação Nacional e Desporto, Departamento de Educação de Adultos e Alfabetização, República Democrático de São Tomé e Príncipe, *A Luta Continua: Segundo Caderno*, pp. 7 and 8.

106. Ibid., p. 56. See also Freire, "Quatro Cartas aos Animadores," p. 141–42; and Ministério da Educação Nacional e Desporto, Departamento de Educação de Adultos e Alfabetização, República Democrático de São Tomé e Príncipe, *A Luta Continua: Primeiro Caderno*, p. 33.

107. Ministério da Educação Nacional e Desporto, Departamento de Educação de Adultos e Alfabetização, República Democrático de São Tomé e Príncipe, *A Luta Continua: Segundo Caderno*, p. 42.

108. Gadotti, *Reading Paulo Freire*, p. 47. See also the interview Sérgio Guimarães conducted with Alda do Espírito Santo and Sinfrônio Mendes in São Tomé in 2002 in Freire and Guimarães, *A África Ensinando a Gente*, pp. 80–81 and 92–94.

109. Freire and Faundez, *Learning to Question*, p. 120. See also "Document No. 5—Adult Literacy and Education Programmes," in WCCA, Working Group on Education 1979/80.

110. Freire and Faundez, *Learning to Question*, p. 133; Faundez, "Programme for Adult Basic Education," in WCCA, Core Groups on Education, Unit III Core Group Meeting, 29 July to 1 August 1980; Ulrich Becker to Freire, 8 July 1982, in WCCA, Education, "Regional Education Secretaries' 1980–1982" Folder.

111. Freire and Faundez, *Learning to Question*, p. 98; see also Ulbrich Becker, "General Report April 8 Working Group Meeting Sub-Unit on Education," in WCCA, Working Group on Education 1979/80; and "Document No. 5—Adult Literacy and Education Programmes," in WCCA, Working Group on Education 1979/80.

112. See, for example, "Minutes of the Joint Working Group," p. 10, and Director's Report/ Regional Education Secretaries Meeting, Sub-Unit on Education, Mt. St. Benedict Trinidad, May 24–31, 1981," in WCCA, Working Group on Education 1981.

Chapter Five

1. The sense that the whole world was watching Nicaragua, particularly during the campaign itself, is demonstrated in, for example, *Encuentro* 16 (1980): 3; and *Documentos del Segundo Congreso Nacional*, pp. 9 and 29.

2. On Nicaragua's political evolution in the first few decades in which the Somozas were in power, see Walter, *Regime of Anastasio Somoza*, particularly pp. xix–xx, 50–65, 85–117, 129–88, and 206–35.

3. Arnove, *Education and Revolution in Nicaragua*, pp. 2–5; Sacasa, *Nicaragua en el CREFAL*, p. 5. For a more objective view, see Waggoner and Waggoner, *Education in Central America*, pp. 89 and 93; UNESCO, "Educational and Cultural Development Project," p. 34; and Juan B. Arrien, "Movilación para la Alfabetización en Nicaragua," in UNESCO, *Alternativas de Alfabetización en America Latina y el Caribe*, p. 244.

4. Gullette, ed., *Nicaraguan Peasant Poetry from Solentiname*, p. 4.

5. See, for example, Belli, *El País Bajo mi Piel*, p. 68, in which she speaks of the veneration with which poets are beheld in her country. Regarding Ernesto Cardenal, see Gullette, ed., *Nicaraguan Peasant Poetry from Solentiname*. Carlos Tünnermann Bernheim credits Ruben Darío with being the first in Nicaragua to call for a literacy campaign. See his "Ruben Darío y Nuestro Nacionalidad," *La Prensa*, 18 January 1980, p. 2.

6. *Campaña de Alfabetización*, pp. 3, 5, 7, 8, and 9; Walter, *Regime of Anastasio Somoza*, pp. 104–5, 111–17, and 129–63.

7. Sacasa, *Nicaraga en el CREFAL*, pp. 3–6 and 8.

8. Maria de los Angeles, "Estudio para la Creación del Museo Fundación Violeta Barrios de Chamorro," unpublished plan for presidential library, Universidad de El Salvador, 2004, available in the Instituto de Historia de Nicaragua y Centro America; Calderón, *Pedro Joaquín*, pp. 177–78; Chamorro, *Dreams of the Heart*, p. 85.

9. Walter, *Regime of Anastasio Somoza*, pp. 111–14 and 131–34; Waggoner and Waggoner, *Education in Central America*, pp. 99–102 and 105–6. On the development of student politics and the university autonomy movement, see Ramírez, *Mariano Fiallos*, pp. 75–80, 83, 117–26, 130–209, and 226–38; and Calderón, *Pedro Joaquín*, pp. 72–77. See also Tünnermann Bernheim, *Pensamiento Universitario Centroamericano*, p. 18; and Castilla, *Educación Y Lucha de Clases en Nicaragua*, pp. 40–42.

10. Zimmermann, *Sandinista*, pp. 33–34, 92, 133, and 180. See also Belli, *El País Bajo mi Piel*, p. 75; Ernesto Cardenal's reflection on Pomares in his *La Revolución Perdida*, pp. 169–70; and Carlos Carrión's discussion of his experience as a member of the FSLN in *Vencimos*, p. 14.

11. Black and Bevan, *Loss of Fear*, p. 26.

12. Cardenal, *La Revolución Perdida*, pp. 131–33.

13. An unusually thoughtful discussion of Nicaraguan class dynamics can be found in Vilas, "Class, Lineage and Politics in Contemporary Nicaragua," particularly pp. 320–22 and 330–33. The best case for the cross-class alliance argument is made in Everingham, *Revolution and the Multiclass Coalition in Nicaragua*, particularly pp. 110–37 and 159–68. See also the editorial "Una Dualidad Nociva," *La Prensa*, 3 July 1980, p. 2. The debate over the use of the term "bourgeois" predates this period. See Chamorro, *Dreams of the Heart*, p. 114, regarding her husband's critique of the Sandinistas' employment of the term. The bourgeois background of many of the Sandinistas is made quite clear in Belli's memoir, *El País Bajo mi Piel*, pp. 90–91.

14. "Primera Proclama de Gobierno de Reconstrucción Nacional," reprinted in *Encuentro* 17 (1980): n.p.

15. The poetic phrase from the draft primer, written by Guillermo Rothschuh, did not appear in the final draft. See Miller, *Between Struggle and Hope*, p. 74. To understand the euphoria among the Sandinistas regarding the new world they felt they were creating, see Cardenal, *La Revolución Perdida*, pp. 331–33, 361, and 364; see also "El 19 de Julio de 1979 se Inició Nuestra Verdadera Historia," *El Nuevo Diario*, 19 July 1980, p. 2; and Miller, *Between Struggle and Hope*, p. 58.

16. See Carrión's comments in *Vencimos*, p. 15; and Miller, *Between Struggle and Hope*, pp. 44–45.

17. Cabestrero, *Ministers of God*, pp. 45–47, 58–59, and 60–62; Miller, *Between Struggle and Hope*, pp. 41–43.

18. "Cronologia de la Cruzada," in Assmann, ed., *Nicaragua Triunfa*, p. 159; Miller, *Between Struggle and Hope*, pp. 46, 55, 64–66, and 77. See also Julio de Santa Ana, "Report on Trip to Nicaragua, September 21–26, 1979," p. 3, in WCCA, CCIAF, Nicaragua 1978–82.

19. Miller, *Between Struggle and Hope*, p. 74; Arnove, *Education and Revolution in Nicaragua*, p 23; see also "Proceso de Elaboración del Cuaderno de Lecto-Escritura," in Assmann, ed., *Nicaragua Triunfa*, pp. 63–66. Note that this document emphasizes the experience in São Tomé.

20. Freire to Ulrich Becker, "Document No. 5—Adult Literacy and Education Programmes," in WCCA, Working Group on Education 1979/80.

21. "Freire Dice: Vengo Aqui a Aprender," *La Prensa*, 25 October 1979, p. 10; "Freire se Marcha Lleno de un Gran Optimismo," *La Prensa*, 2 November 1979, p. 9; "Alfabetizar: Mandato de Nuestra Revolución," *Barricada*, 17 October 1979, p. 7; "Pablo Freire en Nicaragua: Escribió *La Pedagogia del Oprimido*," *Barricada*, 24 October 1979; Miller, *Between Struggle and Hope*, pp. 76–77.

22. For evocations of Freire, see, for example, "Radicalization es Siempre Creadora," which provides information on a speech given by the bishop of Cuernevaca on 25 August 1980, in Assmann, ed., *Nicaragua Triunfa*, p. 177; and the speeches by Swedish union representative Margaret Grape Lantz and the Ebert Foundation's Wolfgang Lutterbach, in *Documentos del Primer Congreso*, pp. 97 and 98, respectively.

23. "Proceso de Elaboración del Cuaderno de Lector-escritura," in Assmann, ed., *Nicaragua*

Triunfa, p. 63; "El Método," *Encuentro* 16 (1980): 26; Miller, *Between Struggle and Hope*, p. 71; Freire, *À Sombra Desta Mangueira*, p. 55.

24. Francisco Lacayo interview in "Logros de la Alfabetización," *Encuentro* 17 (1980): n.p.

25. Bayardo Arce Castaño, "La Educación y la Revolución" and "Significación de la Cruzada en la Revolución Popular Sandinista," in Assman, ed., *Nicaragua Triunfa*, pp. 19, 22, 25, and 39.

26. Sergio Ramírez, "Vamos a Alfabetizar para Cambiar," reprinted in Ramírez, *El Alba de Oro*, pp. 111–12.

27. "Proceso de Elaboración del Cuaderno de Lector-escritura," in Assmann, ed., *Nicaragua Triunfa*, p. 63. See also Alemán Ocampo, *Y También Enséñenles a Leer*, p. 23.

28. Alemán Ocampo, *Y También Enséñenles a Leer*, p. 30.

29. Bayardo Arce Castaño, "Significación de la Cruzada en la Revolución Popular Sandinista," in Assmann, ed., *Nicaragua Triunfa*, p. 44.

30. Miller, *Between Struggle and Hope*, pp. 24 and 68; Stansifer, "Nicaraguan Literacy Crusade," p. 5. The urban literacy campaign received less attention at the time and since.

31. *Amanacer del Pueblo*, pp 58, 66, and 91. See also Fernando Cardenal's comments, for example, in *Documentos del Primer Congreso*, p. 5.

32. Flora, McFadden, and Warner, "Growth of Class Struggle," p. 50; *Documentos del Primer Congreso*, p. 54; Amando López Quintana, "Mensaje del Rector," *Encuentro* 16 (1980): 6; Carlos Tünnermann Bernheim, "Cruzada Nacional de Alfabetización, Prioridad de la Revolución," *Encuentro* 16 (1980): 9. See also "La Alfabetización: Un Projecto Político Prioritario de la Revolución Popular Sandinista," *Encuentro* 16 (1980): 19.

33. See, for example, Bayardo Arce Castaño, "La Educación y la Revolución," p. 17, and "Proceso de Elaboración del Cuaderno de Lecto-escritura," p. 64, in Assmann, ed., *Nicaragua Triunfa*; see also Carrión's comments in *Vencimos*, p. 16; Warner and Bravo, *Testimonios*, pp. 17–18; and Miller, *Between Struggle and Hope*, p. 23. Arnove, in *Education and Revolution in Nicaragua*, says that roughly 20,000 young people participated in the war of liberation. See p. 28.

34. Warner and Bravo, *Testimonios*, p. 19.

35. Stansifer, "Nicaraguan Literacy Crusade," p. 5. See the testimonies collected in Ocampo, *Y También Enséñenles a Leer*, and Aragón López, *Una Misión Noble*, pp. 28–29. See also Hirshon, *And Also Teach Them to Read*, p. 143. For a contrary perspective, see "Correo del Brigadista," *Barricada*, 14 July 1980, p. 7, in which the "ideological unity" that the campaign was creating is stressed. See also Fernando Cardenal, "A Campaña de Alfabetización y la Revolución," in Assmann, ed., *Nicaragua Triunfa*, p. 54; and "Entrevistas y Opiniones," *Encuentro* 16 (1980): 63.

36. "Lo que Usted Desea Saber Sobre la Alfabetización," *Barricada*, 21 January 1980, p. 3; "Preparen Cuadernos para Jornada Alfabetizadora," *Barricada*, 11 December 1979, p. 7.

37. "Entrevistas y Opiniones," *Encuentro* 16 (1980): 63; Cardenal, *La Revolución Perdida*, pp. 398–401; "Logros de la Alfabetización," *Encuentro* 17 (1980): n.p.; "Entrevistas y Opiniones," *Encuentro* 16 (1980): 64. See also appeal made in February 1980 titled "To Youth, Parents of Families, and Citizenry," in *Vencimos*, p. 140–41. See also P. Alexandre von Rechnitz, S.J., "Reflexión para los Padres de la Alfabetización," *La Prensa*, 14 March 1980, p. 2; and "Alfabetización es Revolución," *Barricada*, 14 October 1979, p. 3.

38. Grossman, "Augusto Sandino of Nicaragua," particularly pp. 160 and 163–64; Calderón,

Pedro Joaquín, pp. 73 and 77–80; Cardenal, *La Revolución Perdida*, p. 9; Lesson One in Ministério de Educación, *El Amanacer del Pueblo*; Warner and Bravo, *Testimonios*, p. 68. See also the series of quotations by Pedro Joaquín Chamorro on Sandino's ideology in "Sandino: Nacionalista, pero Nunca Comunista," *La Prensa*, 15 March 1980, p. 2. One of his sons, Carlos Fernando Chamorro B., a deeply committed Sandinista, responded a few days later in his article, "Ni Sandino ni PJCH Legitiman a Reacción," *La Prensa*, 19 March 1979, p. 2. See also Emilio Alvarez Montalva, "Mientras haya Pluralismo no habrá Comunismo," *La Prensa*, 2 August 1980, p. 7.

39. Warner and Bravo, *Testimonios*, p. 68.

40. Sergio Ramírez, *El Alba de Oro*, p. 113.

41. Ministério de Educación, *El Amanacer del Pueblo*, pp. 5, 15, 21, 61, 75, and 78.

42. Ibid., pp. 35, 54, 73, 75, and 95. For economic data, see UNESCO, "Educational and Cultural Development Project: Nicaragua," pp. 16–17.

43. See the Ministério de Educación's multilingual picture book *Cruzada Nacional de Alfabetización*, pp. 14–15 and 20–21.

44. Miller, *Between Struggle and Hope*, p. 175; Stansifer, "Nicaraguan National Literacy Crusade," p. 11. Because of health problems, desertion may have risen as high as 4.6 percent.

45. *Documentos del Primer Congreso*, pp. 51–52; Aragón López, *Una Misión Noble*, pp. 147–48.

46. Flora, McFadden, and Warner, "Growth of Class Struggle," p. 55. See also the "Juramento del Brigadista," in *Vencimos*, p. 151.

47. See Alejandro von Rechnitz, "Diário de un Cura Alfabetizador," in Assmann, ed., *Nicaragua Triunfa*, p. 369; Warner and Bravo, *Testimonios*, p. 20; Aragón López, *Una Misión Noble*, p. 16; and Hirshon, *And Also Teach Them to Read*, p. 143.

48. Hirshon, *And Also Teach Them to Read*, p. 141.

49. Flora, McFadden, and Warner, "Growth of Class Struggle," p. 52.

50. Warner and Bravo, *Testimonios*, p. 74.

51. Ibid., p. 75.

52. "Logros de la Alfabetización," *Encuentro* 17 (1980): n.p.

53. See Warner and Bravo, *Testimonios*, pp. 46, 54, and 95.

54. Aragón López, *Una Misión Noble*, particularly pp. 92 and 141–43.

55. Lorena de Montis, "Las Brigadistas Aprenden a Leer el Libro del los Campesinos," *La Prensa*, 17 July 1980, p. 1.

56. Warner and Bravo, *Testimonios*, pp. 5, 30–35, 46, 53, and 55; Aragón López, *Una Misión Noble*, p. 56.

57. See, for example, Aragón López, *Una Misión Noble*, pp. 81–82; and Zalava Cuadra, "Situación de la Educación," 52.

58. Warner and Bravo, *Testimonios*, p. 92 and 95; Arnove, *Education and Revolution in Nicaragua*, pp. 33–34.

59. Quoted in Ferrari, *Sembrando Utopia*, p. 36; Arnove, *Education and Revolution in Nicaragua*, pp. 34–36.

60. Bayard de Volo, *Mothers of Heroes and Martyrs*, p. 40.

61. Flora, McFadden, and Warner, "Growth of Class Struggle," p. 53.

62. Ibid., p. 60.

63. Ernesto Cardenal, "A Democratização da Cultura," in Brandão, ed., *Lições da Nicaragua*, pp. 37–38. A good source on brigadista attitudes is Flora, McFadden, and Warner, "Growth of Class Struggle," pp. 49 and 51. See also Humberto Ortega, "Tarea de todo el Pueblo: Aplastar la

Contrarevolución," in Assmann, ed., *Nicaragua Triunfa*, p. 179; "Logros de la Alfabetización," *Encuentro* 17 (1980): n.p.; *Documentos del Primer Congreso*, pp. 23, 78, and 111; *Documentos del Segundo Congreso*, pp. 12 and 165; Cardenal, *La Revolución Perdida*, pp. 386–88; Ministério de Educación, *Cruzada Nacional de Alfabetización*, p. 72; Warner and Bravo, *Testimonios*, p. 55–56, 115–16, and 121; and Arnove, *Education and Revolution in Nicaragua*, p. 30. Student enrollment in more technical fields of study increased dramatically, from 42 percent to 70 percent, under the Sandinistas. See Arnove, *Education and Revolution in Nicaragua*, p. 118.

64. Flora, McFadden, and Warner, "Growth of Class Struggle," p. 53.

65. Ibid., p. 55.

66. Guillermo Rothschuh-Tablada, "Alfabetización en Nicaragua," *La Prensa*, 21 October 1979, p. 2.

67. See "La Campaña Nacional de Alfabetización de Nicaragua: Llamamiento de Director General de la UNESCO," reprinted in Assmann, ed., *Nicaragua Triunfa*, pp. 82–83; Miller, *Between Struggle and Hope*, p. 61.

68. UNESCO, "Educational and Cultural Development Project: Nicaragua," p. 19.

69. Gérson Meyer, "Report of the WCC Team Visit to Nicaragua, July 25–31, 1979," pp. 1–3 and 7, in WCCA, CCIAF, Nicaragua 1978–82. See also Julio de Santa Ana, "Report on Trip to Nicaragua, September 21–26, 1979," pp. 3 and 4, in WCCA, CCIAF, Nicaragua 1978–82. Regarding monies disbursed, see the 28 September and 22 November 1979 "Sitreps" by the WCC Programme Unit on Justice and Service, Commission on Inter-Church Aid, Refugee and World Service (CICARWS), and the 3 March 1981 letter from Jean Fischer, Director of CICARWS, in WCCA, CCIAF, Nicaragua 1978–82. See also Fischer's 10 January 1980 letter, pp. 2, 5–6, and 10, in WCCA, CCIAF, Nicaragua 1978–82.

70. Miller, *Between Struggle and Hope*, pp. 52–53. Regarding the role of volunteers in promoting Cuban foreign policy goals generally, see Gleijeses, *Conflicting Missions*, particularly pp. 35–38, 166–69, and 199–206. The best source on Cuban participation in Nicaragua is Rojas, *El Aula Verde*, pp. 9, 12, 32, 38, 70, and 71. See also "Maestros Cubanos en Nicaragua Ejemplos de Internacionalismo," *Barricada*, 2 March 1980, p. 2; "Fidel y lo Nuevo," *El Nuevo Diario*, 1 August 1980, p. 2; *Documentos del Primer Congreso*, p. 18; *Documentos del Segundo Congreso*, p. 177; and Black and Bevan, *Loss of Fear*, pp. 45 and 47.

71. See, for example, "Robelo lider de los Confiscados," *Barricada*, 13 May 1980, pp. 1 and 5; and "Todo lo que Usted Desea Saber Sobre la Cruzada Nacional de Alfabetización," *Barricada*, 15 February 1980, p. 3.

72. Cardenal, *La Revolución Perdida*, pp. 378–79. The CIA contended that Cuban teachers in Cuba were "at times resented in rural areas because of their atheism and the drain they constitute on local housing and food supplies" ("CIA Talking Points—Nicaragua," 21 February 1980, in RAC Machine, NLC-24-6-8-1, Carter Library). See also Robert Pastor, "The Carter Administration and Latin America: An Assessment," 28 October 1980, Zbigniew Brzezinski Collection, Subject File Box 34, Carter Library.

73. *Documentos del Primer Congreso*, p. 13; Miller, *Between Struggle and Hope*, pp. 53 and 62.

74. Luís Carrión interview in Lovo, *História y violencia en Nicaragua*, pp. 340–41.

75. "Lider del MDN Relata su Participación en el Junta," *La Prensa*, 27 May 1980, p. 9.

76. The Costa Rican president's remarks are quoted in Assman, ed., *Nicaragua Triunfa*, p. 176. Regarding the volunteers' experience, see "Entusiasmó a Maestros Ticos la Campaña de Alfabetización," reprinted from Costa Rica's *La Nación* in *La Prensa*, 10 July 1980, p. 6.

77. Stansifer, "Nicaraguan National Literacy Crusade," p. 13. The United States donated roughly $2.2 million, West Germany donated roughly $1.3 million, and Sweden and Switzerland donated roughly $1 million each.

78. Proving the point that memory can play tricks, Luís Carrión noted that Reagan became president "only a few months" after the triumph of the Revolution." See his interview in Lovo, *História y Violencia en Nicaragua*, p. 339.

79. See, for example, Peter Tarnoff to Zbigniew Brzezinski, President Carter's national security adviser, 6 September 1977, in White House Central Files, Subject Files, Countries, Box CO-46, CO 114 1/20/77–1/20/81 Folder, Carter Library. Tarnoff said that "[t]he Guard seems to be heeding President Somoza's recent instructions to avoid human rights violations."

80. As late as 11 June 1979, Carter's presidential review committee projected that Somoza would survive "the latest round of violence," if not until 1981. See its report in Zbigniew Brzezinski Collection, Subject File Meeting SCC, Box 30, Meeting SCC 183 7/17/79 Folder, Carter Library. See also Robert Pastor, "Nicaragua: Planning for the SCC and for the Torrijos Meeting," 1 July 1979, in Zbigniew Brzenzinski Collection, Meeting SCC 175: 7/10/79 National Security Council, Carter Library.

81. Robert Pastor to Zbigniew Brzezinski, "SCC on Central America July 20, 1979," in Zbigniew Brzezinski Collection, Subject File Meeting SCC, Box 30, Meeting SCC 183 7/17/79 Folder, Carter Library. On U.S. policy toward the Sandinistas from July 1979 to January 1981, see Morley, *Washington, Somoza, and the Sandinistas*, pp. 218–307.

82. CIA, Foreign Assessment Center, "Central America: Short-Term Prospects for Insurgency: Part I: Overview: An Intelligence Assessment," August 1979, in RAC Machine, NLC-24-8-5-3-9, p. iii, Carter Library.

83. During the campaign, Robert Pastor noted that the country was "largely directed by pro-Cuban, anti-American Marxists." See his 15 August 1980 memo to Brzezinski, "The Free Press in Nicaragua," in White House Central Files, Subject Files, Countries, Box CO-47, CO 114 1/20/77–1/20/81 Folder, Carter Library. The FSLN anthem is available in Ministério de Educación, *El Amanacer del Pueblo*, p. 123.

84. See "CIA Talking Points—Nicaragua," 21 February 1980, in RAC Machine, NLC-24-37-6-8-1, Carter Library.

85. "El Consejo Ecumenico Blufileñno de las Iglesias Envia una Trascendental Carta al Presidente Jimmy Carter," *El Nuevo Diario*, 12 July 1980, p. 2; "El Respecto que se ha Gando Nicaragua," *El Nuevo Diario*, 12 June 1980, p. 2; "Apertura de Cuba—EE en Managua," *La Prensa*, 21 July 1980, p. 7; and "La Cosecha del Endurecimento," *La Prensa*, 29 July 1980, p. 2. Two of the most thoughtful books on U.S.-Nicaraguan relations during the 1980s are Leogrande, *Our Own Backyard*, and Kagan, *Twilight Struggle*. Regarding Carter's policies, see Leogrande, *Our Own Backyard*, pp. 16–32; and Kagan, *Twilight Struggle*, pp. 27–164. Also useful is Pastor, *Condemned to Repetition*. A useful recent article is John A. Soares Jr., "Strategy, Ideology, and Human Rights," particularly pp. 67–77 and 89–91. See also Barrios de Chamorro, *Dreams of the Heart*, pp. 179–80, 182–83, 188–89, and 208. Regarding U.S. food aid, see "26 Miliones para Alfabetización," *La Prensa*, 6 July 1980, p. 1.

86. Arnove, *Education and Revolution in Nicaragua*, pp. 27–28. Otherwise the rate would be 23 percent, which is certainly a significant drop in any case.

87. UNESCO, "Educational and Cultural Development Project: Nicaragua," p. 17; Miller, *Between Struggle and Hope*, p. 86.

88. Flora, McFadden, and Warner, "Growth of Class Struggle," p. 45.

89. See the statement of the "Conferencia Episcopal de Nicaragua: Compromiso Cristiano en la Cruzada de Alfabetización" by Obando y Bravo and others, reprinted in Assman, ed., *Nicaragua Triunfa*, p. 81; and Conferencia de Religiosos en Nicaragua, "Presencia de los Religiosos en La Cruzada," UCA, pp. 15–16, 29–30, 35 and 55. See also the interviews with the Cardenal brothers and Miguel D'Escoto in Cabestrero, *Ministers of God*; and Jesuit Alejandro von Rechnitz's "Diário de un Cura Alfabetizador," in Assman, ed., *Nicaragua Triunfa*, p. 369. The poster mentioned is reproduced in the photo section in Cardenal, *La Revolución Perdida*; regarding liberation theology, see pp. 439 and 461. See also Ministério de Educación, *El Amanacer del Pueblo*, p. 109; Alemán Ocampo, *Y También Enséñenles a Leer*, pp. 19, 21, 60, and 107; Warner and Bravo, *Testimonios*, pp. 32 and 69; Hirshon, *And Also Teach Them to Read*, p. 11; Aragón López, *Una Misión Noble*, pp. 26 and 157–58. Miller, *Between Struggle and Hope*, pp. 43 and 176–77; Hoyt, *Many Faces of Sandinista Democracy*, pp 11–12; Dodson and O'Shaughnessy, *Nicaragua's Other Revolution*, pp. 3, 5, 30, 121–39, and 143–60; Stansifer, "Nicaraguan National Literacy Crusade," p. 10; Thomas Kugler, "The New Nicaragua Deserves Our Support," accompanying a letter from WCC CICARWS emergencies officer Robin Morrison in WCCA, CCIAF, Nicaragua 1978–82; and Carlos Carrión in *Vencimos*, p. 15.

90. "Hermoso Acto Cristiano y Revolucionario," *Barricada*, 31 August 1980. Luís Carrión suggests that the conflict with the church created "a great distrust of the peasantry toward the Revolution" (Lovo, *História y Violencia en Nicaragua*, p. 343). Rev. José Miguel Torres suggests that pro-Sandinista Christians became active in the mass organizations and stopped being identifiable as a distinctively Christian group. See his "Las Teologias y Pastorale en Nicaragua durante la Revolución Sandinista," in Lovo, *Historia y Violencia en Nicaragua*, p. 390.

91. See Vilas, "Class, Lineage and Politics," pp. 323–24. For examples of Robelo's public stances prior to his break with the Sandinistas, see "Robelo Define Rumbo Hacia el Socialismo," *La Prensa*, 29 October 1979, p. 1, in which he asserted that "we have become aware of Nicaraguan reality. . . . The immoral structures of the past must undergo profound transformations."

92. "Nos Dirigimos Hacia la Democracia: Doña Violeta," *La Prensa*, 19 October, 1979, p. 4; "Texto Oficial de su Renuncia: Cansada, pero Firme," *La Prensa*, 20 April 1980, p. 1; "Seguiré Presente, Dice Doña Violeta," *Barricada*, 20 April 1980, pp. 1 and 3; "Pluralismo Ideologico en Nicaragua," *La Prensa*, 14 October 1980, p. 10.

93. Barrios de Chamorro, *Dreams of the Heart*, is a rich, if somewhat misleading source for at least the public politics of this time period. See ibid., pp. 172–75, 193, and 197–200. In her memoirs, she claims that the literacy campaign was designed by the Cubans; see ibid., p. 196. Regarding Robelo, see, for example, ibid., pp. 178, 180, and 192. See also the praise of Robelo in "Lider del MDN Relata su Participación en el Junta," *La Prensa*, 27 May 1980, p. 9. Robelo gave a brief description of his political evolution in a 16 June 1982 speech in Panama published as a Movimiento Democrático Nicaragüense pamphlet, "Pronunciamiento del Ing. Afonso Robelo C. En Panama," p. 1, UCA.

94. *Documentos del Primer Congreso*, p. 27.

95. Carlos Nuñez's comments are available in ibid., p. 26. Regarding the accusation that the campaign was domesticating the poor, see Carlos Carrión's comments in ibid., pp. 127–29. Regarding opinions of brigadistas and Sandinistas regarding Robelo, see Alemán Ocampo, *Y También Enséñenles a Leer*, p. 147; "Siguen Hostigando a Alfabetizadores," *El Nuevo Diario*, 2

June 1980, p. 1; "Robelo Lider de los Confiscados," *Barricada*, 13 May 1980, pp. 1 and 5; "Coordinador Responde a Robelo," *Barricada*, 17 March 1980, p. 1; and Alfredo Obando P., "Alfabetización es Liberación, no Domesticamiento," *El Nuevo Diario*, 12 June 1980, p. 2. See also letter published in *El Nuevo Diario*, 17 July 1980, p. 2 and Miller, *Between Struggle and Hope*, pp. 177–78. There was concern that Robelo's critique of the campaign was shaping world opinion; see "Nicaragua Launches Vast Campaign Against Illiteracy," a Canadian article reprinted in *Barricada*, 9 June 1980, p. 1. See also "Enfatiza Comandante Borge: Robelo Responsable de lo que Ocurra a Brigadistas," *Barricada*, 14 May 1980, p. 1; "Comandante Borge: 'Iremos a Matiguás," *Barricada*, 19 May 1980, pp. 1 and 5; and "Asesinos son todos los Anticommunistas," *Barricada*, 24 May 1980, p. 1.

96. See references to *La Prensa*'s supposed anti-crusade leanings in Warner and Bravo, *Testimonios*, p. 18; and Hirshon, *And Also Teach Them to Read*, pp. 88–89. See support for the crusade in, for example, "Presentan Paquete de Alfabetización," *La Prensa*, 19 January 1980, p. 2; "Nuestro Heroicos Muchachos: Euforia, Garra y Decisión de Alfabetización," *La Prensa*, 21 March 1980, p. 1; "Revolución Cultural, Unica Forma de Construir el Nuevo Nicaragüense," *La Prensa*, 31 March 1980, p. 2; Joaquín Absalón Pastora, "Alfabetización al Rescate de la Dignidad," *La Prensa*, 2 April 1980, p. 2; "Condenamos Crimen Contra Alfabetizador," *La Prensa*, 26 May 1980, p. 1; "Confirman: 500,000 Alfabetizadas," *La Prensa*, 15 August 1980, p. 1; and "Proclamada Victoria en Managua: Armas de Hoy, 29 Letras," *La Prensa*, 23 August 1980, p. 1.

97. Barrios de Chamorro, *Dreams of the Heart*, p. 203–7.

98. Pablo Antonio Cuadra, "Palabras del Director," *La Prensa*, 9 July 1980, p. 2. Also note the confidence with which the newspaper discusses the distinctiveness of the "Nicaraguan path" in "Entre la Libertad y Igualdad está el Camino Nicaragüense (Un Comentario a Vargas Llosa)," *La Prensa*, 10 July 1980, p. 2.

99. Alejandro von Rechnitz, "Diário de un Cura Alfabetizador," in Assman, ed., *Nicaragua Triunfa*, p. 370.

100. Brown, *Real Contra War*, pp. 44–45 and 57. Lynn Horton does not consider the literacy campaign to have promoted peasant resistance in the rural community of Quilalí. Peasants there viewed the campaign positively, although they had little interest in acquiring anything more than the "basic literacy skills." See Horton, *Peasants in Arms*, pp. 88 and 90–91.

101. Ministério de Educación, *Cruzada Nacional*, p. 37. There is disagreement regarding the origins of the "contras," even among their supporters. See, particularly, Brown, *Real Contra War*, pp. 3–11. Brown worked with the contras in the late 1980s and, as a result of this experience, as well as extensive oral interviews, believes that the contras began as a peasant movement, with strong roots in the anti-Somoza struggle and in traditions of indigenous resistance. From his perspective, anti-Sandinista resistance began with the defeat of Somoza. Many North Americans neglect the Argentine influence on the organization of the contras. For a corrective, see Armony, *Argentina, the United States and the Anti-Communist Crusade*. All supporters of the contras, including Brown, tend to turn a blind eye to contra atrocities. (Brown's book, it must be said, is frustrating, in part because it is inadequately sourced, and in part because his discussion of Argentine involvement seems to be particularly one-sided, assuming, as it does, that Argentines cannot be independent political actors.)

102. Fernando Cardenal in *Documents del Segundo Congreso*, p. 13; Warner and Bravo, *Testimonios*, p. 5; Brown, *Real Contra War*, p. 57.

103. Warner and Bravo, *Testimonios*, pp. 5 and 103–6; Ofelia Morales Gutiérrez, "Ante el De-

safío Contrarevlucionario," *El Nuevo Diario*, 2 August 1980, p. 2; "Condenamos Crimen Contra Alfabetizador," *La Prensa*, 26 May 1980, p. 1; "Entraron de Honduras . . . No Regresarán," *La Prensa*, 30 May 1980, p. 12; "Mató a Georgino porque le Dijeron Ser Comunista," *Barricada*, 2 August 1980, p. 1; "Muerto el Asesino de Georgino," *El Nuevo Diario*, 30 August 1980, p. 1; "Abelardo Sánchez, Otro Brigadistas Asesinado y Amenazas a Alfabetizadores," *La Prensa*, 29 July 1980, p. 5.

104. See *Documentos del Primer Congreso*, pp. 13 and 113.

105. See, for example, Oscar Herdocia Lacayo, "Sobre el Abuso del Término 'Burguesia,'" *La Prensa*, 30 October 1979, p. 2. See also Robelo's critique in "Pronunciamiento," *La Prensa*, p. 3; and the editorials "Una Dualidad Nociva," *La Prensa*, 3 July 1980, p. 2; and "Todos Somos Pueblo," *La Prensa*, 25 July 1980, p. 2.

106. See, for example, Humberto Ortega, "Tarea de Todo el Pueblo: Aplastar la Contrarevolución," in Assman, ed., *Nicaragua Triunfa*, p. 180; "Periodismo Reaccionário y 'Objetividad,'" *Barricada*, 15 May 1980, p. 3; and Raquel Fernandez, "Pueblo vs. Burguesia Vende-Patria," *Barricada*, 4 March 1980, p. 3.

107. Belli, *El País Bajo mi Piel*, p. 336; see also Cardenal's reference to the Club Social de Granada, which he attended when he "was bourgeois," in his *La Revolución Perdida*, p. 339.

108. Calderón, *Pedro Joaquín*.

109. Barrios de Chamorro, *Dreams of the Heart*, pp. 117, 124, 132, and 135; Belli, *El País Bajo mi Piel*, pp. 272–73; Cardenal, *La Revolución Perdida*, pp. 9–12 and 73; Clemente Guido, "Una Dictadura Democrática," *La Prensa*, 19 October 1979, p. 2. For reports on commemorations of Chamorro's assassination, see, for example, "El Grito del 10: Unidad Nacional," *La Prensa*, 8 January 1980, p. 1; "P. J. Chamorro," *La Prensa*, 11 January 1980, pp. 1 and 2; and "Jornada Pro Unidad Nacional 'Dr. Pedro Joaquín Chamorro,'" *Barricada*, 7 January 1980, p. 1. See also Carlos Tünnermann Bernheim, "Pedro Joaquín Chamorro: Simbolo de Unidad Nacional," *La Prensa*, 10 January 1980, p. 2, which lauds his involvement in the 1960s literacy campaign. See also his son Carlos Fernando Chamorro Barrios's critique of those who were using Chamorro "to capitalize on his political legitimacy to benefit positions that try to retard the historical process" in "Ni Sandino ni PJCH Legitiman a Reacción," *La Prensa*, 19 March 1979, p. 2.

110. Belli, *El País Bajo mi Piel*, p. 333.

111. Francisco Hernandez Segura, "Por la Revolución Popular Sandinista, Todo!," *El Nuevo Diario*, 13 July 1980, p. 2; "Revolución de Todos: Robelo," *La Prensa*, 19 July 1980, p. 12; "Que Es Ser Reaccionario?," *La Prensa*, 8 January 1980, p. 2; "Documento del COSEP: Difícil de Refutar," *La Prensa*, 14 December 1979, p. 2; Pablo Antonio Cuadra, "Palabras del Director," *La Prensa*, 9 July 1980, p. 2. Regarding the Council of State, see *Barricada*, 2 May 1980, and the editorial, "La Democracia tiene Un Nuevo Contenido," *Barricada*, 11 April 1980, p. 3. See also Hoyt's discussion of the further evolution of Sandinista thinking in *Many Faces of Sandinista Democracy*, pp. 25–39.

112. "Se Prometió Anunciar Las Elecciones?," *La Prensa*, 1 August 1980, p. 2.

113. On Venezuela under Pérez, see, for example the national intelligence officer for Latin America to Pastor, "Personal and Informal Observations on Cuban Activities in the Caribbean Basin," 11 January 1980, in RAC Machine, NLC-24-15-2-5-2; and RAC Machine, NLC-24-37-6-8-1, p. 7 (on Costa Rica, see RAC Machine, NLC-24-37-6-8-1, p. 8), all in Carter Library. See also CIA, Foreign Assessment Center, "Central America: Short-Term Prospects for Insurgency: Part I: Overview: An Intelligence Assessment," August 1979, p. 3, RAC Machine, NLC-24-8-5-

3-9, Carter Library; and Carlos Guerón, "Introduction," in Tulchin, ed., *Venezuela in the Wake of Radical Reform*, pp. 3–4. For an extensive analysis of Venezuelan foreign policy during this period, consult Toro Hardy, "La Política Exterior," particularly pp. 274–84 and 289–93. Robert Pastor argued that the most important reason for the Sandinista victory was the fact that "our friends, Venezuela, Costa Rica, and Panama, were too obsessed in getting rid of Somoza and preempting Castro that they unwittingly played Castro's game, successfully insulating him from us" (Pastor, "The Carter Administration and Latin America: An Assessment," 28 October 1980, in Zbigniew Brzezinski Collection, Subject File Box 34, Carter Library. See also Pastor, *Condemned to Repitition*, pp. 60 and 126–27. Based on what I argue below, it is important to note that Pastor asserted that, given the fact that Pérez had already left the presidency by the time of the Sandinistas' victory, Venezuela's influence on the Sandinistas had already declined.

114. "Carrión Habla de Elecciones 'Estilo Propio,'" *La Prensa*, 16 August 1980, p. 1. Regarding Venezuelan president Pérez's support for the revolution, see Barrios de Chamorro, *Dreams of the Heart*, pp. 135, 140, and 210; and Cardenal, *La Revolución Perdida*, pp. 34–37. Regarding Costa Rica, see Barrios de Chamorro, *Dreams of the Heart*, p. 184.

115. "Moises Hassan Comenta Sobre Elecciones," *La Prensa*, 29 July 1980, p. 1; "Elecciones y la Esencia del Estado Sandinista," *El Nuevo Diario*, 11 June 1980, p. 2; "Omar Cabezas Habló Sobre Reagan, Robelo, y Elecciones," *La Prensa*, 6 August 1980, p. 7.

116. Humberto Belli P., "Democracia: Poder del Partido, por el Partido Para el Pueblo?," *La Prensa*, 6 August 1980, p. 2. Belli considered this an "incomplete" definition with "a strong paternalistic flavor." See also "Carrión Habla de Elecciones 'Estilo Propio,'" *La Prensa*, 16 August 1980, p. 12.

117. Cardenal, *La Revolución Perdida*, p. 340; "Correo del Brigadista," *Barricada*, 14 July 1980, p. 7; "Obreros Están Claros! Elecciones 'Viejo Juego,'" *Barricada*, 3 August 1980, p. 1; Hoyt, *Many Faces of Sandinista Democracy*, p. 48.

118. "Pueblo Ratificó Voto Para FSLN," *Barricada*, 20 July 1980, p. 1; Juan José Lacayo, "Ofensiva Final Victoriosa," *Barricada*, 2 August 1980, p. 5.

119. "Alfabetización: Voluntad Política del Pueblo," *Barricada*, 8 August 1980, p. 3; "Elecciones Libres, Y Respeto al Resultado," *La Prensa*, 16 August 1980, p. 12; "Elección Auténtica, Compromiso de Honor: 7 Preguntas Candentes al Dr. Arturo J. Cruz," *La Prensa*, 19 August 1980, p. 7.

120. See coverage in *El Nuevo Diario*, 22 August 1980.

121. "El 23 de Agosto y La Hegmonia del Poder Sandinista," *Barricada*, 23 August 1980, p. 3.

122. "El COSEP en Postura Ilógica dicen Jóvenes Profesionales," *Barricada*, 6 August 6, 1980, p. 1. See also "Elecciones en 85! Opciones Sólo dentro de La Revolución," *El Nuevo Diario*, 24 August 1980, p. 1; "Comentarios sobre el Fin de la Gran Cruzada," *El Nuevo Diario*, 24 August 1980, p. 2; and Hoyt, *Many Faces of Sandinista Democracy*, pp. 22–23.

123. "La Gente Opina sobre Elecciones," *La Prensa*, 25 August 1980, p. 1; "En una Democracia, el Lenguaje Debe Corresponder a sus Estructuras," *La Prensa*, 26 August 1980, p. 2.

124. "La Acción Colectiva Patriótica Más Importante de Nuestra Historia," *La Prensa*, 23 August 1980, p. 2; advertisement in *El Nuevo Diario*, 25 August 1980, p. 5.

125. Stansifer, "Nicaraguan National Literacy Crusade," pp. 5 and 7.

126. "Cuaderno de Educación Sandinista: Orientaciones para el Alfabetizador," in Assman, ed., *Nicaragua Triunfa*, p. 632. See also William Alemán Rodriguez, "Al Ejército Popular de

Alfabetización," *El Nuevo Diario*, 7 August 1980, p. 2; and "Dirigentes Sindicales Opinam: Concepción Electoral de COSEP: Pasado Sin Retorno," *Barricada*, 5 August 1980, p. 1.

127. Barrios de Chamorro, *Dreams of the Heart*, p. 176–77. For an opposing perspective, see Cardenal, *La Revolución Perdida*, pp. 344–45.

128. For an analysis of "Sandinista democracy," see Hoyt, *Many Faces of Sandinista Democracy*, particularly pp. 1–2 and 43–48.

129. Arnove, *Education and Revolution in Nicaragua*, pp. 48–68.

130. "Documento Básico de Capacitación," *Documentos del Segundo Congreso*, p. 53; Aragón López, *Una Misión Noble*, pp. 163–64; Carlos Tünnermann Bernheim, "La Educación en la Revolución Sandinista," in Lovo, *História y Violencia en Nicaragua*, p. 360; Juan B. Arrien, "Movilización para la Alfabetización en Nicaragua," in UNESCO, *Alternativas de Alfabetización en América Latina y el Caribe*, p. 281.

131. Tünnermann Bernheim also suggests that the Ministry of Education officials were too passive in their response to the cuts to school funding. See Lovo, *Historia y Violencia en Nicaragua*, p. 365. See also Arrien G. and Matis Lazo, *Nicaragua*, pp. 34–35 and 37; and Sergio Ramírez, "La Revolución que No Fue," *La Prensa*, 19 July 2004, p. 10A.

132. See Carlos Tünnermann Bernheim's comments in a 1991 interview in Ferrari, *Sembrando Utopia*, p. 97.

133. Quoted in Horton, *Peasants in Arms*, p. xiii.

134. Cabestrero, *Ministers of God*, pp. 47–48.

135. See Gustavo Ortega Campos, "Ecos 25 Años Despues: El Sacrificio Traicionada de la Juventud," and "Los Antiguos Dirigentes," *La Prensa*, online edition, 20 July 2004.

136. "El 'Padre' de la Juventud Sandinista," *La Prensa*, online edition, 20 July 2004.

137. One of the more astute critics of the Sandinistas since the 1990s is Sergio Ramírez, former Sandinista vice president of Nicaragua. On 19 July 2004, he wrote in *La Prensa* that if someone were to visit Nicaragua today, he would find it hard to believe that Nicaragua was a country that had ever experienced a revolution. See his editorial on p. 10A. His humanist perspective can be sampled in the introduction to his *Mariano Fiallos*, particularly pp. 17–21. For a North American sympathizer's critique, see Zimmerman, *Sandinista*, p. 224. Regarding the failure of the Sandinista goal of national unity, see Alejandro Serrano Caldera, "En Busca de una Nación," in Lovo, *História y Violencia en Nicaragua*, pp. 21–22. For a discussion of antidemocratic trends in Nicaragua in the 1990s, see the essays in Close and Deonandan, eds., *Undoing Democracy*.

138. Freire and Guimarães, *Aprendendo com a Própria História*, pp. 27–28 and 30. See also Freire's farewell letter to Ulrich Becker, "Document No. 5—Adult Literacy and Education Programmes," in WCCA, Working Group on Education 1979/80.

Chapter Six

1. *WCC Focus*, July 1980. See also Freire's response to interviewers after he returned to Brazil, quoted in Gadotti, Freire, and Guimarães, *Pedagogia*, p. 15.

2. Alves, *State and Opposition in Military Brazil*, pp. 106–14 and 125–28; Skidmore, *Politics of Military Rule*, pp. 284–88; Bacha and Klein, eds., *Social Change in Brazil*, pp. 16–17, 49–51, and 100–105.

3. For a fairly sympathetic treatment of MOBRAL, see Bhola, *Campaigning for Literacy*, pp.

120–37. See also Freitag, *Escola, Estado e Sociedade*, pp. 83–85. For a more critical treatment of the pedagogical aspects of the program, see Januzzi, *Confronto Pedagógico*, particularly pp. 11–12, 21–24, 49–67, 70–79, and 81–84. See also Moacir Gadotti, "Algumas Propostas Educacionais do Partidos dos Trabalhadores," in Damasceno et al., *A Educação como Ato Político Partidário*, p. 31. Regarding the ideological content of literacy training during the military period, see, for example, Rodrigues, *Cartilhas da Dominação*, particularly pp. 16–17, 59–61, and 65–146. For literacy rates, see Skidmore, *Politics of Military Rule*, p. 284. According to a recent study, from 1900 to 1980, illiteracy rates had dropped while the number of illiterates continued to rise. It was only in the 1980s that absolute numbers actually decreased from 19.3 million to 17.7 million. See Costa and Kesel, *Evolução do Analfabetismo no Brasil*, p. 2. In the Brazilian northeast, illiteracy rates still stood at 36 percent in the 1990s. More than half of all Brazilian illiterates live in Freire's native northeast. See Costa and Kesel, *Evolução do Analfabetismo no Brasil*, p. 12.

4. Bhola, *Campaigning for Literacy*, p. 121.

5. Alves, *State and Opposition in Military Brazil*, pp. 210–12.

6. Sader and Silverstein, *Without Fear of Being Happy*, pp. 41–47; Skidmore, *Politics of Military Rule*, pp. 204–6, 212–15, and 222–25; Alves, *State and Opposition in Military Brazil*, pp. 191–210. See also Hélio Bicudo's foreword in Alves, *State and Opposition in Military Brazil*, p. xiii.

7. Alves, *State and Opposition in Military Brazil*, p. 107.

8. Freire, *Pedagogy of the City*, p. 139. See also Freire, *Á Sombra Desta Mangueira*, pp. 64–67; Gadotti and Perreira, *Pra Que PT?*, pp. 8–9 and 11–12; and Damasceno et al., *Educação como Ato Político Partidário*, pp. 7 and 19. A copy of his party membership card is available in Textos Escolhidos, vol. 27, "Angicos," IPF. A good source on the history of the PT in English, written shortly after Lula's defeat in his first presidential campaign, is Sader and Silverstein, *Without Fear of Being Happy*; see particularly pp. 3, 47–51, 55, 59, 80–81, and 107. See also Keck, *Workers' Party*, pp. 3–19, 55–60, 67–85, 108, 162, and 239–53. Regarding popular organizations, see Alves, *State and Opposition in Military Brazil*, pp. 174–82. Regarding new political parties, see Alves, *State and Opposition in Military Brazil*, pp. 212–20; and Skidmore, *Politics of Military Rule*, pp. 220–22. In the 1982 elections, the PT elected six of its eight federal deputies from São Paulo. See Skidmore, *Politics of Military Rule*, p. 235.

9. Gadotti and Perreira, *Pra Que PT?*. See also Olívio de Oliveira Dutra, "Apresentação," in Damasceno et al., *Educação como Ato Político Partidário*, pp. 7–8; Carlos Rodrigues Brandão, "Um Plano Popular de Educação," in Damasceno et al., *Educação como Ato Político Partidário*, pp. 19 and 20; Moacir Gadotti, "Algumas Propostas Educacionais do Partidos dos Trabalhadores," in Damasceno et al., *Educação como Ato Político Partidário*, pp. 29; and Freire, "Partido Como Educador," pp. 3–4, in Manuscritos de Paulo Freire, Textos Selecionados, vol. 3, IPF.

10. Carlos Rodrigues Brandão, "Um Plano Popular de Educação," in Damasceno et al., *Educação como Ato Político Partidário*, p. 19; Moacir Gadotti, "Algumas Propostas Educacionais do Partidos dos Trabalhadores," in Damasceno et al., *Educação como Ato Político Partidário*, p. 29.

11. Damasceno et al., *Educação como Ato Político Partidário*, pp. 10–11, 29, 31, 77, and 126–28; Gadotti, *Uma Só Escola para Todos*, pp. 27 and 30–31.

12. Gadotti, Freire, and Guimarães, *Pedagogia*, pp. 27–28.

13. Skidmore, *Politics of Military Rule*, p. 233.

14. For the PT program, see Comparato, *Muda Brasil!*, particularly pp. 10–12, 15–18, 25, 30, and 79–80. The education program is discussed in ibid., pp. 61–66 and 144–45; see also the English-language text of the Federal Republic of Brazil, "Constitution 1988," pp. 3, 15, and 119; and Sader and Silverstein, *Without Fear of Being Happy*, p. 92.

15. Freire, Pérez, and Martinez, *Diálogos con Paulo Freire*, pp. 5, 13, 14, 16, 22, 29, and 35. A decade after his visit, none of his work had yet been published in Cuba.

16. "1986: International Year of Peace: A Tribute to Paulo Freire," *UNESCO Courier*, December 1986, p. 46.

17. The best source on Freire's thinking at this time available in English is Freire, *Pedagogy of the City*; see particularly pp. 16–17, 19–20, 22–25, 30–31, 41–42, 58, 73–74, 92, 127, and 154–58. See also Secretaria Municipal de Educação, São Paulo, *Cadernos de Formação*, p. 8; Secretaria Municipal de Educação, São Paulo, *Projecto Não a Violência*, p. 6; Secretaria Municipal de Educação, São Paulo, *O Movimento de Reorientação Curricular*, pp. 1 and 3; Antunes, *Aceita um Conselho?*, pp. 11, 13, 105–6, 114, 131, and 139; and the letters contained in "Correspondência Selecionada" in the IPF, such as the 19 January 1989 letter titled "Aos que Fazem a Educação Conosco em São Paulo." Regarding the Erundina administration, see Sader and Silverstein, *Without Fear of Being Happy*, pp. 97–98. For more information on the crisis in primary and secondary education in the 1980s, see Cláudio de Moura Castro, "What is Happening in Brazilian Education?," in Bacha and Klein, eds., *Social Change in Brazil*, pp. 263–81.

18. Luna and Klein, *Brazil Since 1980*, particularly pp. 57–49; Freire, *Pedagogy of the City*, pp. 18 and 27–29. See also Secretaria Municipal de Educação, São Paulo, *Construindo a Educação Pública Popular: Caderno 22 Meses*, p. 3; Secretaria Municipal de Educação, São Paulo, *São Paulo para Todos*, pp. 4–5; Secretaria Municipal de Educação, São Paulo, *Dez Mezes de Administração?*, p. 2; Secretaria Municipal de Educação, São Paulo, *Construindo a Educação Pública Popular: Ano 2*, p. 22; Antunes, *Aceita um Conselho?*, p. 139; and Sader and Silverstein, *Without Fear of Being Happy*, p. 122–24. Erundina's approval rating dipped as low as 16.8 percent in November of 1989. The most thorough analysis of Freire's tenure as secretary of education is O'Cadiz, Wong, and Torres, *Education and Democracy*; see particularly pp. 71–90, 94–102, 107–33, and 135–250.

19. Freire, *Pedagogy of the City*, pp. 26 and 63. See also Secretaria Municipal de Educação, São Paulo, *Construindo a Educação Pública Popular: Caderno 22 Meses*, p. 21; Secretaria Municipal de Educação, São Paulo, *São Paulo para Todos*, p. 8; and Secretaria Municipal de Educação, São Paulo, *Movimento de Alfabetização de Jovens e Adultos*, pp. 2–3, 6–7, and 10. For information on the MOVA campaign, see Stromquist, *Literacy for Citizenship*, pp. 38–49. Stromquist notes that the refusal to adopt a primer resulted from a critical reaction to the MOBRAL program during the military period. See pp. 62–63. For a brief discussion of MOVA, see also O'Cadiz, Wong, and Torres, *Education and Democracy*, pp. 54–61. Regarding Freire's opinion of partisan vs. "popular" hegemony, see Secretaria Municipal de Educação, São Paulo, *Dez Mezes de Administração*, p. 6.

20. Stromquist, *Literacy for Citizenship*, pp. 79–83. Regarding the movement from the northeast to São Paulo, see ibid., p. 103. For "psychological gains," see ibid., pp. 138–48. For reading habits of the newly literate, see ibid., pp. 164–68. Regarding the experience of the teachers, see ibid., pp. 148–50. See also ibid., p. 197.

21. Freire, *Pedagogy of the City*, pp. 136, 152, 153, and 164–65; Stromquist, *Literacy for Citizen-*

ship, pp. 177, 179, and 181; O'Cadiz, Wong, and Torres, *Education and Democracy*, pp. 234–50.

22. See Francis Fukuyama's "The End of History?" His argument was rather more subtle than it was understood to be. See also Berger, "After the Third World?," pp. 27 and 31.

23. A good introduction to this phase of his intellectual life can be found in Freire, *Política e Educação*; see, for example, pp. 29–30 and 34–36. See also Freire, *À Sombra Desta Mangueira*, pp. 19–23 and 28–36; and Freire, *Letters to Cristina*, pp. 120 and 155–57. For an interpretation of Freire's turn to utopian ideas, see Giroux and McLaren, "Paulo Freire," pp. 138–62. Regarding Freire's response to the belief that he was already outmoded in the age of "neoliberalism," see his *El Grito Manso*, pp. 64 and 70. Donald Macedo credits Freire's second wife for helping him remain hopeful, as did Freire himself. See Ana Maria Araújo Freire, *Chronicles of Love*, pp. 3–9.

Epilogue

1. See, for example, McLaren, *Che Guevara*, particularly pp. xix–xxii and 141–82.

2. British Broadcasting Company, "Nepalese Literacy Campaign Begins," 14 January 2009, at <<news.bbc.co.uk>>; UNESCO, *Education for All by 2015*.

3. Bartlett, "Human Capital or Human Connections?," p. 1617. See also UNESCO, *Education for All by 2015*, pp. i and 17–19, 33, 62–65, 198, and 236–43. Since the 1980s, improvements in adult literacy rates have largely taken place in East Asia, particularly China. The number of adult illiterates actually increased in sub-Saharan Africa and some parts of the Arab world.

4. See, for example, Weffort, *Por que Democracia?*.

5. Quoted in Bourne, *Lula of Brazil*, p. 152. My thanks to songwriter Jim White.

6. Weinstein, "Developing Inequality," pp. 5 and 15–18.

Bibliography

Primary Sources

Manuscripts

BRAZIL

Anita Paes Barreto, Depoimento, Centro de Pesquisa e Documentação de História Contemporânea do Brasil, Rio de Janeiro.

Arquivo João Goulart, Série Presidência da República, Centro de Pesquisa e Documentação de História Contemporânea do Brasil, Rio de Janeiro.

Arquivo Público do Estado do Rio de Janeiro.

Arquivo Público Estadual de Pernambuco.

Departamento de Ordem Político e Social, Pernambuco, particularly files of Miguel Arraes de Alencar, Movimento Cultural Popular, and Pelópidas Silveira.

Arquivo Público Estadual de Rio Grande do Norte.

Arquivo Público Estadual de Sergipe.

Fundação Espaço Cultural da Paraíba in João Pessoa, Arquivo Histórico, João Pessoa, Paraíba.

Instituto Histórico e Geográfico do Distrito Federal, Brasília.

Instituto Histórico e Geográfico da Paraíba, João Pessoa, Paraíba.

Instituto Histórico e Geográfico do Rio Grande do Norte, Natal, Rio Grande do Norte.

Instituto Histórico e Geográfico de Sergipe, Aracaju, Sergipe.

Instituto Nacional de Estudos e Pesquisas Anísio Teixeira, Brasília.

Instituto Paulo Freire, São Paulo. Personal Library and Manuscripts.

Lourenço Filho Collection, Centro de Pesquisa e Documentação de História Contemporânea do Brasil, Rio de Janeiro.

Serviço Social de Indústria–Pernambuco, Centro de Ensino Supletivo, Virginia Correa de Oliveira—Biblioteca Paulo Freire, Recife, Pernambuco.

Superior Tribunal Militar, Brasília.

CHILE

Biblioteca del Congreso Nacional de Chile, Santiago, Chile.

Biblioteca Nacional, Santiago, Chile.

FRANCE

United Nations Educational, Scientific, and Cultural Organization, Paris. Correspondence and Mission Files.

NICARAGUA

Universidad Centroamericana, Instituto de Historia de Nicaragua y Centroamérica, Managua.

SWITZERLAND

World Council of Churches, Archives, Geneva
  Churches' Commission on International Activities Files.
  Commission on Churches' Participation in Development Files.
  Office of Education Files.

UNITED STATES

Robert Alexander Papers, Rutgers University, New Brunswick, New Jersey.

Zbigniew Brzezinski Collection, Jimmy Carter Presidential Library, Atlanta, Georgia.

Ralph Dungan Papers, John F. Kennedy Presidential Library, Boston, Massachusetts.

Foreign Affairs Oral History Collection, Association for Diplomatic Studies and Training, Arlington, Virginia.

Charles Steward Kennedy, Interview with Lincoln Gordon, 30 September 1987, The Foreign Affairs Oral History Collection of the Association for Diplomatic Studies and Training, Arlington, Virginia.

Robert F. Kennedy Senate Papers, John F. Kennedy Presidential Library, Boston, Massachusetts.

RAC Machine, Jimmy Carter Presidential Library, Atlanta, Georgia.

Record Group 59, Department of State, National Archives II, College Park, Maryland.

Record Group 84, Department of State, National Archives II, College Park, Maryland.

Record Group 286, U.S. Agency for International Development, National Archives II, College Park, Maryland.

White House Central Files, Jimmy Carter Presidential Library, Atlanta, Georgia.

Published Primary Sources

Album de Esperança. Natal: n.p., 1961.

Arraes, Miguel. *Pensamento e Ação Politica*. Rio de Janeiro: Topbook, 1997.

Assmann, Hugo, ed. *Nicaragua Triunfa en la Alfabetización: Documentos y Testimonios de la Cruzada Nacional de Alfabetización*. San José: Departamento Ecuménico de Investigaciones, 1981.

Cortés Carabantes, Waldemar. *Manual del Método Psico-Social para la Enseñanza de Adultos*. Santiago: Ministério de Educación, 1966.

Documentos del Primer Congreso del Alfabetización "Georgino Andrade": June 9–11. Managua: Ministério de Educación, 1980.

Documentos del Segundo Congreso Nacional de Alfabetización. Managua: Ministério de Educación, 1981.

Documentos Parlamentares 127 Mensagens Presidenciais, 1947–1964. Brasília: Centro de Documentação e Informação, Coordenação de Publicações, Câmara dos Deputados, 1978.

Documentos Primer Congreso Nacional de Educación Popular de Adultos "Augusto Cesar" Managua: Ministério de Educación, 1981.

Federal Republic of Brazil. "Constitution 1988." Translated and revised by Istvan Vajda, Patrícia de Queiroz Carvalho Zimbres, and Vanira Tavares de Souza. Brasília: Federal Senate, Secretariat of Documentation and Information, Undersecretariat of Technical Editions, 1994.

Informe del Ministério de Educación. *La Educación de Adultos en Chile*. Santiago: Ministério de Educación, 1969.

Institute for Cultural Action. *Conscientization and Liberation: A Conversation with Paulo Freire*. Geneva: IDAC, n.d.

———. *Guinea Bissau: Reinventing Education*. Geneva: Institute for Cultural Action Document No. 11/12, 1976.

———. *Guinea-Bissau '79: Learning by Living and Doing*. Geneva: Institute for Cultural Action Document No. 18, 1979.

———. *What Is IDAC?* Geneva: Institute for Cultural Action, 1975.

Godoy, Josina Maria Lopes de, and Norma Porta Carreira Coelho. *Livro de Leitura para Adultos: Movimento de Cultura Popular*. 2nd ed. Rio de Janeiro: Companhia Gráfica Lux, 1963.

Goodall, Norman, ed. *The Uppsala Report 1968: Official Report of the Fourth Assembly of the World Council of Churches Uppsala July 4–20, 1968*. Geneva: World Council of Churches, 1968.

Goulart, João. "Plano Trienal para a Educação." *Revista Brasileira de Estudos Pedagogicos* 89 (January–March 1963): 3–7.

Grupo de Trabalho, Governo do Estado de Pernambuco. *Aliança para o Progresso: Resultado de Inquérito*. Rio de Janeiro: Editora Brasiliense, 1963.

Instituto de Capacitación e Investigación. *La Alfabetización Funcional en Chile*. Santiago: Instituto de Capacitación e Investigación, 1968.

Jefatura de Planes Extraordinarios de Educación de Adultos. *Comunidad: Tercer Nivel*. Santiago: Ministério de Educación, 1967.

———. *Lectura para Adultos: Primer Nivel*. Santiago: Ministério de Educación, 1966.

———. *Lectura para Adultos: Segundo Nivel*. Santiago: Ministério de Educación, 1967.

———. *La Raiz y la Espiga*. Santiago: Ministério de Educación, 1967.

Ministério da Educação Nacional e Desporto, Departamento de Educação de Adultos e Alfabetização, República Democrático de São Tomé e Príncipe. *A Luta Continua*. 5 vols. São Tomé: Ministério da Educação Nacional e Desporto, 1980.

Ministério de Educación. *El Amanecer del Pueblo: Cuaderno de Educación de Lecto-Escritura*. Managua: Ministério de Educación, 1980.

———. *Cruzada Nacional de Alfabetización: Nicaragua Libre 1980*. Managua: Ministério de Educación, 1980.

Ministério de Educación Pública. *Campaña de Alfabetización: Leyes e Instructivo para Alfabetizadores*. Managua: Ministério de Educación Pública, 1951.

Movimento de Educação de Base. *Viver é Lutar: Segundo Livro de Leitura para Adultos*. Rio de Janeiro: n.p., 1963.

Public Papers of the Presidents of the United States. Washington: Federal Register Division, National Archives and Records Service, General Services Administration, 1961–62.

Secretaria Municipal de Educação, São Paulo. *Cadernos de Formação: Alfabetização: Leitura do Mundo, Leitura da Palavra*. São Paulo: Secretaria Municipal de Educação, 1991.

———. *Construiendo a Educação Pública Popular: Ano 2.* São Paulo: Secretaria Municipal de Educação, 1990.

———. *Construiendo a Educação Pública Popular: Caderno 22 Meses.* São Paulo: Secretaria Municipal de Educação, n.d.

———. *Dez Mezes de Administração: O Que Mudou?* São Paulo: Secretaria Municipal de Educação, 1989.

———. *O Movimento de Reorientação Curricular na Secretaria Municipal de Educação de São Paulo.* São Paulo: Secretaria Municipal de Educação, 1990.

———. *Movimento de Alfabetização de Jovens e Adultos da Cidade de São Paulo.* São Paulo: Secretaria Municipal de Educação, 1989.

———. *Projecto Não a Violência.* São Paulo: Secretaria Municipal de Educação, n.d.

———. *São Paulo para Todos: 1989–1992: Relatório Final de Governo.* São Paulo: Secretaria Municipal de Educação, 1992.

Sousa, Itmar de. *Fascículos do Diário de Natal.* Natal: Diário de Natal, 1999.

U.S. Department of State. *Foreign Relations of the United States.* Washington: Government Printing Office, 1958–68.

Vencimos: Nicaragua: Puño en Alto, Libro Abierto para América Latina. Mexico City: Ministério de Educación, 1988.

World Council of Churches. *Handbook: World Conference on Church and Society, July 12–26.* Geneva: World Council of Churches, 1966.

Periodicals

Barricada

Correio da Paraíba

DC—Brasília

Encuentro: Revista de la
 Universidad Centroamericana

Gazeta de Sergipe

El Mercurio

Nô Pintcha

El Nuevo Diario

La Prensa

Punto Final

El Siglo

A União

Secondary Sources

Adriance, Madeleine. *Opting for the Poor: Brazilian Catholicism in Transition.* Kansas City, Mo.: Sheed & Ward, 1986.

Affonso, Almino, Sergio Gómez, Emilio Klein, and Pablo Ramirez. *Movimiento Campesino Chileno.* Vol. 1. Santiago: ICIRA, 1970.

Ahumada, Jorge. *La Crisis Integral de Chile.* Santiago: Editorial Universitaria, 1966.

Albuquerque, Durval Muniz de, Jr. *A Invenção do Nordeste e Outras Artes.* 2nd ed. Recife: Fundação Joaquim Nabuco, 1999.

Alemán Ocampo, Carlos. *Y También Enséñenles a Leer.* Managua: Editorial Nueva Nicaragua, 1984.

Alexander, Robert J. *Juscelino Kubitschek and the Development of Brazil.* Athens: Ohio University Press, 1991.

————. *The Tragedy of Chile*. Westport, Conn.: Greenwood Press, 1978.

Alves, Aluizio. *Memória Viva de Aluizio Alves*. 2nd ed. Natal: Ed. Universidade Federal do Rio Grande do Norte, 1998.

————. *A Primeira Campanha Popular no Rio Grande do Norte*. Natal: Instituto Histórico e Geográfico do Rio Grande do Norte, 1976.

————. *O Que Eu Não Esqueci: Reminiscência Políticas 1933/2001*. Rio de Janeiro: Léo Christiano Editorial, 2001.

————. *Sem Ódio e sem Medo*. 2nd ed. Rio de Janeiro: Nosso Tempo, 1969.

————. *A Verdade que Não é Secreta*. Rio de Janeiro: Nosso Tempo, 1976.

Alves, Márcio Moreira. *O Cristo do Povo*. Rio de Janeiro: Sabiá, 1968.

Alves, Maria Helena Moreira. *State and Opposition in Military Brazil*. Austin: University of Texas Press, 1985.

Ángeles, Maria de los. "Estudio para la Creación del Museo Fundación Violeta Barrios de Chamorro." Unpublished plan for presidential library, Universidad de El Salvador, 2004, available at the Instituto de Historia de Nicaragua y Centro America.

Angell, Alan. "Chile since 1958." In *Chile since Independence*, edited by Leslie Bethell, 129–202. Cambridge: Cambridge University Press, 1993.

Antunes, Ângela. *Aceita um Conselho?: Como Organizar o Colegiado Escolar*. São Paulo: Cortez and Instituto Paulo Freire, 2002.

Aragón López, Miguel Angel. *Una Misión Noble*. Managua: Camino, 2001.

Armony, Ariel C. *Argentina, the United States, and the Anti-Communist Crusade in Central America, 1977–1984*. Athens: Ohio University Press, 1997.

Arnove, Robert F. *Education and Revolution in Nicaragua*. Westport, Conn.: Praeger, 1986.

Arnove, Robert F., and Harvey J. Graff, eds. *National Literacy Campaigns: Historical and Comparative Perspectives*. New York: Plenum Press, 1987.

Arrien G., Juan B., and Roger Matis Lazo. *Nicaragua: 10 Años de Educación en la Revolución: Contexto, Avances, Problemas y Perspectivas de un Proceso de Transformación*. Managua: Ministério de Educación, 1989.

Arruda, Marcos. *Cartas a Lula: Um outro Brasil é Possível*. Rio de Janeiro: Documenta Histórica, 2006.

Austin, Robert. *The State, Literacy, and Popular Education in Chile, 1964–1990*. Lanham, Md.: Lexington Books, 2003.

Azevedo, Fernando de. *Brazilian Culture: An Introduction to the Study of Culture in Brazil*. Translated by William Rex Crawford. New York: Hafner Publishing Company, 1971.

Bacha, Edmar L., and Herbert S. Klein, eds. *Social Change in Brazil, 1945–1985: The Incomplete Transition*. Albuquerque: University of New Mexico Press, 1989.

Barbosa, Letícia Rameh. *Movimento de Cultura Popular: Impactos na Sociedade Pernambucana*. Recife: Edição do autor, 2009.

Barcellos, Jalusa. *CPC da UNE: Uma História de Paixao e Consciência*. Rio de Janeiro: Nova Fronteira, 1994.

Barreiro, Julio. *Educación Popular y Proceso de Concientización*. 8th ed. Mexico City: Siglo Veintiunos Editores, 1984.

Bartlett, Lesley. "Dialogue, Knowledge, and Teacher-Student Relations: Freirean Pedagogy in Theory and Practice." *Comparative Education Review* 49:3 (August 2005): 344–64.

————. "Human Capital or Human Connections? The Cultural Meanings of Education in Brazil." *Teachers College Record* 109:7 (July 2007): 1613–36.

Bayard de Volo, Lorraine. *Mothers of Heroes and Martyrs: Gender Identity Politics in Nicaragua, 1979–1999.* Baltimore: Johns Hopkins University Press, 2001.

Beiseigel, Celso de Rui. *Estado e Educação Popular (Um Estudo sobre a Educação de Adultos).* São Paulo: Livraria Pioneira Editora, 1974.

Belli, Gioconda. *El País Bajo mi Piel: Memorias de Amor y Guerra.* Managua: Anamá, 2001.

Berger, Mark T. "After the Third World? History, Destiny and the Fate of Third Worldism." *Third World Quarterly* 25:1 (February 2004): 9–39.

Berlinck, Manoel Tosta. *O Centro Popular de Cultura da UNE.* Campinas: Papirus, 1984.

Bhola, H. S. *Campaigning for Literacy: Eight National Experiences of the Twentieth Century, with a Memorandum to Decision-Makers.* Paris: UNESCO, 1984.

Bittencourt, Ademar, org. *Fundos e Campanhas Educacionais (Coletânea de Atos Oficiais).* Vol. 1, *1942–1958.* Rio de Janeiro: Departamento Nacional de Educação, 1959.

Black, George, and John Bevan. *The Loss of Fear: Education in Nicaragua before and after the Revolution.* London: Nicaragua Solidarity Campaign: World University Service, 1980.

Bock, Paul. *In Search of a Responsible World Society: The Social Teachings of the World Council of Churches.* Philadelphia: Westminster Press, 1974.

Bojunga, Claudio. *JK: O Artista do Impossível.* Rio de Janeiro: Objetiva, 2001.

Bomeny, Helena. *Os Intelectuais da Educação.* Rio de Janeiro: Jorge Zahar, 2001.

Bourne, Richard. *Lula of Brazil: The Story So Far.* Berkeley: University of California Press, 2008.

Brandão, Carlos Rodrigues, ed. *Lições de Nicaragua: A Experiência da Esperança.* 2nd ed. Campinas: Papirus, 1985.

Brown, Timothy C. *The Real Contra War: Highlander Peasant Resistance in Nicaragua.* Norman: University of Oklahoma Press, 2001.

Burnett, Ben G. *Political Groups in Chile: The Dialogue between Order and Change.* Austin: University of Texas Press, 1970.

Burns, E. Bradford. *A History of Brazil.* 3rd ed. New York: Columbia University Press, 1993.

Cabestrero, Teofilo. *Ministers of God, Ministers of the People: Testimonies of Faith from Nicaragua.* Translated from the Spanish by Robert R. Barr. Maryknoll, N.Y.: Orbis Books, 1983.

Caetano, Maria do Rosário. *Paulo Freire e a Educação Brasileira.* Brasília: Correio Braziliense, 1982.

Calderón, Edmundo Joaquín. *Pedro Joaquín: Juega!* Managua: Ediciones Centroamericanas, 1998.

Callado, Antonio. *Tempo de Arraes: A Revolução sem Violência.* 3rd ed. Rio de Janeiro: Paz e Terra, 1980.

Cardenal, Ernesto. *La Revolución Perdida (Memorias Tomo III).* Managua: Anamá Ediciones Centroamericanas, 2003.

Cardoso, Miriam Limoeiro. *Ideologia do Desenvolvimento Brasil: JK–JQ.* Rio de Janeiro: Paz e Terra, 1977.

Carron, G., and A. Bordia, eds. *Issues in Planning and Implementing National Literacy Programmes.* Paris: UNESCO: International Institute for Educational Planning, 1985.

Castilla, Miguel de. *Educación Y Lucha de Clases en Nicaragua*. Managua: Universidad Centromericana, 1980.

Castro, Pedro. *La Educación en Chile de Frei a Pinochet*. Salamanca: Tierra, 1977.

Cechin, Antonio. "Evangelizing Men as They Are." In *The Medellín Papers*, edited by Johannes Hofinger and Terence J. Sheridan, 117–36. Manila: East Asian Pastoral Institute, 1969.

Chabal, Patrick. *Amílcar Cabral: Revolutionary Leadership and People's War*. London: Hurst & Company, 2002.

——, ed. *A History of Postcolonial Lusophone Africa*. Bloomington: Indiana University Press, 2002.

——. *Political Domination in Africa: Reflections on the Limits of Power*. New York: Cambridge University Press, 1986.

Chamorro, Violeta Barrios de, with Sonia Cruz de Baltodano and Guido Fernandez. *Dreams of the Heart: The Autobiography of President Violeta Barrios de Chamorro of Nicaragua*. New York: Simon and Schuster, 1996.

Chilcote, Ronald H. *The Brazilian Communist Party: Conflict and Integration, 1922–1972*. New York: Oxford University Press, 1974.

Chonchol, Jacques. *El Desarrollo de America Latina y la Reform Agraria*. 2nd ed. Santiago: Editorial del Pacifico, 1965.

——. *La Reforma Agraria como Proceso Dinámico de Integracióm en una Sociedad que se Transforma*. Santiago: INDAP, 1967.

——. "Poder y Reforma Agraria en la Experiencia Chilena." In *Chile Hoy*. 3rd ed. Santiago: Editorial Universitaria, 1971.

Chonchol, Jacques, and Julio Silva S. *Hacia un Mundo Comunitario: Condiciones de una Political Social Cristiana*. Santiago: Estudos Sociales, 1951.

Cittadino, Monique, et al. *Estrutura de Poder na Paraíba*. João Pessoa: Universidade Federal da Paraíba, 1999.

Clark, Charles E. *Uprooting Otherness: The Literacy Campaign in NEP-Era Russia*. Selinsgrove: Susquehanna University Press, 2000.

Close, David, and Kalowatie Deonandan, eds. *Undoing Democracy: The Politics of Electoral Caudillismo*. Lanham, Md.: Lexington Books, 2004.

Cohn, Amélia. *Crise Regional e Planejamento: Processo de Criação da SUDENE*. São Paulo: Editora Perspectiva, 1973.

Collier, Simon, and William Sater. *A History of Chile, 1808–1994*. Cambridge: Cambridge University Press, 1996.

Comparato, Fábio Konder. *Muda Brasil! Uma Constituição para o Desenvolvimento Democrático*. 2nd ed. São Paulo: Brasiliense, 1986.

Cooper, Frederick. *Colonialism in Question: Theory, Knowledge, History*. Berkeley: University of California Press, 2005.

Cortés Carabantes, Waldemar. "Formas Muertas y Dinámicas en nuestra Educación de Adultos." *Revista de Educación* 93–94 (July–December 1963): 11–25.

——. "Los Planes Extraordinarios de Educación de Adultos." *Revista de Educación* 7 (June 1968): 28–35.

Costa, Maria das Graças Moreira, and Leo Kesel. *Evolução do Analfabetismo no Brasil, 1980–1990*. MEC: Brasília, 1993.

Cullather, Nick. "Development? It's History." *Diplomatic History* 24:4 (Fall 2000): 641–53.

———. "Miracles of Modernization: The Green Revolution and the Apotheosis of Technology." *Diplomatic History* 28:2 (April 2004): 227–54.

Cunha, Luiz Antônio, and Moacyr de Góes. *O Golpe na Educação*. Rio de Janeiro: Jorge Zahar, 1985.

Cury, Carlos Roberto Jamil. *Ideologia e Educação Brasileira*. São Paulo: Cortez & Moraes Ltda., 1978.

Damasceno, Alberto, et al. *A Educação como Ato Político Partidário*. São Paulo: Cortez, 1989.

Dantas, José Ibaré Costa. *Os Partidos Politicos em Sergipe (1889–1964)*. Rio de Janeiro: Tempo Brasileiro, 1989.

———. *A Tutela Militar em Sergipe: 1964–1984*. Rio de Janeiro: Tempo Brasileiro, 1997.

Davidson, Basil. *The Liberation of Guiné: Aspects of an African Revolution*. Hammondsworth, Middlesex, United Kingdom: Penguin Books, 1979.

Dávila, Jerry. *Diploma of Whiteness: Race and Social Policy in Brazil, 1917–1945*. Durham: Duke University Press, 2003.

Dawson, Andrew. "A Very Brazilian Experiment: The Base Education Movement, 1961–1967." *History of Education* 31:2 (March 2002): 185–94.

Dhada, Mustafah. *Warriors at Work: How Guinea Was Really Set Free*. Niwot: University Press of Colorado, 1993.

Dodson, Michael, and Laura Nizzi O'Shaughnessy. *Nicaragua's Other Revolution: Religious Faith and Political Struggle*. Chapel Hill: University of North Carolina Press, 1990.

Droit, Roger-Pol. *Humanity in the Making: Overview of the Intellectual History of UNESCO, 1945–2005*. Paris: UNESCO, 2005.

Duarte, Sérgio Guerra. *Por Que Existem Analfabetos no Brasil?* Rio de Janeiro: Editora Civilização Brasileiro, 1963.

Duggan, William Redman, and John R. Civille. *Tanzania and Nyerere: A Study of Ujamaa and Nationhood*. Maryknoll, N.Y.: Orbis Books, 1976.

Dulles, John W. F. *Castelio Branco: The Making of a Brazilian President*. College Station: Texas A&M University Press, 1978.

Ekbladh, David. "'Mr. TVA': Grass-Roots Development, David Lilienthal, and the Rise and Fall of the Tennessee Valley Authority as a Symbol for U.S. Overseas Development, 1933–1973." *Diplomatic History* 26:3 (Summer 2002): 349–70.

Engerman, David C. *Modernization from the Other Shore: American Intellectuals and the Romance of Russian Development*. Cambridge: Harvard University Press, 2003.

Engerman, David C., Nils Gilman, Marh H. Haefele, and Michael E. Latham, eds. *Staging Growth: Modernization, Development, and the Global Cold War*. Amherst: University of Massachusetts Press, 2003.

Engerman, David C., and Corinna R. Unger. "Introduction: Towards a Global History of Modernization." *Diplomatic History* 33:3 (June 2009): 375–85.

Escobar, Arturo. *Encountering Development: The Making and Unmaking of the Third World*. Princeton: Princeton University Press, 1995.

Escobar, Samuel. *Paulo Freire: Una Pedagogia Latinoamericana*. Mexico City: Kyrios, 1993.

Everingham, Mark. *Revolution and the Multiclass Coalition in Nicaragua*. Pittsburgh: University of Pittsburgh Press, 1996.

Fagen, Richard R. *The Transformation of Political Culture in Cuba*. Stanford: Stanford University Press, 1969.

Faria, Góis Sobrinho. "O Ensino e a Renovação Social." *Revista Brasileira de Estudos Pedagógicas* 29 (April–June 1958): 33–41.

Faria, Herminio Augusto. *Três Pesquisas: O Voto do Analfabeto, A Lei de Diretrizes e Bases, A Divisão da Guanabara em Municípios*. Rio: Fundação Getúlio Vargas, 1964.

Faundez, Antonio. *Cultura Oral, Cultura Escrita y Proceso de Alfabetización en São Tomé e Príncipe*. Quito: Corporación Ecuatoriana para el Desarrollo de la Comunicación, 1984.

Fávero, Osmar, ed. *Cultura Popular Educação Popular: Memória dos Anos 60*. 2nd ed. Rio de Janeiro: Ediçoes Graal, 2001.

Fernandes, Francisco Calazans, and Antonio Terra. *40 Horas de Esperança: Politica e Pedagogia na Experiência Pioneira de Educação*. São Paulo: Cortez, 1996.

Ferrari, Sergio. *Sembrando Utopia: Reportajes y Conversaciones*. Managua: Ediciones Nicarao, 1992.

Ferreira, Maria Edy. *Tendencias del Poder entre los Campesinos Asentados*. Santiago: ICIRA, 1970.

Figueiredo, Ariosvaldo. *História Política de Sergipe*. Vols. 2 and 5. Aracaju: Gráfica Editora J. Andrade, 1996.

Figueiredo, Betânia Gonçalves. "A Criação do SESI e SESC: Do Enquadramento da Preguiça a Produtivade de Ocio." Unpublished master's thesis, Universidade Estadual de Campinas, 1991.

Fischer, Brodwyn. *A Poverty of Rights: Citizenship and Inequality in Twentieth-Century Rio de Janeiro*. Stanford: Stanford University Press, 2008.

Fitzpatrick, Sheila, ed. *Cultural Revolution in Russia, 1928–1931*. Bloomington: Indiana University Press, 1978.

———. *Education and Social Mobility in the Soviet Union*. Cambridge: Cambridge University Press, 1979.

Fleet, Michael. *The Rise and Fall of Chilean Christian Democracy*. Princeton: Princeton University Press, 1985.

Flora, Jan L., John McFadden, and Ruth Warner. "The Growth of Class Struggle: The Impact of the Nicaraguan Literacy Crusade on the Political Consciousness of Young Literacy Workers." *Latin American Perspectives* 10:1 (Winter 1983): 45–61.

Foracchi, Marialice M. *O Estudante e a Transformação da Sociedade Brasileira*. São Paulo: Companhia Editora Nacional, 1965.

Frei, Eduardo. "The Aims of Christian Democracy." *The Commonweal*, 9 October 1964, 63–66.

Freire, Ana Maria Araújo. *Chronicles of Love: My Life with Paulo Freire*. Translated by Alex Oliveira. New York: Peter Lang, 2001.

———. *Paulo Freire: Uma História de Vida*. Indaiatuba: Villa das Letras, 2006.

Freire, Paulo. *Actividades Desarrolladas en el Año de 1968: Informe Anual*. Santiago: ICIRA, 1969.

———. "The Adult Literacy Process as Cultural Action for Freedom." *Harvard Educational Review* 40:2 (May 1970): 205–25.

———. *El Asentamiento como una Totalidad*. Santiago: ICIRA, 1968.

———. *El Compromiso del Profesional con la Sociedad*. Santiago: ICIRA, 1968.

———. *Educação e Atualidade Brasileira*. São Paulo: Cortez, 2001.

———. "Education, Liberation and the Church." *Study Encounter* 9:1 (1973): 1–16.

———. *Extensión o Comunicación*. Santiago: ICIRA, 1969.

———. "Freire Speaks on Freire." *Church and Community* 31:4 (June 1974): 4–7.

———. *El Grito Manso*. Buenos Aires: El Siglo XXI Editores Argentina, 2003.

———. *Letters to Cristina: Reflections on My Life and Work*. Translated by Donald Macedo with Quilda Macedo and Alexandre Oliveira. New York: Routledge, 1996.

———. "Paulo Freire: Educação e Prática da Liberdade." *Tempo e Presença* 15:4 (October 1979): 3–6.

———. *Pedagogy in Process: The Letters to Guinea-Bissau*. Translated by Carman St. John Hunter. New York: Seabury Press, 1978.

———. *Pedagogy of Hope: Reliving Pedagogy of the Oppressed*. Translated by Robert R. Barr. New York: Continuum, 1994.

———. *Pedagogy of the City*. Translated by Donald Macedo. New York: Continuum, 1993.

———. *Política e Educação*. São Paulo: Cortez, 2003.

———. *A Propósito de uma Administração*. Recife: Imprensa Universitária, 1961.

———. "Quatro Cartas aos Animadores de Círculos de Cultura de São Tomé e Príncipe." In *A Questão Política da Educação Popular*, compiled by Carlos Rodrigues Brandão. São Paulo: Brasiliense, 1980.

———. *El Rol de Trabajador Social en el Proceso de Cambio*. Santiago: ICIRA, 1968.

———. *À Sombra Desta Mangueira*. São Paulo: Olho d'Água, 1995.

Freire, Paulo, and Antonio Faundez. *Learning to Question: A Pedagogy of Liberation*. Geneva: World Council of Churches, 1989.

Freire, Paulo, and Sérgio Guimarães. *A África Ensinando a Gente: Angola, Guiné Bissau, São Tomé e Príncipe*. São Paulo: Paz e Terra, 2003.

———. *Aprendendo com a Própria História*. 2 vols. Rio de Janeiro: Paz e Terra, 1987, 2002.

Freire, Paulo, Sérgio Guimarães, and Donald Macedo. *Literacy: Reading the Word and the World*. Westport, Conn.: Bergin & Garvey, 1987.

Freire, Paulo, Sérgio Guimarães, Rosiska Darcy de Oliveira, Miguel Darcy de Oliveira, and Claudius Ceccon. *Vivendo e Aprendendo: Experiência do Idac em Educação Popular*. São Paulo: Brasiliense, 1980.

Freire, Paulo, Esther Pérez, and Fernando Martinez. *Diálogos con Paulo Freire*. Havana: Editorial Caminos, 1997.

Freitag, Barbara. *Escola, Estado e Sociedade*. São Paulo: EDART, 1978.

Freitas, Marcos Cezarde. *Álvaro Vieira Pinto: A Personagem Histórica e Sua Trama*. São Paulo: Cortez, 1998.

French, John D. *Drowning in Laws: Labor Law and Brazilian Political Culture*. Chapel Hill: University of North Carolina Press, 2004.

———. "Workers and the Rise of Adhemarista Populism in São Paulo, Brazil, 1945–47." *Hispanic American Historical Review* 68:1 (February 1988): 1–43.

Fukuyama, Francis. "The End of History?" *The National Interest*, Summer 1989.

Gadotti, Moacir. *Reading Paulo Freire: His Life and Work*. Translated by John Milton. Albany: State University of New York Press, 1994.

———. *Uma Só Escola para Todos: Caminhos da Autonomia Escolar*. Petrópolis: Vozes, 1990.

Gadotti, Moacir, Paulo Freire, and Sérgio Guimarães. *Pedagogia: Diálogo e Conflito*. 5th ed. São Paulo: Cortez, 2000.

Gadotti, Moacir, and Octaviano Perreira. *Pra Que PT? Origem, Projeto e Consolidação do Partido dos Trabalhadores*. São Paulo: Cortez, 1989.

Gajardo, Marcela. "Apreciaciones Criticas sobre la Concientización y la Educación Popular en los Paises Latinoamericanos." Documento de Trabajo Programa/FLACSO-Chile No. 437, Noviembre 1989.

———. "Educación de Adultos: De Nairobi a Paris." Documento de Trabajo/FLACSO Chile No. 472, Noviembre 1985.

Galvão, Mailde Pinto. *1964, Aconteceu em Abril*. Natal: Ed. Clima, 1994.

Garrido, R., José Cristián Guerrero, and María Soledad Valdés. *Historia de la Reforma Agraria en Chile*. Santiago: Editorial Universitaria, 1988.

Gazmuri, Cristián, Patricia Arancibia, and Álvaro Góngora. *Eduardo Frei y su Época*. Vol. 2. Santiago: Aguilar Chilena de Ediciones, Ltda., 2000.

Gerhardt, Heinz Peter. "Angicos—Rio Grande do Norte—1962/63 (A Primeira Experiência com O Sistema Paulo Freire)." *Educação e Sociedade*, Maio 1983, 5–28.

Germano, José Willington. *Lendo e Aprendendo: "A Campanha de Pé no Chão."* São Paulo: Cortez, 1982.

Gil, Federico G. *The Political System of Chile*. Boston: Houghton Mifflin, 1966.

Giroux, Henry, and Peter McLaren. "Paulo Freire, Postmodernism, and the Utopian Imagination: A Blochian Reading." In *Not Yet: Reconsidering Ernest Bloch*, edited by Jamie Owen Daniel and Tom Moylan, 138–62. New York: Verso, 1997.

Gleijeses, Piero. *Conflicting Missions: Havana, Washington, and Africa, 1959–1976*. Chapel Hill: University of North Carolina Press, 2002.

Gould, Jeffrey L. *To Lead as Equals: Rural Protest and Political Consciousness in Chinandega, Nicaragua, 1912–1979*. Chapel Hill: University of North Carolina Press, 1990.

Graff, Harvey J. *The Labyrinths of Literacy: Reflections on Literacy Past and Present*. London: Falmer Press, 1987.

Grossman, Richard. "Augusto Sandino of Nicaragua: The Hero Never Dies." In *Heroes and Hero Cults in Latin America*, edited by Samuel Brunk and Ben Fallaw, 149–70. Austin: University of Texas Press, 2006.

Guedes, Nonato, ed. *O Jogo da Verdade: Revolução de 64: 30 Anos*. João Pessoa: A União, 1994.

Gullette, David, ed. *Nicaraguan Peasant Poetry from Solentiname*. Albuquerque, N.M.: West End Press, 1988.

Gutiérrez, Gustavo. *A Theology of Liberation*. Translated and edited by Sister Caridad Inda and John Eagleson. Maryknoll, N.Y.: Orbis Books, 1973.

Hamuy B., Eduardo. "Chile: El Proceso de Democratización Fundamental." *Cuadernos del Centro de Estudios Socioeconomicos* 4 (April 1967): 15–37.

Harasim, Linda. "Literacy and National Reconstruction in Guinea Bissau: A Critique of the Freirean Literacy Campaign." Unpublished Ph.D. dissertation, University of Toronto, 1983.

Hernández, Isabel. *Educação e Sociedade Indígena*. São Paulo: Cortez, 1981.

Hinzen, H., and V. H. Hundsdorfer, eds. *The Tanzanian Experience: Education for Liberation and Development*. Hamburg: UNESCO Institute for Education, 1979.

Hirshon, Sheryl L. *And Also Teach Them to Read = Y, Tambien, Enséñeles a Leer*. Westport, Conn.: L. Hill, 1983.

Hobsbawm, Eric. *The Age of Extremes: A History of the World, 1914–1991*. New York: Vintage, 1996.

Horton, Lynn. *Peasants in Arms: War and Peace in the Mountains of Nicaragua, 1979–1994*. Athens: Ohio University Press, 1998.

Horton, Myles, and Paulo Freire. *We Make the Road by Walking: Conversations on Education and Social Change*. Philadelphia: Temple University Press, 1990.

Hoyt, Katherine. *The Many Faces of Sandinista Democracy*. Athens: Ohio University Press, 1997.

Instituto Superior de Estudos Brasileiros. *Introdução aos Problemas do Brasil*. Rio de Janeiro: Ministério de Educação/ISEB, 1956.

Jaccoud, Luciana de Barros. *Movimentos Sociais e Crise Política em Pernambuco, 1955–1968*. Recife: Fundação Joaquim Nabuco, Editora Massangana, 1990.

Jaksic, Iván, ed. *The Political Power of the Word: Press and Oratory in Nineteenth-Century Latin America*. London: Institute of Latin American Studies, 2002.

Januzzi, Gilberta. *Confronto Pedagógico: Paulo Freire e Mobral*. São Paulo: Cortez & Moraes, 1979.

Jolly, Richard, Louis Emmerij, Dharam Ghai, and Frédéric Lapeyre. *UN Contributions to Development Theory and Practice*. Bloomington: Indiana University Press, 2004.

Jones, Phillip W. *International Policies for Third World Education: UNESCO, Literacy and Development*. New York: Routledge, 1988.

Jorrin, Miguel, and John D. Martz. *Latin American Political Thought and Ideology*. Chapel Hill: University of North Carolina Press, 1970.

Judt, Tony. *Postwar: A History of Europe since 1945*. London: William Heinemann, 2005.

Kagan, Robert. *A Twilight Struggle: American Power and Nicaragua, 1977–1990*. New York: Free Press, 1996.

Kaufman, Robert R. *The Politics of Land Reform in Chile, 1950–1970: Public Policy, Political Institutions, and Social Change*. Cambridge: Harvard University Press, 1972.

Keck, Margaret E. *The Workers' Party and Democratization in Brazil*. New Haven: Yale University Press, 1992.

Kennedy, William B. "Education in the World Ecumenical Movement." *Ecumenical Review* 27:2 (April 1975): 147–56.

Kipnow, Karl Ernest. "Alienation, Liberation, Community: The Educational Policy of the WCC before and after Nairobi." *Ecumenical Review* 30:2 (April 1978): 139–54.

Kirkendall, Andrew J. *Class Mates: Male Student Culture and the Making of a Political Class in Nineteenth-Century Brazil*. Lincoln: University of Nebraska Press, 2002.

———. "Entering History: Paulo Freire and the Politics of the Brazilian Northeast, 1958–1964." *Luso-Brazilian Review* 41:1 (Summer 2004): 168–89.

———. "Kennedy Men and the Fate of the Alliance for Progress in LBJ-Era Brazil and Chile." *Diplomacy & Statecraft* 18:4 (December 2007): 745–72.

———. "Paulo Freire, Eduardo Frei, Literacy Training and the Politics of Consciousness

Raising in Chile, 1964–1970." *Journal of Latin American Studies* 36:4 (November 2004): 687–717.

———. "Paulo Freire, l'Unesco et la Lutte Contre l'Analphabétisme des Adultes dans le Monde de la Guerre Froide." *60 Ans D'Histoire de l'Unesco: Actes du Colloque International, Paris, 16–18 Novembre 2005*. Paris: UNESCO, 2007.

———. "Student Culture and Nation-State Formation." In *Beyond Imagined Communities: Reading and Writing the Nation in Nineteenth-Century Latin America*, edited by Sara Castro-Klarén and John Charles Chasteen, 84–111. Baltimore: Johns Hopkins University Press, 2003.

Kolakowski, Leszek. *Main Currents of Marxism*. Translated by P. S. Falla. New York: W. W. Norton & Company, 2005.

Kozol, Jonathan. *The Night Is Dark and I am Far from Home*. Boston: Houghton Mifflin, 1975.

Latham, Michael E. *Modernization as Ideology: American Social Science and "Nation Building" in the Kennedy Era*. Chapel Hill: University of North Carolina Press, 2000.

Leacock, Ruth. *Requiem for Revolution: The United States and Brazil, 1961–1969*. Kent, Ohio: Kent State University Press, 1990.

Lefever, Ernest. *Amsterdam to Nairobi: The World Council of Churches and the Third World*. Washington: Ethics and Public Policy Center, 1979.

Lehmann, David. *Democracy and Development in Latin America: Economics, Politics and Religion in the Post-War Period*. Philadelphia: Temple University Press, 1990.

———. "Peasant Consciousness and Agrarian Reform in Chile." *Archives Européenes de Sociologie*. 13:2 (1972): 296–325.

———. "Political Incorporation versus Political Instability: The Case of the Chilean Agrarian Reform, 1965–70." *Journal of Development Studies* 7:4 (July 1971): 365–95.

Leogrande, William. *Our Own Backyard: The United States in Central America, 1977–1992*. Chapel Hill: University of North Carolina Press, 1998.

Lernoux, Penny. *Cry of the People: The Struggle for Human Rights in Latin America—The Catholic Church in Conflict with U.S. Policy*. New York: Penguin Books, 1982.

Levinson, Jerome, and Juan de Onís. *The Alliance that Lost Its Way: A Critical Report on the Alliance for Progress*. Chicago: Quadrangle Books, 1970.

Lima, Haroldo, and Aldo Arantes. *História da Ação Popular: da JUC ao PC do B*. São Paulo: Editora Alfa-Omega, 1984.

Lopes, Carlos. *Guinea-Bissau: From Liberation Struggle to Independent Statehood*. Boulder, Colo.: Westview Press, 1987.

Lourenço Filho, Manoel Bergstrom. *Introdução ao Estudo da Escola Nova: Bases, Sistemas e Diretrizes da Pedagogia Contemporânea*. 12th ed. São Paulo: Melhoramentos, 1978.

Love, Joseph L. *Crafting the Third World: Theorizing Underdevelopment in Rumania and Brazil*. Stanford: Stanford University Press, 1996.

———. "Political Participation in Brazil, 1881–1969." *Luso-Brazilian Review* 7:2 (December 1970): 3–24.

Loveman, Brian. *Struggle in the Countryside: Politics and Rural Labor in Chile, 1919–1973*. Bloomington: Indiana University Press, 1976.

Lovo, Anastasio. *História y Violencia en Nicaragua*. Managua: Nos-Otros, 1997.

Luhn, Christina Anne. "The 'Catechism of Development': America's Cold War Commitment

to Education, Democracy and Development in Northeast Brazil, 1960–1964."
Unpublished Ph.D. dissertation, University of Missouri–Kansas City, 2003.

Luiz, Mackson. *SESI: 50 Anos*. Rio de Janeiro: Dórea Books and Art, 1996.

Luna, Francisco Vidal, and Herbert S. Klein. *Brazil Since 1980*. Cambridge: Cambridge University Press, 2006.

Lynch, Edward A. *Latin America's Christian Democratic Parties: A Political Economy*. Westport, Conn.: Praeger, 1993.

Lyra, Carlos. *As Quarenta Horas de Angicos: Uma Experiência Pioneira de Educação*. São Paulo: Cortez, 1996.

Malkin-Fontecchio, Tia. "Citizens or Workers: The Politics of Education in Northeast Brazil, 1959–1964." Unpublished Ph.D. dissertation, Brown University, 2003.

Mallon, Florencia. *Courage Tastes of Blood: The Mapuche Community of Nicolás Ailío and the Chilean State, 1906–2001*. Durham: Duke University Press, 2005.

Mallorquin, Carlos. *Celso Furtado: Um Retrato Intellectual*. São Paulo: Contraponto, 2005.

Maranhão, Djalma. *Cartas de um Exilado*. Natal: CLIMA, 1984.

Mariz, Marlene da Silva, and Luiz Eduardo Brandão Suassuna. *História do Rio Grande do Norte Contemporâneo 1934 a 1990; Estado, Evolução, Política, Social e Económica*. Natal: CDF Gráfica e Editora, 2001.

McCullough, Jock. *In the Twilight of Revolution: The Political Theory of Amilcar Cabral*. London: Routledge & Kegan Paul, 1983.

McDonald, Theodore. *Making a New People: Education in Revolutionary Cuba*. Vancouver: New Star Books, 1985.

McLaren, Peter. *Che Guevara, Paulo Freire, and the Pedagogy of Revolution*. Lanham, Md.: Rowman & Littlefield, 2000.

Medary, Marjorie. *Each One Teach One: Frank Laubach, Friend to Millions*. New York: Longmans, Green and Co., 1954.

Medeiros, Adailson, Argentina Rosas, Maria Nayde dos Santos Lima, and Zélia Maria Soares Jófili, eds. *Paulo Rosas, Um Construtor da Cidade*. Recife: Prefeitura do Recife, 2005.

Miller, Valerie. *Between Struggle and Hope: The Nicaraguan Literacy Crusade*. Boulder, Colo.: Westview Press, 1985.

Monarcha, Carlos. *A Reinvenção da Cidade e da Multidão: Dimensões da Modernidade Brasileira: A Escola Nova*. São Paulo: Cortez, 1989.

Moniz Bandeira, Luiz Alberto. *O Governo João Goulart: As Lutas Sociais no Brasil, 1961–1964*. 7th ed. Rio de Janeiro: Revan, 2001.

Moraes, Dênis de. *A Esquerda e o Golpe de 64: Vinte e Cinco Anos Depois, as Forças Populares Repensam Seus Mitos, Sonhos e Ilusões*. Rio de Janeiro: Espaço e Tempo, 1989.

Morley, Morris H. *Washington, Somoza, and the Sandinistas: State and Regime in U.S. Policy toward Nicaragua, 1969–1981*. Cambridge: Cambridge University Press, 1994.

Najafizadeh, Mehrangiz, and Lewis Mennerick. "Worldwide Educational Expansion from 1950 to 1980: The Failure of the Expansion of Schooling in Developing Countries." *Journal of Developing Areas* 22:2 (April 1988): 333–58.

Nava, Carmen. "Pátria and Patriotism: Nationalism and National Identity in Brazilian Public Schools, 1937–1974." Unpublished Ph.D. dissertation, University of California, Los Angeles, 1995.

O'Cadiz, Maria del Pilar, Pia Lindquist Wong, and Carlos Alberto Torres. *Education and Democracy: Paulo Freire, Social Movements, and Educational Reform in São Paulo*. Boulder, Colo.: Westview Press, 1998.

Oliveira, Francisco de. *Elegia para uma Re(li)gião: SUDENE, Nordeste. Planejamento e Conflito de Classes*. Rio de Janeiro: Paz e Terra, 1977.

Oliveira, Ernesto Luiz de, Jr. *Doze Ensaios sobre Educação e Tecnologia*. Rio de Janeiro: Campanha Nacional de Aperfeiçoamento de Pessoal de Nível Superiores, 1956.

Oman, Charles P., and Ganeshan Wignaraja. *The Postwar Evolution of Development Thinking*. New York: St. Martin's Press, 1991.

Orrego Vicuña, Claudio. *Soldidaridad o Violencia: El Dilema de Chile: La Revolución en Libertad: Una Racionalidad Democratica para el Cambio Social*. Santiago: Editorial Zig-Zag, 1969.

Page, Joseph A. *The Revolution that Never Was: Northeast Brazil, 1955–1964*. New York: Grossman Publishers, 1972.

Paiva, Vanilda Pereira. *Educação Popular e Educação de Adultos*. 4th ed. São Paulo: Ediçoes Loyola, 1987.

———. *Paulo Freire e o Nacionalismo-Desenvolvimentista*. Rio de Janeiro: Editora Civilização Brasileira, 1980.

Pastor, Robert A. *Condemned to Repetition: The United States and Nicaragua*. Princeton: Princeton University Press, 1987.

Paton, David, ed. *Breaking Barriers: Nairobi 1975: The Official Report of the Fifth Assembly of the World Council of Churches*. Grand Rapids, Mich.: Wm. B. Eerdmans, 1976.

Pécaut, Daniel. *Os Intelectuais e a Política no Brasil: Entre o Povo e a Nação*. Translated from the French by Maria Júlia Goldwasser. São Paulo: Ática, 1990.

Pelandré, Nilcéa Lemos. *Ensinar e Aprender com Paulo Freire: 40 Hora, 40 Anos Depois*. São Paulo: Cortez, 2002.

Petras, James, and Hugo Zemelman Merino. *Peasants in Revolt: A Chilean Case Study, 1965–1971*. Translated by Thomas Flory. Austin: University of Texas Press, 1972.

Pinsky, Jaime, and Carla Bassanezi Pinsky, eds. *História da Cidadania*. São Paulo: Contexto, 2003.

Pinto, Álvaro Vieira. *Consciência e Realidade Nacional*. Rio de Janeiro: ISEB, 1960.

Pompei, Gian Franco, et al. *In the Minds of Men: UNESCO 1946 to 1971*. Paris: UNESCO, 1972.

Porto, Dores Paiva de Oliveira, and Iveline Lucena da Costa Lage. *CEPLAR: História de um Sonho Coletivo: Uma Experiência Popular na Paraíba Destruída pelo Golpe de Estado de 1964*. João Pessoa: Conselho Estadual de Educação, 1994.

Pratt, Cranford. *The Critical Phase in Tanzania, 1945–1968: Nyerere and the Emergence of a Socialist Strategy*. Cambridge: Cambridge University Press, 1976.

Rabe, Stephen G. *The Most Dangerous Area in the World: John F. Kennedy Confronts Communist Revolution in Latin America*. Chapel Hill: University of North Carolina Press, 1999.

Ramírez, Sergio. *El Alba de Ora: La História Viva de Nicaragua*. Mexico City: Siglo Veintiuno Editores, 1983.

———. *Mariano Fiallos: Biografía*. 2nd ed. León, Nicaragua: Editorial Universitaria, 1997.

Ramos, Alberto Guerrero. *Condições Sociais do Poder Nacional*. Rio de Janeiro: ISEB, 1957.

Ramos-Reyes, Mario. "The Impact of Jacques Maritain [sic] Political Thought in Twentieth

Century Latin America." Unpublished Ph.D. dissertation, University of Kansas, 1996.

Reese, Roger R. *Stalin's Reluctant Soldiers: A Social History of the Red Army, 1925–1941*. Lawrence: University Press of Kansas, 1996.

Reis Filho, Casemiro dos. *A Educação e a Ilusão Liberal em São Paulo*. São Paulo: Cortez, 1981.

Rezende, Antônio Paulo, ed. *Recife: Que História é Essa?*. Recife: Prefeitura do Recife, 1987.

Ridenti, Marcelo. *Em Busca do Povo Brasileiro: Artistas da Revolução, do CPC à Era da TV*. Rio de Janeiro: Editora Record, 2000.

Riquelme, Alfredo. "Promoción Popular y la Educación para la Participación." *Proposiciones* 15 (January 1990): 132–47.

Rodrigues, Marlene. *Cartilhas da Dominação*. Curitiba: Ed. Da UFPR, 1991.

Roett, Riordan. *The Politics of Foreign Aid in the Brazilian Northeast*. Nashville: Vanderbilt University Press, 1972.

Rojas, Marta. *El Aula Verde*. Havana: Unión de Escritores y Artistas da Cuba, 1982.

Rosas, Paulo. *Papéis Avulsos sobre Paulo Freire, 1*. Recife: Centro Paulo Freire and Universidade Federal de Pernambuco, 2003.

Rosemblatt, Karin Alejandra. *Gendered Compromises: Political Cultures and the State in Chile, 1920–1950*. Chapel Hill: University of North Carolina, 2000.

Roux, Jorge. *Álvaro Vieira Pinto: Nacionalismo e Terceiro Mundo*. São Paulo: Cortez, 1990.

Roxborough, Ian. *Theories of Underdevelopment*. London: Macmillan, 1979.

Roxborough, Ian, Philip O'Brien, and Jackie Roddick. *Chile: The State and Revolution*. New York: Holmes and Meier, 1977.

Sabato, Hilda. "On Political Citizenship in Nineteenth-Century Latin America." *American Historical Review* 106:4 (October 2001): 1298–99.

Sacasa, Crisanto. *Nicaragua en el CREFAL*. Managua: Ministério de Educación, 1955.

Sader, Emil, and Ken Silverstein. *Without Fear of Being Happy: Lula, the Workers Party and Brazil*. London: Verso, 1991.

Saldaña-Portillo, María Josefina. *The Revolutionary Imagination in the Americas and the Age of Development*. Durham: Duke University Press, 2003.

Santos, Paulo de Tarso. "Capacitación en Reforma Agraria (La Experiencia de ICIRA en Chile)." Paper presented by ICIRA at II Reunión de Ejecutivos de Reforma Agraria, Santiago, 16 December 1967.

———. *Os Cristãos e a Revolução Social*. Rio de Janeiro: Zahar, 1963.

———. "Educação e Desenvolvimento (Modelos Alternativos, com Dados da Realidade Brasileira)." In *Projeto Educação (Conferências, Pronunciamentos e Depoimentos)*. Vol. 2. Brasília: Senado Federal, Comissão de Educação e Cultura, 1978.

———. "Educación Agrícola y Desarrollo Rural: Versión Preliminar." Conferencia Mundial Sobre Enseñanza y Capacitación Agrícola, Copenhagen, 1970.

———. *64 e Outros Anos: Depoimentos a Oswaldo Coimbra*. São Paulo: Cortez, 1984.

Sater, William. *Chile and the United States: Empires in Conflict*. Athens: University of Georgia Press, 1990.

Schlesinger, Arthur M., Jr. *A Thousand Days: John F. Kennedy in the White House*. Boston: Houghton Mifflin, 1965.

Scoguglia, Afonso Celso. *Educação Popular: Do Sistema Paulo Freire aos IPMs da Ditadura*. São Paulo: Cortez, 2001.

———. *A História das Idéias de Paulo Freire e a Atual Crise de Paradigmas*. 4th ed. João Pessoa: Editora Universitária, 2003.

———. "Paulo Freire e a CEPLAR da Paraíba (1961–1964)—História de uma Experiência Pioneira do Alfabetização Política com o Método," Unpublished manuscript, Instituto Paulo Freire.

Scott, James C. *Seeing Like a State: How Certain Schemes to Improve the Human Condition Have Failed*. New Haven: Yale University Press, 1998.

Seixas Dória, João de. *Eu, Reu sem Crime*. Rio de Janeiro: Editora Equador, Ltda., 1964.

———. *Recortes de uma Jornada*. Aracaju: Fundação Oviédo Teixeira, 2001.

Sewell, James P. *UNESCO and World Politics: Engaging in International Relations*. Princeton: Princeton University Press, 1975.

Shor, Ira, and Paulo Freire. *A Pedagogy for Liberation: Dialogues on Transforming Education*. Westport, Conn.: Bergin & Garvey, 1987.

Sigmund, Paul E. *Liberation Theology at the Crossroads: Democracy or Revolution?* New York: Oxford University Press, 1990.

———. *The Overthrow of Allende and the Politics of Chile, 1964–1976*. Pittsburgh: University of Pittsburgh Press, 1977.

———. *The United States and Democracy in Chile*. Baltimore: Johns Hopkins University Press, 1993.

Silva, Geraldo Bastos. *Educação e Desenvolvimento Nacional*. Rio de Janeiro: MEC/ISEB, 1957.

Silva, Justina Iva de A. *Estudantes e Politica: Estudo de um Movimento, 1960–1969*. São Paulo: Cortez, 1989.

Silva, Pontes da, ed. *Poder e Política na Paraíba: Uma Análise das Lideranças, 1960–1990*. João Pessoa: A União, 1993.

Skidmore, Thomas E. *Politics in Brazil, 1930–1964: An Experiment in Democracy*. New York: Oxford University Press, 1967.

———. *The Politics of Military Rule in Brazil, 1964–1985*. New York: Oxford University Press, 1988.

Smith, Christian. *The Emergence of Liberation Theology: Radical Religion and Social Movement Theory*. Chicago: University of Chicago Press, 1991.

Soares, John A., Jr. "Strategy, Ideology, and Human Rights: Jimmy Carter Confronts the Left in Central America, 1979–1981." *Journal of Cold War Studies* 8:4 (Fall 2006): 57–91.

Soares, José Arlindo. *A Frente do Recife e o Governo do Arraes: Nacionalismo em Crise: 1955–1964*. Rio de Janeiro: Paz e Terra, 1982.

Souza, Francisco de Assis Lemos de. *Nordeste: O Vietnã que Não Houve: Ligas Camponesas e o Golpe de 64*. Londrina: Universidade Federal de Londrina, 1996.

Souza, João Francisco de. *Uma Pedagogia da Revolução: A Contribuição do Governo Arraes (1960–1964) à Reinvenção da Educação Brasileira*. São Paulo: Cortez, 1987.

Stallings, Barbara. *Class Conflict and Economic Development in Chile, 1958–1973*. Stanford: Stanford University Press, 1978.

Stansifer, Charles. "The Nicaraguan National Literacy Crusade." Hanover, N.H.: American Universities Field Staff Reports, 1981.

Staples, Amy L. S. *The Birth of Development: How the World Bank, Food and Agriculture*

Organization, and World Health Organization Changed the World. Kent, Ohio: Kent State University Press, 2006.

Stromquist, Nelly. *Literacy for Citizenship: Gender and Grassroots Dynamics in Brazil*. Albany: State University of New York Press, 1997.

Szuchman, Mark D. *Order, Family, and Community in Buenos Aires, 1810–1860*. Stanford: Stanford University Press, 1988.

Taffet, Jeffrey F. "Alliance for What? United States Development Assistance in Chile during the 1960s." Unpublished Ph.D. dissertation, Georgetown University, 2001.

———. *Foreign Aid as Foreign Policy: The Alliance for Progress in Latin America*. New York: Routledge, 2007.

Taussig, Michael. *The Devil and Commodity Fetishism in South America*. Chapel Hill: University of North Carolina Press, 1980.

Teixeira, Anísio. *A Educação e a Crise Brasileira*. São Paulo: Companhia Editora Nacional, 1956.

———. *Educação Não é Privilégio*. Rio de Janeiro: Livraria José Olympio, 1957.

Thiesenhusen, William C., ed. *Searching for Agrarian Reform in Latin America*. Boston: Unwin Hyman, 1989.

Tinsman, Heidi. *Partners in Conflict: The Politics of Gender, Sexuality, and Labor in the Chilean Agrarian Reform, 1950–1973*. Durham: Duke University Press, 2002.

Toledo, Caio Navarro de Toledo. "ISEB Intellectuals, the Left and Marxism." *Latin American Perspectives* 98:25 (January 1998): 109–35.

———, org. *Intelectuais e Política no Brasil: A Experiência do ISEB*. Rio de Janeiro: Revan, 2005.

———. *ISEB: Fábrica de Ideologias*. São Paulo: Ática, 1977.

Tomás, António. *O Fazedor de Utopias: Uma Biografia de Amílcar Cabral*. Lisbon: Tinta-da-China, 2007.

Toro Hardy, Alfredo. "La Política Exterior durante los Últimos Quince Años." In *Venezuela Contemporanea, 1974–1989*. Caracas: Fundación Eugenio Mendoza, 1989.

Torres, Carlos Alberto, and Adriana Puiggrós, eds. *Latin American Education: Comparative Perspectives*. Boulder, Colo.: Westview Press, 1997.

Trindade, Sérgio Luis Bezerra. *Uma Síntese da Abertura Política no Rio Grande do Norte, 1974–1979*. Natal: n.p., 1998.

Triviños, Augusto Nibaldo Silva, and Balduíno Antonio Andreola. "Da Opressão para a Esperança: O Tempo do Exílio de Ernani Maria Fiori e Paulo Freire no Chile: Contribuição de Fiori e de Freire para a Educação Chilena." Relatório de Pesquisa, Universidade Federal do Rio Grande do Sul, Faculdade de Educação, 1994. Available in Instituto Paulo Freire.

Tulchin, Joseph S., ed. *Venezuela in the Wake of Radical Reform*. Boulder, Colo.: Lynne Rienner, 1993.

Tünnermann Bernheim, Carlos. *Pensamiento Universitario Centroamericano*. San José: EDUCA, 1980.

United Nations Educational, Scientific, and Cultural Organization. *Alternativas de Alfabetización en América Latina y el Caribe*. Santiago: UNESCO, 1988.

———. "Educational and Cultural Development Project: Nicaragua." Paris: UNESCO, 1983.

———. *Education for All by 2015: Will We Make It?* Paris: UNESCO, 2007.

———. *International Development Strategy: Action Programme of the General Assembly for the*

Second United Nations Development Decade. New York: United Nations Department of Economic and Social Affairs, 1970.

———. *World Illiteracy at Mid-Century: A Statistical Study.* Westport, Conn.: Greenwood Press, 1970.

United Nations Department of Economic and Social Affairs. *International Development Strategy: Action Programme of the General Assembly for the Second United Nations Development Decade.* New York: United Nations Department of Economic and Social Affairs, 1970.

Unsicker, Jeffrey Glenn. "Adult Education, Socialism and International Aid in Tanzania: The Political Economy of the Folk Development Colleges." Unpublished Ph.D. dissertation, Stanford University, 1987.

Valderrama, Fernando. *A History of UNESCO.* Paris: UNESCO, 1995.

Van den Heuvel, Albert, ed. *Unity of Mankind: Speeches from the Fourth Assembly of the World Council of Churches.* Geneva: World Council of Churches, 1969.

Vasconcelos, Adirson. *Taguatinga: Cidade Progresso.* Brasília: Instituto Histórico e Geográfico do Distrito Federal—Serie Cidades—Satélites de Brasília No. 1, 1988.

Vaughan, Mary Kay. *Cultural Politics in Revolution: Teachers, Peasants, and Schools in Mexico, 1930–1940.* Tucson: University of Arizona Press, 1997.

———. *The State, Education, and Social Class in Mexico, 1880–1928.* DeKalb: Northern Illinois University Press, 1982.

Vilas, Carlos M. "Class, Lineage and Politics in Contemporary Nicaragua." *Journal of Latin American Studies* 24:2 (May 1992): 309–41.

Waggoner, George R., and Barbara Ashton Waggoner. *Education in Central America.* Lawrence: University Press of Kansas, 1971.

Walter, Knut. *The Regime of Anastasio Somoza, 1936–1956.* Chapel Hill: University of North Carolina Press, 1993.

Wanderley, Luiz Eduardo W. *Educar para Transformar: Educação Popular, Igreja Católica e Política no Movimento de Educação de Base.* Petrópolis: Vozes, 1984.

Warner, Ruth, and Luis Bravo. *Testimonios de Brigadistas: Cruzada Nacional de Alfabetización.* Managua: Instituto Nicaragüense de Investigación y Educación Popular, 1995.

Weffort, Francisco Corréa. *O Populismo na Politica Brasileira.* 2nd ed. Rio de Janeiro: Paz e Terra, 1978.

———. *Por que Democracia?* São Paulo: Brasiliense, 1984.

Weinstein, Barbara. "Developing Inequality." *American Historical Review* 113:1 (February 2008): 1–18.

———. *For Social Peace in Brazil: Industrialists and the Remaking of the Working Class in São Paulo, Brazil, 1920–1964.* Chapel Hill: University of North Carolina Press, 1996.

Weis, W. Michael. *Cold Warriors and Coups D'État: Brazilian-American Relations, 1945–1964.* Albuquerque: University of New Mexico Press, 1993.

Weiss, Thomas G., Tatiana Carayannis, Louis Emmerij, and Richard Jolly. *UN Voices: The Struggle for Development and Social Justice.* Bloomington: Indiana University Press, 2005.

Wertheim, Jorge, and Juan Díaz Bordenave, eds. *Educação Rural no Terceiro Mundo: Experiências e Novas Alternativas.* Rio de Janeiro: Paz e Terra, 1981.

Westad, Odd Arne. *The Global Cold War: Third World Interventions and the Making of Our Times.* Cambridge: Cambridge University Press, 2007.

Williamson Castro, Guillermo. *Paulo Freire: Educador para una Nueva Civilización*. Temuco, Chile: Ediciones Universidad de la Frontera, 1999.

Wynne, J. Pires. *História de Sergipe*. Vol. 2, 1930–1972. Rio de Janeiro: Editora Pongetti, 1975.

Zalava Cuadra, Xavier. "Situación de la Educación." *Revista del Pensamiento Centroamericano* 40 (January–March 1985): 42–53.

Zimmermann, Matilde. *Sandinista: Carlos Fonseca and the Nicaraguan Revolution*. Durham: Duke University Press, 2000.

Index